MAKING WOODEN CLOCK CASES

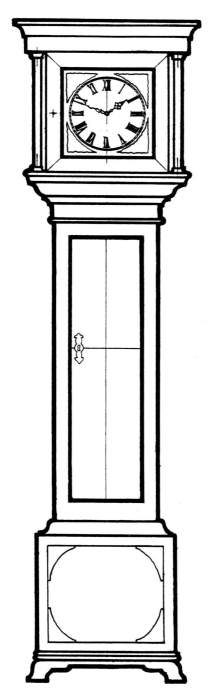

MAKING
WOODEN
CLOCK
CASES

Tim and Peter Ashby

LINDEN PUBLISHING

246897531

MAKING WOODEN CLOCK CASES

Library of Congress Cataloging-in-Publication Data

Ashby, Tim.
    Making wood clock cases / Tim and Peter Ashby.
        p. cm.
    Includes bibliographical references and index.
    ISBN 0–941936–21–X:
    1. Woodwork. 2. Clocks — Design and construction.
  I. Ashby, Peter.   II. Title.
TT200.A68   1992   92–5333
684.1′6--dc20   CIP

Published 1992 by
LINDEN PUBLISHING CO. INC.
3845 N. Blackstone
Fresno CA 93726

Printed in Hong Kong

CONTENTS

CLOCK PLANS

Dedication

In memory of my father and co-author, Peter Ashby (1925–1990): architect, designer-craftsman, publisher, humanist and environmentalist.

Thank you, Peter, for all that you gave to this world.

Introduction

Within the pages of this book is a collection of our clock designs that were created when we were running Ashby Design Workshop in Frome, Somerset.

The workshop activities up to 1990, when Peter died, included furniture making, antique restoration, commission work, boxes and clocks of a traditional and contemporary nature.

The first few clock plans were developed in co-operation with the Bath Clock Company and later extended as part of the Ashby Design Workshop 'Plans Service' which included traditional and modern furniture in 'Planpack' format. Further details are to be found in Appendix I.

As designer craftsmen, we felt that the plans should give the maker the practical information he or she needed to move straight to the workbench, having previously understood the project. Consequently, you will find fully dimensioned elevations, plans, sections, profiles, cutting lists, exploded diagrams, and schedules of operations included in the book and, in a larger 'workshop format', within the original A1 size 'Planpacks'. There is a chapter on reading plans for those who need to familiarise themselves with the process.

Dimensions

The drawings are dimensioned in both imperial and metric dimensions and are designed to work as 'stand-alone' systems of measurement and should NOT be mixed. This is especially apparent with the anomalies between the two systems for measuring plywood or mouldings. In metric, commonly used thicknesses of plywood are in 3 millimetre increments with their imperial counterparts in ⅛" increments:

3mm, 6mm, 9mm, 12mm, 15mm, 18mm, 21mm and 24mm correspond with ⅛", ¼", ⅜", ½", ⅝", ¾", ⅞" and 1" thicknesses.

These measurements are, however, nominal as ½" plywood, for instance, is in reality 12.7mm and ¾" ply is 19mm. So if you had two stacks of, say, four or five 'corresponding though differing' laminates of metric and imperial plywood, the stacks would naturally have differ-

ent final thicknesses. Consequently, it is impossible to have an exact conversion of dimensions, as in engineering, as nominal sized dimensions of material are used: the dimensions can only work in a 'stand-alone' format with slightly different sized clock cases resulting with the metric and imperial systems. Do not be alarmed if you occasionally see, for instance, both 15 and 16mm equalling ⅝" or a stack of metric plywood not equalling the stated imperial dimensions — they are stand-alone systems and NOT direct conversions.

The Cutting Lists are designed to show the *finished* component sizes, enabling the maker to cross reference sizes with the dimensions given on the drawings. When ordering materials, however you should take the following considerations into account:

Solid Timber (Hardwoods and Softwoods)

If you are machining the components yourself, allow surplus material in the thickness for planing and thicknessing, taking into account any warping, bowing or cupping in the wood. It is also advisable to allow surplus material in the length for saw thicknesses and for any shakes and defects that may occur at the end of a chosen plank.

Manufactured Boards (Plywood, Medium Density Fibreboard)

When purchasing manufactured boards it is worth mapping out in diagram form the components you will be cutting to allow for saw cuts and to ensure that you are buying economically; a number of timber merchants will be happy to supply you with eighth, quarter or half sheets, so plan ahead.

Mouldings

The Cutting Lists specify *minimum* lengths of mouldings: these are, in fact, the final lengths of moulding after construction so you will need to be reasonably generous to allow extra material for saw cuts and the trimming of mitres. If you are machining your own mouldings, you might need even more surplus length when machining with a router or a spindle moulder.

Veneers

The Cutting Lists do not specify how much veneer you will need for a project as this is virtually an impossible task when you consider the multitudinous shapes and sizes of veneer sheets available. This is a personal task that you will have to map out for yourself according to the materials you can acquire.

An important aspect of creating any object is naturally the materials that are employed. Whilst, let's say, a rustic gate would only need some easily obtained green timber and ironware, clock cases would obviously need more specialised equipment and materials and 'Product and Supplier Charts' are included in Appendix II to help the maker in tracking down these items. Many suppliers will be happy to supply you with the materials you need for your project as well as with appropriate tooling. I anticipate that machined kits will be available for selected designs from the book and when these are launched they will be announced with leaflets in the Planpacks and this book and in Ashby Design Workshop's 'Catalogue and Sourcebook' and Stockist Network (see Appendix I and II).

The Clock Component Lists, which follow the cutting lists, feature the clock components and hardware (excluding screws and pins) that are required for each project. I have avoided giving specific reference or model numbers for each component as these numbers can vary significantly between different stockists and manufacturers; furthermore, product lines can be deleted or introduced by stockists and manufacturers and, in a variable commercial world, new companies can appear on the market and established ones can, sadly, go out of business. Consequently, I have given the following 'critical information' which will allow you, the maker, to establish with your chosen supplier which components are available at the time of your enquiry.

Mechanical Movements

With pendulum movements, the pendulum length is given as the distance between the centre of the handshaft and the centre of the pendulum bob; the pendulum swing is the maximum distance that the pendulum bob should travel within the confines of the clock case; maximum plate size dimensions (roughly equivalent to the size of the front face of the movement) and the depth of the movement give an idea of the maximum size of movement allowable without having to change the clock case dimensions; the length of handshaft is variable between different movements and should be checked against the thickness of your dial-board; chime options are also given. These criteria can generally be satisfied by models from established manufacturers such as Hermle and Kieninger and from models by Urgos who went out of business in 1991. With custom made and antique models and with movements from less well-known manufacturers, you should check the 'critical information' and adjust the size of your case if necessary.

Quartz Movements

The main critical dimension when purchasing a quartz movement is the length of the handshaft and its corresponding fixing nut — these relate to the thickness of your dial-board and dial. Short, medium and long shafts are generally specified by manufacturers and suppliers, though do check that the actual dimensions will satisfy your requirements. The pendulum on a pendulum movement is usually decorative, rather than functional, and can consequently be cut to your required length, though do check the overall swing of the pendulum. The overall dimensions of the movement case are not usually critical as they are compact, though melody/chiming movements can be bulkier. Well-known manufacturers include Emes, Junghans, Kienzle, Hechinger, Seiko, Staiger and Talley UK/Westclox.

Dials

Overall dial dimensions are given with options for the use of chapter rings, where appropriate. Various materials and finishes are available.

Clock Hands

Check that these are bushed to fit the handshaft of your chosen quartz or mechanical movement. The hands should suit the size of your dial and it is normal practice for suppliers to specify the length of the minute hand from the centre of the handshaft to the tip of the hand as the critical dimension. Many styles and patterns are available.

Brassware

There is a truly vast range of brassware available for clock cases and the component lists specify critical sizes and suggested patterns for various brass components.

Skill

Skill is another factor that affects the quality of an object; obviously a collection of woodworking projects, with drawings and schedules of operations, cannot give a person the skill needed for a project, though the skills chapter and further reading section suggest further ways of improving your skills. The clocks are also graded with a star system allowing the reader to ascertain the degree of skill required, though this can only ever be an approximate indication as peoples' ability and preferences for different woodworking processes can vary considerably.

Whilst the plans and drawings give specific design and making information, which is especially useful for traditionally styled clock cases, there is plenty of room for manoeuvre for the maker to breathe his or her own spirit in the making process and to express the beauty of wood and the materials that are being used. There is, of course, nothing to stop you changing any detail to suit any personal preferences or to suit the materials and tooling that you have available.

Examples of 'Variations on a Theme' are illustrated in the book with the following corresponding plans which are similar in concept and construction but employ different sized dials and cases, varying proportions and decorative details:

The 'Yeoman' and the 'Half Cased Wall Clock'
The 'Deacon' and the 'Full Cased Wall Clock'
The 'Sexton' and the George III Bracket Clock
The 'Chorister' and 'Curate'
Long-case Clocks: 17th century Long-case and Grand-daughter Clock
and Vienna Regulators: Large and Small.

Whichever projects you choose to make, I trust that you will have as much pleasure in their creation as Peter and I had in preparing the drawings and building the prototypes. The style of the drawings evolved from Peter's many years in architecture and developed into the wood based drawings after both he and I had been immersed in our activities with Ashby Design Workshop. I hope you like what you see.

Tim Ashby
1992

CHAPTER ONE

Woodworking Skills & Workmanship

You don't have to be a master craftsman to be able to build a clock case!

The plans and projects in this book are suitable for woodworkers of varying skill and there is a star grading for each plan to indicate the difficulty of the project: one star plans are suitable for beginners and this progresses to five star plans which are for advanced woodworkers.

The star system can only ever *indicate* the level of skill required for a project due to one main variable — people! A relative beginner could, for instance, complete a three star project successfully simply if he or she has plenty of patience and no time limitations for the project, whereas a skilled professional, with commercial restrictions, might have to limit his or her time and effort in order to make the job profitable (this does not necessarily mean that good workmanship will not be used).

Quite simply, if you gave the same project to twelve woodworkers of similar ability, you will undoubtedly have twelve different results. Workmanship is a personal expression and is also an essential ingredient of the finished design: the craftsman or manufacturer has as much influence over the *quality* of a product as the designer, the budget or the materials used.

I believe, after seventeen years in design, making, teaching and publishing, that quality workmanship cannot be taught or given to someone; it is something that is acquired by the individual through practice, pleasure and persistence, albeit with the influence of teachers, customers and other woodworkers. There are, however, certain considerations that aid the woodworker in his striving to produce quality workmanship:

an understanding of the design and how it works;

an understanding of the working processes required to transform the design from 2-dimensional ideas on paper to a 3-dimensional object;

choice of materials;

interpretation of the nature of the chosen materials and how they can be used to best effect;

the correct use of tools;

soundness of construction;

treatment of surfaces and how they are finished;

working rhythm;

costs;

time;

added ingredients: patience, care, imagination, attention to detail, motivation, experience and an attitude that does not crumble everytime that something goes wrong with a project. Even the most experienced craftsman has problems with many tasks he encounters — solving these problems is part of the joy of creativity.

One of the great pleasures of woodworking is that there is always something new to learn and there are many ways to improve your skills. To reverse the example above, if one woodworker were to make the same piece twelve times, say over twelve years, each finished item will undoubtedly look different, reflecting the change of personal skills and attitudes over the years.

If, however, I were put on the spot and asked for one *essential* ingredient for quality workmanship, I would say that whatever the task, and its difficulty, the main thing is to have fun doing it! Good workmanship does not evolve from negativity.

CHAPTER TWO

How To Read Plans

The old cliché that a single picture is worth a thousand words is nevertheless as true today as when it was first coined. A drawing is as much a message as any letter or telegram, but it is far more concise and enables a swift impression of the object illustrated to be obtained. A written message might well have to be read completely before an understanding of the object described is gained. Although the cry 'it's very complicated' is often heard, if a drawing is read in the same way as a letter — word for word and phrase by phrase — it can be just as easy as reading words.

When a child learns to read he has to understand that words are made up of sounds and that sounds are shown by the letters of the alphabet. In a like manner, to follow technical drawings it is necessary to understand the principles used to create the drawing and to know some of the rules used.

We all know what a drawing is; it is a representation on paper of a three-dimensional object. We are also used to seeing pictures which have been drawn to look as lifelike as possible, and the artist who creates those pictures uses perspective to obtain the semblance of life.

However, that method gives only a general impression of the object illustrated. It would be difficult to create a replica of the original object using only the information contained in the perspective drawing. For example, what are the heights and widths of the object? How has it been made and with what materials? What are the details of the parts not actually shown in the picture?

From these questions, it is clear that some other method of drawing the object is required. Apart from this, the artist's perspective drawing is devised on the assumption that the object is viewed from one position only — the position that his eye happens to be in when he makes the drawing.

Reference to Fig 1A will show that when this principle is followed the real size of the object is distorted when it is illustrated.

In order to overcome this distortion, the draughtsman makes a different assumption from that of the artist. He concludes that his eye moves to line up with every feature that he wants to draw. In this way his eye 'projects' the feature and thus eliminates perspective distortion. Fig. 1B shows that this method gives accurate sizes of the object drawn.

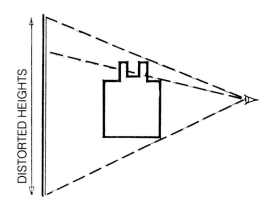

FIGURE 1A

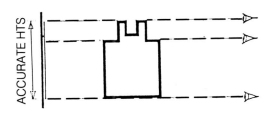

FIGURE 1B

Again, the artist shows on his perspective drawing more than one face of his object, while the draughtsman in his elevations shows only one face of the object at a time.

In order to understand how these elevations are obtained, reference should now be made to Fig. 2A.

In that diagram it is assumed by the draughtsman that the object to be illustrated is 'floating in mid air'. To show how the object would appear from above, each of the features is projected downwards to fall on an imaginary piece of paper positioned below the floating object. When the points of intersection with the paper are joined up the end result is a Plan view which faithfully reproduces the appearance of the top surface of the floating object.

the relevant portion of the drawing or, more generally, in the title panel.

With the views created so far, it would be awkward to

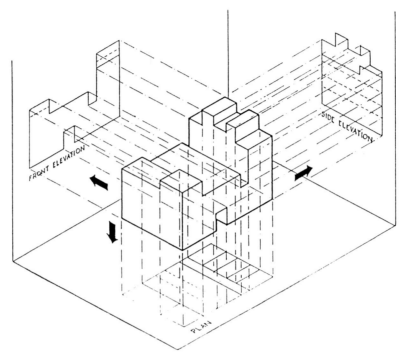

FIGURE 2A

In a similar manner, the Front Elevation can be created by projecting the features on the front of the object onto a further imaginary piece of paper held vertically behind the object. The result, in this case, is a front view which faithfully reproduces the features on the front of the object.

A similar approach is made to create views of the two sides and the back face of the object.

Measuring all the sizes of the Plan and the Elevations will show that all dimensions which should agree do, in fact, do so.

So far, our draughtsman has worked on the assumption that he is drawing the object to its actual size. However, this is obviously hard to do in the case of a large object, such as a wardrobe.

When this difficulty arises, the object is 'drawn to scale'. This may sound daunting to the beginner, but it simply means that the illustrator decides in advance, for instance, that he will draw everything to a quarter of the real size and perhaps illustrate only selected parts of the construction to full size.

When this approach is made, the draughtsman will make a note on the drawing of the scale used. This may be under

have several different pieces of paper, each bearing a different view of the object. The draughtsman, therefore, brings all the views together on a single sheet of paper. This also helps with understanding the object since it is then easier to compare the various views, one with the other.

These views are usually arranged in an accepted position on the one sheet. The Plan is normally located in the lower left-hand corner with the Front and Back Elevations positioned immediately above it. The Side Elevations are then drawn to the right of the front and back elevations.

Fig. 2B shows a typical layout for a detailed working drawing.

In a perfect world it should be easy for the person using the drawing to just measure the various sizes of features as drawn by the illustrator. However, the paper used by the draughtsman may shrink or stretch with varying air humidity, as will the paper on which the drawing is later printed. A good draughtsman will, therefore, always state actual calculated dimensions for each view drawn.

On the Plan or the Elevations there may be drawn dotted or broken lines. These are a device to indicate critical hidden details essential to the understanding of the object

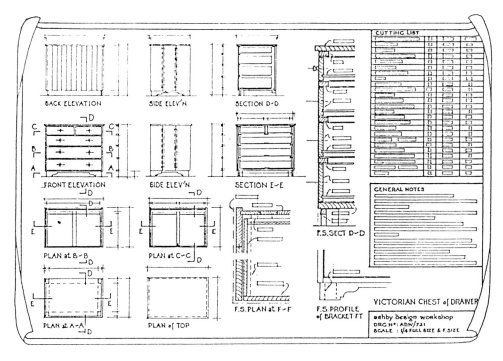

FIGURE 2B

drawn.

So far, the illustrator has drawn all the views of how the completed object will look. However, it may be essential to show parts of the construction which will be concealed when the object has been built.

This is done in a manner using the same principle of projection, but with one difference: the draughtsman imagines that the object he is drawing has been cut through in the part he wishes to detail.

Reference to Fig. 3 will show how this is done. The position where the assumed cut has been made is shown as a thick line on the Plan or Elevation and is usually labelled A-A, B-B, etc. The projected Section is labelled in a similar manner.

The Section may further elaborate on a particular feature by means of small sketches drawn in a special projection known as Isometric Projection. These sketches are self-explanatory, and it is not essential for the person reading the drawing to know how they are created. Sometimes these sketches are used to show the general arrangement of the component parts of the object by assuming that the object in question has 'exploded'.

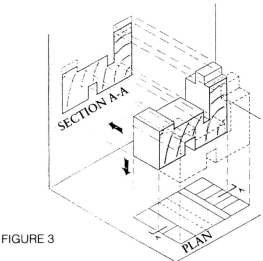

FIGURE 3

A draughtsman often labels the component parts of the object where they appear on the various views, *Eg* '32 × 18 Stretcher'. He will also include any minor notes needed to fully explain the design.

If step by step instructions are needed they are usually shown separately in a Schedule of Operations.

A woodwork working drawing will also schedule a cutting list for all the component parts of the object illustrated.

CHAPTER THREE

Materials

Having chosen which design you are going to build and having read and understood the plans and schedules, the next stage is to acquire all the materials (except the glass which is fitted at the end of the project) that you require for the project — prior to construction. You might, for instance, need to make sure your timber is seasoned or have the clock dial, movement or brass fittings available to check for fit with the clock case you are making.

Clock Movements

The clock movements specified in this collection of designs are either quartz, mechanical or insertion movements. There are a number of makes, manufacturers and specifications for each category of movement. A guide for choosing the right movement is outlined below and there is also a Product and Supplier listing in Appendix II showing from which suppliers you can obtain clock components.

Quartz Movements

Basically, a quartz movement is a very accurate timepiece which has a piece of quartz resonating at a fixed frequency within an electronic circuit — the quartz crystal has replaced the pendulum used on mechanical clocks. The accuracy of a quartz movement is usually within plus or minus one minute a year. The power is supplied from a battery which can last from 12–18 months (depending on the make); this means that the end users of the clock need never think about winding up the clock on a daily or weekly basis and, due to the simple plastic housing of the movement, need not concern themselves with cleaning and maintenance. If the movement fails at any time in the future, it will be cheaper to replace a new movement rather than repair the old one.

From the woodworker's point of view, he will need to know the following two facts before purchasing a quartz clock movement:

— the length of the 'centre fixing nut' that secures the movement to the clock case's 'dial-board'. The thickness of the dial-board (which can be 3mm, 6mm or 9mm/⅛″, ¼″ or ⅜″ plywood/MDF) plus the thickness of the applied metal dial (if used) will determine the length of the required fixing nut;
— the length of the 'spindle' which passes through the centre fixing nut and has the second, minute and hour hands secured to it. The common spindle lengths are 11mm, 16mm and 21mm/⅜″, ⅝″ and ⅞″ and you will have to make sure that it is suitable for the established fixing nut. You will also need to ensure that the spindle is not too long that it will foul any glass door that is a part of the clock case design.

In addition to the basic model of quartz movement, you can also get pendulum movements, though the pendulum does not affect the timekeeping of the movement as it is purely decorative. Pendulum lengths are variable and the longer 'pendulum rods' can be cut to a shorter length if required. Spun brass 'pendulum bobs' are available in different diameters.

Other types of quartz movements on the market include: melody or chiming models, which can have one or more melodies (e.g. Whittington or Westminster) and tend to have bulkier casings; high torque movements which are suitable for driving longer and heavier clock hands; anti-clockwise movements, (a novelty item) and mini-pendulum movements.

Insertion Movements

These are all-in-one pieces comprising a 'drum' quartz movement, hands, a circular dial (various styles) and a protective bezel and glass. Insertion movements/dial/bezel combinations come in different diameters and are simply fixed to a clock case by being pushed into an appropriate sized hole (springs on the side of the drum movement keep the movement in place). The Carter, Ostler, Coachman and

Groom clocks all employ this type of movement.

Mechanical Movements

The history and development of mechanical clocks is extensive and stretches over centuries; it is a fascinating subject in its own right though there is no need to be an 'horological expert' in order to create one of the clock cases from this book. The main information you need to acquire is firstly, whether the movement will fit the case; secondly, how to fit the movement to the case; thirdly, how to set and operate the movement; and fourthly, how to maintain it. This information should be freely forthcoming from your supplier or manufacturer.

There are four main types of traditional clock cases that employ mechanical movements in the book and within these categories there are many variables and choices — this emphasises the need for you to purchase your clock movement *before* you commence construction of the clock case. Further information is given below to help you in your choice of movements, though do please refer to your supplier who will also have useful literature available.

Long-case Clocks

These include grandfather, grandmother and granddaughter versions — these are populist terms that have evolved in the last century (long-case was the original term) and indicate the overall height of the clock case and the appropriate size of movement. The height of the clock cases can vary from approximately 1520mm/60 inches (granddaughter) to 2790mm/110 inches (largest grandfather).

Long-case Movements

These can be 'weight-driven' and wound up with a key which raises lead weights (with brass shells) that are attached to the movement via cables and pulleys — the descending weights drive the clock movement usually for a period of eight days, though this can vary; 'chain-driven' movements are also driven by weights though these are raised by pulling chains rather than winding a key; 'spring-driven' movements have no weights and are wound up with a key. All three types of movement have pendulums which act as oscillators — it is important that the overall swing of the pendulum does not exceed the inside width of the trunk

of the clock case. Similarly, the height of the trunk should also accommodate the 'drop' of the weights (assuming that the movement is weight driven) as this varies with granddaughter, grandmother and grandfather movements.

Long-case Chimes

Chimes can incorporate any one, or a combination, of the following features: single bell strike, double bell strike, bim-bam, Westminster, Whittington, and St Michael chimes, either rod gongs, coil gongs or bells and night-silence switches (automatic and manual).

Long-case Dials

Dials can either be square or arched and come in a variety of styles, patterns, materials, colours and finishes. Many of the dials available are quite ornate incorporating decorative cast and engraved brasswork or imaginative paintwork. Specialist dials, connected to specialist movements, can incorporate separate moon phase, calendar and second dials as well as triple-chime and night-silence switches.

Vienna Regulator Clocks

These are wall hung clocks which are based around an elongated glass and wood-frame box that houses and displays the movement, dial, pendulum and weights. Visually, the glass and wood case would be embellished with crests, mouldings, carvings and turnings — this could either be in a restrained fashion, as with the two examples in this book, or in a highly ornate form as seen with many exuberent traditional examples. The height of the clocks can vary from 760–1520mm/30–60 inches.

Vienna Regulator Movements

Movements are usually 'weight-driven' with the weights being wound up with a key. The dial is integral with the movement and is normally made from brass and white enamel. The movements have pendulums which are either straight wooden rods with a brass bob or a more elaborate 'lyre' design which comprises steel and brass rods and plates. As with the longcase clocks, a number of chime options are also available.

Wall Clocks

Whilst regulator clocks are a common form of traditional wall clock, other traditional wall clocks include simple round 'dial clocks' (sometimes known as school clocks) and 'drop dial clocks' which have a box attached to the dial/dial rim that accommodates the movement and a pendulum — an example of an English Drop Dial clock is included in the book.

Wall Clock Movements

These are available in a number of sizes, with or without pendulums, and have a number of chime options. Again refer to your supplier for details.

Wall Clock Dials

Circular wall clock dials are generally available in 152, 203, 254 and 305mm/6, 8, 10 and 12 inch diameters. Circular brass bezels and glass can be used to protect the dial and hands and these are purchased separately from the dials, though special bezel and dial combinations are available. Square dials are also available in different sizes and styles.

'Table' Clocks

These have included, historically, a variety of designs such as bracket, carriage, drum, desk, lantern, balloon, lancet, mantel, shelf and skeleton clocks; they are all designed to sit on a horizontal surface as opposed to floorstanding or wall hung designs.

Table Clock Movements

Whilst a quartz movement could be simply used for any of the table clocks in the book, many people will prefer mechanical movements and these are available in a variety of sizes and with chime options.

Table Clock Dials

These are available in round or square patterns and in a number of sizes and styles. Dial/bezel combinations are also available.

Fixtures and Fittings

Browsing through the Product List in Appendix I, or through a clock supplier's catalogue will quickly give you an idea of the specialist clock fixtures and fittings currently available on the market. Books on antique clocks reveal what is possible with custom-made fittings in both metal and wood, and will also show the various historical styles and trends.

Metal Fixtures and Fittings

The metal fixtures used in the book's collection of plans all use components that are generally available though, from time to time, manufacturers or suppliers can delete or change certain items from their ranges, for various reasons, so do check the availability *before* commencing any construction work. Most metal fixtures for clocks tend to be in brass for decorative reasons and are available in various styles and sizes. They include finials, paterae, spires, clock case feet, door handles, carrying handles, column bases/capitals, spandrels, hinges, locks and escutcheons.

Wooden Fixtures and Fittings

The wooden fixtures, such as mouldings, finials, carvings, fretwork and pillars will, I am assuming, be home-made, though there are quality manufactured versions available from different suppliers. This is handy especially if, for instance, you haven't a lathe for turning finials or columns. If, in the case of turned work where you have no lathe and cannot track down standard manufactured items, you might consider asking a woodturner with the right equipment to turn the items for you. Where appropriate, the plans show standard manufactured mouldings which are available in limited timber species only. If you want your mouldings to match the timber in the rest of your clock case, you will have to make your own out of matching wood and this can be done with appropriate router cutters or with moulding planes.

Clock Hands

Clock hands are available in a variety of sizes, patterns and finishes. Choosing which ones to use on your clock really is a matter of personal preference, though the hands do need to be the right length to match in with the diameter of your clock dial. For quartz movements, the 'bushes' that fix the hands to the movement's spindle are standard — no problem; however, bushes for hands suitable for mechanical movements do vary, so again, check before purchasing. If you are adventurous and wish to make your own clock hands, you will need to obtain separate bushes for the task.

Chapter Rings & Numerals

Whilst clock dials were specifically covered in the clock movement section, it is worth mentioning 'chapter rings' which are clock dials with the centre removed. In effect, you have a large washer with numerals, minute marks and decorative motifs that are printed or etched on the ring itself. A number of styles and sizes are available and they tend to be made with a brass, aluminium or silvered finish. Because of the centre hole, chapter rings can be especially effective when they are fixed to a decorative surface such as a burr wood panel as this will allow this material to be seen.

Various 'applied numerals' are used to create a clock dial and these can be made from cast, fettled and polished metal or sticky-back plastic. Roman and Arabic numerals are available as well as specialist designs such as the signs of the zodiac.

Whilst each plan in the book specifies the movement, dial and fixtures and fittings that are suitable for the project, it really is up to you, the maker, to make a personal choice from the wide range of options on the market. This wide choice also emphasises the need to acquire these materials before commencing construction. As mentioned before, the glass is the only exception to this and this should be measured and cut to fit appropriate openings in doors after construction — if you are not skilled at cutting glass, your local glazier/supplier should be able to provide this service for you.

Timber — Making the Right Choice

Timber Species

The number of timber species on the planet is truly vast and you would naturally not expect to see the full gamut on display at your local timber merchant. You might, how-ever, be surprised at the range available, especially as veneers, and it is worth investigating which suppliers have varied woods in stock both locally and in the national woodworking magazines. The supply of timber species will vary from time to time according to which logs have been farmed recently or which logs have been shipped into the country at any one time.

Other factors that will affect your choice of species are the exciting bits! The colour of the wood, its figure and graining, its vibrancy and aroma, its workability, the condition of the boards available and the price of the timber can all send your heart racing! The cost of the materials for one of the smaller clocks in the range would generally be very moderate unless, of course, you choose rare and exotic species in which case you would expect the material to command a higher price. If you are using old and existing timber, which is a form of recycling, the price would be considerably less.

On an environmental note, whether you are using home-grown or imported timber, you might like to quiz your timber merchant as to whether your chosen species have come from a sustainable and renewable woodland. Trees really are extraordinary living forms that provide immense benefits to our climate, our environment, our economies, our cultures and our spirits *if* they are farmed, harvested and replanted correctly. Just as you, the consumer, changed attitudes in the food industries, you can, by asking your timber supplier about renewable sources, create a demand for sensitively farmed timber.

Further reading on timber species is suggested in the Bibliography and a number of timber merchants supply lists and catalogues of their timber stocks. Whilst many merchants offer a mail order/carriage service for timber and veneers, it is worthwhile actually selecting the timber for yourself (if the merchant will allow it) as this will enable you to make personal choices as regards the all important decisions of colour and figure — you might want a delicate figure for a small clock whereas the merchant, choosing for you, might select timber with a bold figure. Seeing the timber before purchase might also prompt you into making artistic decisions which you otherwise would have ignored, for example, spotting particularly beautiful book matched veneers in some corner of the merchant's store.

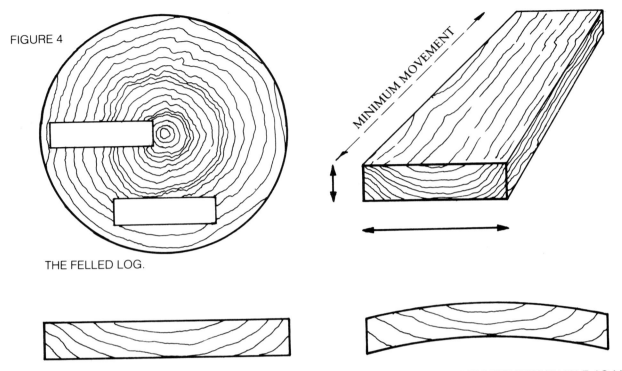

FIGURE 4

THE FELLED LOG.

THE PLAIN-SAWN PLANK TENDS TO MOVE MOSTLY ACROSS ITS WIDTH AND APPROXIMATELY HALF AS MUCH THROUGH ITS THICKNESS.

THE QUARTER-SAWN PLANK HAS THE GREATEST MOVEMENT IN ITS THICKNESS WHERE IT IS RELATIVELY UNIMPORTANT AND MOVES ABOUT HALF AS MUCH THROUGH ITS THICKNESS.

Solid vs Veneered Timber — Timber Behaviour

Each of the plans in the book specifies whether solid or veneered timber should be used for the project, though in some cases it is possible to use solid instead of veneered material as long as the maker understands how timber behaves and adjusts the construction accordingly.

The main thing to remember about solid timber is that it moves, even if it is very well seasoned. Timber has a natural moisture level which, although by seasoning can be reduced from approximately 50% down to 10%, never remains constant. As the humidity of the air changes, so does the moisture content of the wood (visualise leaving timber in a damp cellar compared with a south facing window!)

Timber will swell and contract as the moisture content changes and this almost always occurs across the width and thickness of a board rather than across its length (see Fig. 4).

Once you accept that solid timber does move — you've no choice in the matter — you should then make sure that the construction allows for this movement. Examples of this can be seen in traditionally framed and panelled doors which allow the solid panels to move within grooves within the framework. See Fig. 5.

FIGURE 5

There are two distinct advantages that veneered materials have over solid timber:

— One, the veneers are usually glued and pressed to a core material such as plywood or Medium Density Fibreboard (MDF). These manufactured boards are, unlike solid wood, inherently stable and will not warp in reasonable atmospheric conditions; this stability is further increased with the bonding of the veneers on both surfaces of the boards with facing veneers and backing veneers.

— Two, the range of decorative options is greatly increased as each leaf of veneer sliced from a log is virtually identical to its adjacent leaf, thus allowing for 'running', 'book', 'quarter' and 'radial' matching (see Chapter 5). Furthermore, a number of exotic and difficult to work burr timbers are more suited to veneer work rather than solid work, and the use of veneers therefore increases your choice of timber species.

The main disadvantage of using veneers over solid wood is that they are not as durable in terms of accidents and damage, though this is not such an essential requirement for a clock which is rarely handled in everyday life.

As designers, we have gone through the process of allowing for timber movement on each plan and have specified accordingly. If, however, you want to replace specified veneered material in a plan with solid timber, think carefully and make sure that you can accommodate timber movement.

Timber Seasoning

Solid timber is either air or kiln dried and can be part or wholly seasoned. Check with your timber merchant prior to buying: using partly or unseasoned timber will only cause grief later. Generally it can be said that air dried timber has a better colour than kiln dried material. If you want to season your own timber you will need knowledge (gained from further reading and talking to people), suitable storage space and lots of patience!

It is worth noting that after your timber has been machined from raw sawn boards to planed and thicknessed components, it is wise to let the newly machined components settle in your workshop for a week or two prior to any construction work. Also, bear in mind the environment in which the finished project is intended to be used.

Veneers are often ready for working immediately after purchase, though if you are going to keep them for any period you will need to store them flat, away from direct heat or sunshine and covered with polythene sheeting — this will prevent them from drying out. If the veneers are dried out and brittle and buckled, they will need to be flattened again (see veneering section in Chapter 5).

Adhesives

There are two basic adhesive requirements when building a clock case: firstly, an adhesive is needed for any structural work such as carcass assembly, the gluing of mouldings and door frames etc; secondly, different adhesives are required for veneer work.

Structural work

The easiest adhesive to use for structural work is a PVA based adhesive that requires no mixing — use it straight from the bottle. There are three common types of PVA glue: exterior PVA; interior PVA; fast grab PVA. For clock case work, there is no real advantage in using exterior types and the interior glues are more than adequate for structural requirements. With both interior and exterior PVA adhesives, you will need to cramp the work that you are gluing.

You might find the fast grab glues (which 'grab' within a few minutes and 'set' and 'cure' within a few hours) useful for work where it is difficult to use cramps, for instance, with mouldings.

Other common types of adhesive suitable for construction work are casein glues, animal glues (which are good for fast grab work) and a variety of synthetic resin adhesives. All of these require different working processes and it is important to familiarise yourself with the manufacturers' instructions and, if necessary, to experiment until you are happy with the use of your chosen adhesive.

Veneer Work

There are a number of adhesives available for veneer work and the choice of adhesive largely depends on the facilities you have in your workshop, the size of area that you are gluing and personal preference. For larger areas and panels (say, above ½ square metre or 2 square feet) it is *generally* easier to use adhesives that are suitable for hot or cold presses though this is not a hard and fast rule (see Chapter 5 for techniques on veneering without a press).

The adhesives that are commonly used for hot veneer presses (usually found in production workshops) are either in the 'phenol resin' or 'urea formaldehyde' groups and are available in a number of formulae.

For cold veneer presses, the adhesives used are often in the 'cold pressing urea formaldehyde' groups and can also include 'PVA' and 'casein' type glues.

Woodworkers without the luxury of a veneer press might like to consider cramping and gluing the veneers to the 'groundwork' (the material being veneered) by cramping the groundwork/veneer between two stout boards. Other highly satisfactory options are to use 'contact' adhesives, 'glu-film' and hot 'animal glues' (see Chapter 5).

Finishes

French polish, lacquers, varnishes, polyurethanes, cellulose, waxes, oils, stains, paints, marbled effects, limed effects, leather effects, wrinkle effects, spatter effects, pearl effects, two-tone effects, pickled pine effects, and ebonised effects are just a few examples of a vast range of finished surfaces that are available to the woodworker.

Where do you start? Especially if you are a beginner. There are hundreds of finishes that have been developed over the centuries and, if you chose, you could spend all your time getting acquainted with these finishes and become truly expert in their use, though this will obviously leave you little time for woodwork!

Decisions have to be made as to the type of finish you use and, for the beginner, I would suggest that you initially focus your attention on just a few finishes until you become

good at their use — once you have this 'base knowledge' you can then expand your horizons and start to experiment a little.

In choosing which finishes to use, you will need to take the following considerations into account:

— the type of timber you are finishing. A close grained burr walnut, an open grained oak and a medium density fibreboard, for instance, will all require different treatments and 'artistic interpretations';
— the type of surface you prefer. This could be a full gloss, a semi-matt or a matt finish and can also include painted and textured surfaces;
— colour. Whilst many timbers can be stunning in their natural state, there are often occasions when a timber can be enhanced with stains or with coloured polishes;
— favoured methods for applying the finish. This can include brush finishes, 'rubber' finishes (used with french polishes) and spray finishes.

In Chapter 5, methods for applying certain *basic* finishes are explained so as to allow beginners at the craft to achieve highly satisfactory results with their completed clock case/s.

For those of you who wish to find out more about finishing and polishing, I would recommend that you purchase a copy of Frederick Oughton's 'Complete Manual of Wood Finishing' which is published by Stobart Davies — this book will not only tell you how to apply various finishes, but will also inspire you to experiment with a variety of recipes. Short one and two-day wood finishing courses are available (look in the adverts in the magazines), and can give a boost to finishing skills for beginners and accomplished wood finishers. You will also find that many finish and polish manufacturers give instructions on the use of their products. Above all, practice makes perfect!

CHAPTER FOUR

Tools

An important part of planning and completing a project is the tools that you will use for that job. It is often said that a good workman never blames his tools and whilst this statement has an element of truth, it is worth considering the nature of tools to realise the statement's limitations.

The Nature and Use of Tools

In essence, a tool can be considered as a 'shape-determining system' (to quote David Pye) or, alternatively, as a 'jig'. Consider the shape of your thumb: if you are a potter, this could play an important role in determining the shape of, say, the handle of a jug. Or let's assume that you wish to draw a straight line with a pencil: by drawing freehand, it is unlikely that you will achieve this aim; however, with the introduction of a straight edge or ruler — a shape-determining system — you will eliminate much of the risk involved and you should be able to achieve your aim of drawing a reasonably straight line.

When you consider woodworking tools as shape-determining systems, this will give you a better insight as to *how* you should use these tools. For instance, a bench is a shape-determining system that allows you to work on a horizontal surface and to plane woodworking components flat — assuming that the bench top is itself reasonably flat. Chisels, planes, gouges, drills, saws and even cramps can all determine certain shapes assuming that the right energy, or force, is exerted during the use of the tool.

In order to become proficient in the use of tools, there are certain basics that must be understood:

— The purpose of the tool: what shape will it determine.

How the tool is designed to achieve a specific shape: for instance, planes, chisels, flat files and rasps can all be used to create flat shapes; moulding planes, scratch-stocks and electric routers can be used for moulded shapes. A question of choice of tool also comes in here in terms of 'fitness for purpose' and the 'context of your work': a workshop made scratchstock might be what is needed to create a small piece of moulding in the restoration of an antique, whereas a router might be more appropriate if there are many metres of mouldings required for a bookcase.

The material that the tool is designed to cut: for instance, wood, plastic, stone or metal.

The energy, or force, that is required to direct a tool to achieve a specific shape or result. Hand tools, portable power tools, fixed machinery and even robots and computers require some form of human energy to make them work and produce useful results. It is a matter of learning what is required of you, the maker or operator, in the mastering of a tool, or a process, and this is the fun (and agonising) bit that takes time, patience and energy — with rewards.

The maintenance of tools: blunt chisels or pencils, worn drill bits and badly calibrated machines will not produce the results that are intended. Not only is there an art to be learned in the usage of tools, but also in the maintenance and safety aspects of that usage.

Assuming that you know the principle of a specific tool and the tasks that it can be expected to perform, you then need to know *how* to use it. Basic methods for acquiring knowledge and skill in the use of tools include the reading of books, magazines and tool catalogues, training courses and the all important hands-on experience.

Choosing and Buying Tools

When deciding *which* tools to purchase, your first consideration should be the tasks that *you* need to perform — you should then be able to establish which tools, or shape-determining systems, will assist you in fulfilling those tasks. This could entail researching what is available on the market through magazines, books and tool catalogues.

Basic considerations when deciding on the purchase of a

tool are: will it perform the tasks that are expected of it; the options available on the market; its construction, quality and durability; cost and value for money; labour saving potential — you might like to consider power tools in many situations; the services your tool dealer can offer; guarantees and maintenance; your ability to use the tool — in the case of machinery or power hand tools you might need to consider training in usage and safety.

When purchasing machinery, which is often your most expensive investment, it is important to consider the effect on your cash flow: is it best to buy with cash and gain a possible discount or will stage payments, hire purchase, leasing or bank loans suit your financial situation better?

A good way of building up your collection of smaller tools, without too much pain in the wallet, is to buy these items as you need them for specific jobs — it is surprising how large your collection will grow over the course of a year or two. Check out the second-hand shops and car boot sales — you never know what bargains you will come across.

It is also worth attending the major woodworking shows as you can *see* what is available; how differing makes and models work and what services different companies offer. Apart from anything else it makes for a good day out.

Hand Tools

The hand tools you require for making a clock case are really not much different from those you would use for many woodworking projects and cover the following main tasks and categories:

Benches

The bench that you work at can be viewed as the most important tool in your workshop. Quite simply, if the bench top is not flat, you will never be able to plane a piece of wood flat! The bench is your base on which your project will be built and will inevitably incorporate that all important tool — the woodworking vice.

There are a number of bench options on the market as well as plans for you to build your own versions. With bought-in manufactured benches, the specifications naturally vary according to price though it is worth spending as much as you can as this tool will affect your work for many

years to come. Ideally, you should have a bench with a laminated solid wood top as this will not only be a sound base to work on but will also be a stable surface with little wood movement. Manufactured benches have a number of vice options, including end vices linked to 'dogs' which enable you to hold planks and strips of wood flat on the bench for planing etc. Research the vice options before you buy. There are also a number of 'workcentres' and 'power tool tables' that you might wish to investigate.

Hand Tools

Listed below, are a range of *basic* hand tools that will cover most of your needs for the majority of projects in this book. There are, of course, hundreds of different types of hand tools on the market including many specialist tools.

Carving

Whilst most of the clock projects in this book do not have a carving element, it is always worth having a few carving tools in your kit. If you studied the carving market, you will find that an enormous range of gouge, chisel and knife profiles are available as well as various carving accessories. Even professional woodcarvers will rarely use this full range of profiles and will frequently use just half a dozen favourite tools. I would recommend that the beginner starts his collection with a limited range of five or six gouges and chisels which can be bought individually or as a set. There are also a number of options in the quality of tools available and, inevitably, those with the best grade steel command a higher price.

Cramping and Holding

During the course of a woodworking project, you will need cramps and holding devices for the making and the assembly and gluing of components. The main holding devices that are continually used are the woodworking vices that are attached to your bench. A bench 'holdfast' which cramps components onto the flat surface of your bench is also a useful accessory. For assembling main carcass work, a set of four sash cramps will be needed: these are adjustable and available in a variety of lengths and you will need to decide on cramp sizes according to the scale of your work. (A long-case clock will obviously need larger cramps than a mantel clock). G-cramps (also called C-clamps) are also invaluable for many varied woodworking tasks and are available in a range of sizes and styles (*Eg* deep throat and quick action G-cramps). It is worthwhile building up a collection of different G-cramps in your workshop as they are inevitably used in most woodworking projects.

Cutting

The main hand tools used for cutting or slicing wood are chisels, knives, scalpels, planes (which are dealt with later), spokeshaves and gouges. If you are just starting your tool collection, I would suggest, as with the carving tools, that you purchase a good set of four or five chisels that will vary enough in size to perform many tasks — you can always add to your collection later. Knives often used in woodworking include pen/whittling/carving knives, marking knives (with a single bevel that allows you to mark square shoulders) and scalpels.

Drilling

With the wide range of specialised drill bits available, I would suggest that your best choice for clock case making would be a set of metalworking twist drills, a set of dowel/spur woodworking bits and a countersink bit. Other specialist drills such as forstner and saw tooth bits are highly desirable though these can be purchased gradually as the need, or your finances, allow. Hand drilling tools (as opposed to bits) include carpenter's braces and wheel braces (sometimes simply known as hand drills).

Filing

Files, rasps and rifflers (shaped files for carving) are not tools that I favour for woodworking as they tend to tear the fibres of wood rather than slice them. However, they can prove useful for difficult cleaning jobs (*Eg* cleaning up mouldings), and for filing surplus veneer after it has been stuck down (at the edge of the veneered board). It is handy to have a collection of different sectioned files, (*Eg* flat, round, triangular) for different woodworking tasks and, in some cases, Surforms can also prove to be valuable additions to your tool chest. Metal files and a set of needle files might also be needed for fettling fixtures and fittings as well as delicate fretwork.

Hammering

The three main types of hammer are cross pein, ball pein and claw hammers and these are available in various weights and sizes. For clock case work, I would recommend that you acquire a light 3½ or 4 ounce cross pein 'pin hammer' which you will need for delicate work (*Eg* fitting glazing beads to glass doors) and 8 and 12 ounce cross pein hammers for heavier work. Carpenter's mallets for general joinery work and carver's mallets are also essential tools to have in your collection.

Jointing Jigs

Whilst a skilled craftsman can happily create joints without special jigs, it is worth investigating which jointing jigs are available on the market for they can help in terms of speed and accuracy. Traditional devices that help in the cutting of joints include mitre boxes, bench hooks, shooting boards and dowelling jigs — these can be made in the workshop or purchased as manufactured items. In recent years, a number of advanced jointing systems have also been developed to assist in the cutting of dovetails, tenons and various decorative joints.

Measuring and Marking

Tools in this category that are useful for making clock cases include *sharp* pencils, marking knives/scalpels, tape measures, rules, try/combination squares, sliding bevels (for marking varied angles), dividers, calipers and dovetail markers. It is always worth having simple heavyweight straight edges (as opposed to rulers) for marking and cutting operations — these are generally available up to a metre or 3 feet long.

Planing

This is a subject that holds a lot of passion for woodworkers as planing is such an important part of hand work. There are many styles of plane on the market, not only for different types of work, but also in the materials used and the manufacturing methods employed, *Eg* wooden planes, custom made and mass production models. I would recommend that the beginner should have three basic planes in his tool collection: a large fore or try plane that is suitable for planing larger stuff; a smoothing plane whose tasks are suited to its name; a block plane, preferably with an 'adjustable mouth' that will allow you to plane small section stuff, end grain and will help in planing stubborn or difficult areas of timber. Traditional wooden moulding planes and combination/plough planes can also be useful for a range of shaping tasks, though these tools have largely been superceded by the electric router

Sanding

The main hand tool used for sanding is the simple cork sanding block which has abrasive paper wrapped round it whilst sanding flat surfaces. Other useful sanding tools are generally home/workshop made items such as dowels and shaped blocks which allow abrasive paper to be wrapped around specific profiles for specific operations. The shape of your hand or fingers can also prove occasionally useful!

Sawing

The main groups of handsaws that you would use freqently are: rip saws for ripping along the grain of solid timber; panel or cross cut saws for sawing across the grain of solid timber and for manufactured boards such as plywood and MDF; tenon saws for crosscut work and for joint making; gents and dovetail saws for fine joint work; fret and coping saws for scroll and pattern work. You might also like to investigate Japanese saws (which cut as you pull the saw blade towards you) as these can produce remarkably fine saw cuts.

Scraping

The cabinet scraper is a small piece of hardened steel sheet that is sharpened (with practice) to produce a burr — the burr is then used for scraping difficult or torn timber and can be much more effective than sandpaper for such tasks. Cabinet scrapers are also available in curved and kidney shapes and whilst they are difficult tools to sharpen and master, I would suggest that it is well worth the time and effort in becoming proficient in their use.

Sharpening

You might as well use a knife and fork rather than work with blunt tools! A basic sharpening set-up can include a bench grinder for grinding correctly angled hollowed bev-

els on your gouges, chisels and plane irons and flat and curved honing stones which will give you your final cutting edge. There are a number of variations available for both grinders and honing stones and it is worth looking at the options before you purchase.

Veneering

It is surprising what you can achieve in veneering with a straight edge and a scalpel. There are more specialised veneering tools such as veneer edge trimmers and punches and these are worth investigating if you intend to do a lot of veneering work. If you are gluing your veneers with hot animal glues, a gluepot and veneer hammer will also be needed.

Machinery

Machines can be viewed as motorised hand tools and usually require as much skill to operate as their hand counterparts. The main advantages of machines are their labour saving potential and their accuracy (if they are set up and operated correctly and if sharp tooling/cutters are employed).

Woodworking machinery can be divided into two main categories: portable power tools and floor/bench standing machinery. To give full descriptions of all the machinery options available could be counter-productive as this is an involved subject in its own right: magazines, books and machinery catalogues are your best source for detailed information. An overview of basic machines that are suitable for clock case making will, however, give the beginner an insight as to which items will be most useful without draining your bank account.

Portable Power Tools

An electric drill is perhaps the most extensively used DIY tool and is always worth having in your collection. Prices, quality and specifications vary and, as with all tools, I would suggest that you buy the best that your budget will allow. Drill presses that can accommodate portable electric drills are worth considering for accurate vertical drilling and if you can, at some time, afford a full-blown pillar drill, you will find this a continually useful workshop item. Other accessories are available for electric drills and can include circular saw, lathe, sanding and polishing attachments.

Portable circular saws are useful for ripping or crosscutting boards and panels of timber or manufactured boards. They are limited in their scope in that they cannot be directed freehand and should always be used with a fence. Jigsaws and electric scrollsaws, however, are inevitably directed freehand and can be used for curved or straight work though they will not produce the straight lines that are associated with circular saws linked to a fence.

Electric routers are always worth having in your collection due to their versatility for making mouldings, joints, housings, rebates, inlays and varied shaped work. When linked to routing jigs and tables, their versatility can be extended even further.

Portable planers are useful labour saving devices though they are not essential if you can get your timber planed and thicknessed on either your own or another woodworker's/company's planer/thicknesser.

Electric sanders include orbital, belt and palm sanders and are useful labour saving devices.

Dust extractors are always worth considering for health and safety reasons and for their usefulness in keeping your work area clean. Many portable power tools have in-built dust bags/extractors though you might like to consider a purpose-built dust extractor that can be connected to a number of portable and floorstanding/bench machines. Vacuum cleaners are also a useful workshop accessory.

Floorstanding and Bench Machinery

Personally, if I were forced to choose one major floorstanding or bench machine on a low budget, I would opt for a bandsaw due to its flexibility for cutting curved, straight and mitred work; they can also be used for cutting veneers from a block of wood and, with the right blades, are suitable for metal, wood and plastics. A good motorised fretsaw will also handle many bandsaw operations, albeit on thinner stock and they are, of course, also useful for fretwork!

If you run a one- or two-man workshop, it is worth considering a combination machine which can accommodate a planer/thicknesser, a saw bench/table for crosscutting and ripping, a spindle moulder and a slot morticer. These machines when new are not cheap and reconditioned or second-hand bargains at a much lower price can occasionally be found if you're working to a tight budget. Combination machines for the small workshop are, however, a sound long-term investment that can save you hundreds, if not thousands of hours of sweat and toil. They are also much cheaper than their individual counterparts.

Another highly versatile piece of machinery is the radial arm saw which is a circular saw that travels across an arm that is above bench height. Their primary function is one of crosscutting timber at 90 degrees though, due to the adjustability of the arm and the saw's motor, the machine can also be set for ripping timber with parallel cuts as well as for a variety of angles for mitre and compound mitre cuts. Dado cutters (a combination of saw blades that can be set to varying widths) can be used for cutting housings and tenons on the radial arm saw and it is even possible to obtain, with some models, a spindle moulder head accessory for shaped work.

In addition to the bandsaw, fretsaw, combination machine and radial arm saw, there are many individual machines available that are devoted to single operations such as saw benches, planers, thicknessers, morticers, tenoners, overhead routers, spindle moulders, pad and drum sanders and drilling machines, though these are only worth investigating seriously if you run a production workshop.

The woodturning lathe I would recommend to anyone who not only wishes to turn wood, but also to those who would like to extend the range and variety of shaped components that they can make in their workshop. There are, nowadays, many jigs, chucks and accessories that have been developed that extend woodturning beyond the realms of bowls, platters and cylinder work, though these three basic forms are still the basis of most turning work.

A final note on machines and machining. Whichever items of machinery you choose to have in your workshop, whether they are purchased from a qualified tool dealer or second-hand through an auction or an advertisement in your local paper, you really must learn how to operate the machines correctly and safely and, just as importantly, how to maintain them in good working order. Machining can be really rewarding as long as you learn safe procedures, though it only takes a split second mistake to find out that they can cut more than just wood! Once safe machining procedures become an automatic part of your working attitude, you will find that there is not only little danger of hurting yourself but also that you will produce better quality work.

CHAPTER FIVE

Construction — General Rules

Each clock project in this book is accompanied by working drawings, cutting and material lists and by 'Schedules of Operations'. These schedules/instructions guide the woodworker through the project suggesting an order of operations. The schedules cannot tell someone how to operate a tool and neither can they be looked on as gospel, for we are all different and have our own way of coping with problems according to personal preference and the tools, materials and workshop environment that we have available.

There are, however, general procedures that are common in cabinet making or clock case work:

The Design

Before cutting into beautiful and possibly expensive materials, it is wise to make sure that you fully understand the nature of the project that you are embarking on, whether it is based on your own design, a design from a detailed drawing/plan or even from sketches for a carving project. This research stage should reveal what materials and tools you require and also possible workloads. (Bear in mind that on a new project, most tasks take a lot longer than you first anticipate).

Materials

Order and acquire your materials and fixtures and fittings.

Marking and Measuring

This is a process that is used throughout a project, from the initial 'rough conversion' of boards of solid timber to the final planing and dimensioning of components, the cutting of joints, the assembly of carcasses and through to the fitting and hanging of doors. It is wise to acquire a traditional woodworking habit of 'measure twice and cut once' as a safety measure against mistakes.

Converting and Machining Solid Timber

If you buy solid boards of *sawn* timber, you will need to know their approximate moisture content prior to any machining and planing work — check this with your timber merchant if you have no moisture meter. If you have too much moisture in the timber, consider either leaving it to season for a longer period or ask your timber merchant if he has kiln drying facilities.

Study the boards to establish what the figure and grain looks like — you might need to do an initial surface planing/thicknessing in order to reveal the figure. Note: with 'wany edged' boards you will need, for safety reasons, to straighten the irregular edges (with a band, hand or jigsaw) prior to feeding the board through a planing machine.

Establish, in pencil, which components will come out of your board/s, allowing for figure/pattern, colour and grain direction. The ends of the boards frequently have shakes, splits and cracks and these should be left as waste material unless you wish to incorporate these unstable defects into your design!

You will then need to consider how you are going to cut the components from the boards (*Eg* hand, band, circular or jig saw) and will need to allow for the thickness of your saw blades in your dimensioning. At this stage, it is better to cut everything oversize to allow for final dimension cutting and planing at a later stage. If you have a number of small components, it is better to combine these in one larger component for the planing and thicknessing operations prior to final dimensioning.

Cut/saw your boards into oversized components (or groups of small components) and then surface plane and thickness these components to a few millimetres (approx ⅛″) over your required thickness — it is then wise to leave the components to settle for a week or two as the heat from the machining will make the timber move — you can then do a final 'skim' machining and finish off with a hand plane.

Once the components are planed to their final thickness, you can then proceed in planing one 'straight and square edge' along the length of the grain: this will give you a 'baseline' to accurately measure and mark the other lines of your component with either a try square and marking knife for the square edges or a marking gauge for parallel edges.

Your 'baseline straight and square edge' will also allow you to feed the material against the fence of a circular saw or bandsaw for final sawn dimensioning — allow a little surplus for you will then need to plane, by machine and hand, the length-grain sawn edges down to their final dimension lines. With end-grain, you might be able to come straight from the saw or alternatively, you might need to plane down to your final knife line with a blockplane (a mitre trimmer can also be extremely useful for squaring off end grain).

If you have machinery, but are unfamiliar with machining practice, it is essential to get some training and there are a number of part time courses available — check the magazines. If you have no machinery, it is worthwhile asking local joinery companies or timber merchants — many of these companies will be happy to machine up your basic components from a cutting list so you can then proceed with the handwork and the construction of your project. Further reading is also suggested in the Bibliography.

Converting Man-made Boards

The beauty of man-made boards such as plywood or MDF is that they are inherently stable and you do not have to consider seasoning and timber movement and warpage. Furthermore, the planing and thicknessing operations are not necessary and you only have to consider sawing and planing straight, square and parallel edges for rectangular components (unless, of course, your components have a curved profile).

Jointwork

Once you have sawn and planed your components to their final dimensions, you can then proceed to measure, mark and cut any required joints. Check the plans so that you know exactly what is required; if you are unsure about the procedure for cutting specific joints, there are a number of books on the subject. If you are marking and cutting a joint that is new to you, it might be worth having a practice run on scrap material.

If you have a number of repetitive joints, it is worthwhile getting into a rhythm by doing all the measuring and marking in one stage, followed by the sawing and chiselling operations. if you have machining facilities such as circular saws and routers, a number of accurate joint cutting operations are also possible with this equipment. You might also like to consider the use of 'Jointing Jigs/Systems' which are available on the market.

Check your joints for an *initial* fit — try to avoid pushing them right home until you are getting ready for assembly, as the more you work the joints, the sloppier they will become.

Carcass Assembly

Many of the clocks in this book have a main carcass, or box section, that can be constructed from veneered man-made boards: if you wish to use solid timber you should preferably employ the traditional framed and panelled method of construction which allows for timber movement.

The box section is the main unit of the clock to which other components are attached such as mouldings, dial-boards, doors, crests, finials and fixtures/fittings. It is therefore essential that this box section is accurately made and assembled as it will affect the rest of the clock case construction.

The starting point for the box or carcass is usually the backboard which acts like the keel of a boat from which the other components spring, (see the long-case clock plans as a good example of this). If you make this accurate, square and straight the rest of the carcass will be easier to construct.

Once you have made the components for the main carcass, it is wise to assemble them 'dry', without glue, using G or sash cramps: you can then check that the carcass will glue together squarely and without any twisting or warping: checking that the diagonals of a square or rectangle are equal is the favoured method for ensuring square-ness though the use of squares, and your sight, will also help. You might need to fine adjust components, joints or the position of your cramps at this stage to ensure that you have a truly accurate carcass.

Prior to final gluing, you might also need to consider sanding, cleaning and polishing/painting the interior surfaces as these might be inaccessible later — this is a matter of personal preference and common sense. For instance, the interiors of the long-case clocks might never see the light of day in which case black paint will be sufficient and this can be applied after assembly; with the regulator clocks, however, the interiors are a major visual feature and you will want as good a finish on both the interior and exterior surfaces.

When you come to the final gluing, take the phone off the hook and bite off anyone's head who interrupts you midway through the process (!) for you cannot allow the glue to grab until your components are accurately cramped in position. Any surplus glue that squeezes out of the joints should be wiped off, firstly with a slightly damp rag and then with a dry one to remove any moisture. Some woodworkers favour leaving the surplus glue to go hard and chiselling it off afterwards though I find that this can either tear the fibres of bare unfinished wood or, if you have pre-finished the components, it can remove the surface of the finish.

Veneer Work

A common myth about veneers is that they are inferior to solid timber. Whilst this may be true in terms of future physical damage to your woodwork (solid wood can obviously take heavier blows), veneered boards are inherently more stable than solid wood boards.

A trip around a quality veneer store or a browse through historical books which illustrate the achievements of veneered work over the centuries will soon dispel the 'inferior' myth. There are things that you can do with veneer work in terms of veneer matches (*Eg* book, quarter, radial and running matches) and in terms of marquetry and inlay that are just not feasible with solid timber. Furthermore, there are a number of beautiful timbers, especially as burrs (or burls), which are unsuitable for solid timber construction work, but are ideal for veneer work. When these are sliced into veneers and are book or quarter matched, they can produce quite stunning results.

Another advantage of veneers is their controllability over a large area in terms of grain and figure matching. When a log is sliced into a number of thin, closely matching sheets (they obviously vary gradually as they progress through the

log), it is possible to cover complete walls and rooms with a closely matching figure — this would not be possible with solid boards.

Veneers can be virtually as easy to lay as wallpaper, or as difficult as . . . well it depends on how wild the grain and figure is, the condition of the veneers and how easy the species of timber is to work. Most straight grain veneers can be glued directly to the groundwork whereas some of the wild burrs might need damping and flattening prior to gluing. Details are given in W.A. Lincoln's 'Complete Manual of Wood Veneering' which is a valuable book to have in your workshop collection of publications.

Before the introduction of man-made boards such as plywood, blockboard and medium density fibreboard (MDF), veneers were glued to a solid wood groundwork. This groundwork would traditionally be made from single or laminated boards (see Fig. 6) and would be veneered on two surfaces with a decorative veneer on the outer surface and a plain 'balancing' veneer on the unseen inner surface — veneering on one surface only would pull the board out of true and the balancing veneer would correct this warpage.

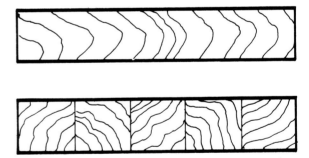

FIGURE 6

The two veneered surfaces help the stability of the solid wood especially with items such as table leaves. In box or carcass constructions however, you will frequently find with antique furniture that there was no balancing veneer on the inner surfaces as they were not needed — the strength of the construction was sufficient to keep the solid boards of timber flat.

Whilst veneers helped with the stability of solid wood groundwork on antique furniture, this could not totally prevent the groundwork from moving — consequently, one of the ongoing tasks with antique restorers is to replace veneer that has blistered or cracked as a result of groundwork movement. This is not a problem when stable man-made boards such as plywood or MDF are used for the groundwork and I am sure that many of the craftsmen from previous centuries would have favoured using these materials, if they had been available for the base of their quality veneer, inlay and marquetry work.

To lay veneers, the following procedure is usually adopted:

The groundwork must be free of defects such as cracks, bumps or dents — these will show through the veneers if they are not filled or sanded clean.

The groundwork must be sanded clean and flat and all dust removed.

If your groundwork is made from a particularly absorbent material, it is advisable to size the groundwork with a thin glue-size first (this could be a watered-down PVA or animal glue or even a decorator's paste).

Edge Lippings and Facings

Prior to gluing the veneers to the main surfaces of a panel, you will need to consider the edges of the panel. If these edges will not be seen in the final construction, you can ignore them. If they are exposed, you should cover them either with a hardwood lipping, a strip of veneer or, if appropriate to the design, with a moulding (see Fig. 7).

WHEN VENEERING EDGES OF PLYWOOD OR MDF, IT IS ADVISABLE TO SIZE THESE EDGES WITH GLUE FIRST

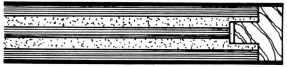

LIPPINGS CAN BE BUTTED & GLUED DIRECTLY TO THE EDGES, THOUGH A TONGUED & GROOVED JOINT WILL PRODUCE A STRONGER RESULT.

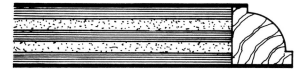

WHEN GLUING MOULDINGS DIRECTLY TO PLYWOOD OR MDF EDGES, IT IS ADVISABLE TO SIZE THESE EDGES FIRST WITH GLUE.
FIGURE 7

Once the edges have been treated, you can then proceed to veneer the main flat surfaces of the panel and the way in which this is done largely depends on the adhesives and gluing options that you adopt.

Adhesives and Gluing Options

CONTACT (OR IMPACT) ADHESIVES

These include adhesives such as 'Thixofix', 'Time Bond' and 'Evo Stik' which are spread on both the groundwork and the veneer surfaces: once the adhesive has become touch dry on both surfaces, the veneer can then be bonded to the groundwork and this can initially be done with hand pressure — I usually find it is then best to apply a harder pressure either with a wooden roller or a veneering hammer. Contact adhesives do not require a veneer press.

GLU-FILM

This is a relatively new technique that involves the use of a paper backed adhesive film which bonds veneers to the groundwork with the use of a domestic iron. The adhesive film, which is available in 1 metre or 36 inch widths, is cut to size and sandwiched between the veneer and the groundwork; the paper backing is used to protect the veneer from scorching by the iron (usually set on a low setting) and the heat will set off the glue-film between the veneer and the groundwork. Glue-film does not require the use of a veneer press.

HOT GLUES AND HAMMER VENEERING

This is a traditional process that uses animal adhesives such as Scotch glue or modern alternatives such as Croid Aero Scotch Glue. The glue is heated in a special gluepot (this can be an electric or a traditional stove version) to approximately 120 degrees Farenheit (as hot as your finger can bear); the glue is then spread thinly over both the groundwork and the veneer with a brush and allowed to become 'tacky'; the veneer is pressed down in position and is then *lightly* sponged with hot water to prevent the glue from sticking to an electric iron (set on a low setting) which is then worked over the surface of the veneer to draw the adhesive into the veneer pores; a veneer hammer, or squeegee, is then worked along the grain working from the centre of the veneer out towards the edges in a zig-zag fashion — this removes any air bubbles and surplus glue. A veneer press is not needed for this process.

GLUES FOR VENEER PRESSES

Standard cabinetmaking and woodworking glues such as Cascomite and PVA can also be used for veneering, though some form of veneer press will be needed — this could be a traditional 'cold veneer press' which is usually an expensive item of equipment, or it could be a workshop made press, or caul, where the veneer/groundwork is cramped between two stout boards. The glues will need a few hours to set and cure in a cold press, though Cascomite (and various 'phenolic resin' adhesives) can be used in hot presses where the setting and curing time takes only a matter of minutes. These hot presses, however, are more suited for production woodwork.

Veneer Trimming

When the veneer has been laid and glued to the edges or the main surfaces of the groundwork, you should ensure that there is surplus material projecting beyond these surfaces, this surplus will then need to be trimmed.

There are a number of veneer trimming tools available, though I find that a scalpel and patience can be just as effective. Certainly in the case of burr veneers with a wild grain, a scalpel may be superior as you have more control over how your cutting edge reacts with the grain.

When trimming the edge, be careful not to undercut the veneer: it is preferable to leave a slight surplus for filing flat afterwards and this is dependent on how you angle the blade of your scalpel and the position of the bevel on the blade. A blunt file is preferable as this will not tear the fibres and this should be pushed into the groundwork to help seal the edges (see Fig. 8).

Mouldings

Whether you are using bought-in mouldings or those hand-made in your workshop with scratchstocks, moulding planes, plough planes, routers or spindle moulders, you should ensure that you have surplus length available as you will lose a certain amount of material when you cut your mitres.

When you are 'wrapping' a moulding around a box section or carcass, it is advisable to start at the front face then move to the two side faces and finally to the rear face. This is simply because moulding mitre joints can be difficult to cut and it may be necessary to fine adjust the mitre surfaces for a good fit — if you are going to have difficulties, it is most likely to occur with the final moulding you fit and it is as well that this happens where it will

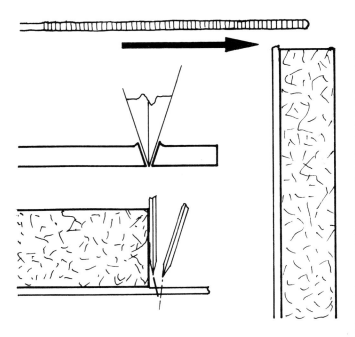

FIGURE 8

not be so noticeable at the rear of the carcass.

(Note: Frequently there is no moulding specified on the rear face).

Mark and cut your front moulding mitres to fit as in Fig. 9A. I usually find that it is worth gluing this front moulding at this stage as it then becomes a 'stable baseline' that will not shift around. Mark and cut mitres on the side mouldings that will join the front mouldings and check for fit, Fig. 9B ; mark and cut the opposing mitres on the side mouldings that will fit the rear face moulding (if there is one in the design), and glue in position, Fig. 9C ; finally, mark and cut the two mitres on the rear moulding to fit exactly between the side mouldings, Fig. 9D. This is the trickiest bit and could involve a certain amount of trial and error.

When cutting mitres by hand, a mitre box and a fine saw can produce a reasonably clean surface though you will need to clean this surface with a sharp chisel if you are to achieve a truly accurate joint.

Other accessories for cutting mitres by hand include mitre trimmers (frequently used in picture framing) and mitre saws. You can also cut mitres on a circular saw (table saw or radial arm versions) and on the bandsaw, though you will most likely have to clean up the surface with a chisel afterwards.

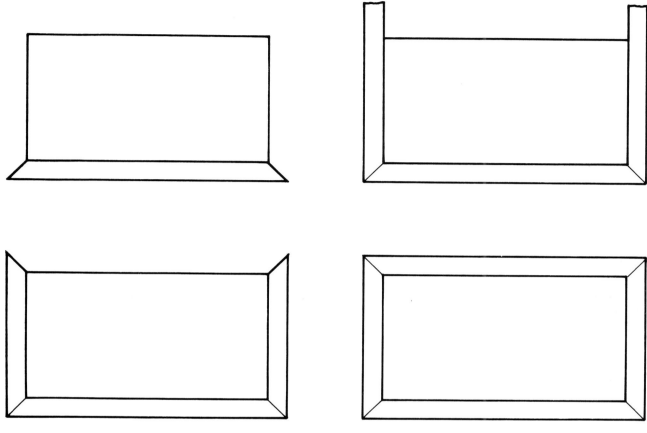

FIGURE 9

Woodturning

Personally, I have always found woodturning to be a highly pleasurable aspect of woodworking and, with clock case making, it can be a useful extra skill for turning individual components such as columns, finials and paterae. if you have no lathe or do not wish to take up woodturning, these components may be bought in as ready-made manufactured items or, alternatively, you may find a woodturner who can turn the items you require.

Although turned components and designs are detailed in some of the clock projects, it is not possible to instruct the beginner in how to turn wood within the scope of this book as it is a subject that needs investigating in its own right and obviously requires hands-on experience. If you do not already turn and wish to find out more about the subject, there are now many books, videos and woodturning courses available as the craft has enjoyed a resurgence in recent years. Though beware, should you catch the woodturning bug, you might find that you have less time for those other 'important things' in life!

Sanding, Scraping and Cleaning

This can be a controversial subject in its own right amongst woodworkers. Some argue that a wood surface has a lot more vibrancy when it is unsanded and is left as a cut surface straight from a plane, chisel, gouge or cabinet scraper; it is argued that sanding with an abrasive, either with an electric sander or by hand, will knead the wood's fibres and give a cloudy appearance.

Whilst this is undoubtedly true, it is not always practical to work straight from a cutting edge, especially with veneers and with those 'difficult' timbers which have the grain going in a number of directions. Invariably, some timbers will have the occasional torn surface where the cutting edge has gone against the grain and these blemishes will need to be removed. Generally the cabinet scraper, if correctly sharpened, will be the best tool for this job, though it is likely that a little abrasive work will be needed as well.

Furthermore, with burr timbers where the grain travels in every possible direction, it is almost impossible to produce a clean surface, without tears, straight from a cutting tool — abrasives are usually needed. It might also be necessary with burrs to 'size' the timber with a watered-down glue (*Eg* 90% water: 1% glue), in order to bind the wood fibres together prior to sanding.

Ultimately it is up to you, the maker, who is intimate with the timbers that you are working, to decide how you are going to clean your work, whether it is with a scraper, plane or abrasives. You might even wish to experiment. I have found that wet and dry paper (as opposed to the usual glass and garnet papers) can produce a very fine surface and if this is then worked with fine wire wool (*Eg* 0000 grade), which has a metal cutting action, you can get close to that initial shimmering surface that you will get from a cutting tool.

Whichever way you choose to clean your wood, clean it you must, for any blemishes, tears or grubby marks will become magnified when you come to apply your chosen finish or polish. Be careful when you are cleaning timber not to overdo it and significantly change the shape of the components that you had previously machined and planed: it is very easy to round off a narrow flat surface or the shoulders of a carefully cut joint. You will also need to consider how you will finish the arrises (the corners/edges where two surfaces meet) for if these are left sharp, your polish will 'crawl' away from them later: you might wish to just take off the sharp edges with a wipe of glasspaper or you might prefer a light or an exaggerated chamfer — this can be an important feature in the finished product.

Finishing and Polishing

In Chapter 3, I mentioned that there are hundreds of finishes and polishes available on the market and that this is an area of expertise in its own right. I also mentioned that, for the beginner, it is worthwhile becoming acquainted with a few basic finishing techniques that will give good results for a number of wood finishing projects.

Before moving onto basic finish/polish applications, it is worth considering the reasons *why* wood needs to be finished.

Freshly cut or sanded wood is beautiful. The problem is that it will not stay that way. Wood is like blotting paper and unless it is sealed, it will absorb moisture and accommodate greasy and dirty marks. Furthermore, if you experiment in your workshop by planing a piece of wood and you leave it for a few weeks you will find, on your return, that the surface and colour have dulled from oxidisation — try planing the piece again and you will see the difference!

Wood needs some form of finish applied to it for the following reasons:

As wood is like blotting paper, wood pores need sealing to minimise the absorption of moisture in damp weather and the evaporation of moisture in dry weather. As wood tends to move according to the current humidity of the air, a finish/polish will reduce this moisture change and will minimise wood movement.

A finish/polish will protect the surface of the wood from disfiguring marks, stains and scratches.

A finish/polish can enhance the natural beauty of wood. Matt and semi-matt/satin finishes enrich the colouring, figure and pattern of wood and high gloss lacquers can act as a magnifier of these features, though there is the danger of the eye being distracted by the reflective surfaces of such finishes.

Finishes and polishes can also retard the oxidisation of the wood surface. There is a trade-off here, however, in that some polishes (*Eg* french polish and polyurethane varnish) will, themselves, oxidise and change colour — this is apparent with antique furniture which, over the centuries, fade to a different colour: purple rosewood, for instance, becomes yellow though if you remove the french polish, the darker colour can be revealed again, though there is naturally some oxidisation of the wood surface as well.

One of your first considerations before choosing *which* finish you are going to use for a particular project will be whether you want a matt, semi-matt/ satin or a high gloss surface. This is a matter of personal preference though the nature of the wood itself and the object you are creating can help you determine the sort of surface that is best. For instance, a high gloss surface on a timber that has a really open grain could be inappropriate unless the grain is filled: light reflecting from the crevices of the open grain could contrast uncomfortably with the light reflecting from the flat surfaces of the wood.

To avoid these uncomfortable variations of reflection,

you can choose to fill open grained timber either with a proprietary grainfiller prior to polishing or with the polish itself, though this will usually require a build up of many coats of polish which are rubbed flat before each new application of polish. French polishing also employs a process called 'spiriting' which helps to fill the grain and achieve a mirror finish. It is also possible to fill grain with wax after you have applied your 'liquid polishes', though this might require many coats applied over a period of weeks. Only once the grain has been filled can a true 'mirror finish' be achieved.

A matt or semi-matt/satin finish can work well on an open grained timber that has not been filled as light reflections are minimal.

Another decision is one of colour. In many cases the natural colour of the wood is all that is needed, though it is worth remembering that even a transparent polish can make the colour a little darker. You might, however, wish to enrich or darken the colour further or even change it completely with a red, blue, green, yellow or black stain or dye — this again is a matter of personal preference. There are a number of stains available on the market which tend to be either water, oil or spirit based; coloured varnishes and lacquers are also available though these will produce a different result from colouring the actual wood.

For the beginner, these decisions may sound a little daunting though a few experiments on scrap samples of your timber with different finishes will soon help you in your choice (it is usually worth having a few variations in stock in your finishing cupboard). You should find that the following options could cover many of your requirements:

Wax Finishes

Waxes can really enhance the beauty of wood and are usually fun to apply, though a certain amount of elbow grease is needed to burnish the surface and create a good sheen. Generally, if you apply wax directly to freshly cut/sanded timber, the first few coats will dull after a short period as the wax is absorbed into the wood fibres — however, many *light* coats of wax polish built up and burnished over a period fo time can create a beautiful lustrous shine or patina, though you have to be patient.

To avoid having to apply many coats of wax, you can use a sanding sealer which seals the surface of the timber making it less absorbant. Sealers are usually shellac or cellulose based and are brushed onto the timber prior to waxing and are then wire wooled down to flatten the surface and remove any blemishes and 'nibs'. You will find that you only need one or two coats of wax on top of a sanding sealer to create a good lustrous sheen.

Waxes can also be applied on top of french polish and varying brands of varnish and will help in achieving a full gloss shine.

There are a number of proprietary waxes available on the market, which are usually petroleum or beeswax based and there are also a number of traditional recipes that you can mix yourself (*Eg* beeswax and turpentine). Waxes tend to have good moisture resistance though they have little protection against heat and scratches, though this might not be a problem with clocks which are not usually subjected to much handling.

Oil Finishes

There are two basic categories of oil finishes: linseed oils and teak oils.

Linseed oils (raw and boiled) are fairly stain resistant though they do not protect the timber from changes in atmospheric humidity and resulting timber movement and I would not recommend their use for the projects in this book.

Teak oils (which include Danish and Tung oils), however, seal wood well and provide protection against atmospheric humidity whilst giving a hard wearing durable finish. Many woodworkers feel that teak oils offer the best solution for finishing wood without changing its nature significantly as is the case with lacquers, varnishes and french polishes which tend to have a surface 'skin'. These oils can provide a matt finish or, if a few coats are applied, a beautiful lustrous sheen can be achieved that really enhances the character of the wood.

Application of teak oils is really quite easy compared with lacquers in that the oil is brushed well into the timber and then surplus liquid is simply wiped off with a soft rag leaving a smooth surface (there is little danger of building up 'dribbles' or 'runs', as there is with various lacquers). If you are applying a number of coats, you will need to rub each one down with fine wire wool before proceeding to the next coat. There is rarely a need to grain-fill timber when using teak/tung oils as you are not aiming for a full gloss finish and will not have those 'uncomfortable reflections' mentioned above. With some proprietary brands of teak oil, it is also possible to apply wax afterwards.

Thinners used for teak oils tend to be white spirit or turpentine based.

French Polish and Shellac Finishes

French polishes began to be extensively used during Georgian times and achieved a real popularity during the Victorian era, mainly due to the fact that the owner of a piece of furniture would not need to regularly wax the piece: the protective skins of polish would provide a virtually maintenance free surface for many years as long as the surface was not damaged by liquids (*Eg* water, wine or whisky!) or by heat (*Eg* hot tea).

French polish is shellac based (shellac is derived from 'lac' beetle) and, over the years, many types of french polish have been developed including button, garnet, white, transparent and heavy french polishes. The process of french polishing can be varied to give light semi-matt finishes or, if the polish is built up with numerous light layers, can be used to achieve a 'mirror finish' with a fully 'choked' grain. Application is initially with a brush and then a 'rubber' (wadding wrapped in cotton rag) is used to build up successive layers of thin coats of polish until the required effect is achieved.

To look good, french polish needs to be expertly applied and this is only possible after much practice — there are, however, a number of 'amateur french polishing kits' available on the market and the beginner might like to experiment with these initially. Shellac based sanding sealers are also suitable for the beginner and are simple brush coats that can be rubbed down with wire wool and then waxed.

There are a number of french polishing training courses available including one or two day and evening courses. I would also recommend Frederick Oughton's book 'The Complete Manual of Wood Finishing' for further enlightenment on the subject; french polish manufacturers frequently provide literature on the use of their products and these are also worth investigating.

Thinners used for french polishes tend to be methylated spirit based.

Cellulose Finishes

Cellulose has been used extensively during the 20th century in mass produced furniture as a tough, heat, moisture and spirit resistant finish.

In its simplest form, cellulose has been developed as a brush coat 'sanding sealer' where only one or two coats need to be applied — these can be rubbed down with wire wool and then waxed and can be easily used by beginners.

Most cellulose finishes, however, tend to be designed for application with a spray gun and can include acid catalyst, pre-acid catalyst, melamine and coloured lacquers (as used on cars). These are only worth investigating if you wish to set up your own spray booth in your workshop.

Special cellulose thinners are used for cellulose lacquers.

Polyurethane Finishes

As with cellulose, these are also tough, heat, moisture and spirit resistant finishes. They are available in matt, semi-matt and gloss formulae and include transparent and coloured versions.

Polyurethane finishes have largely been developed for application by brush and there are many brands available that are suitable for the DIY market.

White spirit and turpentine are used for thinning polyurethane varnishes.

Acrylic Finishes

A number of polish manufacturers have been developing acrylic based finishes in recent years and these tend to be easy to apply brush finishes giving a satin appearance.

Water is used as a thinner for acrylic finishes.

Finishing Abrasives

I would like to give you an exaggerated scenario where you have applied, let's say, a polyurethane varnish, which has gone on a little thickly with runs and dribbles and has a closer resemblance to marmalade rather than a beautiful polish. Don't panic! The careful use of finishing abrasives can rectify the situation.

Wet and dry paper and silicon carbide papers such as 'Lubrasil' and 'Flour Paper' have been developed for rubbing finishes and polishes flat and smooth. Wire wool is also available in a number of grades (0000 grades are commonly used) for flatting finishing and, when rubbed in the direction of the wood grain, can give a good satin effect. Fine abrasive powders and liquids are also available such as pumice powder, rottenstone, burnishing cream and even Brasso and these can be used as a very fine abrasive process giving a final highly polished surface prior to waxing.

The rubbing down of polishes can be as important a part of achieving a quality finish as the application of the finish itself, though if the original finish is applied neatly, less rubbing down will be needed. Be careful not to over rub or sand a finish as there is a danger of cutting through it to the bare wood which will produce a patchy result.

Conditions for Finishing and Polishing

Whichever finish you choose to use, it is worth making sure that you are applying it in clean, dust free conditions. Furthermore, it is better for your workshop to be dry and moderately warm as cold and damp conditions could affect the performance of the finish you are using, *Eg* cellulose can 'bloom' and go white in a damp atmosphere.

Another important condition for applying finishes is the state of your mind! You may have spent hundreds of hours making a beautiful wooden object only to spoil it by rushing the final finishing stage. You will need, especially with some of the liquid finishes and lacquers, to develop a concentrated working rhythm that is smooth, quick and deliberate without being hasty and, above all, you will need patience. If you are unsure about the use of a finishing product, practice on scrap material until you get it right. If the telephone goes whilst you are in mid flow, ignore it. If you mess things up, don't panic — most things are repairable and your patience will help in achieving a quality result.

Fitting Fixtures and Fittings

The final stage of making a clock case includes the hanging of doors and the fitting of brassware, wooden fixtures and glass. Be warned, this is not a five-minute job if you wish to achieve a quality result and inevitably takes longer than first anticipated.

If you are working on components that have been finished and polished, it is worth having squares of carpet on your workbench to protect them from damage. Watch out for small screws or glazing bead pins — these are easily overlooked and can cause much damage to finished wood-work when left lying around.

When fixing screws, make sure that the correct size pilot holes are drilled. With brass screws, it is worth first creating a 'lubricated thread' in the pilot hole with a steel screw of the same size and a wax candle: this will reduce friction and lessen the danger of damaging the head of the brass screw (which is a soft metal) with your steel screw driver (it also helps if the thickness of the screwdriver fits snugly in the slot in your screw head). Where there are a number of screws, it is also worth considering the final position and alignment of the screw head slots as these could visually enhance the end product.

Hanging doors and fixing door locks, hinges and catches is a real patience job: you are a lucky person if, after fixing these items the door opens and closes perfectly first time — fine adjustments are almost inevitable. You will frequently find that the cause of a door not working perfectly lies with how the hinges sit in their recesses, the depth of the recesses and possible binding between the edges of the doors and the carcass it sits in. Take your time and explore in fine detail what is happening; only then can you rectify any problems.

Care is needed when fixing glass. It is usually worth having the glass cut a few millimetres smaller than the size of the opening it sits in so as to avoid any fouling. Glazing beads should be drilled with clearance holes to loosely accommodate the glazing bead pins. When driving the pins home, a 3½ or 4 ounce pin hammer is the best tool for the job and this should lie flat on the glass as you are hammering the pins with a sliding action — do not worry, there is less danger in breaking the glass with this method than with the normal swinging action of a hammer. Never use glue with the glazing beads: the pins will be sufficient to hold the beads in place and, if the glass is broken at any time in the future, both it and the beads will be easy to replace.

When you have finally finished the clock case with all its fixtures and fittings, you can then attach the dial, movement and hands (checking with any manufacturer's instructions), lovingly rub the polished woodwork with a soft rag, stand back and admire the final result and think about photography — but then that is another subject altogether!

1. Grand-daughter Clock Case

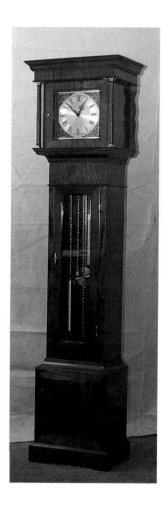

The Grand-daughter clock is a comparative latecomer in the field of long-case clocks and is, in effect, a smaller version of the traditional taller clocks.

Because of the smaller sizes of modern homes, there is a continued demand for these dainty timepieces which are eminently suitable for use in rooms such as a study or on staircase landings and all the features of the traditional long-case (or grandfather) clocks are incorporated in this elegant design.

The plans specify only standard DIY mouldings and the ingenious construction method for making the doors eliminates the necessity for mortice and tenon joints required in traditional framed door construction.

A wide range of mechanical and easy to fit quartz clock movements may be used, thus widening the element of choice.

(Note: The trunk door can be made either glazed to show the pendulum movement as illustrated above, or as solid veneered quarter matched panels in fine timber as outlined in the plan's instruction.)

Overall dimensions: 390 wide × 228 deep × 1493–1556mm high

15⅜″ wide × 9″ deep × 58¾″–61¼″ high

Skill level ＊＊＊＊

Schedule of Operations

You will note that this design is suitable for use with various sizes and makes of clock movements. It will obviously be necessary at an early stage to decide which of those movements you intend to use and to adjust on the drawings any minor differences in dimensions. It is recommended that you obtain your movement, dial, etc., before you commence work on construction. Manufacturers do, from time to time, alter the specifications of their products or even decide to withdraw a model from the market.

TRUNK CONSTRUCTION, ASSEMBLY & VENEERING

In preparing these drawings the Designers have assumed that the main carcass of the case will be built in good quality plywood and then veneered.

Cut out the various components to the sizes shown on the cutting list and ensure that all cut surfaces are square. It is suggested that mouldings are not cut to length at this stage. For parts that are to match, check one against the other to ensure that they are, in fact, identical. The sizes shown in the cutting list are finished sizes and due allowance must be made for planing, etc.

Take the backboard component and carefully mark out the profile given on the drawings and cut out accurately. Any error at this stage will be reflected in the completed project.

Make the trunk sides, ensuring that they are identical and form the rebate at the rear vertical edges. Make the trunk front and cut out the rectangular door opening.

Lay the backboard on a horizontal surface and fix the trunk sides to it using PVA adhesive and glue blocks. Ensure that the trunk sides are at right angles to the backboard and use temporary bracing battens as necessary. Be careful that the bottoms of the trunk sides are in line with each other.

After the adhesive has set hard remove any temporary bracing battens and fix the trunk front to the sides with PVA, glue blocks and long panel pins. Plane off any projections beyond the trunk sides.

Mark for and fix with PVA and screws the upper base framing to the lower outer faces of the trunk sides and front.

Make the base sides and form the rebate at the rear vertical edges. Fix in position on the lower part of the backboard with PVA and glue blocks and to the upper base framing with PVA and long panel pins. Check for squareness with the other components and then fix the base front using PVA, glue blocks and long panel pins. Plane off any minor projections.

Mark for and fix in position the lower base framing using PVA and screws to the lower inner faces of the base sides and front. Note that the lower part of the framing is to be set projecting to later accept the feet or skirting.

Punch in the heads of all exposed panel pins, fill and sand all outer surfaces, taking care not to round over any arrises. Dust off any sanding dust and then veneer all outer surfaces of the trunk and base, including the reveal of the door opening, to the patterns shown on the drawings. It is suggested that an impact adhesive is used in accordance with the manufacturer's instructions.

After veneering, sand the main surfaces of the trunk and base using progessively finer grades of abrasive paper and working in the general direction of the grain.

TRUNK MOULDINGS & FEET

Using standard mouldings and scrap softwood, make up lengths of the upper base mouldings and the upper trunk mouldings to the profiles shown on the drawings. Sand the completed composite mouldings to a finish and cut to lengths, forming neat mitres at the corners. Fix in position with PVA adhesive.

Make the ogee feet in the following manner. Take a long length of the component named in the cutting list and form a rebate on the outer top surface. Carefully mark out the position of the actual feet and glue on pieces of scrap softwood where the splay of the feet occurs. Round over the edge of the rebate already formed and then with a spokeshave or chisel from the splay to each foot, working to the profile shown on the drawings. Cut to lengths required, forming neat mitres at the corners. Mark out for and form, using a bandsaw or coping saw, the inner shapes shown on the elevations. Fix in position to the projecting parts of the lower base framing, using PVA and sash cramps. Carefully clean up with abrasive and veneer as indicated on the drawings. Sand veneer to a finish.

Take the lower base moulding and sand to a finish. Cut to lengths and mitre at corners and fix in position with PVA adhesive.

Protect all arrises and corners on the trunk/base assembly with masking tape to prevent any accidental damage.

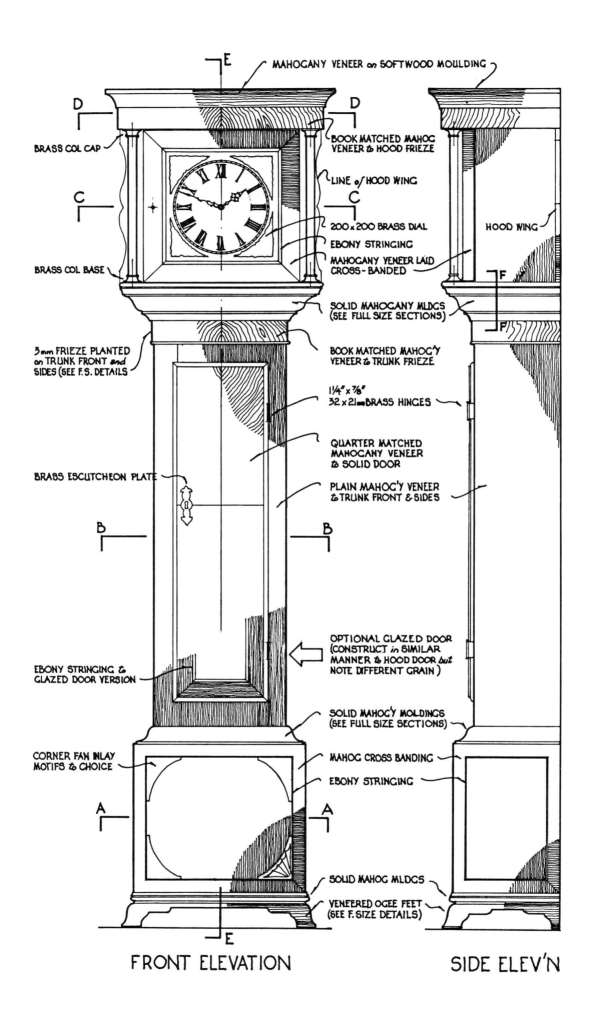

MAHOGANY VENEER on SOFTWOOD MOULDING

BOOK MATCHED MAHOG.
VENEER to HOOD FRIEZE

LINE of HOOD WING

BRASS COL CAP

200 x 200 BRASS DIAL

EBONY STRINGING

MAHOGANY VENEER LAID
CROSS-BANDED

HOOD WING

BRASS COL BASE

SOLID MAHOGANY MLDGS
(SEE FULL SIZE SECTIONS)

3mm FRIEZE PLANTED
on TRUNK FRONT and
SIDES (SEE F.S. DETAILS

BOOK MATCHED MAHOG'Y
VENEER to TRUNK FRIEZE

1¼" x ⅞"
32 x 21mm BRASS HINGES

QUARTER MATCHED
MAHOGANY VENEER
to SOLID DOOR

BRASS ESCUTCHEON PLATE

PLAIN MAHOG'Y VENEER
to TRUNK FRONT & SIDES

OPTIONAL GLAZED DOOR
(CONSTRUCT in SIMILAR
MANNER to HOOD DOOR but
NOTE DIFFERENT GRAIN)

EBONY STRINGING to
GLAZED DOOR VERSION

SOLID MAHOG'Y MOLDINGS
(SEE FULL SIZE SECTIONS)

CORNER FAN INLAY
MOTIFS to CHOICE

MAHOG CROSS BANDING

EBONY STRINGING

SOLID MAHOG MLDGS

VENEERED OGEE FEET
(SEE F. SIZE DETAILS)

FRONT ELEVATION   SIDE ELEV'N

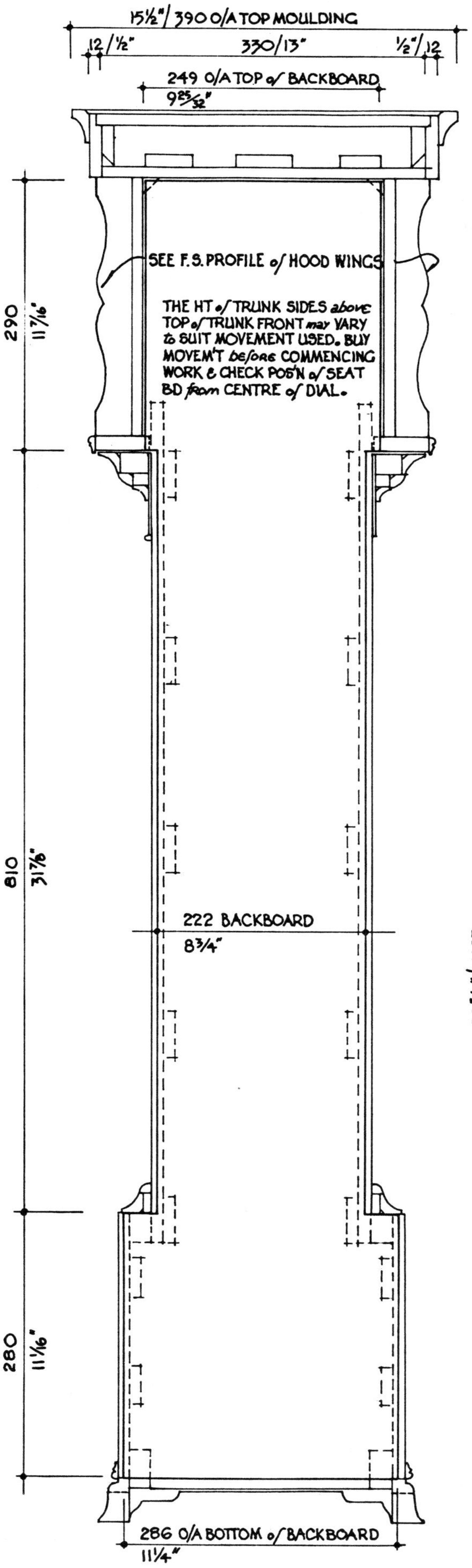
15½"/390 O/A TOP MOULDING
12/½"
330/13"
½"/12
249 O/A TOP of BACKBOARD
9 25/32"
SEE F.S. PROFILE of HOOD WINGS
THE HT of TRUNK SIDES above TOP of TRUNK FRONT may VARY to SUIT MOVEMENT USED. BUY MOVEM'T before COMMENCING WORK & CHECK POS'N of SEAT BD from CENTRE of DIAL.
290
11 7/16"
810
31 7/8"
222 BACKBOARD
8¾"
280
11 1/16"
286 O/A BOTTOM of BACKBOARD
11¼"

REAR ELEVATION

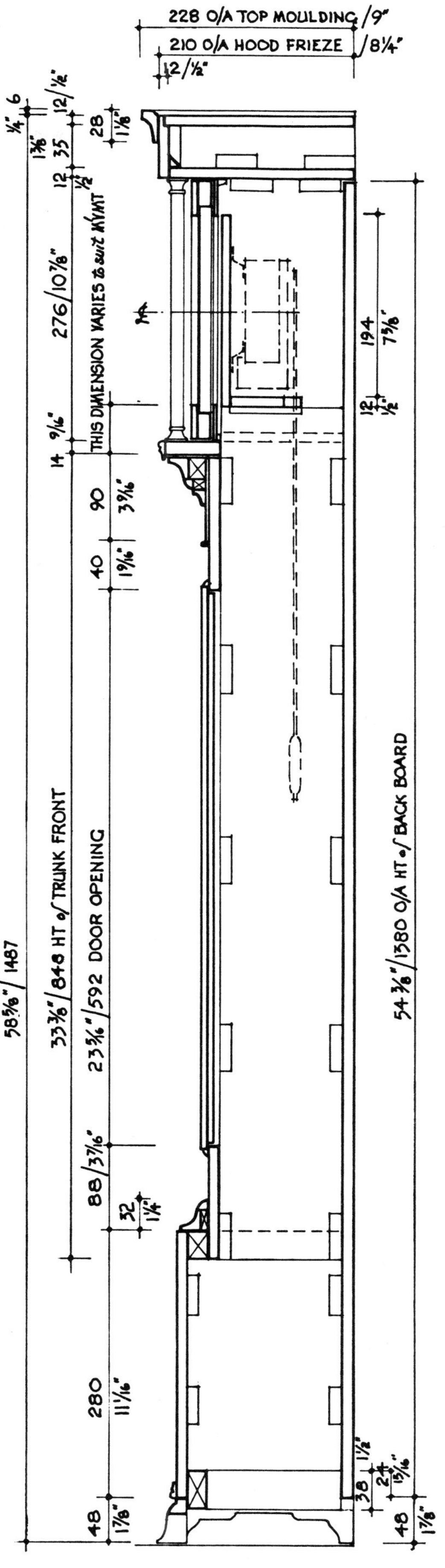
228 O/A TOP MOULDING/9"
210 O/A HOOD FRIEZE/8¼"
12/½"
¼" 6
12/½"
28
1⅛"
1⅜" 35
12 ½"
276/10⅞"
THIS DIMENSION VARIES to suit MVMT
14 9/16"
90
3 9/16"
40
1 9/16"
58⅝"/1487
33⅜"/848 HT of TRUNK FRONT
23 5/16"/592 DOOR OPENING
88/3 7/16"
32
1¼"
280
11 1/16"
48
1⅞"
194
7⅝"
12
½
54⅜"/1380 O/A HT of BACK BOARD
1½"
38
24
15/16"
48
1⅞"

SECTION E-E

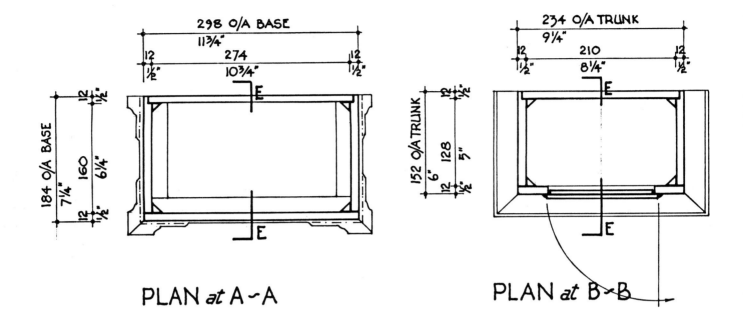

PLAN at A-A

PLAN at B-B

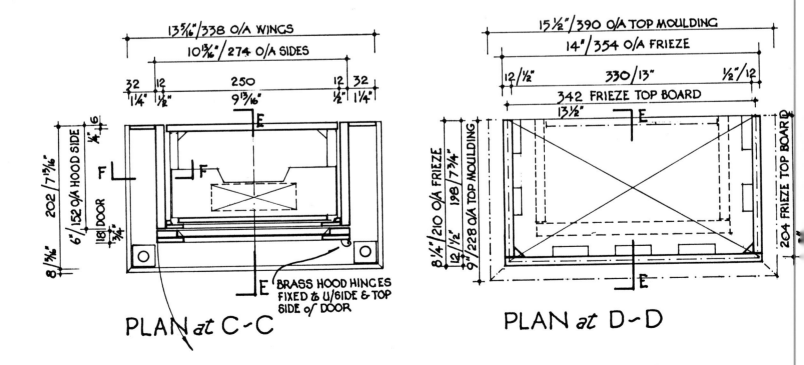

PLAN at C-C

BRASS HOOD HINGES
FIXED to U/SIDE & TOP
SIDE of DOOR

PLAN at D-D

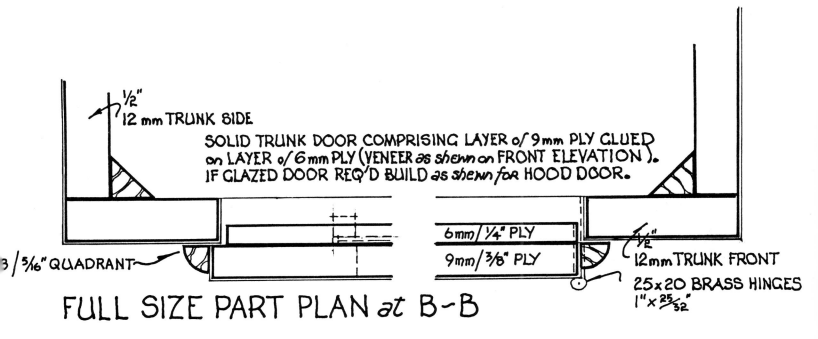

½"
12 mm TRUNK SIDE

SOLID TRUNK DOOR COMPRISING LAYER of 9 mm PLY GLUED
on LAYER of 6 mm PLY (VENEER as shewn on FRONT ELEVATION).
IF GLAZED DOOR REQ'D BUILD as shewn for HOOD DOOR.

6 mm / ¼" PLY
9 mm / ⅜" PLY

½"
12 mm TRUNK FRONT
25 x 20 BRASS HINGES
1" x 25⁄32"

3 / 5⁄16" QUADRANT

FULL SIZE PART PLAN at B-B

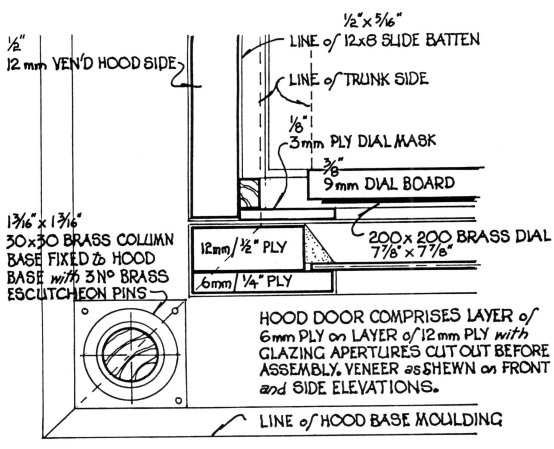

½"
12 mm VEN'D HOOD SIDE

½" x 5⁄16"
LINE of 12x8 SLIDE BATTEN

LINE of TRUNK SIDE

⅛"
3 mm PLY DIAL MASK

⅜"
9 mm DIAL BOARD

1³⁄16" x 1³⁄16"
30x30 BRASS COLUMN
BASE FIXED to HOOD
BASE with 3 N° BRASS
ESCUTCHEON PINS

12mm / ½" PLY

6mm / ¼" PLY

200 x 200 BRASS DIAL
7⅞" x 7⅞"

HOOD DOOR COMPRISES LAYER of
6 mm PLY on LAYER of 12 mm PLY with
GLAZING APERTURES CUT OUT BEFORE
ASSEMBLY. VENEER as SHEWN on FRONT
and SIDE ELEVATIONS.

LINE of HOOD BASE MOULDING

F.SIZE PART PLAN at C-C

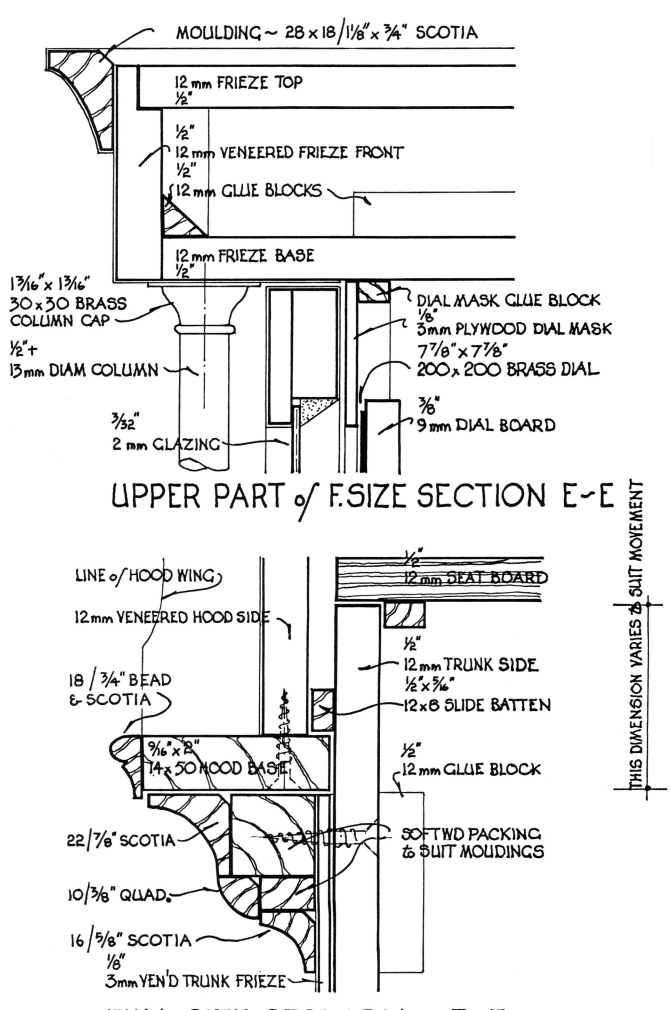

MOULDING ~ 28 × 18 / 1⅛″ × ¾″ SCOTIA

12 mm FRIEZE TOP
½″

½″
12 mm VENEERED FRIEZE FRONT
½″
12 mm GLUE BLOCKS

12 mm FRIEZE BASE
½″

1³⁄₁₆″ × 1³⁄₁₆″
30 × 30 BRASS
COLUMN CAP

½″+
13 mm DIAM COLUMN

³⁄₃₂″
2 mm GLAZING

DIAL MASK GLUE BLOCK
⅛″
3 mm PLYWOOD DIAL MASK
7⅞″ × 7⅞″
200 × 200 BRASS DIAL

⅜″
9 mm DIAL BOARD

UPPER PART of F.SIZE SECTION E~E

LINE of HOOD WING

12mm VENEERED HOOD SIDE

½″
12 mm SEAT BOARD

½″
12 mm TRUNK SIDE
½″ × ⁵⁄₁₆″
12 × 8 SLIDE BATTEN

18 / ¾″ BEAD
& SCOTIA

⁹⁄₁₆″ × 2″
14 × 50 HOOD BASE

½″
12 mm GLUE BLOCK

22 / ⅞″ SCOTIA

SOFT WD PACKING
to SUIT MOULDINGS

10 / ⅜″ QUAD.

16 / ⅝″ SCOTIA

⅛″
3mm VEN'D TRUNK FRIEZE

THIS DIMENSION VARIES to SUIT MOVEMENT

FULL SIZE SECTION at F~F

F. SIZE SECTION E~E

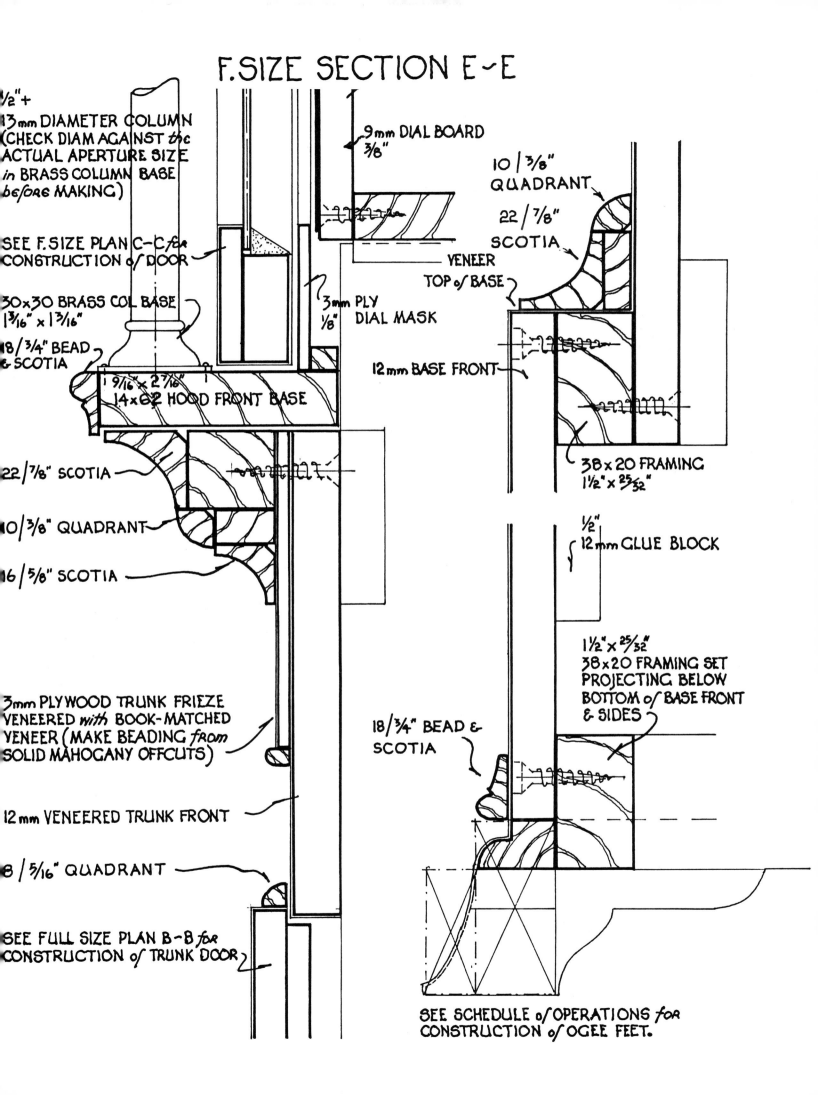

½"+
13mm DIAMETER COLUMN
(CHECK DIAM AGAINST the
ACTUAL APERTURE SIZE
in BRASS COLUMN BASE
before MAKING)

SEE F. SIZE PLAN C~C for
CONSTRUCTION of DOOR

30×30 BRASS COL BASE
1³⁄₁₆" × 1³⁄₁₆"

18/¾" BEAD
& SCOTIA

9/16" × 2⁷⁄₁₆"
14×62 HOOD FRONT BASE

22/⁷⁄₈" SCOTIA

10/³⁄₈" QUADRANT

16/⁵⁄₈" SCOTIA

3mm PLYWOOD TRUNK FRIEZE
VENEERED with BOOK-MATCHED
VENEER (MAKE BEADING from
SOLID MAHOGANY OFFCUTS)

12mm VENEERED TRUNK FRONT

8/⁵⁄₁₆" QUADRANT

SEE FULL SIZE PLAN B~B for
CONSTRUCTION of TRUNK DOOR

9mm DIAL BOARD
³⁄₈"

3mm PLY
⅛"
DIAL MASK

VENEER
TOP of BASE

10/³⁄₈"
QUADRANT

22/⁷⁄₈"
SCOTIA

12mm BASE FRONT

38×20 FRAMING
1½" × ²⁵⁄₃₂"

½"
12mm GLUE BLOCK

1½" × ²⁵⁄₃₂"
38×20 FRAMING SET
PROJECTING BELOW
BOTTOM of BASE FRONT
& SIDES

18/¾" BEAD &
SCOTIA

SEE SCHEDULE of OPERATIONS for
CONSTRUCTION of OGEE FEET.

TRUNK DOOR

Make the trunk door in the manner shown on the drawings, using two layers of plywood glued and pinned together. Punch home any panel pin heads, fill and sand down. Veneer the inner face of the door with any common veneer to act as a balancer. Veneer the arrises of the door before veneering the face of the door with quarter matched veneers to the pattern shown on the drawings. Sand the veneers to a finish and fix the door moulding in position with PVA, forming neat mitres at the corners. Sand to a finish when adhesive has set hard.

Offer up the trunk door to the trunk assembly and carefully mark the positions of the unequal leg hinges on the door and the door opening. Chop out for the hinges in the door opening and the door, cutting through the door moulding as required to accommodate the hinges. Carefully mark out for the door lock and neatly cut the key escutcheon opening. Fix the lock and hinges and the escutcheon plate.

HOOD ASSEMBLY

Take the hood front base and hood side bases and form the hood base, assembling with PVA and sash cramps. It is important that this sub-assembly is square and flat and is a loose sliding fit over the top of the trunk. It will be found helpful to fix a temporary batten across the back of the door sub-assembly.

Next, take the hood sides and wings and check for squareness and matching. Cut the wing shaped profile as shown on the drawing below. Sand the hood sides and wings and veneer to the graining shown on the plan. Sand the veneer to a finish.

Make the freize sub-assembly. Check that the freize sides are identical and form the rebate at the top to take the frieze top. Form the similar rebate at the top of the frieze front. Check the frieze bottom for size and squareness and fix the frieze sides and front to it using PVA and glue blocks. As necessary, pin the front and sides.

Punch home the heads of any panel pins used and fill, and after sanding veneer the underside of the frieze bottom where exposed and then veneer the vertical surfaces of the frieze sub-assembly. Sand the veneering to a finish.

Fix the hood sides to the hood base sub-assembly, using PVA and screws. It is essential to ensure that the sides are exactly at right angles to the base so use temporary bracing battens as necessary. Fix the wings to the sides and hood base using PVA and cramps.

Fix the frieze sub-assembly to the hood sides, using PVA and screws. After adhesive has set, make the frieze top and glue into position in the rebates already formed at the top of the sides and front frieze members.

Take the softwood moulding for the top of the hood. Sand down and then veneer laying the veneer with grain longitudinally. Sand to a finish, cut to lengths and neatly mitre at corners and fix in position with PVA.

Remove any temporary battens at the back of the hood assembly and offer up the hood to the top of the trunk assembly. Carefully mark the positions where the slide battens are to occur. Remove the hood assembly and fix the slide battens to the trunk sides with PVA and pins.

Make the dial mask to exactly fit between the hood sides and between the underside of the frieze bottom and the top of the front hood base. Carefully mark the opening to be cut out, using the brass dial as a guide. The opening should be slightly less than the overall size of the dial. Fix in position using glue blocks as shown on the drawings.

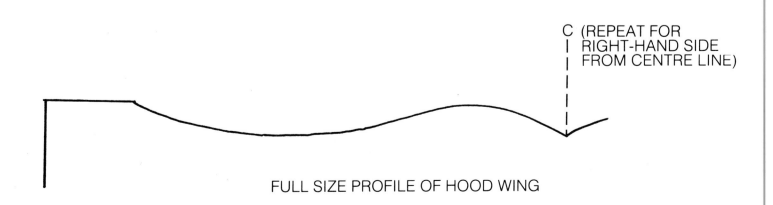

C (REPEAT FOR
RIGHT-HAND SIDE
FROM CENTRE LINE)

FULL SIZE PROFILE OF HOOD WING

HOOD DOOR

Take the two components for the hood door and check for size and squareness against the hood assembly. Carefully mark out for and form the square opening in the outer leaf, using the hole already formed in the dial mask as a guide. Mark out for and form the larger square opening in the inner leaf. Fix the two leaves together with PVA and panel pins. Sand down and veneer to the pattern shown on the drawing and sand veneer to a finish.

Take the flat, horned, hood door hinges and chop out to suit the shapes on the under and upper surfaces of the door. Offer up the door, with hinges, to the hood assembly and mark for and drill the holes for the hinge fixing pins but do not fix at this stage.

On the lathe turn the two hood columns, checking that the ends of the columns are a tight fit into the sockets of the brass column caps and bases. Check the length of each column against the available height in the hood assembly. Sand the columns to a finish while still mounted in the lathe. It is best to apply the final finish to the columns while they are still mounted in the lathe.

MOVEMENT, DIAL & SEAT BOARD LOCATION

Take the member for the seat board and form fixing holes and slot for pendulum rod in accordance with the movement manufacturer's instructions. Fix the softwood locating battens (make from scrap) to the base of the seat board and offer up to the top of the trunk sides to check that it is a snug fit. The seat board is never fixed to the trunk.

Some mechanical movements are not made to fit to the seat board, but have fixing lugs on the front of the movement. In these cases it will be necessary to make and fix a dial-board to the front of the seat board in the manner shown on the drawings. A similar arrangement is necessary for quartz movements.

Fit the brass dial to the dial-board and fix the movement to the seat board or dial-board as the case may be. Offer up this complete assembly on the top of the trunk sides. Offer up the hood assembly and check that the dial fits neatly behind the dial mask without gaps. It may be necessary to slightly reduce the trunk sides or pack up under the seat board to obtain a snug fit.

Leave the seat board and movement in position and slide off the hood assembly. Hang the pendulum rod in position at the rear of the movement and check that the pendulum can swing freely. Remove the pendulum rod and then remove the seat board with the movement still attached and carefully put aside for later positioning.

FINISHING & FINAL ASSEMBLY

The recommended finish for the completed clock case is to grain fill and french polish in the traditional method. However, for those who have no experience in this, an attractive finish may be obtained with any good polyurethane varnish. Thoroughly clean the case of any dirty marks and ensure that all surfaces are free from sanding dust. Apply one coat of polyurethane, brushing well into the grain of the wood. When absolutely dry and hard light sand with fine abrasive, working in the same direction as the grain of the wood. Apply a further coat of polyurethane and when dry and hard, flat down with 0000 grade wire wool, again working in the direction of the wood grain. Repeat the process until a good body of finish has been obtained. Finally, lightly flat down with wire wool as before and bring to a final gloss with solid wax polish lightly applied and brought to a shine with a lint-free cloth. The use of a soft haired brush in the crevices of mouldings will be found of help both in applying wax and final polishing.

After the finishes are complete, fix the column caps, bases and columns in position on the hood. It may, in some cases, be necessary to drill fixing holes in the brassware. The bases and caps should be fixed using brass escutcheon pins rather than screws.

Glaze the hood door with 2mm picture glass, using glazier's sprigs and putty. If you are able to obtain old picture glass with flaws and bubbles the final result will appear more authentic.

Set up the seat board and movement in position and hang the pendulum and fix the hands in accordance with the manufacturer's instructions. The whole clock case should stand upright on a level floor. In the case of a floor that is out of level this may be corrected by inserting small wooden wedges under the feet.

For the first three or four months after the clock has been completed keep the finish free from finger marks and dust by use of a soft polishing cloth *without* wax. Wax may be applied at two or three monthly intervals thereafter but only sparingly. The use of excessive amounts of wax will only create a thick layer which will attract dust and which will never give a satisfactory shine.

Cutting list

COMPONENT	QUANTITY	SECTION	LENGTH
Backboard	1	12 × 286	1380
	1	½″ × 11¼″	54⅜″
Lower Base Side Frames	2	20 × 38	140
	2	²⁵/₃₂″ × 1½″	5¹⁵/₃₂″
Upper Base Side Frames	2	20 × 38	140
	2	²⁵/₃₂″ × 1½″	5¹⁵/₃₂″
Lower Base Front Frame	1	20 × 38	274
	1	²⁵/₃₂″ × 1½″	10¾″
Upper Base Front Frame	1	20 × 38	274
	1	²⁵/₃₂″ × 1½″	10¾″
Ogee Foot Members (Total Length)	1	22 × 48	800
	1	⅞″ × 1⅞″	31½″
Base Sides	2	12 × 184	280
	2	½″ × 7¼″	11¹/₁₆″
Base Front	1	12 × 298	280
	1	½″ × 11¾″	11¹/₁₆″
Trunk Sides	2	12 × 140	900
	2	½″ × 5½″	35⁷/₁₆″
Trunk Front	1	12 × 234	848
	1	½″ × 9¼″	33⅜″
Trunk Frieze (Total length)	1	3 × 90	544
	1	⅛″ × 3⁹/₁₆″	21½″
Slide Battens	2	8 × 12	140
	2	⁵/₁₆″ × ½″	5½″
Lower Base Moulding (Total Length)	1	9 × 18	702 minimum
	1	⅜″ × ¾″	27¾″
Lower Trunk Moulding (Composite) (Total Length)	1	30 × 32	658 minimum
	1	1³/₁₆″ × 1¼″	26″ minimum
Upper Trunk Moulding (Composite) (Total Length)	1	45 × 48	718 minimum
	1	1¾″ × 1⅞″	28¼″ minimum
Trunk Door (Inner Leaf)	1	6 × 152	592
	1	¼″ × 6″	23⁵/₁₆″
Trunk Door (Outer Leaf)	1	9 × 158	598
	1	⅜″ × 6¼″	23⁹/₁₆″
Trunk Door Moulding (Total Length)	1	8 × 8	1576 minimum
	1	⁵/₁₆″ × ⁵/₁₆″	62⅛″ minimum
Hood Sides	2	12 × 152	276
	2	½″ × 6″	10⅞″
Hood Side Bases	2	14 × 50	202
	2	⁹/₁₆″ × 2″	7¹⁵/₁₆″

Hood Front Base	1	14 × 62	338
	1	9/16″ × 2 7/16″	13 5/16″
Dial Mask	1	3 × 250	276
	1	1/8″ × 9 13/16″	10 7/8″
Seat Board	1	12 × 76	234
	1	1/2″ × 3″	9 1/4″
Dial-Board	1	9 × 206	206
	1	3/8″ × 8 1/8″	8 1/8″
Hood Frieze Base	1	12 × 198	330
	1	1/2″ × 7 3/4″	13″
Hood Frieze Sides	2	12 × 59	198
	2	1/2″ × 2 3/8″	7 3/4″
Hood Frieze Front	1	12 × 59	354
	1	1/2″ × 2 3/8″	14″
Hood Frieze Top	1	12 × 204	342
	1	1/2″ × 8″	13 1/2″
Hood Wings	2	6 × 32	276
	2	1/4″ × 1 1/4″	10 7/8″
Hood Door (Inner Leaf)	1	12 × 274	274
	1	1/2″ × 10 13/16″	10 13/16″
Hood Door (Outer Leaf)	1	6 × 274	274
	1	1/4″ × 10 13/16″	10 13/16″
Hood Columns (Turn from square)	2	18 × 18	275
	2	3/4″ × 3/4″	10 27/32″
Lower Hood Moulding (Total Length)	1	9 × 18	778 minimum
	1	3/8″ × 3/4″	30 11/16″ minimum
Upper Hood Moulding (Total Length)	1	18 × 28	846 minimum
	1	3/4″ × 1 1/8″	33 1/2″ minimum
Glue Blocks	Make from scrap		

Clock Components and Hardware (excluding screws and pins)

CLOCK MOVEMENT — OPTIONS:

1. Mechanical/weight driven movement.
   Maximum length of pendulum (centre of hand shaft to centre of bob) should be 689mm/27 1/8″.
   Maximum overall swing of the pendulum should be 200mm/7 7/8″.
   Maximum drop of the weights should be 1041mm/41″ or adjust overall height of clock case to suit movement.
   Maximum overall dimensions of movement not to exceed hood's interior dimensions.
   Chime options: Single/twin bell strike; Whittington; Westminster; St Michael; Triple-Chime.

2. Mechanical/spring driven movement (no pendulum/bracket clock movements)

   Maximum overall dimensions of movement not to exceed hood's interior dimensions.

   Chime options: Single/twin bell strike; Whittington; Westminster; St Michael; Triple-Chime.

3. Quartz movements

   Various pendulum and chiming/melody movements available.

   Hand shaft/fixing nut length: to suit 11mm/$^7/_{16}$" dial-board/dial thickness.

CLOCK DIAL — OPTIONS:

- 200 × 200mm/7$^7/_8$"7$^7/_8$".
- Solid brass, alloy, aluminium and hand painted models available.
- Note: if front winding mechnaical movement is used, drill holes in the dial and bush to accommodate winding keys.

CLOCK HANDS:

- Bushed to suit chosen mechanical or quartz movement.
- Length to suit dial size.
- Pattern to suit individual choice.

BRASSWARE:

- Hinges:

  Trunk door: one pair of odd-sided hinges — 32 × 21mm/1$^1/_4$" × $^7/_8$".

  Hood door: a) pins fixed into column or b) 32mm/1$^1/_4$" butt hinges.
- Door Locks:

  Trunk door: one cupboard lock 50 × 12.5mm/2" × $^1/_2$" to pin.

  Hood door: one concealed bullet catch.
- Filagree plate escutcheon — pattern to suit individual taste.
- Column Caps/Bases

  Full diameters: Two pairs to suit 21mm/$^7/_8$" diameter columns.

  Quarter diameters: Two pairs to suit 21mm/$^7/_8$" diameter columns.

INLAYS:

- Corner Fan Inlays.
- Stringing: black or white line, to suit carcass veneer.

GLASS:

- To suit hood door.

2. *17th Century Long-case Clock*

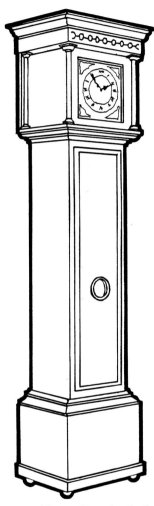

In 1693, during the reign of William and Mary, Peter Abbott of London built an elegant long-case clock standing just 6′6″ high. Because of the unreliability of the movements in those days a lenticle glass was incorporated in the trunk door so that the owner could see the swing of the pendulum.

Many earlier long-case clocks were covered with florid marquetry work, but this clock case has matched burr and crown cut walnut veneers which enhance the beautiful lines.

The fully detailed construction plans will enable you to build a virtual replica of Peter Abbott's masterpiece. A precision-built brass movement and dial may be obtained from the suppliers listed in Appendix II index.

The case may be built in either solid wood or veneered plywood.

Overall dimensions: 470 wide × 275 deep × 1985mm high
18½″ wide × 10¾″ deep × 6′6″ high

Skill level ✳✳✳✳✳

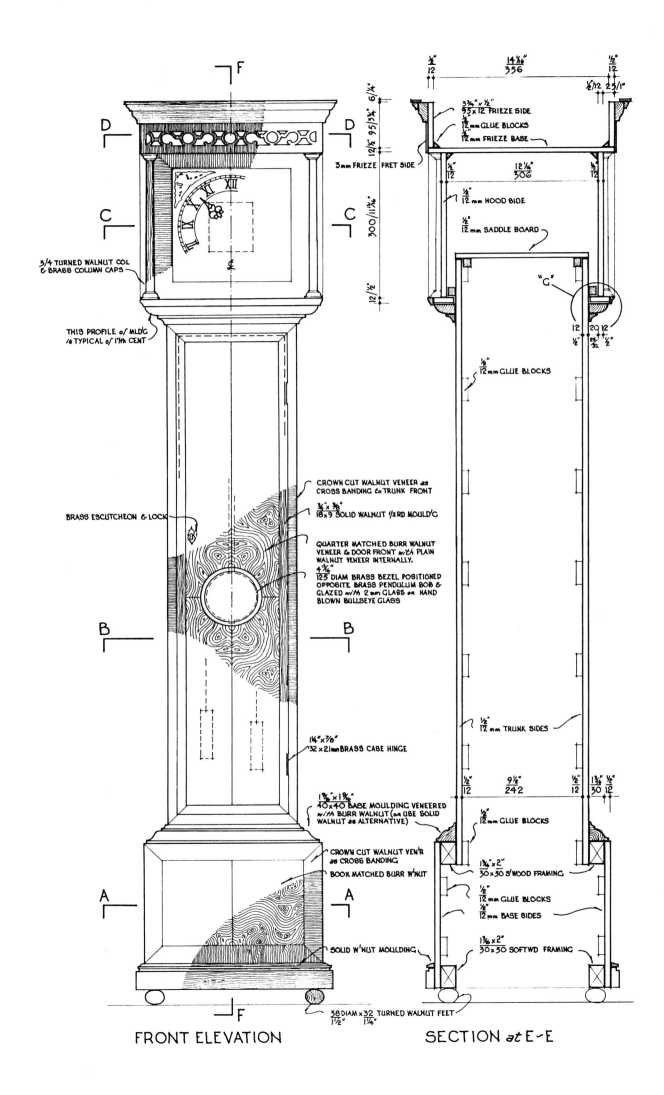

FRONT ELEVATION

SECTION at E-E

3/4 TURNED WALNUT COL & BRASS COLUMN CAPS

THIS PROFILE of MLD'G is TYPICAL of 17th CENT

BRASS ESCUTCHEON & LOCK

CROWN CUT WALNUT VENEER as CROSS BANDING to TRUNK FRONT

$\frac{3}{4}$" × $\frac{3}{8}$"
18×9 SOLID WALNUT 1/2 RD MOULD'G

QUARTER MATCHED BURR WALNUT VENEER to DOOR FRONT with PLAIN WALNUT VENEER INTERNALLY.

$4\frac{15}{16}$"
125 DIAM BRASS BEZEL POSITIONED OPPOSITE BRASS PENDULUM BOB & GLAZED with 2mm GLASS or HAND BLOWN BULLSEYE GLASS

$1\frac{1}{4}$" × $\frac{7}{8}$"
32 × 21mm BRASS CASE HINGE

$1\frac{9}{16}$" × $1\frac{9}{16}$"
40×40 BASE MOULDING VENEERED with BURR WALNUT (or USE SOLID WALNUT as ALTERNATIVE)

CROWN CUT WALNUT VEN'R as CROSS BANDING

BOOK MATCHED BURR W'NUT

SOLID W'NUT MOULDING

38 DIAM × 32 TURNED WALNUT FEET
$1\frac{1}{2}$" $1\frac{1}{4}$"

$\frac{1}{2}$
12   $\frac{14\frac{1}{16}"}{356}$ $\frac{1}{2}$ 12

$\frac{1}{2}$/12 $\frac{25}{1}$"

$3\frac{1}{4}$" × $\frac{1}{2}$"
55 × 12 FRIEZE SIDE

$\frac{1}{2}$
12 mm GLUE BLOCKS

$\frac{1}{2}$
12 mm FRIEZE BASE

3mm FRIEZE FRET SIDE

$6\frac{1}{4}$"
$\frac{1}{2}$/12 $9\frac{5}{3}$/$3\frac{3}{4}$"

$12\frac{1}{2}$

$\frac{\frac{1}{4}}{12}$ $\frac{12\frac{1}{16}"}{306}$ $\frac{\frac{1}{2}}{12}$

$\frac{1}{2}$
12 mm HOOD SIDE

$\frac{1}{2}$
12 mm SADDLE BOARD

"G"

300/$11\frac{3}{4}$"

$12\frac{1}{2}$

12 20 12
$\frac{1}{2}$ $\frac{3}{32}$ $\frac{1}{2}$

$\frac{1}{2}$
12 mm GLUE BLOCKS

$\frac{1}{2}$
12 mm TRUNK SIDES

$\frac{1}{2}$
12   $\frac{9\frac{1}{2}"}{242}$ $\frac{1}{2}$
12   $\frac{1\frac{3}{16}}{30}$ $\frac{1}{2}$
12

$\frac{1}{2}$
12 mm GLUE BLOCKS

$1\frac{3}{16}$" × 2"
30 × 50 S'WOOD FRAMING

$\frac{1}{2}$
12 mm GLUE BLOCKS

$\frac{1}{2}$
12 mm BASE SIDES

$1\frac{3}{16}$" × 2"
30 × 50 SOFTWD FRAMING

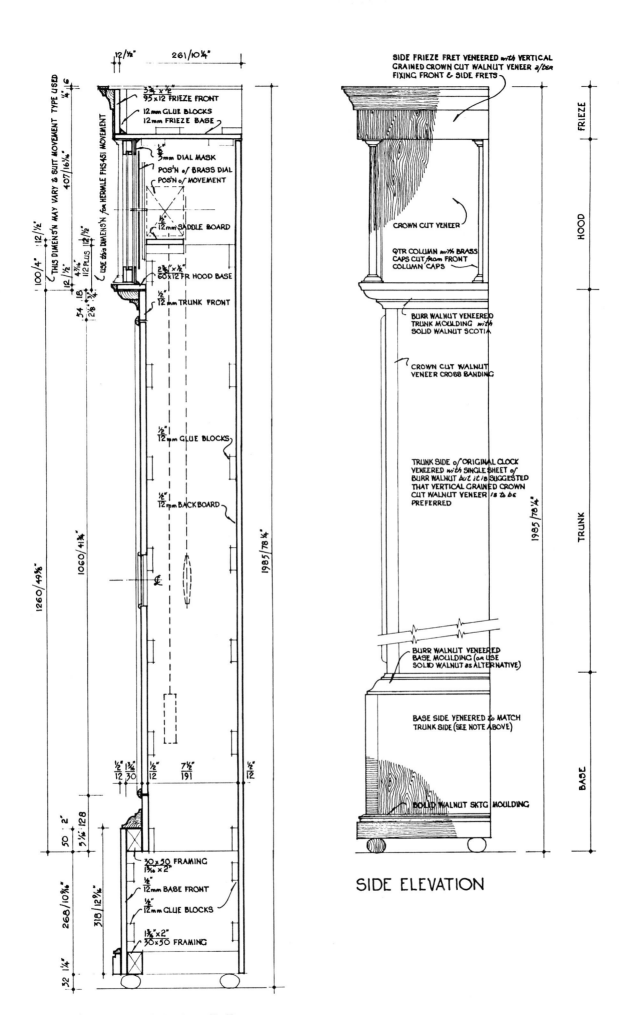

12/½" 261/10¼"

4/16 4/6

3¾ x ½"
95 x 12 FRIEZE FRONT
12mm GLUE BLOCKS
12mm FRIEZE BASE

THIS DIMEN'S'N MAY VARY to SUIT MOVEMENT TYPE USED

USE this DIMEN'S'N for HERMLE FHS451 MOVEMENT

3mm DIAL MASK
POS'N of BRASS DIAL
POS'N of MOVEMENT

100/4" 12/½"

407/16¼"

12mm SADDLE BOARD

12/½" 4/16
12/½" 112 PLUS 112/½"

2⅜" x ½"
60 x 12 FR HOOD BASE

½"
12mm TRUNK FRONT

54 18
2⅜ 57½

½"
12mm GLUE BLOCKS

1060/41⅞"

½"
12mm BACKBOARD

1260/49⅝"

1985/78¼"

½" 1³⁄₁₆" ½" 7½" ½"
12 30 12 191 12

50 2"
5⅛ 128

30 x 50 FRAMING
1³⁄₁₆ x 2"

½"
12mm BASE FRONT

½"
12mm GLUE BLOCKS

1³⁄₁₆" x 2"
30 x 50 FRAMING

268/10⅝"

318/12⅝"

52¼

SECTION at F-F

SIDE FRIEZE FRET VENEERED with VERTICAL
GRAINED CROWN CUT WALNUT VENEER a/bsn
FIXING FRONT & SIDE FRETS

FRIEZE

HOOD

CROWN CUT VENEER

QTR COLUMN with BRASS
CAPS CUT from FRONT
COLUMN CAPS

BURR WALNUT VENEERED
TRUNK MOULDING with
SOLID WALNUT SCOTIA

CROWN CUT WALNUT
VENEER CROSS BANDING

TRUNK SIDE of ORIGINAL CLOCK
VENEERED with SINGLE SHEET of
BURR WALNUT but it is SUGGESTED
THAT VERTICAL GRAINED CROWN
CUT WALNUT VENEER is to be
PREFERRED

TRUNK

1985/78¼"

BURR WALNUT VENEERED
BASE MOULDING (or USE
SOLID WALNUT as ALTERNATIVE)

BASE

BASE SIDE VENEERED to MATCH
TRUNK SIDE (SEE NOTE ABOVE)

SOLID WALNUT SKTG MOULDING

SIDE ELEVATION

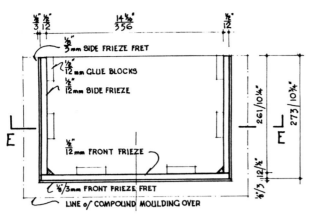

PLAN *at* D~D

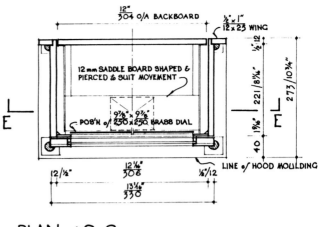

PLAN *at* C~C

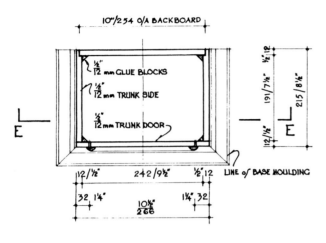

PLAN *at* B~B

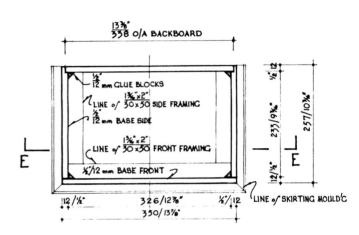

PLAN *at* A~A

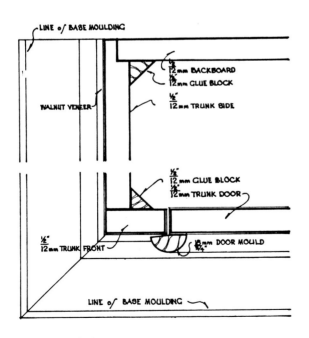

PART PLAN B~B

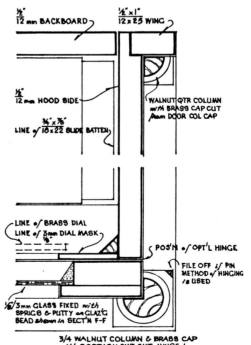

PART PLAN C~C

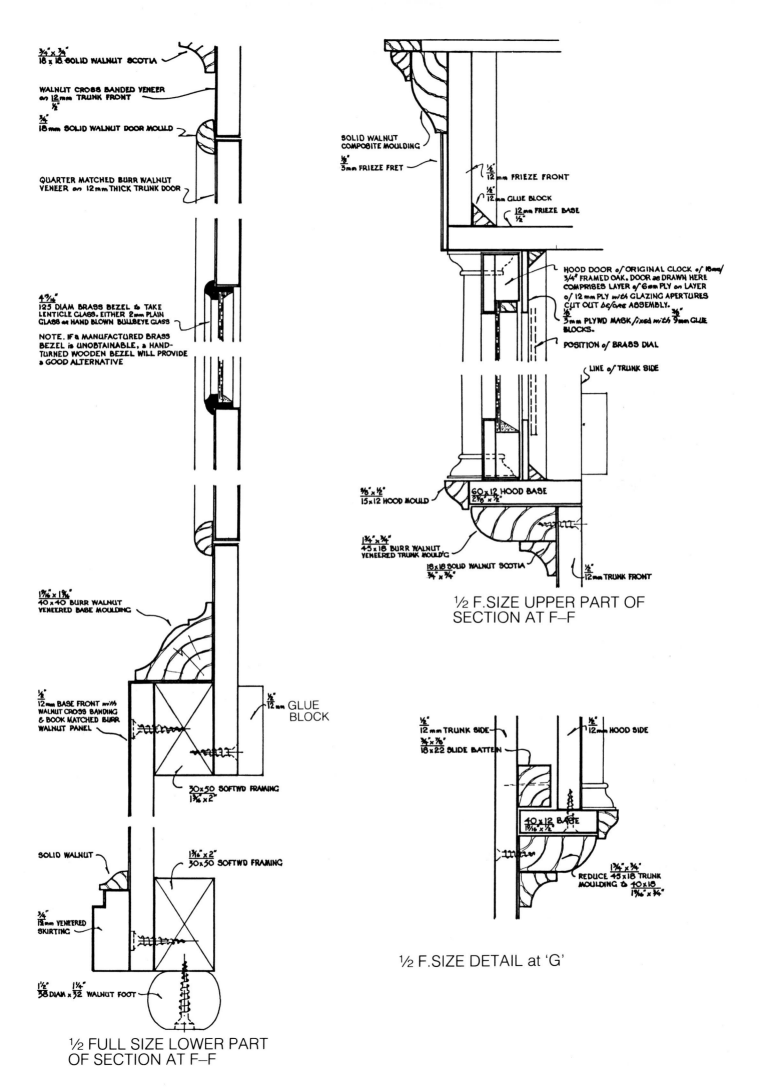

¾" x ¾"
18 x 18 SOLID WALNUT SCOTIA

WALNUT CROSS BANDED VENEER
on 12mm TRUNK FRONT
½"

¾"
18mm SOLID WALNUT DOOR MOULD

QUARTER MATCHED BURR WALNUT
VENEER on 12mm THICK TRUNK DOOR

4⁹⁄₁₆"
125 DIAM BRASS BEZEL to TAKE
LENTICLE GLASS. EITHER 2mm PLAIN
GLASS or HAND BLOWN BULLSEYE GLASS

NOTE. IF a MANUFACTURED BRASS
BEZEL is UNOBTAINABLE, a HAND-
TURNED WOODEN BEZEL WILL PROVIDE
a GOOD ALTERNATIVE

1⁹⁄₁₆" x 1⁹⁄₁₆"
40 x 40 BURR WALNUT
VENEERED BASE MOULDING

½"
12mm BASE FRONT with
WALNUT CROSS BANDING
& BOOK MATCHED BURR
WALNUT PANEL

½"
12mm GLUE BLOCK

GLUE
BLOCK

30x50 SOFTWD FRAMING
1³⁄₁₆" x 2"

SOLID WALNUT

1³⁄₁₆" x 2"
30 x 50 SOFTWD FRAMING

¾"
18mm VENEERED
SKIRTING

1½"   1¼"
38 DIAM x 32 WALNUT FOOT

½ FULL SIZE LOWER PART
OF SECTION AT F–F

SOLID WALNUT
COMPOSITE MOULDING

½"
3mm FRIEZE FRET

½"
12mm FRIEZE FRONT

¼"
12mm GLUE BLOCK

12mm FRIEZE BASE
½"

HOOD DOOR o/ ORIGINAL CLOCK o/ 18mm/
¾" FRAMED OAK. DOOR as DRAWN HERE
COMPRISES LAYER o/ 6mm PLY on LAYER
o/ 12mm PLY with GLAZING APERTURES
CUT OUT before ASSEMBLY.

½"   ³⁄₈"
3mm PLYWD MASK fixed with 9mm GLUE
BLOCKS.

POSITION o/ BRASS DIAL

LINE o/ TRUNK SIDE

⁵⁄₈" x ½"
15 x 12 HOOD MOULD

60 x 12 HOOD BASE
2³⁄₈" x ½"

1¾" x ¾"
45 x 18 BURR WALNUT
VENEERED TRUNK MOULD'G

18 x 18 SOLID WALNUT SCOTIA
¾" x ¾"

½"
12mm TRUNK FRONT

½ F.SIZE UPPER PART OF
SECTION AT F–F

½"
12mm TRUNK SIDE
¾" x ⁷⁄₈"
18 x 22 SLIDE BATTEN

½"
12mm HOOD SIDE

40 x 12 BASE
1¹¹⁄₁₆" x ½"

1¾" x ¾"
REDUCE 45 x 18 TRUNK
MOULDING to 40 x 18
1⁹⁄₁₆" x ¾"

½ F.SIZE DETAIL at 'G'

Schedule of Operations

TRUNK CONSTRUCTION, ASSEMBLY & VENEERING

Cut out the various components to the sizes shown on the cutting list and ensure that all cut surfaces are square. It is suggested that mouldings are not cut to length at this stage. For parts that are to match, check one against the other to ensure that they are identical.

Take the backboard component and carefully mark the profile given on the plan and cut out accurately. Any error at this stage will be reflected in the completed project. Make sure that cut edges are at right angles to the adjacent surfaces.

Take the trunk side and form the rebate at the rear vertical edges. Take the trunk front and cut out the rectangular door opening. Be sure to remove the waste in one piece, since this is used later for the trunk door.

Lay the backboard on a horizontal surface and fix the trunk sides to it using PVA adhesive and glue blocks. Ensure that the trunk sides are at right angles to the backboard and use temporary bracing battens if necessary. Be careful that the bottoms of the trunk sides line up one with the other.

After PVA has set hard fix the trunk front to the sides with PVA, glue blocks and panel pins. Plane off any projections beyond the trunk sides.

Mark for and fix with PVA and screws the upper softwood framing to the lower outer faces of the trunk sides and front.

Take the base sides and form the rebate at the rear vertical edges. Fix in position on the lower part of the backboard with PVA and glue blocks and to the upper softwood framing with PVA and panel pins. Check for squareness with the other components and then fix the base front using PVA, glue blocks and panel pins. Plane off any minor projections.

Mark for and fix in position with PVA and screws the lower softwood framing to the lower inner faces of the base sides and front.

Punch in the heads of all exposed panel pins, fill and sand outer surfaces, taking care not to round over any arrises. Dust off any sawdust and then veneer all surfaces of the trunk and base, including the reveal of the door opening to the patterns shown on the drawings. It is suggested that the veneering be carried out with a contact adhesive.

After veneering the main surfaces of the trunk and base carefully sand to a finish.

MOULDINGS

Cut to length the base moulding with accurate mitres at the intersections and fix in position using PVA adhesive and sash cramps. Repeat the process with the skirting and skirting mouldings.

Mark out for and fix, as last, the mouldings at the head of the trunk. Great accuracy is required here if the clock hood is to sit properly in position. Sand all mouldings.

Protect all arrises and corners on the assembly with masking tape to prevent accidental damage.

HOOD ASSEMBLY

Take the hood base sides and front and form the hood base, assembling with PVA and sash cramps. It is important that this assembly is square and flat and is a loose sliding fit over the top of the trunk. It will be found helpful to fix a temporary batten across the back of the hood base assembly. Veneer the upper face and sand down.

Next, take the hood sides and wings and check for squareness and matching. Form the rebates at the rear of the sides to take the wings. Veneer the sides and wings as indicated on the plans and sand to a finish. Fix the wings in position at the rear of the sides with PVA and panel pins.

Make the dial mask, ensuring that the overall sizes given on the plans are followed and that all corners are right angles. Using the mask as a jig, mark on the top of the hood base assembly the position to be occupied by the sides and wings and fix to the base with PVA and screws. Fix the dial mask in position with PVA and glue blocks. It will be helpful to fit a temporary batten across the rear of the sides.

Take the frieze base and check for size and squareness. Veneer the underside and sand down. Fix in position on top of the sides and wings with PVA and screws.

Take the frieze front and sides and check for size and squareness and fix with PVA and glue blocks to form the box on top of the frieze base. Trim off minor projections.

Take the frieze front fret. Veneer the outer face and sand down. Mark out the frieze fret pattern and cut out the pattern with a fret saw. Clean up the cut pattern with needle files and sand to remove saw kerfs. Cover the back of this component with crimson or black cloth and glue in position on the frieze front. Take the frieze fret sides and glue onto the frieze sides. File off any minor projections at the junction with the frieze fret front and veneer the sides,

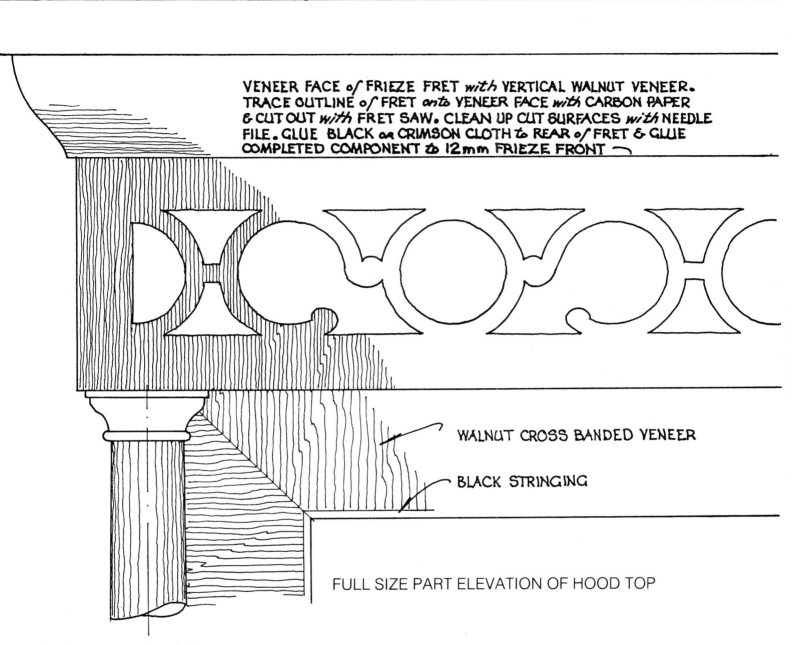

VENEER FACE of FRIEZE FRET with VERTICAL WALNUT VENEER.
TRACE OUTLINE of FRET onto VENEER FACE with CARBON PAPER
& CUT OUT with FRET SAW. CLEAN UP CUT SURFACES with NEEDLE
FILE. GLUE BLACK or CRIMSON CLOTH to REAR of FRET & GLUE
COMPLETED COMPONENT to 12mm FRIEZE FRONT ⌐

WALNUT CROSS BANDED VENEER

BLACK STRINGING

FULL SIZE PART ELEVATION OF HOOD TOP

carrying the veneer over the cut edge of the frieze fret front.

Cut to length and fix in position all hood mouldings with PVA forming neat mitres at the corners. Sand down the mouldings and afford temporary protection with masking tape.

Remove any temporary battens across the back and offer up the whole hood assembly to the top of the trunk. Mark the positions where the slide battens are to occur. Remove the hood assembly and fix the slide battens to the trunk sides with PVA and panel pins.

HOOD DOOR & COLUMNS

Take the two components for the hood door and check for size and squareness against the hood assembly. Cut the square holes for the door window in each component and then fix the two together with PVA and panel pins, thus forming a rebated opening. Veneer all surfaces as shown on the plans and sand.

On the lathe turn each ¾ and ¼ column for the hood, using the split spindle method. Check that each end of the columns are a tight fit in the sockets of the brass column caps. Sand on the lathe to a finish and then split off the ¼ column. Remove all traces of paper from the columns.

From each brass column cap carefully cut out a ¼ section using a piercing saw. Clean the cut surfaces with a needle file. Glue the columns in the positions shown on the plans. Drill the sides of the column caps for fixing pins and fix the column ends with brass panel pins.

MOVEMENT, DIAL & SADDLE BOARD LOCATION

Take the saddle board and form holes and slots as shown on the manufacturer's movement instructions. Fix the softwood locating battens at the base of the saddle board and offer up at the top of the trunk sides to check that it is a snug fit. The saddle board is never fixed to the trunk.

Fix the movement to the saddle board in accordance with the maker's instructions and fit the dial to the dial plate attached to the movement. Offer up this complete assembly on the top of the trunk sides. Offer up the hood assembly and check that the dial fits neatly behind the dial mask without gaps. It may be necessary to reduce the height of the trunk sides or to pack up under the saddle board to achieve a good fit.

Leave the saddle board and movement in position and slide off the hood assembly. Hang the pendulum rod and bob in position at the rear of the movement and mark on the hood front a light pencil mark showing the exact height at which the centre of the bob occurs. Remove the pendulum rod and bob and then the movement and dial still attached to the saddle board.

TRUNK DOOR

Take the waste material cut from the door opening in the trunk front. True up all round with a plane and check for size and fit against the trunk front. The door should be a loose fit into the door opening and allowance should be made for veneer thickness on the cut surfaces of the door. Mark on the door the exact centre line of the pendulum bob where previously marked on the trunk front. Mark for and cut out the hole for the brass bezel of the lenticle glass and check that the bezel is fitting snugly. Remove the bezel. (Note: The brass bezel has, on occasions, been difficult to obtain in recent years. In case of difficulty an attractive alternative is to make a turned wooden bezel in matching timber.)

Veneer the edges and outer face of the trunk door with quarter matched burr walnut veneer and the inside face of the door with any common veneer to act as a balancer. Sand all surfaces to a finish. Cut the half round edge mouldings to lengths, neatly mitre the corners and fix in position with PVA and clamps. Sand mouldings to a finish and fix the brass lenticle bezel in position.

Chop in for and fix in position the brass lock and ornamental brass escutcheon and chop in for and fix the brass hinges to the trunk door.

Study the plan and select your preferred method for hanging the hood door.

FINISHING & FINAL ASSEMBLY

On the lathe, turn the solid walnut feet to the profile shown on the plan. Drill for and fix in position with PVA and screws to the underside of the lower softwood framing of the base.

The original clock case had been grainfilled and french polished and it is suggested that a similar finish will give the most authentic appearance. Alternatively, any method of grainfilling with a system of varnishing should prove satisfactory but in such case it is suggested that the final coat of varnish or polyurethane be flatted down with very fine grade wire wool and then brought back to a gloss with wax finish.

After the finishes are complete, glaze the hood door with 2mm sheet glass, using glazier's sprigs and putty. If you are able to obtain old picture glass with occasional flaws and bubbles, the final result will appear more authentic. Glaze the lenticle bezel with hand blown bullion (or bullseye) glass or 2mm sheet glass.

Set up the saddle board and movement assembly, hang the pendulum and weights and fix hands etc, in accordance with the maker's instructions. The whole clockcase should stand upright on a level floor. In the case of a floor that is out of level this may be corrected by inserting small wooden wedges under the feet.

Cutting list

COMPONENT	QUANTITY	SECTION	LENGTH
Backboard	1	12 × 338	1840
	1	½″ × 13⅜″	72½″
Base Front	1	12 × 350	318
	1	½″ × 13⅞″	12⁹⁄₁₆″
Base Sides	2	12 × 245	318
	2	½″ × 9¹¹⁄₁₆″	12⁹⁄₁₆″
Base Framing (Front)	2	30 × 50	326
	2	1³⁄₁₆″ × 2″	12⅞″
Base Framing (Sides)	4	30 × 50	203
	4	1³⁄₁₆″ × 2″	8″
Base Skirting (Front)	1	18 × 45	386
	1	¾″ × 1¾″	15⅜″
Base Skirting (Sides)	1	18 × 45	275
	1	¾″ × 1¾″	10¹⁵⁄₁₆″
Base Skirting Mould (Front)	1	12 × 15	380
	1	½″ × ⅝″	15⅛″
Base Skirting Mould (Sides)	2	12 × 15	272
	2	½″ × ⅝″	10¹³⁄₁₆″
Base Moulding (Front)	1	40 × 40	346
	1	1⁹⁄₁₆″ × 1⁹⁄₁₆″	13⅝″
Base Moulding (Sides)	2	40 × 40	255
	2	1⁹⁄₁₆″ × 1⁹⁄₁₆″	10¹⁄₁₆″
Trunk Front	1	12 × 266	1260
	1	½″ × 10½″	49⅝″
Trunk Sides	2	12 × 203	1360
	2	½″ × 8″	53⅝″
Trunk Door (Cut from Middle of Trunk Front)	1	12 × 202	1060
	1	½″ × 8″	41¾″
Trunk Door Moulding	2	18 × 9	220
	2	¾″ × ⅜″	8¾″
Trunk Door Moulding	2	18 × 9	1078
	2	¾″ × ⅜″	42½″
Trunk Scotia (Front)	1	18 × 18	302
	1	¾″ × ¾″	12″
Trunk Scotia (Sides)	2	18 × 18	233
	2	¾″ × ¾″	9¼″
Trunk Moulding (Front)	1	45 × 18	346
	1	1¾″ × ¾″	13⅝″
Trunk Moulding (Sides)	2	40 × 18	260
	2	1⁹⁄₁₆″ × ¾″	10¼″

Hood Slide Battens	2	18 × 22	153
	2	¾″ × ⅞″	6″
Hood sides	2	12 × 233	300
	2	½″ × 9³⁄₁₆″	11¹¹⁄₁₆″
Hood Base (Front)	1	12 × 60	346
	1	½″ × 2⅜″	13⅝″
Hood Base (Sides)	2	12 × 40	260
	2	½″ × 1⁹⁄₁₆″	10¼″
Hood Base Moulding (Front)	1	12 × 15	370
	1	½″ × ⅝″	14⅝″
Hood Base Moulding (sides)	2	12 × 15	273
	2	½″ × ⅝″	10¾″
Hood Door Front	1	6 × 330	300
	1	¼″ × 13¹⁄₁₆″	11¹³⁄₁₆″
Hood Door Back	1	6 × 330	300
	1	¼ × 13¹⁄₁₆″″	11¹³⁄₁₆″
Hood Dial Mask	1	3 × 306	300
	1	⅛″ × 12¹⁄₁₆″	11¹³⁄₁₆″
Movement Saddle Board	1	12 × 102	266
	1	½″ × 4″	10½″
Hood Columns	2	ex 25	300
	2	ex 1″	11¹³⁄₁₆″
Hood Quarter Columns	2	ex 25	300
	2	ex 1″	11¹³⁄₁₆″
Hood Wings	2	12 × 25	300
	2	½″ × 1″	11¹³⁄₁₆″
Hood Frieze Base	1	12 × 273	380
	1	½″ × 10¾″	15¹⁄₁₆″
Frieze Front	1	12 × 95	380
	1	½″ × 3¾″	15¹⁄₁₆″
Frieze Sides	2	12 × 95	261
	2	½″ × 3¾″	10¼″
Frieze Fret (Front)	1	3 × 65	386
	1	⅛″ × 2⁹⁄₁₆″	15⁵⁄₁₆″
Frieze Fret (Sides)	1	3 × 65	273
	1	⅛″ × 2⁹⁄₁₆″	10¾″
Hood Top (Composite) Mould (Front)	1		456
	1		18¹⁄₁₆″
Hood Top (Composite) Mould (Sides)	2		308
	2		12⅛″

Clock Components and Hardware (excluding screws and pins)

CLOCK MOVEMENT — OPTIONS:
- Mechanical/weight driven movement.
- Maximum length of the pendulum should be 930mm/36⅝″.
- Maximum overall swing of the pendulum should be 220mm/8¹¹⁄₁₆″.
- Maximum overall dimensions of movement not to exceed hood's interior dimensions.
- Chime options: Single Bell Strike; Bim-Bam; Whittington; Westminster; St Michael; Triple-Chime.

CLOCK DIAL — OPTIONS
- 250 × 250mm/9⅞″ × 9⅞″.
- Solid brass, alloy, aluminium and hand painted models available.
- Note: if front winding mechanical movement is used, drill holes in the dial and bush to accommodate winding keys.

CLOCK HANDS:
- Bushed to suit chosen mechanical movement.
- Length to suit dial size.
- Pattern to suit individual choice.

BRASSWARE:
- Lenticle Bezel: Brass versions now difficult to obtain. Consider a hand turned hardwood bezel/ring.
- Hinges:
  Trunk Door: one pair of odd-sided hinges — 32 × 21mm/1¼″ × ⅞″.
  Hood Door: a) pins fixed into column or b) 32mm/1¼″ butt hinges.
- Door Locks:
  Trunk Door: one cupboard lock 50 × 12.5mm/2″ × ½″ to pin.
  Hood Door: one concealed bullet catch.
- Filagree plate escutcheon: pattern to suit individual taste.
- Column Caps/Bases
  Full diameters: two pairs to suit 21mm/⅞″ diameter columns.
  Quarter diameters: two pairs to suit 21mm/⅞″ diameter columns.

GLASS:
- To suit hood door.
- To suit lenticle bezel.

3. *George III Period Bracket Clock*

The plan details a very handsome example of a traditional bracket clock of the George III period.

The clock cases of this period were often veneered in mahogany or, more rarely, in walnut. Today, it is not often possible to find veneers in Spanish mahogany and the 'equivalent' offered is usually somewhat coarse grained. It is, therefore, suggested that European walnut would give a better result. Occasionally clock cases were given a japanned finish but this option is really only open to those woodworkers experienced in that technique.

The construction method has been amended to suit modern techniques and uses standard DIY mouldings, and either mechanical or quartz movements may be used.

Overall dimensions: 278 wide × 160 deep × 460mm high inc handle
11″ wide × 6″ deep × 18¼″ high inc handle

Skill level ****

Schedule of Operations

MAIN CASE CONSTRUCTION

Take the 12mm/½″ plywood for the two cheekboards and carefully set out the dimensions given on the drawing. Plane to those dimensions with both sheets clamped together in a vice to ensure an identical result between the two components. Run the vertical stopped rebates at the rear of the cheekboards to later accept the 12mm/½″ backboard. Run the horizontal through rebate on the lower outer face of each cheekboard. Refer to Section D-D on the drawing and it will be seen that the depth of rebate is to suit the picture frame moulding chosen. Run the horizontal rebates on the inside upper faces to later accept topboard A. Set aside for later use.

Take the 18mm/¾″ ply for baseboard B and set out the dimensions given on the drawing. Plane to size and set aside for later use.

Take the 12mm/½″ ply for the backboard and set out the dimensions given on the drawing. Check the setting out against the length of baseboard B and the depth of the stopped rebate in the cheekboards. Plane to final size.

Set out the rectangular rear access aperture and cut out with a fret saw. Set aside for later use.

In 6mm/¼″ plywood set out the final size of baseboard A. Reference to Section B-B on the drawing will show that the front to back dimension for this component also depends on the picture frame moulding of your choice. Plane to final size and set aside for later use.

Take the 18mm/¾″ ply component for topboard A and set out the final size required. The length of this will be the same as the width of the backboard and the front to back dimension should equal that of baseboard A. Plane to final size and set aside for later use.

Take the 18mm/¾″ ply component for baseboard C and set out final size. Check sizes against components already made and plane to size.

Take the 12mm/½″ ply component for baseboard D set out for and plane to final size. Note that the dimensions for this component are dependent on the size of the lower scotia mould. See Sections B-B and D-D.

Note: At this stage it is better not to cut topboards B to 'F' since the final sizes of these depend upon the main case assembly.

SIDE FRETS IN CHEEKBOARDS

These are an optional feature but nonetheless an important one. In addition to adding an authentic touch the sound of the clock strike will be much improved.

Various patterns of pierced brass frets are available from specialist stockists. Having made your choice mark out for and fret suitable openings in the cheekboards. It should be noted that the frets are located in the centre of the completed case (which includes the thickness of the door) rather than in the centre of the cheekboard itself. See Side Elevation on the drawing.

MAIN CASE ASSEMBLY

Once the veneer is well stuck down trim back any surplus veneer from the edges and round the side fret apertures.

Offer up the cheekboards to the sides of baseboard B and pin and glue in position using PVA adhesive. Check that the cheekboards are at right angles to the baseboard.

Offer up topboard A to the rebates at the top of the cheekboards and glue and pin in position.

Slide baseboard A on to the top of baseboard B and between the cheekboards and glue and pin down. Remove any surplus adhesive with a damp rag.

While the above sub-assembly is setting hard, veneer the inner face of the backboard with common veneer. Trim off surplus. Veneer the inside cut edges of the rear aperture. Veneer the outer face of the backboard with decorative veneer. Trim off surplus.

Offer up the backboard to the rear of the case sub-assembly and glue in position using glue blocks. Set the case sub-assembly to one side to set hard.

DOOR

Use the case sub-assembly to measure the size required for the door and mark out for this overall size on both the ply door layers and plane as a pair to that size. Mark out on each layer the sizes of the apertures for glazing and cut these accurately with a fret saw. Fettle the cut edges of the apertures to remove any saw kerfs.

Glue and pin the two layers together and clamp. Do not attempt to dispense with the pins since the layers may slip out of position if you use clamps only. When set hard, clean up any surplus glue before veneering.

Veneer the outer and inner cut edges of the door sub-assembly with decorative veneer. Note the use of ebony strings on the edge adjacent to the glass. Trim off surplus.

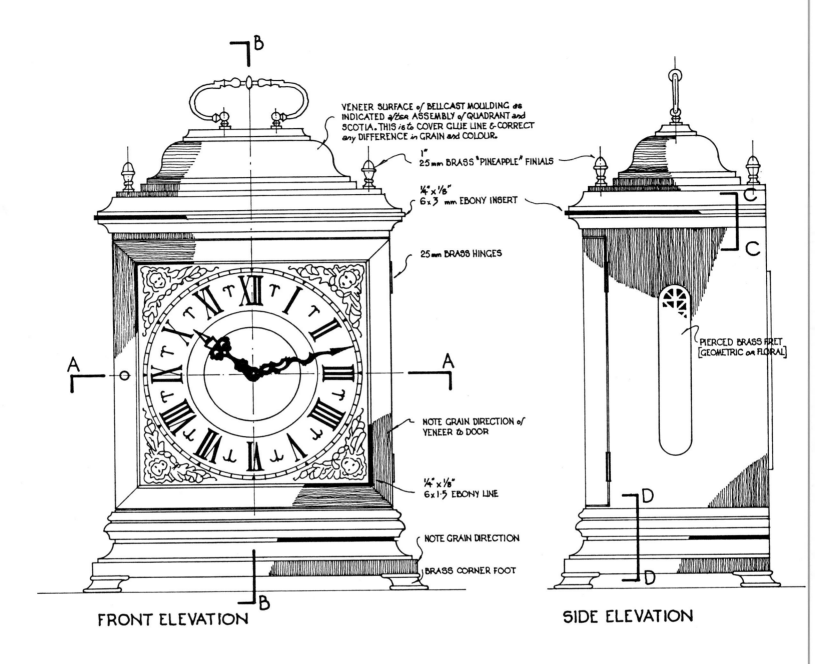

VENEER SURFACE of BELLCAST MOULDING as INDICATED after ASSEMBLY of QUADRANT and SCOTIA. THIS is to COVER GLUE LINE & CORRECT any DIFFERENCE in GRAIN and COLOUR.

1"
25mm BRASS "PINEAPPLE" FINIALS

¼" x ⅛"
6 x 3 mm EBONY INSERT

25mm BRASS HINGES

NOTE GRAIN DIRECTION of VENEER to DOOR

¼" x ⅛"
6 x 1·5 EBONY LINE

NOTE GRAIN DIRECTION

BRASS CORNER FOOT

PIERCED BRASS FRET
[GEOMETRIC or FLORAL]

FRONT ELEVATION

SIDE ELEVATION

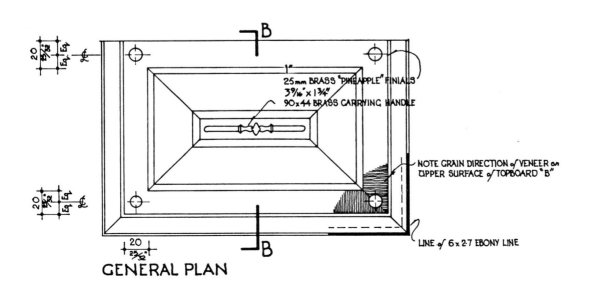

1"
25mm BRASS "PINEAPPLE" FINIALS
3⁹⁄₁₆" x 1¾"
90 x 44 BRASS CARRYING HANDLE

NOTE GRAIN DIRECTION of VENEER on UPPER SURFACE of TOPBOARD "B"

LINE of 6 x 2·7 EBONY LINE

GENERAL PLAN

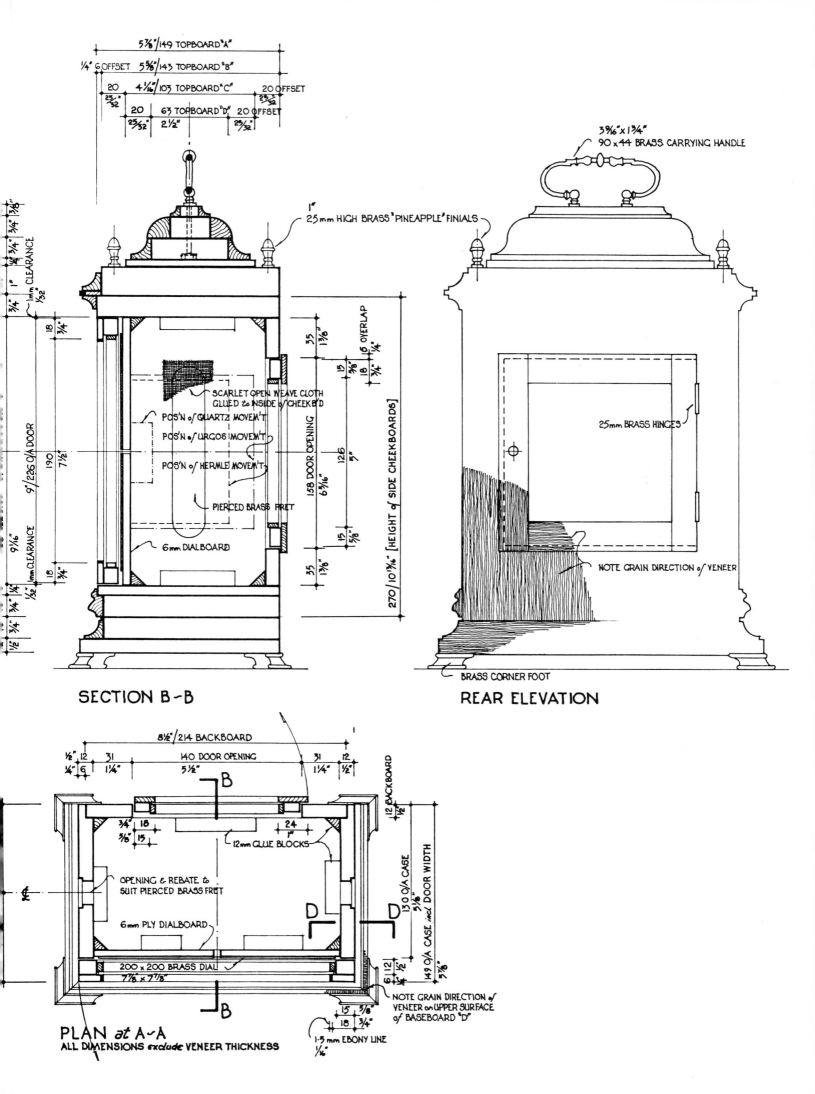

SECTION B-B

REAR ELEVATION

PLAN at A-A
ALL DIMENSIONS *exclude* VENEER THICKNESS

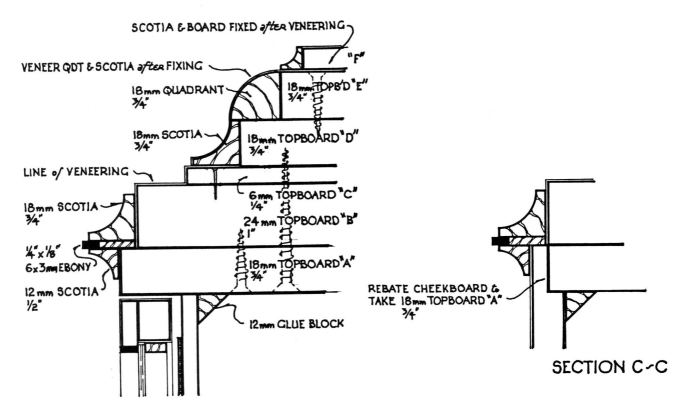

SCOTIA & BOARD FIXED *after* VENEERING

VENEER QDT & SCOTIA *after* FIXING

18mm QUADRANT
3/4"

18mm SCOTIA
3/4"

LINE *of* VENEERING

18mm SCOTIA
3/4"

1/4" x 1/8"
6x3mm EBONY

12mm SCOTIA
1/2"

18mm TOPB'D "E"
3/4"

"F"

18mm TOPBOARD "D"
3/4"

6mm TOPBOARD "C"
1/4"

24mm TOPBOARD "B"
1"

18mm TOPBOARD "A"
3/4"

12mm GLUE BLOCK

UPPER PART *of* SECTION B~B

REBATE CHEEKBOARD &
TAKE 18mm TOPBOARD "A"
3/4"

SECTION C~C

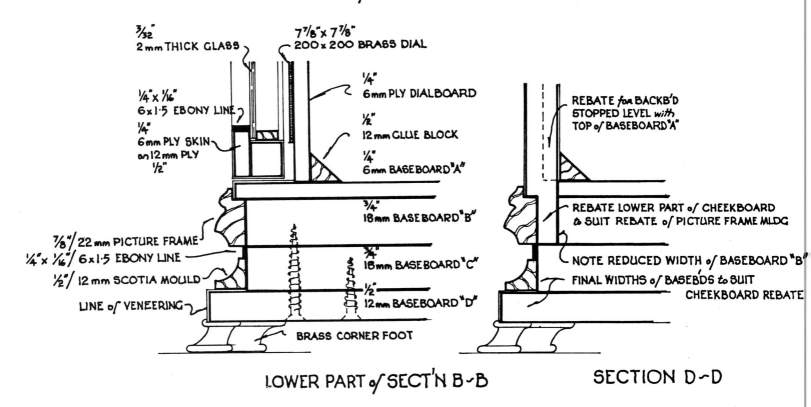

3/32"
2mm THICK GLASS

1/4" x 1/16"
6x1.5 EBONY LINE

1/4"
6mm PLY SKIN
on 12mm PLY
1/2"

7/8" 22mm PICTURE FRAME
1/4" x 1/16" 6x1.5 EBONY LINE
1/2" 12mm SCOTIA MOULD

LINE *of* VENEERING

7 7/8" x 7 7/8"
200 x 200 BRASS DIAL

1/4"
6mm PLY DIALBOARD

1/2"
12mm GLUE BLOCK

1/4"
6mm BASEBOARD "A"

3/4"
18mm BASEBOARD "B"

3/4"
18mm BASEBOARD "C"

1/2"
12mm BASEBOARD "D"

BRASS CORNER FOOT

REBATE *for* BACKB'D
STOPPED LEVEL *with*
TOP *of* BASEBOARD "A"

REBATE LOWER PART *of* CHEEKBOARD
to SUIT REBATE *of* PICTURE FRAME MLDG

NOTE REDUCED WIDTH *of* BASEBOARD "B"

FINAL WIDTHS *of* BASEBDS *to* SUIT
CHEEKBOARD REBATE

LOWER PART *of* SECT'N B~B

SECTION D~D

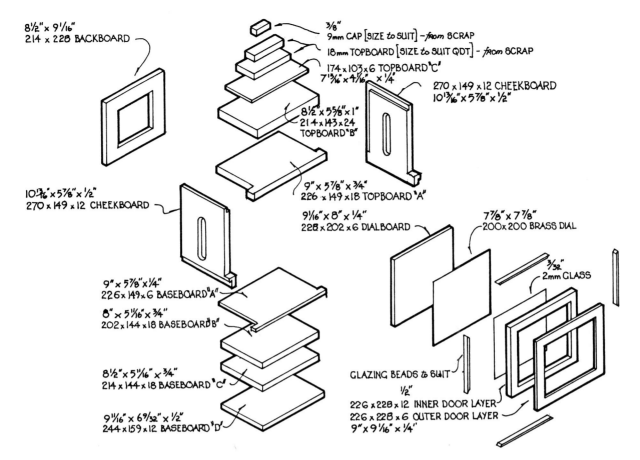

8½" x 9 1/16"
214 x 228 BACKBOARD

3/8"
9mm CAP [SIZE to SUIT] –from SCRAP

18mm TOPBOARD [SIZE to SUIT QDT] –from SCRAP

174 x 103 x 6 TOPBOARD "C"
7 13/16" x 4 1/16" x ¼"

270 x 149 x 12 CHEEKBOARD
10 13/16" x 5 7/8" x ½"

8½" x 5 5/8" x 1"
214 x 143 x 24
TOPBOARD "B"

9" x 5 7/8" x ¾"
226 x 149 x 18 TOPBOARD "A"

10 13/16" x 5 7/8" x ½"
270 x 149 x 12 CHEEKBOARD

9 1/16" x 8" x ¼"
228 x 202 x 6 DIALBOARD

7 7/8" x 7 7/8"
200 x 200 BRASS DIAL

3/32"
2mm GLASS

9" x 5 7/8" x ¼"
226 x 149 x 6 BASEBOARD "A"

8" x 5 11/16" x ¾"
202 x 144 x 18 BASEBOARD "B"

8½" x 5 11/16" x ¾"
214 x 144 x 18 BASEBOARD "C"

9 11/16" x 6 9/32" x ½"
244 x 159 x 12 BASEBOARD "D"

GLAZING BEADS to SUIT

½"
226 x 228 x 12 INNER DOOR LAYER
226 x 228 x 6 OUTER DOOR LAYER
9" x 9 1/16" x ¼"

EXPLODED ISOMETRIC DIAGRAM of CARCASS
[NOTE:- GLUE BLOCKS and MOULDINGS OMITTED for CLARITY]

NOTE CUTBACK on HINGE STILE

DOOR CONSTRUCTION SIMILAR to
DIAL DOOR but NOTE ALTERNATIVE
HARDWOOD OUTER LAYER SHOWN HERE

CHEEKBOARD & BACKBOARD to be
VENEERED INTERNALLY before ASSEMBLY

½"
12 mm CHEEKBOARD
½"
12 mm GLUE BLOCK
¼"
6mm DIALBOARD

DRILL DIALBOARD to SUIT DIAM
of HANDSHAFT of MECHANICAL
MOVEMENT or DIAM of FIXING
BUSH of QUARTZ MOVEMENT

BRASS HINGE

200 x 200 BRASS DIAL 7 7/8" x 7 7/8"

3/32"/2mm GLASS

DOOR CONSTRUCTED of 2 LAYERS of
PLYWOOD with DIFFERING SIZES of
CUTOUTS. VENEER as INDICATED

BRASS CORNER FOOT

PLAN at A-A

Veneer the front and inside faces of the door with decorative veneers. Trim off surplus.

Sand all veneered surfaces of the door using progressively finer grades of abrasive paper and a sanding block. Work in the general direction of the grain.

Dust off all surfaces and apply finish as later described before marking out for and chopping in brass hinges.

FINISHES GENERALLY

The best finish to use is french polish but pleasing results may be obtained with varnish, cellulose or polyurethane. In the latter cases, grain fill before applying the initial coat (which should be flowed on rather than brushed in). When this first coat has dried hard flat down with grade 0000 wire wool, working in the direction of the grain. Repeat the process until satisfactory results are obtained. Flat down the final coat and apply solid wax polish for a final gloss.

Before applying finishes take note of any area which will accept glue in the final assembly process and mask these off with cellotape.

VENEERING CASE

Veneer the rear and front edges of cheekboards with decorative veneers set vertically. Trim off surplus.

Veneer the outer faces of cheekboards with matched decorative veneer. Trim off surplus. Veneer the front of baseboard A where indicated on Section B-B with decorative veneer set as cross-banding. Trim off surplus. Veneer only the front edge of the topboard A with decorative veneer set cross-banded. Trim off surplus.

Sand down all surfaces veneered so far to a finish. Dust off and apply finishes as described.

DIAL-BOARD

Carefully measure inside the case assembly to ascertain the final size required for the dial-board. Mark out this size on the 6mm/¼″ sawn component and plane to final size. Offer up the brass dial and ascertain the exact position which will be taken by the handshaft of the movement. With the dial still in position mark position and diameter of winding shafts. Remove the dial and drill holes in the dial-board for hand and key shafts.

The margins of the dial-board will project beyond the edges of the brass dial and it is best to paint these margins matt black before fixing the dial-board in the case assembly with PVA and glue blocks.

BASEBOARD ASSEMBLY

Refer to the drawings and ascertain the position to be taken up by baseboard C but take actual dimensions from the case sub-assembly. On the 18mm/¾″ sawn ply component set out those dimensions and plane to final size.

Drill pilot and clearance holes for fixing screws and glue and screw baseboard C to the underside of baseboard B. Wipe off any surplus glue.

In a like manner ascertain the size required for baseboard D. Mark out on 12mm/½″ ply and plane to final size. Drill pilot and clearance holes for fixing screws. Before fixing offer up baseboard D to baseboard C and mark on the margin of the area to be veneered on the top surface. Veneer with decorative veneer, roll down and trim off. Apply decorative veneer set cross-banded to the cut edges of baseboard D, roll down and trim off.

Sand the above named veneers to a finish, dust off and apply finishes.

Glue and screw baseboard D to the underside of baseboard C.

MOULDINGS GENERALLY

The scotias and quadrant shown on the drawing are standard DIY sections. If you are unable to obtain these in a matching timber to the wood chosen for veneers it will be necessary to stain them to a similar colour.

Pre-sand the mouldings in long lengths and, if necessary, apply stain.

It is best to apply finishes to the total lengths of mouldings before cutting.

Cut the pre-finished lower scotia and picture frame mouldings to the lengths required, mitring at the intersections and glue in position on the case assembly.

Cut the pre-finished 12mm/½″ scotia to lengths etc and glue in position on the front edge of topboard A and the upper part of the cheekboards.

TOPBOARDS

Using a length of 18mm/¾″ scotia as a guide ascertain the size of topboard B. (Line up the front of the 18mm/¾″ scotia with the front edge of the 12mm/½″ scotia — the back of the larger scotia will give the line required).

Mark out the sizes so obtained on 24mm/1″ plywood (or use 2 layers of 12mm/½″ and plane to final size).

Veneer the top surface of topboard B with decorative veneer, and trim off surplus.

Veneer the edges of topboard B with decorative veneer set crossbanded. Sand all veneer to a finish, dust off and apply finishes.

Glue and screw topboard B to topboard A (see Section B-B).

From scrap wood make the backing strip for the ebony stringing above the 12mm/½″ scotia, cut to length and glue in position. Cut the ebony string to length with neat mitres at intersections and glue in position.

Cut 18mm/¾″ scotia to length with mitres at intersections and glue in position against topboard B.

Mark out and plane to final size 6mm/¼″ topboard C. Veneer as indicated on drawing, roll down and trim off, sand to a finish and apply finishes before gluing and screwing in position above topboard B.

Mark out and plane to final size topboard D and glue and screw to topboard C as shown on Section B-B.

Cut lengths of 18mm/¾″ scotia with mitres at intersections and glue in position to the edges of topboard D. If necessary plane off the top of the scotia exactly flush with the upper surface of this topboard.

Take the 18mm/¾″ quadrant and offer it up on the top of the last named scotia with the front edges exactly, coinciding. The inner face of the quadrant will give the size required for topboard E. Mark out and plane to size 18mm/¾″ ply for topboard E. Glue and screw topboard E to the top of topboard D. Cut quadrant to lengths with mitres at intersections and glue in position to the edges of topboard E.

It may be necessary at this stage to fettle the join between the quadrant and scotia. The resultant compound mould should be veneered with decorative veneer to cover the join and any difference in colour between the scotia and quadrant. Continue the veneer right across the top of this topboard. Sand veneers to a finish and dust off and apply finishes.

Make topboard F in 9mm/⅜″ ply and glue in position on top of topboard E. Cut pre-finished 9mm/⅜″ scotia to

lengths with mitres at intersections and glue in position. Veneer across the top of the board and scotia with decorative veneer. Sand to a finish, dush off and apply finishes.

HANGING FRONT DOOR

Offer up the door to the case assembly and carefully mark the position of the hinges on the front vertical face of the cheekboards.

Remove door and chop in hinges to cheekboards.

Remove hinges from door and glaze the door using glazing beads made from scrap hardwood.

Screw the hinges to the cheekboards and then to the door. Check the snugness of fit and the swing of the door and adjust as required.

REAR DOOR

measure the aperture in the backboard and make the rear door in a similar manner to that described for the front door.

Finish, glaze and hang the rear door in the same way as the front door.

BRASSWARE

Fix all the various items of brassware as indicated on the drawings, including the brass dial.

SETTING UP

Carefully follow the maker's instructions and fix the movement in position to the rear face of the dial-board.

Fit the hands to the handshaft and wind the movement. Rotate the hands to the hour mark and check the strike of the bell. Some minor adjustment to the hammer arm may be necessary.

Over a period of days check the time-keeping of the clock and adjust on the 'fast or slow' arm at the back of the movement as necessary. You may find that several adjustments are needed over a period before the right position is found.

Cutting list

COMPONENT	QUANTITY	SECTION	LENGTH
Baseboard A	1	6 × 149	226
	1	¼″ × 5⅞″	9″
Baseboard B	1	18 × 144	202
	1	¾″ × 5¹¹⁄₁₆″	8″
Baseboard C	1	18 × 144	214
	1	¾″ × 5¹¹⁄₁₆″	8½″
Baseboard D	1	12 × 159	244
	1	½″ × 6⁹⁄₃₂″	9¹¹⁄₁₆″
Cheekboards	2	12 × 149	270
	2	½″ × 5⅞″	10¹³⁄₁₆″
Dial-board	1	6 × 202	228
	1	¼″ × 8″	9¹⁄₁₆″
Backboard	1	12 × 214	228
	1	½″ × 8½″	9¹⁄₁₆″
Topboard A	1	18 × 149	226
	1	¼″ × 5⅞″	9″
Topboard B	1	24 × 143	214
	1	1″ × 5¹¹⁄₁₆″	8½″
Topboard C	1	6 × 103	174
	1	¼″ × 4¹⁄₁₆″	6¹⁵⁄₁₆″
Topboard D	1	18 × 63	134
	1	¾″ × 2½″	5⅜″
Topboard E (adjust size to suit overlapping quadrant)	1	18 × 33	104
	1	⅜″ × 1¼″	4⅛″
Capboard F (adjust size to suit scotia)	1	9 × 15	86
	1	⅜″ × ½″	3⅜″
Inner layer to Rear Door (ply)	1	9 × 138	156
	1	⅜″ × 5⁷⁄₁₆″	6¼″
Outer Layer to Rear Door (stripwood — hinge stile)	1	6 × 22	164
	1	¼″ × ⅞″	6⁹⁄₁₆″
Outer Layer to Rear Door (stripwood — handle stile)	1	6 × 28	164
	1	¼″ × 1⅛″	6⁹⁄₁₆″
Outer Layer to Rear Door (stripwood for rails)	2	6 × 28	93
	2	¼″ × 1⅛″	3⅝″
Inner Layer to Front Door	1	12 × 226	226
	1	½″ × 9″	9″
Outer Layer to Front Door	1	6 × 226	226
	1	¼″ × 9″	9″
Baseboard Scotia (Total Length)	1	12 × 12	550 minimum
	1	½″ × ½″	21⅞″ minimum

Baseboard Moulding (Total Length)	1	22 × 12	538 minimum
(Picture Frame)	1	⅞″ × ½″	21⅜″ minimum
Topboard A Scotia (Total Length)	1	12 × 12	572 minimum
	1	½″ × ½″	22¾″ minimum
Topboard B Scotia (Total Length)	1	18 × 18	572 minimum
	1	¾″ × ¾″	22¾″ minimum
Topboard D Scotia (Total Length)	1	18 × 18	538 minimum
	1	¾″ × ¾″	21¼″ minimum
Topboard E Quadrant (Total Length)	1	18 × 18	418 minimum
	1	¾″ × ¾″	16¾″ minimum
Capping Scotia (Total Length)	1	9 × 9	274 minimum
	1	⅜″ × ⅜″	10¾″ minimum
Glue Block Triangles (Total Length)	1	12 × 12	1712 minimum
	1	½″ × ½″	68″ minimum
Glazing Beads	1	3 × 8 ·	1500
	1	⅛″ × ⁵⁄₁₆″	59″

Clock Components and Hardware (excluding screws and pins)

CLOCK MOVEMENT — OPTIONS:

1. Mechanical Bracket Clock Movements:
   Spring driven.
   Maximum 'plate size' (front face of movement): 165 × 165mm/6½″ × 6½″.
   Maximum depth (to suit depth of clock case): 115mm/4½″.
   handshaft: check length and adjust thickness of plywood dial-board.
   Chime Options: Single/twin bell strike (half and one hour); Westminster; Whittington; St Michael; Triple Chime.

2. Quartz Clock Movements:
   Hand shaft/fixing nut length; to suit 6–8mm/¼″ – ⁵⁄₁₆″ dial-board and dial thickness.
   Standard or melody movements available.
   Manufacturers.

CLOCK DIAL — OPTIONS:
 – 200 × 200mm/7⅞″ × 7⅞″.
 – Drill holes in dial for front winding mechanical movements.
 – Solid brass, alloy, aluminium and hand painted models available.
 – Note: If front winding mechanical movement is used, drill holes in dial and bush to accommodate winding keys.

CLOCK HANDS:
 – Bushed to suit chosen mechanical or quartz movement.
 – Length to suit dial size.
 – Pattern to suit individual choice.

GLASS:
 – To suit front door.

BRASSWARE:
 – Hinges: two pairs of 25mm/1″ butts.
 – Front door handle: 9mm/⅜″ brass knob.
 – Rear door handle: 9mm/⅜″ brass knob/latch.
 – Front door lock: one 6mm/¼″ ball catch.
 – Carrying handle: 90 × 40mm/3⁹⁄₁₆″ × 1¾″.
 – Four 25mm/1″ pineapple finials.
   Additional patterns: acorn, flame and urn.
 – Four corner feet: 35 × 35 × 12mm/1⅜″ × 1⅜″ × ½″.
 – Two pierced frets: 152 × 22mm/6″ × ⅞″ or nearest.

4.   19th Century French Mantel Clock

Based on a typical design of the 19th century French period, this handsome addition to the mantelshelf may be finished in veneer or spray painted to simulate the original alabaster.

A quartz or a mechanical movement may be used.

Overall dimensions: 240 wide × 140 deep × 310mm high excl eagle
9⁷⁄₁₆″ wide × 5½″ deep × 12³⁄₁₆″ high excl eagle.

Skill level ✳ ✳ ✳

Schedule of Operations

This project depends, to some extent, on marrying up certain components to the sizes of some items of brassware. It is, therefore, suggested also that you get all the items of brassware at an early stage.

There are two options with regard to suitable finishes for this project and your choice in this regard will affect the types of veneer required. The clocks of this period were often cased with alabaster and it is possible to mimic this material with satin spray paint (do not attempt this approach unless you are experienced in spray painting) in which case only common veneer will be required. The second option is to use a decorative veneer with hardwood for the turned columns. obviously, it would be prudent to select a veneer that is compatible with the timber chosen for the columns. European walnut is a good choice since it is close grained and may be obtained in both solid and veneer.

MAIN CASE CONSTRUCTION
Cut out the various plywood items to the sawn sizes given in the Cutting List.

Take the 18mm/¾″ thick ply laminates B, C, D and E and clamp them together in a vice. Plane one edge of the cluster truly straight and square. This edge will give a base line for setting out.

On laminate D mark out the centre line of the main circle at a right angle to the base line, returning the centre line across the baseline edge.

Carefully mark out the clearance slot for the pendulum as shown on the drawing. Saw along those lines towards the centre but do not remove any wood at this stage.

Take laminates B, C, D and E and with the base line edges accurately married up one with the other glue and pin the laminates together and apply clamps. Take care to ensure that any pins do not occur where you will be sawing later. If clamps are applied without pinning the laminates may slip out of position.

When this laminate assembly has set hard clean up the baseline edge of any surplus glue. Draw out the profile shown on the drawing on to the ply face.

Cut out the shape on the bandsaw starting with the outer curves. When you come to cut out the inner circle it will be necessary to cut across the plywood to reach the perimeter of the inner circle. This saw cut can later be filled with veneer slips and glue.

After removing the inner circle of the laminate cluster remove the pre-cut pendulum slot.

In 6mm/¼″ ply, mark out for and cut the large disc which forms laminate A. Check the diameter carefully against the main laminate cluster.

Repeat the process in 6mm/¼″ ply to form laminate F and remove the centre circle.

Glue and pin laminates A and F to the main laminate cluster taking care to align the outer edges accurately. Set aside to set hard.

It may be necessary at this time to 'fettle' the cut edges of the main case sub-assembly to remove saw kerfs and any irregularities in the cut edges. use a medium wood file, sanding block and abrasive paper for this. The inside curves are best fettled with a half round file of suitable diameter and abrasive paper wrapped round a dowel. In carrying out the fettling part of the project take very great care not to create any 'flat spots' and do not round off any arrises. A blemish at this stage will show through on any veneer later applied.

In 6mm/¼″ ply, mark out for and cut laminates G, checking the diameters against the main case sub-assembly. Do not attach laminates G at this stage.

VENEERING MAIN CASE ASSEMBLY
Veneer the rear face of the case sub-assembly with decorative veneer set vertically. Make sure that the veneer is free from any bubbles etc.

Veneer the lower faces of the rear of laminate E with decorative veneer set horizontally. In this instance it will be necessary to pre-shape the edge of the veneer where it will butt against the perimeter of laminate F. Roll down and trim off surplus veneer.

Veneer the perimeter of laminate F where it immediately abuts the area last veneered. Do not continue this veneer strip all round the main drum of the case. Roll down and trim off.

To the front face of laminate B apply veneer in a similar manner to that described for laminate E above. Take the veneer right across the area to be later occupied by laminates G. Roll down and trim off.

Veneer the perimeter of laminate A where it immediately abuts the area last veneered. Do not continue this veneered strip right round the rest of the drum. Roll down and trim off.

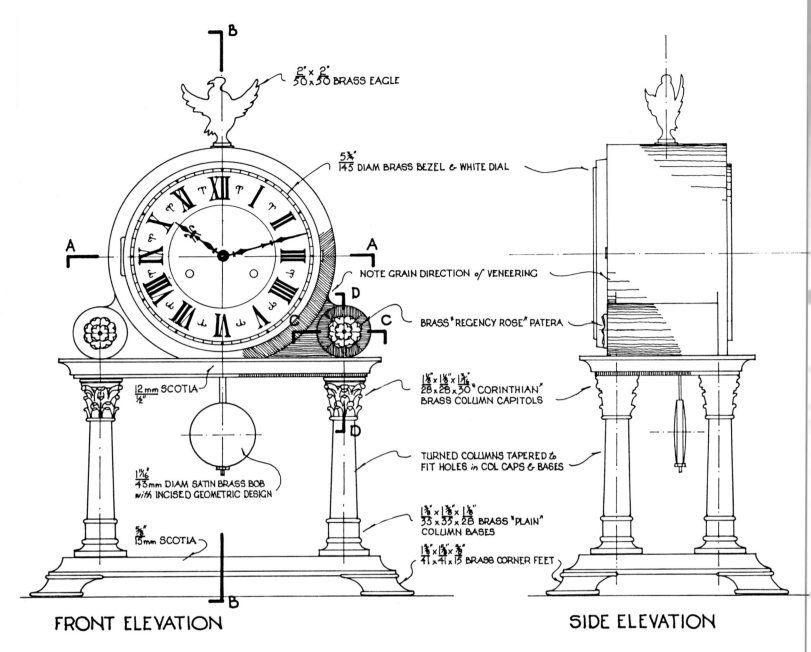

$\frac{2"\times 2"}{50 \times 50}$ BRASS EAGLE

$\frac{5\frac{5}{8}"}{145}$ DIAM BRASS BEZEL & WHITE DIAL

NOTE GRAIN DIRECTION of VENEERING

BRASS "REGENCY ROSE" PATERA

$\frac{1\frac{1}{8}"\times 1\frac{1}{8}"\times 1\frac{3}{16}"}{28 \times 28 \times 30}$ "CORINTHIAN" BRASS COLUMN CAPITOLS

$\frac{12\,mm}{\frac{1}{2}"}$ SCOTIA

TURNED COLUMNS TAPERED to FIT HOLES in COL CAPS & BASES

$\frac{1\frac{11}{16}"}{43\,mm}$ DIAM SATIN BRASS BOB with INCISED GEOMETRIC DESIGN

$\frac{1\frac{3}{8}"\times 1\frac{3}{8}"\times 1\frac{1}{8}"}{35 \times 35 \times 28}$ BRASS "PLAIN" COLUMN BASES

$\frac{5}{8}"$ $\frac{15\,mm}$ SCOTIA

$\frac{1\frac{5}{8}"\times 1\frac{5}{8}"\times \frac{5}{8}"}{41 \times 41 \times 15}$ BRASS CORNER FEET

FRONT ELEVATION

SIDE ELEVATION

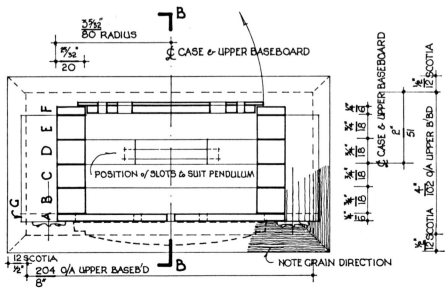

$\frac{3\frac{5}{32}"}{80}$ RADIUS

$\frac{\frac{13}{32}"}{20}$

$\mathrm{C\!\!\!\!L}$ CASE & UPPER BASEBOARD

$\mathrm{C\!\!\!\!L}$ CASE & UPPER BASEBOARD

D E F
C D E
B C
A B

POSITION of SLOTS to SUIT PENDULUM

$\frac{12}{\frac{1}{2}"}$ SCOTIA 204 O/A UPPER BASEB'D $8"$

NOTE GRAIN DIRECTION

PLAN at A-A

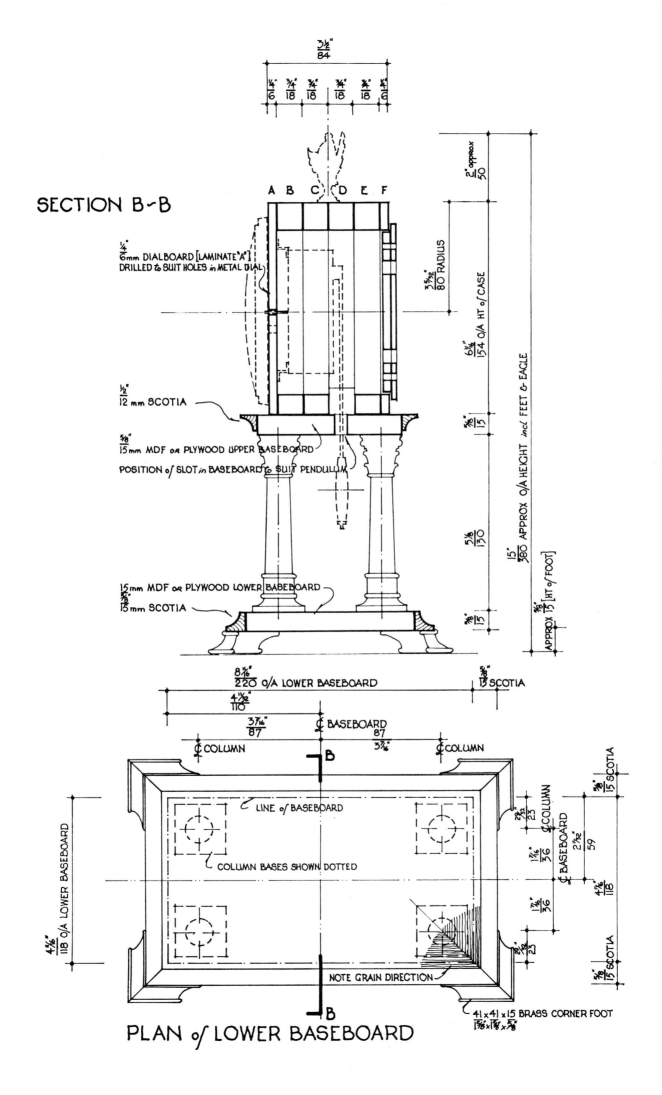

SECTION B-B

$\frac{3\frac{1}{2}"}{84}$

$\frac{\frac{1}{4}"}{6}$ $\frac{3/4"}{18}$ $\frac{3/4"}{18}$ $\frac{3/4"}{18}$ $\frac{3/4"}{18}$ $\frac{\frac{1}{4}"}{6}$

A B C D E F

$\frac{2"}{50}$ approx

$\frac{3\frac{5}{32}"}{80}$ RADIUS

$\frac{6\frac{1}{16}"}{154}$ O/A HT of CASE

$\frac{\frac{1}{4}"}{6}$/6mm DIALBOARD [LAMINATE "A"]
DRILLED to SUIT HOLES in METAL DIAL

$\frac{\frac{1}{2}"}{12}$ mm SCOTIA

$\frac{5/8"}{15}$

$\frac{5/8"}{15}$ mm MDF or PLYWOOD UPPER BASEBOARD

POSITION of SLOT in BASEBOARD to SUIT PENDULUM

$\frac{5\frac{1}{8}"}{130}$

$\frac{15"}{380}$ APPROX O/A HEIGHT incl FEET & EAGLE

15mm MDF or PLYWOOD LOWER BASEBOARD
$\frac{5/8"}{15}$ mm SCOTIA

$\frac{5/8"}{15}$

APPROX $\frac{5/8"}{15}$ [HT of FOOT]

$\frac{8\frac{11}{16}"}{220}$ O/A LOWER BASEBOARD

$\frac{5/8"}{13}$ SCOTIA

$\frac{4\frac{11}{32}"}{110}$

$\frac{3\frac{7}{16}"}{87}$

₵ BASEBOARD $\frac{87}{3\frac{7}{16}}$

₵ COLUMN

₵ COLUMN

LINE of BASEBOARD

COLUMN BASES SHOWN DOTTED

$\frac{5/8"}{15}$ SCOTIA

$\frac{29}{32}"}{23}$ ₵ COLUMN

₵ BASEBOARD

$\frac{1\frac{7}{16}"}{36}$

$\frac{2\frac{5}{16}"}{59}$

₵ BASEBOARD

$\frac{4\frac{11}{16}"}{118}$ O/A LOWER BASEBOARD

$\frac{1\frac{7}{16}"}{36}$

$\frac{4\frac{11}{16}"}{118}$

$\frac{29}{32}"}{23}$

$\frac{5/8"}{15}$ SCOTIA

NOTE GRAIN DIRECTION

41 x 41 x 15 BRASS CORNER FOOT
$\frac{1\frac{5}{8}" \times 1\frac{5}{8}" \times \frac{5}{8}"}{}$

PLAN of LOWER BASEBOARD

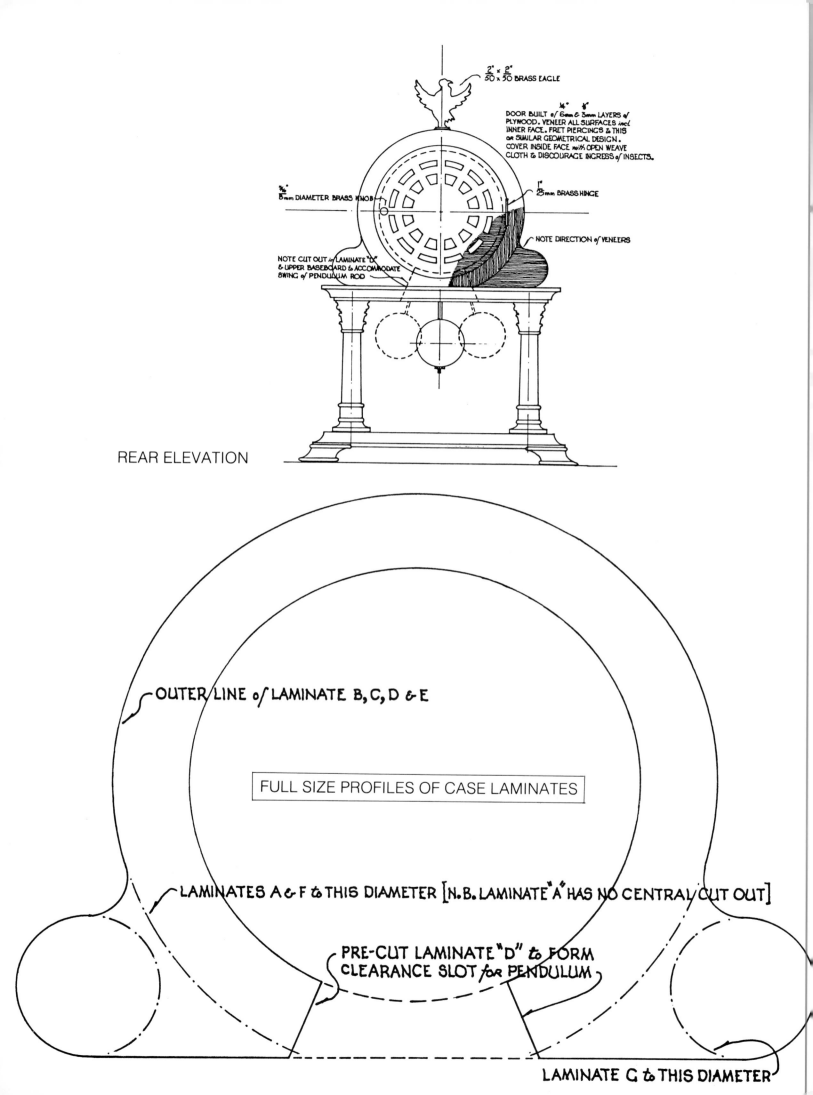

2" × 2"
50 × 50 BRASS EAGLE

¼" ⅛"
DOOR BUILT o/ 6mm & 3mm LAYERS o/
PLYWOOD. VENEER ALL SURFACES incl
INNER FACE. FRET PIERCINGS to THIS
or SIMILAR GEOMETRICAL DESIGN.
COVER INSIDE FACE with OPEN WEAVE
CLOTH to DISCOURAGE INGRESS o/ INSECTS.

⅜"
8mm DIAMETER BRASS KNOB

1"
25mm BRASS HINGE

NOTE DIRECTION o/ VENEERS

NOTE CUT OUT in LAMINATE "D"
& UPPER BASEBOARD to ACCOMMODATE
SWING o/ PENDULUM ROD

REAR ELEVATION

OUTER LINE o/ LAMINATE B, C, D & E

FULL SIZE PROFILES OF CASE LAMINATES

LAMINATES A & F to THIS DIAMETER [N.B. LAMINATE "A" HAS NO CENTRAL CUT OUT]

PRE-CUT LAMINATE "D" to FORM
CLEARANCE SLOT for PENDULUM

LAMINATE G to THIS DIAMETER

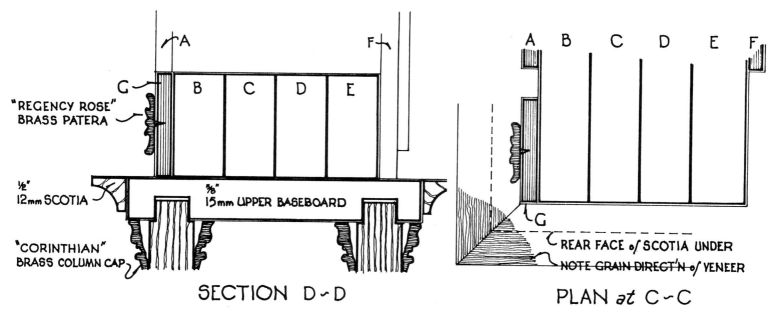

G

"REGENCY ROSE"
BRASS PATERA

½"
12mm SCOTIA

"CORINTHIAN"
BRASS COLUMN CAP

⅝"
15mm UPPER BASEBOARD

SECTION D~D

REAR FACE of SCOTIA UNDER

NOTE GRAIN DIRECT'N of VENEER

PLAN at C~C

NOTE: ASSEMBLE LAMINATE B, C, D and E FIRST
and VENEER FRONT & REAR FACES before FIXING
LAMINATES A, F and G

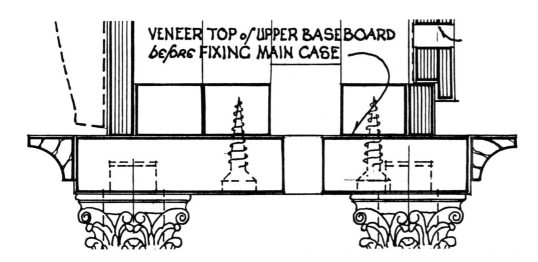

VENEER TOP of UPPER BASEBOARD
before FIXING MAIN CASE

FULL SIZE DETAIL FROM SECTION B–B FOR BASEBOARD FIXING

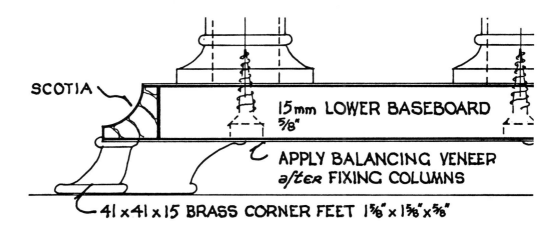

SCOTIA

15mm LOWER BASEBOARD
⅝"

APPLY BALANCING VENEER
after FIXING COLUMNS

41 x 41 x 15 BRASS CORNER FEET 1⅝" x 1⅝" x ⅝"

Veneer the perimeter of laminates B, C, D and E. Roll down and trim off. Glue laminates G with PVA spread very thinly and pin in position to the face of laminate B. Punch home any projecting pin heads.

Veneer the whole of the drum with decorative veneer set cross banded and starting at the top centre line. Roll down with care and trim off. Repeat the process with the other half of the drum, making sure that you obtain a good join at top centre. Roll down and trim off.

Veneer the faces of laminates G with quarter matched decorative veneer and roll down and trim off.

Veneer the *whole* of the face of laminate A with quarter matched decorative veneer and roll down and trim off.

Carefully sand all the veneered surfaces of the main case to a finish using progressively finer grades of abrasive paper. Generally work in the direction of the grain only and take care that the surface of the veneer is not rubbed through, particularly at the arrises. Set the whole of the case sub-assembly to one side for later finishing and final assembly.

REAR DOOR

Refer to the main case assembly and ascertain the actual diameter, of the rear access opening and in 6mm/¼" ply cut a circle to that size *less* allowance for thickness of future veneer to the perimeter. Fettle the cut edge.

In 3mm/⅛" ply cut a circle for the outer layer of the door allowing 3mm/⅛" overlap *all round*. Fettle the cut edge as required.

With PVA adhesive glue and pin the two layers together ensuring that the inner layer is set exactly central to the outer layer. Clamp together as needed and set to one side to set hard.

VENEERING DOOR

Veneer the whole of the inner face of the door assembly with common veneer. Roll down and trim off.

Veneer the perimeter of the inner layer with common veneer. Roll down and trim off.

Veneer the perimeter of the outer layer with decorative veneer. Roll down and trim off.

Veneer the outer face of the outer layer with decorative veneer set with the grain horizontal. Roll down and trim off.

FRETTING DOOR

Sand down the door surfaces to a semi finish. Carefully set out with compasses and a straight edge the geometrical pattern shown on the drawing (or any other of your choice). Make sure that in marking out you do not bruise the face of the veneer.

With a fret saw with a *very fine* blade carefully cut out the shapes just marked out. As needed, fettle the fretted cuts with needle files.

Sand the whole of the rear door assembly to a finish and set aside for later use.

UPPER BASEBOARD

Take the sawn plywood component for the upper baseboard and accurately mark out the sizes shown on the drawing. Carefully plane back to that size.

Take the clock movement and measure the position taken up by the pendulum rod. Also referring to the drawing mark that position on the upper baseboard. Allowing oversize in width and length for the swing of the pendulum mark out for and cut a through slot in the plywood.

With decorative veneer lay cross-banding to all four planed edges of the upper baseboard.

Take a length of 12mm/½" scotia and sand down. Brush off and stain to match main veneer if required. Cut the scotia to the lengths required with neat mitres at intersections. Offer up and glue to the edge of the baseboard.

When scotias have set hard veneer the whole of the upper surface of the upper baseboard including the top of the scotia.

To the underside of the upper baseboard mark out for and drill the pilot and clearance holes for screws which will ultimately attach the case assembly to the upper baseboard. Don't assemble these units yet.

LOWER BASEBOARD

Working as described for the upper baseboard, plane the lower baseboard to the size shown on the drawings. Prepare lengths of the 18mm/¾" scotia as before, mitre at intersections and glue to the edges of the lower baseboard.

With decorative veneer, cover the whole of the upper surface of the baseboard including the top of the scotia. Set aside for later work.

TURNED COLUMNS

On the lathe, turn the supporting columns noting the taper required to suit the differing diameters of the sockets in the brass column caps and bases. At one end of each column turn a spigot as indicated on the drawing. Accurately mark the total length required between spigot shoulder and the base of the column. At this stage dismount the column from the lathe and check that a good fit has been made to the brass column sockets. Remount the column on the lathe, sand to a finish and apply finishes of your choice.

On the lathe make the other columns to the *exact* length of the first. Still check each individual column against the sockets in its brass caps — there may be minor differences in diameter between the brassware.

SETTING OUT FOR COLUMN FIXING

Using the Corinthian brass column caps as a guide, carefully mark out on the under surface of the upper baseboard the centres required for sockets to accept the column spigots. Drill for those spigots and check that a good tight fit has been obtained.

On the upper side of the lower baseboard accurately mark out the centres required for the screw fixing of the columns. Note: The dimensions centre to centre of these holes should be *exactly* the same as the dimensions centre to centre of the spigot sockets in the upper baseboard. Drill the pilot and clearance holes for screws.

FINISHES GENERALLY

The best finish to use is french polish but pleasing results may be obtained with varnish, cellulose or polyurethane finishes. In the latter cases, grain fill the wood before you apply the initial coat (which should be flowed on rather than brushed in). When this first coat has dried hard flat down with grade 0000 wire wool, working in the direction of the grain. Repeat the process until satisfactory results are obtained. Flat down the final coat and apply solid wax polish to obtain a final gloss.

Before applying finishes to any components, check the areas that will be required to accept glue and carefully mask these off with cellotape.

APPLY FINISHES

Apply finishes to the whole of the case assembly except the underside which is to be glued and screwed to the upper baseboard. Do not fix brassware at this stage.

Apply finishes to the whole of the upper baseboard except for the underside which has yet to be veneered.

Apply finishes to the whole of the lower baseboard except for the underside which has yet to be veneered.

ASSEMBLY

Glue and screw the upper baseboard to the underside of the case assembly. Use the adhesive sparingly and remove any surplus from adjacent surfaces.

When the above has set hard fill the screw head holes with proprietary filler. Sand down flush with adjacent surfaces. Veneer the underside of the upper baseboard. Roll down, trim off round edges and trim round holes for column spigots. Sand down and apply finishes. Set aside for final assembly.

Place the brass column bases and caps in position on the pre-finished turned hardwood columns. Fix spigots in to sockets on underside of upper baseboard using PVA adhesive.

Before the spigots have set hard glue and screw the lower baseboard to the lower ends of the columns. Check that the whole assembly is true and square and set aside for adhesive to set hard.

When this has occurred, fill the screw head holes with filler, sand down and veneer the underside of the base with common veneer. Roll down and trim off, sand down and apply finish.

FINAL ASSEMBLY INCLUDING BRASSWARE

Following the maker's instructions fix the movement to the inside of the dial-board (laminate A) but do *not* hang the pendulum at this stage.

Fix the dial to the outer face of the dial-board and fix the hands to the movement handshaft.

Fix the brass hinge to the door and hang the door in position. Check that it swings easily and is a good fit in to the opening. (The fit should be such that the door stays closed by friction). Fix the brass door knob in position.

Screw the brass corner feet in position on the lower baseboard.

Drill for and fix in position the brass eagle, making sure that it is at the exact centre of the drum top.

Set the completed clock upright on a true and level surface and hang the pendulum.

Wind the movement, set the hands to the correct time and swing the pendulum to set the movement in motion.

It is unlikely that the clock will keep accurate time at first and it will, therefore, be necessary to adjust the pendulum bob over a period of some days. This is achieved by using the small nut immediately under the bob. (Tighten the nut UP to speed the clock UP and turn the nut DOWN to slow DOWN the clock).

Cutting list

COMPONENT	QUANTITY	SECTION	LENGTH
Lower Baseboard	1	15 × 118	220
	1	5/8″ × 4¹¹/₁₆″	8¹¹/₁₆″
Upper Baseboard	1	15 × 102	204
	1	5/8″ × 4″	8″
Laminates A (Dial-board)	1	6 × 160	–
	1	¼″ × 6⁵/₁₆″	–
Laminates B, C, D & E	4	18 × 155	212
	4	¾″ × 6⅛″	8⅜″
Laminate F	1	6 × 160	–
	1	¼″ × 6⁵/₁₆″	–
Laminate G	2	6 × 38	–
	2	¼″ × 1½″	–
Inner Layer of Door	1	6 × 120	–
	1	¼″ × 4¾″	–
Outer Layer of Door	1	3 × 130	–
	1	⅛″ × 5⅛″	–
Lower Baseboard Scotia	1	15 × 15	796 minimum
	1	5/8″ × 5/8″	31¾″ minimum
Upper Baseboard Scotia	1	12 × 12	708
	1	½″ × ½″	28″
Columns	4	ex 24 × 24	152
	4	ex 1″ × 1″	6″

Clock Components and Hardware (excluding screws and pins)

CLOCK MOVEMENT — OPTIONS:

1. Mechanical Bracket Clock Movement.
   Spring driven.
   90mm/3⁹/₁₆″ diameter movement.
   85mm/3⅜″ depth of movement.
   Pendulum length: 170mm/6¹¹/₁₆″.
   Pendulum swing: 130mm/5⅛″ approx.
   Pendulum bob: 43mm/1¹¹/₁₆″ diameter.
   Manufacturers: this clock was designed specifically to suit a Hermle 131–080 movement. Other mechanical bracket clock movements might be suitable, though adjustments to the size of the clock case might be necessary.

2. Quartz pendulum movements.
   Standard/pendulum or melody/pendulum models available.
   Pendulum length: can be cut to size.
   Pendulum swing: variable — check with make of movement.
   Pendulum bob: 43mm/1¹¹/₁₆″ diameter or nearest equivalent.
   Handshaft/fixing nut length: to suit 6–8mm/¼″ – ⁵/₁₆″ dial-board and dial thickness.
   Note: Whichever movement is chosen, adjust size and position of slot in upper baseboard to suit pendulum position and swing.

CLOCK DIAL — OPTIONS:
   - The case is designed to suit 147mm/5¹³/₁₆″ diameter integral bezel and dial combination. Keyholes drilled in dial for front winding movement.
   - If alternative dials/bezels are used (Eg 152mm/6″ diameter), slight adjustments in the size of the main case laminates will be needed.

CLOCK HANDS:
   - Bushed to suit mechanical or quartz movement.
   - Length to suit dial size.
   - Pattern to suit individual choice.

BRASSWARE:
   - One 25mm/1″ butt hinge.
   - One 9mm/⅜″ knob/latch for rear door.
   - Column Caps/Bases:
     Four 35 × 35 × 28mm/1⅜″ × 1⅜″ × 1⅛″ 'plain' brass column bases.
     Four 28 × 28 × 30mm/1⅛″ × 1⅛″ × 1³/₁₆″ 'Corinthian' brass capitols.
   - One 50 × 50mm/2″ × 2″ brass eagle.
   - Four 41 × 41 × 15mm/1⅝″ × 1⅝″ × ⅝″ corner feet.
   - Two 21mm/⅞″ diameter 'Regency Rose' paterae, or similar.

GLASS:
   - To suit bezel diameter, if not supplied with dial/bezel combination.

5.   18th Century Balloon Clock

The design of balloon mantel clocks probably reached a peak of perfection at the turn of the century.

The simple but elegant lines of that period are recreated in this plan with complete profiles of the shapes. Basic construction is simple and the case may be finished with easily obtained veneers and inlay motifs.

The same dial, bezel and mechanical or quartz movements used in the lancet clock may be incorporated in this clock.

Overall dimensions: 244 wide × 134 deep × 425mm high
                     9⅝″ wide ×   5¼″ deep × 16¾″ high.   Skill level * * *

Schedule of Operations

BODY ASSEMBLY & LAMINATES

The shaping and assembly of the laminates forming the main part of the clock case may be done in different ways, depending upon the workshop equipment available.

If you own a bandsaw, it is suggested that the type 'Y' laminates are assembled with PVA adhesive and pins before attempting any shaping. Once the adhesive has set hard, carefully mark out the profiles shown on the plan, including the large diameter hole which will later accept the movement. Working slowly to reduce kerf lines, accurately bandsaw the outer shape. Clean off any kerf marks with a file and sanding block. Cut out the large diameter hole with the bandsaw, cutting through the perimeter at the top centre line. After the central waste wood has been removed, fill the top centre saw cut with a veneer slip using PVA adhesive.

If you do not own a bandsaw, the profiles should be cut out on the individual laminates before assembly, using a coping saw. Take great care in cutting the shapes, ensuring that the saw is held upright. Check each shaped laminate, one against the other, to ensure that you have obtained a good match. Carefully assemble the laminates, using PVA adhesive and pins. Once the adhesive has set hard, clean up the shapes with a file and sanding block.

Accurately cut out the sub dial-board, using the main laminate assembly as a marking out template. Fix to the main laminate assembly with PVA adhesive and pins. Clean up saw kerfs with a file and sanding block.

Accurately cut out laminate 'X' in the same manner and fix to the rear of the main laminate assembly as last. Clean up any saw kerfs with a file and sanding block, paying close attention to the inner edge of the large diameter hole. Accuracy here will help you later to obtain a good fit to the rear door assembly.

Mark out the dial-board with compasses, checking the diameter against the main laminate assembly. Mark the centre lines before carefully cutting out the perimeter. Check the diameter of the movement spindle and drill the dial-board at dead centre. The resultant hole should achieve a 'sloppy' fit with the spindle. Offer up the movement to the *rear* of the dial-board and accurately mark out the position of the winder pins (front wind mechanical movements only). Drill for the winder pins to a diameter giving a 'sloppy' fit with the winder key. On the main laminate assembly mark the exact top centre line.

Carefully aligning the respective centre lines, fix the dial-board to the main assembly with PVA adhesive and pins. Clean up saw kerf marks with a file and sanding block.

Check over the whole of the body assembly, punching in the heads of pins. Fill the punch holes and any holes in the cut edges of plywood with stopping compound. Sand off stoppings flush with the surrounding surfaces.

VENEERING

Veneer the whole of the under surfaces of the body assembly, using a contact adhesive. Trim off any surplus veneer using a sharp craft knife.

Veneer the whole of the rear of the body assembly and trim off surplus veneer as last, paying particular attention to the edge of the rear door opening.

Veneer the whole of the side faces of the body assembly, taking particular note of the grain directions indicated on the plan. Trim off surplus veneer.

Veneer the face and underside of the sub dial and trim off surplus veneer.

Veneer the face of the dial-board, cutting the veneer in segmental areas first, so as to maintain the visual impression of cross banding radiating from the dial centre. Trim off surplus veneer, including around the spindle and winder holes.

Take the inlay motif of your choice and carefully mark out the perimeter of the motif in the centre of the veneer sheet to be used in the front of the body assembly. Accurately cut out for and insert the inlay motif, holding it in position in the veneer sheet with masking tape or cellotape. Mark out for and cut out at the top of the sheet the curve of the sub dial underside, checking against the sub dial for accuracy of fit. Lay the veneer on the body assembly with a contact adhesive, taking great care to ensure that the inlay motif is central relative to the sides of the body. Trim off surplus veneer and remove the masking tape from the motif.

Generally, sand all veneered surfaces of the body assembly to a finish, using progressively finer abrasive papers and working parallel to the grain.

SUB FINIAL BASE

Make the sub finial base in softwood to the shape and sizes shown on the plan. In order to ensure a really accurate fit with the rounded top of the body assembly, tape a sheet of fine abrasive paper to the rounded top and rub the finial

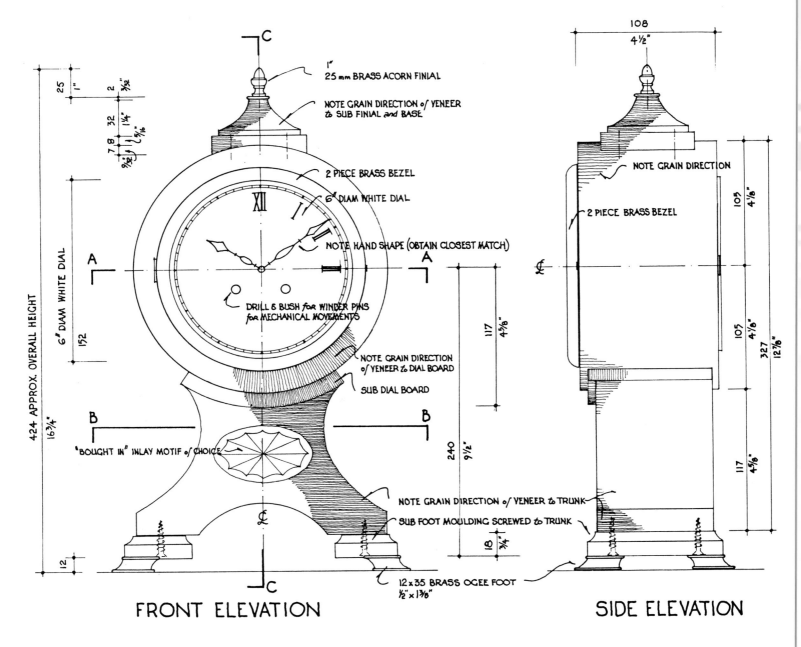

FRONT ELEVATION

1" 25 mm BRASS ACORN FINIAL

NOTE GRAIN DIRECTION of VENEER to SUB FINIAL and BASE

2 PIECE BRASS BEZEL

6" DIAM WHITE DIAL

NOTE HAND SHAPE (OBTAIN CLOSEST MATCH)

DRILL & BUSH for WINDER PINS for MECHANICAL MOVEMENTS

NOTE GRAIN DIRECTION of VENEER to DIAL BOARD

SUB DIAL BOARD

"BOUGHT IN" INLAY MOTIF of CHOICE

NOTE GRAIN DIRECTION of VENEER to TRUNK

SUB FOOT MOULDING SCREWED to TRUNK

12 x 35 BRASS OGEE FOOT ½" x 1⅜"

424 APPROX. OVERALL HEIGHT 16¾"

6" DIAM WHITE DIAL 152

25 1" 2 2 3/32"

7 8 32 9/32" 5/16" 1/4"

117 4⅝"

240 9½"

18 ¾"

12

SIDE ELEVATION

108 4½"

NOTE GRAIN DIRECTION

2 PIECE BRASS BEZEL

105 4⅛"

105 4⅛"

327 12⅞"

117 4⅝"

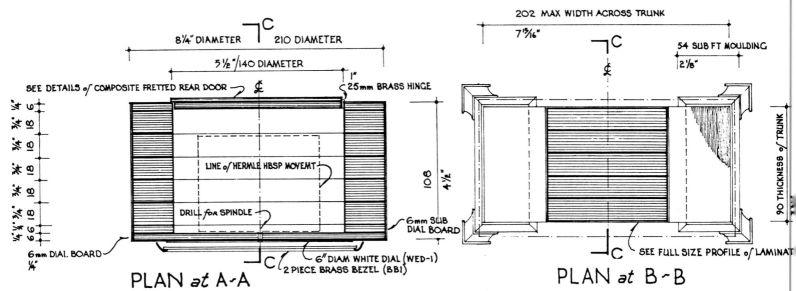

PLAN at A-A

8¼" DIAMETER 210 DIAMETER

5½"/140 DIAMETER

1"

SEE DETAILS of COMPOSITE FRETTED REAR DOOR

25mm BRASS HINGE

LINE of HERMLE HBSP MOVEM'T

DRILL for SPINDLE

6mm SUB DIAL BOARD

6mm DIAL BOARD ¼"

6" DIAM WHITE DIAL (WED-1) 2 PIECE BRASS BEZEL (BB1)

6 18 18 18 6 ¼" ¾" ¾" ¾" ¼"

PLAN at B-B

202 MAX WIDTH ACROSS TRUNK

7¹⁵⁄₁₆"

54 SUB FT MOULDING 2⅛"

90 THICKNESS of TRUNK

108 4½"

SEE FULL SIZE PROFILE of LAMINAT

SEE FULL SIZE PROFILE of LAMINAT

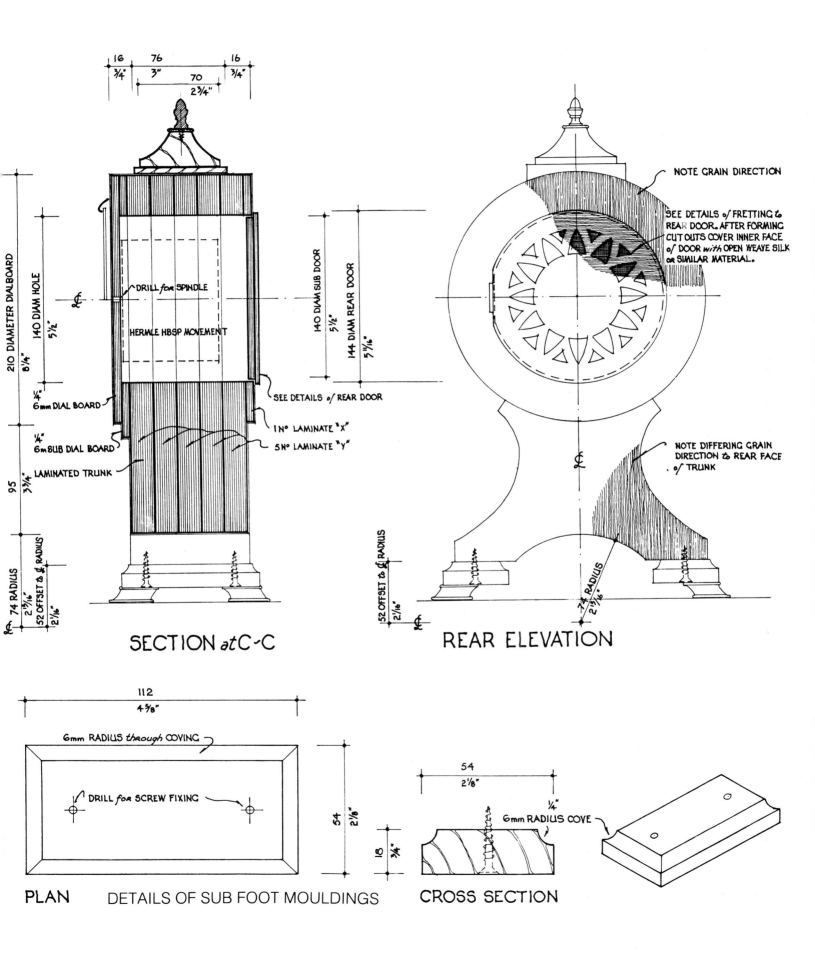

SECTION at C-C

REAR ELEVATION

PLAN   DETAILS OF SUB FOOT MOULDINGS   CROSS SECTION

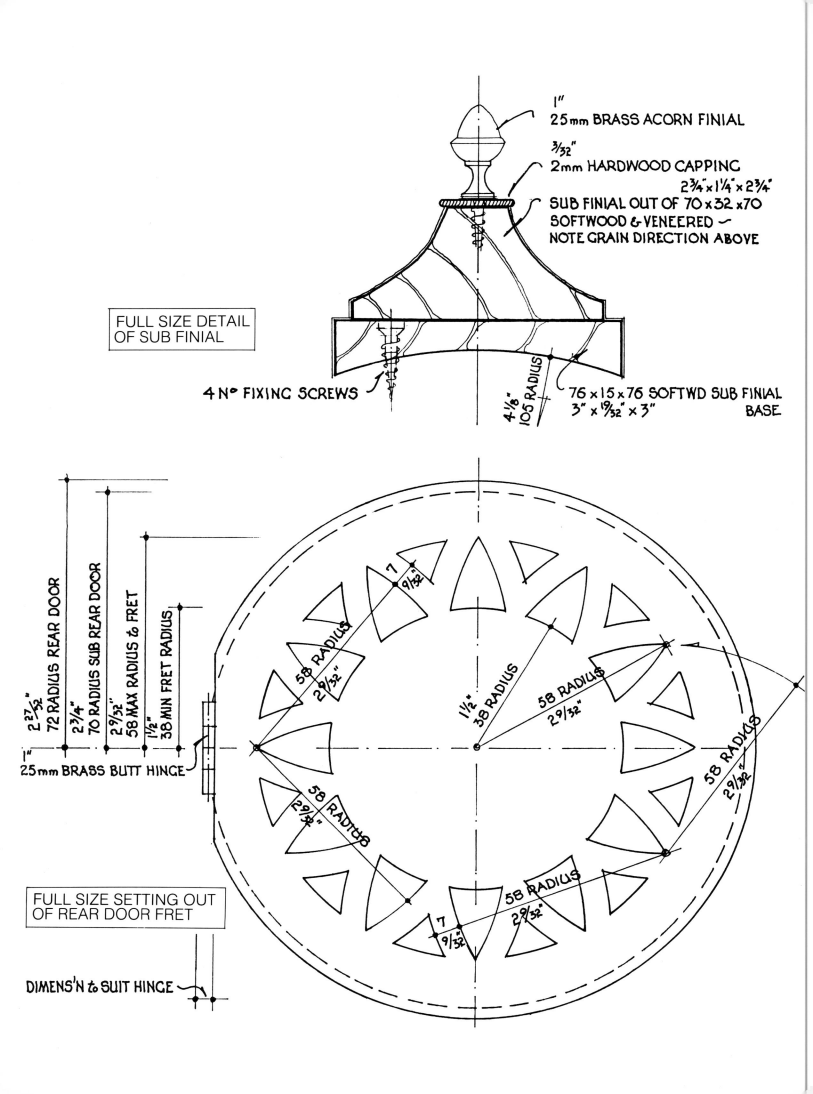

1"
25mm BRASS ACORN FINIAL

3/32"
2mm HARDWOOD CAPPING

2¾" × 1¼" × 2¾"
SUB FINIAL OUT OF 70 × 32 × 70
SOFTWOOD & VENEERED —
NOTE GRAIN DIRECTION ABOVE

FULL SIZE DETAIL
OF SUB FINIAL

4 Nº FIXING SCREWS

4⅛"
105 RADIUS

76 × 15 × 76 SOFTWD SUB FINIAL
3" × 19/32" × 3"   BASE

2 27/32"
72 RADIUS REAR DOOR

2¾"
70 RADIUS SUB REAR DOOR

2 9/32"
58 MAX RADIUS to FRET

1½"
38 MIN FRET RADIUS

1"
25mm BRASS BUTT HINGE

7
9/32"

58 RADIUS
2 9/32"

1½"
38 RADIUS

58 RADIUS
2 9/32"

58 RADIUS
2 9/32"

58 RADIUS
2 9/32"

58 RADIUS
2 9/32"

58 RADIUS
2 9/32"

7
9/32"

FULL SIZE SETTING OUT
OF REAR DOOR FRET

DIMENS'N to SUIT HINGE

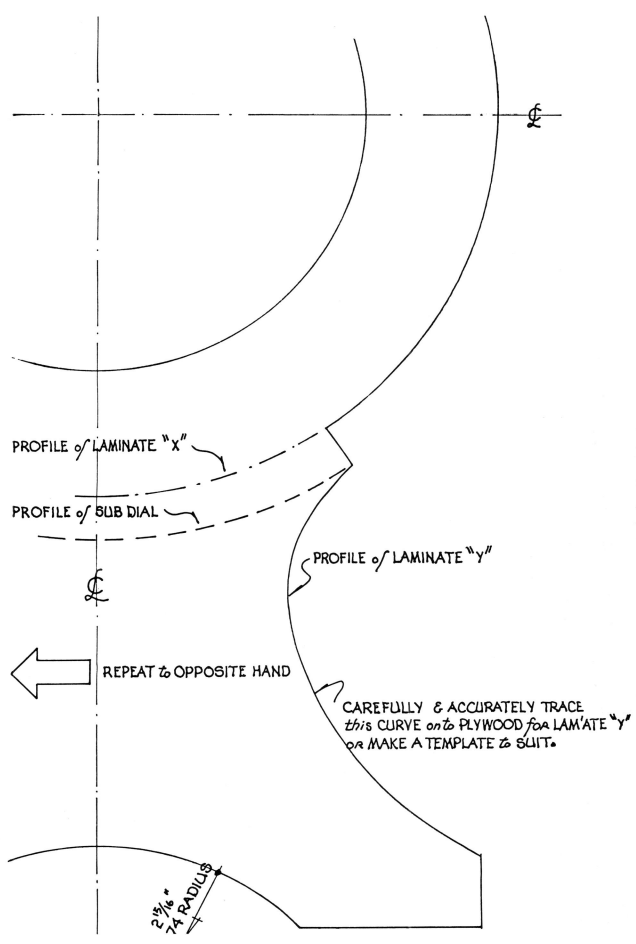

PROFILE of LAMINATE "X"

PROFILE of SUB DIAL

PROFILE of LAMINATE "Y"

REPEAT to OPPOSITE HAND

CAREFULLY & ACCURATELY TRACE
this CURVE onto PLYWOOD for LAM'ATE "Y"
or MAKE A TEMPLATE to SUIT.

2 13/16 "
74 RADIUS

FULL SIZE PROFILES OF LAMINATES

base on this until a perfect fit has been obtained.

Veneer the exposed surfaces of the sub finial base and sand to a finish. Set to one side.

Make the softwood sub finial to the shape shown on the plan. It is suggested that the curved profiles are cut with a bandsaw or coping saw, but with a longer block of wood than required. After carefully cleaning up the curved surfaces, cut off any surplus length of wood to obtain the required height. Veneer all surfaces with the grain direction as indicated on the plan, sand to a finish and set to one side.

REAR DOOR

Cut out the rear door and sub rear door components. Offer up the smaller diameter component to the rear door opening and check for a loose but accurate fit. Clean up the saw kerf marks to all cut edges and glue the two compon—ents together. Veneer the cut edges of the larger perimeter and trim off surplus veneer. Veneer the outer face of the door, laying on the veneer with grain in the direction shown on the plan. Sand down veneer, but not to a final finish.

On the outer face of the rear door, mark out the fretted pattern to the setting out detail shown on the plan. Accurately cut out the fretted parts with a fine toothed fretsaw. As necessary, clean up the fretted edges with needle files to remove any kerf marks. Sand all surfaces to a final finish.

FINISHING & FINAL ASSEMBLY

Brush off all sanding dust before applying finishes and work in a dust free environment. Seal all surfaces with a meths-based sanding sealer and polish all surfaces with button polish or heavy french polish. when bone dry, flat down the final coat with very fine wire wool and bring

back to a gloss with wax polish. Alternatively, after applying the sanding sealer, apply three coats of polyure-thane varnish, flatting down each coat when dry and bringing final coat to a gloss with wax polish.

Glue the sub finial assembly in position at the top of the body assembly, taking very great care to ensure that it is placed accurately. The slightest misplacement will spoil the final appearance of your clock.

Fix the dial to the dial-board with small screws or pins. Offer up the brass bezel and fix in position, making sure that it is exactly central relative to the dial.

Where winder holes have been formed in the dial for a front wind mechanical movement, neatly bush the holes before fixing the movement in position. Fix the movement to the inner face of the dial-board and fix the hands to the main spindle in accordance with the manufacturer's instructions.

Screw the sub foot mouldings in position at the bottom of the body assembly, being careful to ensure that they are accurately positioned. Screw the brass ogee feet in position on the sub foot mouldings.

Carefully cover the inner face of the rear door with a contrasting colour open weave silk or similar material. Use a general household adhesive for this. Apply the adhesive sparingly to the wood surface only and make sure that the sheet of material is stretched tight without wrinkles.

Fix the brass hinge to the rear door and hang the door in position. If the door is a loose fit in the opening fit a small brass side hook to retain the door in the closed position.

Drill for and fix the brass acorn finial in position.

Note: Since this clock case features an extensive use of veneers, the completed clock should not be placed directly above any localised heat source.

Cutting list

COMPONENT	QUANTITY	SECTION	LENGTH
Dial-board (Plywood)	1	6 × 210	—
	1	¼″ × 8¼″	—
Sub Dial-board (Plywood)	1	6 × 210	222
	1	¼″ × 8¼″	8¼″
Rear Door (Plywood)	1	3 × 144	—
	1	⅛″ × 5¹¹/₁₆″	—

Sub Rear Door	1	6 × 140	—
	1	¼″ × 5½″	—
Laminate 'X'	1	6 × 210	—
	1	¼″ × 8¼″	—
Laminate 'Y'	5	18 × 210	327
	5	¾″ × 8¼″	12⅞″
Sub Foot Moulding (Hardwood)	2	18 × 54	112
	2	¾″ × 2⅛″	4⅝″
Sub Finial (Softwood)	1	32 × 70	70
	1	1¼″ × 2¾″	2¾″
Sub Finial Base (Softwood)	1	15 × 76	76
	1	⅝″ × 3″	3″

Clock Components and Hardware (excluding screws and pins)

CLOCK MOVEMENT — OPTIONS:

1. Mechanical Movements.

   Spring driven bracket clock movement without pendulum.

   Front winding or rear winding versions available.

   Overall size of movement, including swing of gong/bell hammers, not to exceed size of 'movement hole' — 140mm dia × 90mm/5½″ dia × 3¾″.

   Handshaft: check length and adjust thickness of dial-board if necessary.

   Compact circular and rectangular movements available.

   Single bell strike and twin bell strike options available.

2. Quartz Movements.

   Standard or melody movements available.

   Shaft length/fixing nut: to suit 6mm/¼″ dial-board.

CLOCK DIAL — OPTIONS:

- 152mm/6″ diameter.
- Steel dial with enamel paint finish; aluminium dial with sprayed paint finish.
- Note: if front winding mechanical movement is used, drill holes in the dial and bush to accommodate winding keys.

CLOCK HANDS:

- Bushed to suit chosen mechanical or quartz movements.
- Length to suit dial size. Pattern to suit individual choice.

BRASSWARE:

- Bezel: to suit 152mm/6″ dial. All-in-one dial and bezel combinations are also available.
- One 25mm/1″ butt hinge for rear door. Door latch for rear door.
- One 25mm/1″ acorn finial. Additional patterns: flame, pineapple, urn.
- Four ogee/corner feet: 35 × 35 × 12mm/1⅜″ × 1⅜″ × ½″.

INLAYS: — Inlay motif various motif patterns and sizes available. GLASS: — To suit brass bezel.

6.   'Shepherdess' Clock

This is a traditional 'American styled' mantel clock that can also be used with an optional wall bracket as illustrated in our picture. The double glazed door allows the viewer to see both the clock dial and the movement of a pendulum. The lower portion of glass can also be painted with numerous decorative designs and we have shown a selection of four attractive floral and fruit examples.

Overall dimensions: 228 wide × 96 deep × 343mm high
9″ wide × 3⅞″ deep × 13⅝″ high

Schedule of Operations

BOX CARCASS

The design of this clock case is based on the principle of a box carcass constructed with simple butt joints and glue blocks.

After carefully studying the plan and the Schedule of Operations, take the sheet of 12mm/½″ plywood and carefully mark out the overall sizes of the faceboard and' the side cheekboards. The latter may be set out in the area to be cut out of the middle of the faceboard. Also mark out the exact shape of the topboard.

Take the sheet of 6mm/¼″ plywood and carefully mark out the shapes of the backboard and the bottom board.

Cut out the overall sizes of each component and cut out the various holes and slots in the backboard, faceboard and topboard using a tenon saw and coping saw.

Check all the components for squareness with a trysquare and similarly check all cut edges for squareness to the adjacent main surfaces. Correct where necessary using a plane and check the cheekboards against each other to ensure that they are identical.

Working on a table or bench top, lay the backboard flat and in turn hold the cheek boards in position ensuring that the surfaces which will later be glued marry up closely and then, using a trysquare check that the cheekboards sit at right angles to the backboard and the faceboard. Check the top and bottom boards against the back and face boards to ensure correct length.

Fix the glue blocks in the positions shown on the details of carcass boards. The initial fixing of the glue blocks is best achieved using veneer or moulding pins and PVA adhesive. Clean off any surplus adhesive which may have spread onto adjacent surfaces.

When all the glue blocks have set hard lay the backboard flat on the bench top and hold the left-hand cheekboard at right angles to it. Lightly tap in moulding pins to the sides of the glue blocks on the cheek boards but don't tap them home at this stage. Remove the cheekboard and thinly spread adhesive on the surface of the glue block and the cut edge of the backboard. Offer up the cheekboard again to the backboard and tap home the moulding pins. Repeat this whole process for the right-hand cheek. Clean off excess adhesive.

Next, glue the baseboard and topboard in position and hold in place by means of moulding pins. Offer up the faceboard to the carcass thus far assembled, drill for and screw partly home the screws where indicated on the drawing. Check all surfaces for squareness and remove the screws. Thinly spread adhesive on the cut edges of the cheekboards and again offer up the faceboard, this time screwing the screws fully home. Remove excess adhesive and set the assembly aside for all glue to harden and set.

When the carcass assembly has properly set, neatly trim off any projecting surfaces with a block plane and lightly sand down with 150 grit garnet paper.

PILASTER, PLINTH & DIAL-BOARD

Take the remainder of the sheet of 12mm/½″ thick plywood and carefully mark out the pilaster strips to the full height of the assembled carcass. Mark out the 25mm/1″ high plinth strips.

Take the remainder of the 6mm/¼″ thick sheet of plywood and mark and cut out the plinth packing piece and the dial-board. Check for squareness.

Next, cut to length the 9mm/⅜″ square softwood bearer strips for the dial-board and screw and glue in the positions shown on the drawing. Take the dial-board and check against the assembled carcass for fit. Drill in the dial-board for the movement spigot, ensuring that it is correctly positioned. Glue and pin the dial-board in position and remove any surplus adhesive.

Glue and pin in position the plinth packing piece at the front of the carcass assembly and glue and pin in position all the plinth strips, cutting to length as required. Remove surplus adhesive and when glue has set and hardened trim off any excess wood projections with a block plane.

DOOR ASSEMBLY

Take the remainder of the 12mm/½″ and 6mm/¼″ plywood and mark out and cut out the shapes for the door assembly. Check the two components for squareness as previously described. Thinly coat with adhesive the surfaces to be joined and offer up one to the other, ensuring that the outer cut edges co-incide, one with the other. Clamp the two surfaces together or, in the absence of clamps, pin together. set the door assembly to one side to harden and set, having first removed any surplus adhesive.

Offer up the door assembly to the opening in the faceboard to check for fit. Since the meeting surfaces of the door and the faceboard are to be veneered it is essential that due allowance is made for the thickness of the veneer. If it is necessary to remove wood from the edge of the door assembly this should be done with a block plane equally all

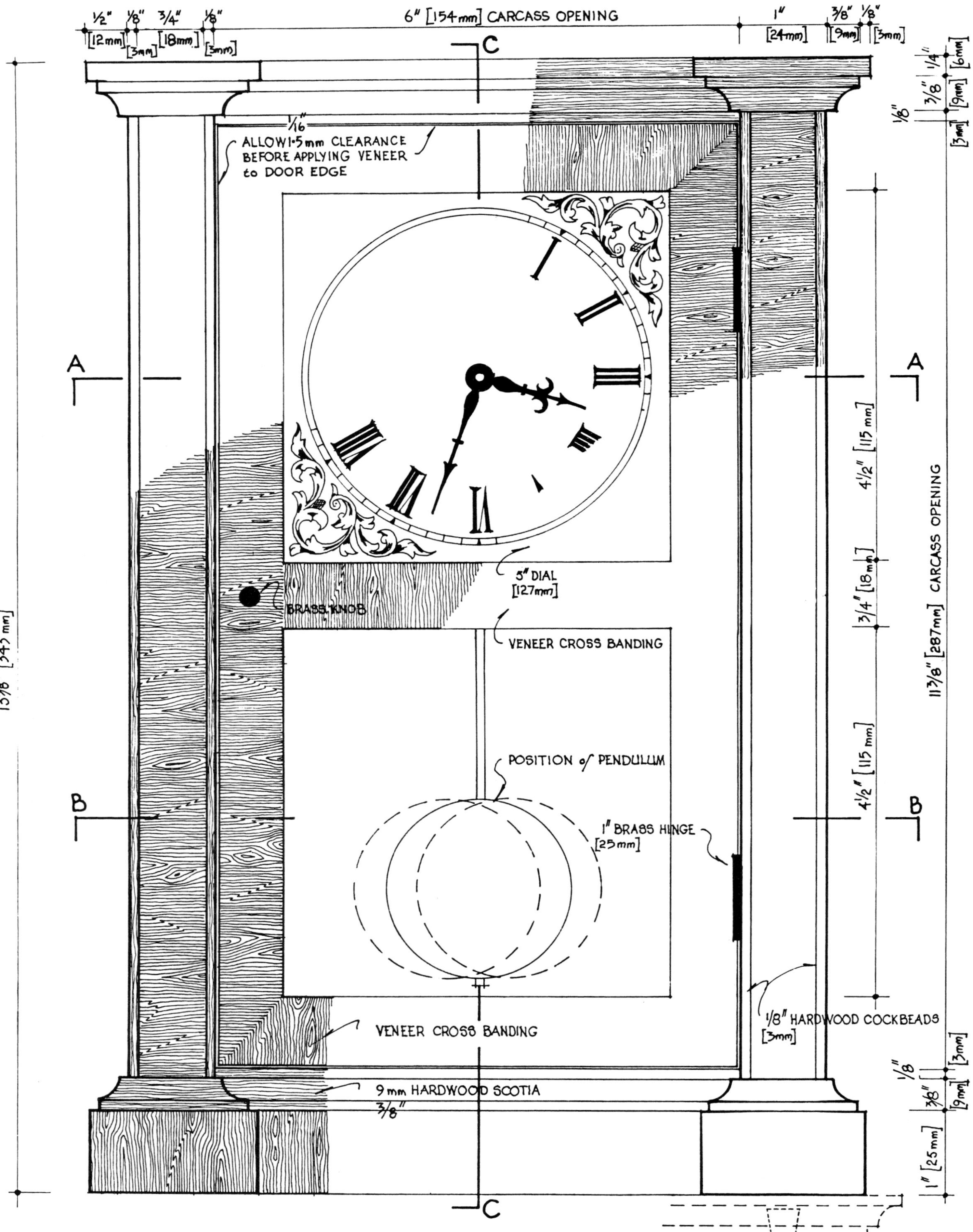

1/2" 1/8" 3/4" 1/8"
[12mm] [3mm] [18mm] [3mm]
6" [154mm] CARCASS OPENING
1" 3/8" 1/8"
[24mm] [9mm] [3mm]
1/4" [6mm]
3/8 [9mm]
1/8" [3mm]
C
1/16"
ALLOW 1·5mm CLEARANCE BEFORE APPLYING VENEER to DOOR EDGE
A
A
4 1/2" [115 mm]
11 3/8" [287mm] CARCASS OPENING
13 5/8" [343 mm]
5" DIAL [127mm]
BRASS KNOB
3/4" [18mm]
VENEER CROSS BANDING
POSITION of PENDULUM
4 1/2" [115 mm]
B
B
1" BRASS HINGE [25mm]
1/8" HARDWOOD COCKBEADS [3mm]
VENEER CROSS BANDING
1/8" [3mm]
9 mm HARDWOOD SCOTIA
3/8"
3/8" [9mm]
1" [25mm]
C
POS'N of OPTIONAL SHELF & BRACKET

FRONT ELEVATION

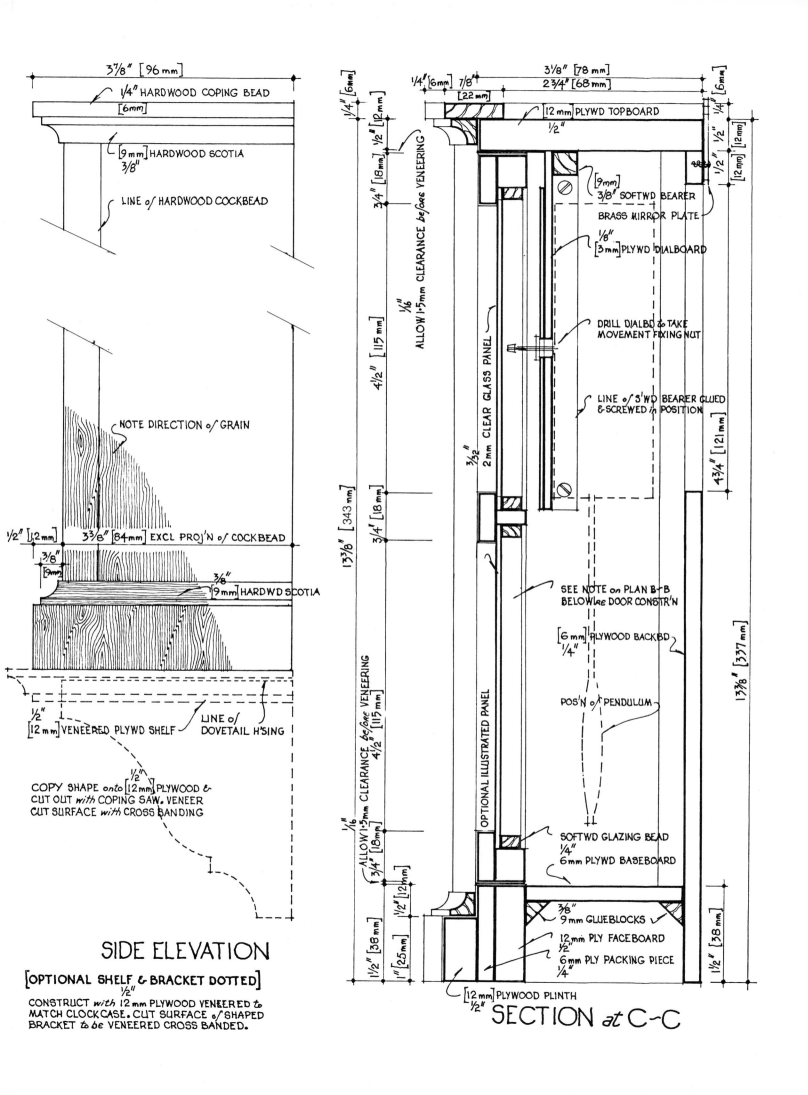

3⅞" [96 mm]

¼" HARDWOOD COPING BEAD [6 mm]

[9 mm] HARDWOOD SCOTIA 3/8"

LINE of HARDWOOD COCKBEAD

NOTE DIRECTION of GRAIN

½" [12 mm]

3/8" [9 mm]

3⅜" [84 mm] EXCL PROJ'N of COCKBEAD

3/8" 9 mm HARDWD SCOTIA

½" [12 mm] VENEERED PLYWD SHELF

LINE of DOVETAIL H'SING

COPY SHAPE onto ½" [12 mm] PLYWOOD & CUT OUT with COPING SAW. VENEER CUT SURFACE with CROSS BANDING

SIDE ELEVATION

[OPTIONAL SHELF & BRACKET DOTTED]

CONSTRUCT with 12 mm PLYWOOD VENEERED ½" to MATCH CLOCK CASE. CUT SURFACE of SHAPED BRACKET to be VENEERED CROSS BANDED.

¼" [6 mm]

¼" [6 mm]

½" [12 mm]

¾" [18 mm]

ALLOW 1·5 mm CLEARANCE before VENEERING 1/16"

13⅜" [343 mm]

4½" [115 mm]

3/4" [18 mm]

4½" [115 mm]

ALLOW 1·5 mm CLEARANCE before VENEERING

ALLOW 1·5 mm CLEARANCE 1/16"

¾" [18 mm]

1/16"

½" [12 mm]

1½" [38 mm]

1" [25 mm]

OPTIONAL ILLUSTRATED PANEL

3/32" 2 mm CLEAR GLASS PANEL

3⅛" [78 mm]

2¾" [68 mm]

7/8" [22 mm]

¼" [6 mm]

12 mm PLYWD TOPBOARD ½"

½" [12 mm]

½" [12 mm]

¼"

½" [12 mm]

[9 mm] 3/8" SOFTWD BEARER

BRASS MIRROR PLATE

1/8" [3 mm] PLYWD DIALBOARD

DRILL DIALBD to TAKE MOVEMENT FIXING NUT

LINE of 3'WD BEARER GLUED & SCREWED in POSITION

4¾" [121 mm]

SEE NOTE on PLAN B-B BELOW re DOOR CONSTR'N

[6 mm] PLYWOOD BACKBD ¼"

POS'N of PENDULUM

13⅜" [337 mm]

SOFTWD GLAZING BEAD ¼" 6 mm PLYWD BASEBOARD

3/8" 9 mm GLUEBLOCKS

12 mm PLY FACEBOARD ½" 6 mm PLY PACKING PIECE ¼"

[12 mm] PLYWOOD PLINTH ½"

1½" [38 mm]

SECTION at C-C

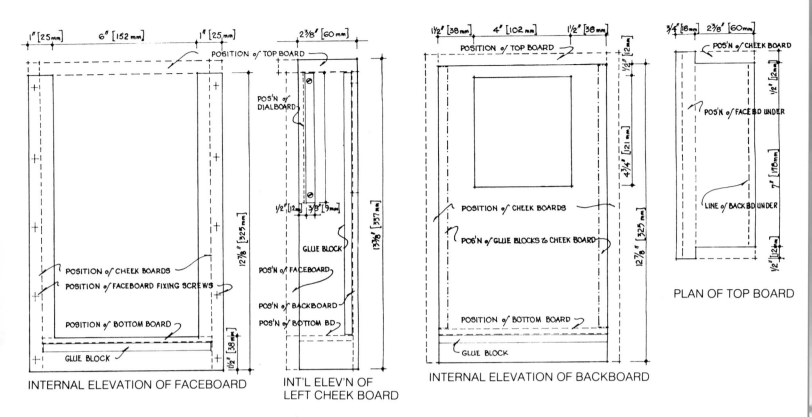

1" [25mm] 6" [152 mm] 1" [25mm] 2⅜" [60 mm]

POSITION of TOP BOARD

POS'N of DIALBOARD

½" [12mm] ⅜" [9mm]

GLUE BLOCK

12⅞" [325mm]

13⅛" [337 mm]

POSITION of CHEEK BOARDS
POSITION of FACEBOARD FIXING SCREWS

POS'N of FACEBOARD

POSITION of BOTTOM BOARD

POS'N of BACKBOARD

POS'N of BOTTOM BD

1½" [38 mm]

GLUE BLOCK

INTERNAL ELEVATION OF FACEBOARD

INT'L ELEV'N OF LEFT CHEEK BOARD

½" [38 mm] 4" [102 mm] 1½" [38 mm]

POSITION of TOP BOARD

½" [12 mm]

POSITION of CHEEK BOARDS

POS'N of GLUE BLOCKS to CHEEK BOARD

4¾" [121 mm]

12⅞" [325 mm]

POSITION of BOTTOM BOARD

GLUE BLOCK

INTERNAL ELEVATION OF BACKBOARD

¾" [18mm] 2⅜" [60 mm]

POS'N of CHEEK BOARD

½" [12mm]

POS'N of FACE BD UNDER

7" [178mm]

LINE of BACK BD UNDER

½" [12mm]

PLAN OF TOP BOARD

DETAILS OF CARCASS BOARDS

IF YOU ARE PAINTING THE LOWER PORTION OF GLASS OR PERSPEX HERE, BELOW AND RIGHT, ARE FOUR DECORATIVE DESIGN EXAMPLES TO CONSIDER.

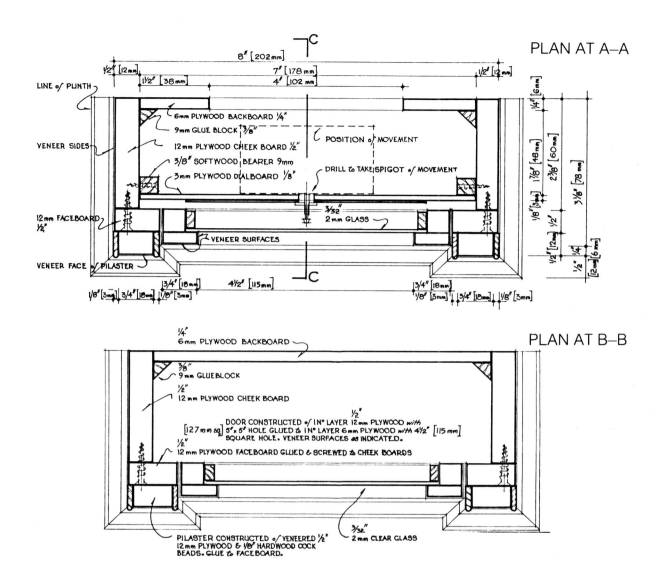

PLAN AT A–A

LINE of PLINTH

8" [202mm]
7" [178 mm]
4" [102 mm]
1/2" [12mm]
1 1/2" [38 mm]
1/2" [12 mm]

6mm PLYWOOD BACKBOARD 1/4"
9mm GLUE BLOCK 3/8"
12mm PLYWOOD CHEEK BOARD 1/2"
3/8" SOFTWOOD BEARER 9mm
3mm PLYWOOD DIALBOARD 1/8"

POSITION of MOVEMENT
DRILL to TAKE SPIGOT of MOVEMENT

VENEER SIDES

12mm FACEBOARD 1/2"

3/32" 2mm GLASS

VENEER SURFACES

VENEER FACE of PILASTER

3/4" [18mm]
1/8" [3mm] 3/4" [18mm] 1/8" [3mm]
4 1/2" [115mm]
3/4" [18mm]
1/8" [3mm] 3/4" [18mm] 1/8" [3mm]

1/4" [6mm]
1/8" [3mm]
1 7/8" [48mm]
2 3/8" [60mm]
3 1/8" [78mm]
1/8" [3mm] 1/2"
1/2" [12mm]
1/2" [12mm] 1/4"
1/2" 1/4" [12mm 6mm]

PLAN AT B–B

1/4" 6mm PLYWOOD BACKBOARD

3/8" 9mm GLUEBLOCK

1/2" 12mm PLYWOOD CHEEK BOARD

1/2"
DOOR CONSTRUCTED of 1 N° LAYER 12mm PLYWOOD with
[127mm sq] 5"x 5" HOLE GLUED to 1 N° LAYER 6mm PLYWOOD with 4 1/2" [115 mm]
SQUARE HOLE. VENEER SURFACES as INDICATED.

1/2" 12mm PLYWOOD FACEBOARD GLUED & SCREWED to CHEEK BOARDS

PILASTER CONSTRUCTED of VENEERED 1/2"
12mm PLYWOOD & 1/8" HARDWOOD COCK
BEADS. GLUE to FACEBOARD.

3/32" 2mm CLEAR GLASS

THESE DESIGNS CAN BE ENLARGED ON A ZOOM-LENS PHOTOCOPIER TO THE REQUIRED SIZE

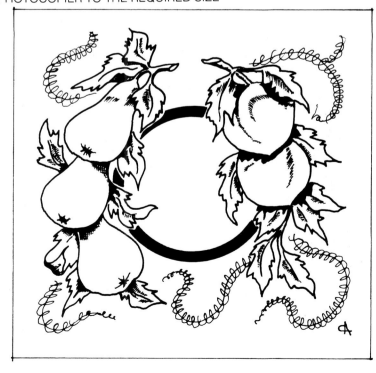

the way round. If wood is removed from one side only, the glazing openings in the door will not be central.

CASE & PLINTH VENEERING

Set the door assembly to one side and commence the veneering of the case. First veneer the cut edges of the opening in the faceboard and then the main surfaces of the cheekboards. The surfaces of the plinth may be veneered next and the front face of the pilasters last of all. Sand down all veneered surfaces of the main case assembly with 150 grit garnet paper and 240 grit wet and dry paper. Grain fill all surfaces and sand down with wet and dry paper.

COCKBEADS & MOULDINGS

Sand down generally all exposed surfaces of the 9mm/⅜" hardwood scotia moulding while still in strip form. Cut to the various lengths required, cutting mitres where required. Glue the scotia mouldings in the positions shown on the drawings, pinning as required; punch home the pin heads and fill and neatly sand down with wet and dry paper, paying particular attention to the mitre joints. Sand down, cut out, mitre and glue and pin in position the 6 × 9mm/¼" × ⅜" hardwood strips to form the coping at the top of the case. Punch home pin heads and fill as before. Sand down as before. Grain fill and sand down scotias and coping with wet and dry paper.

Take the 3mm/⅛" hardwood strips and cut to an accurate length to suit the exact height of the pilasters. Place these strips loosely in position on each side of the pilaster strips. It should be found that they project slightly beyond the veneered surfaces of the cheekboards and the opening in the faceboard. Remove the strips and round the front edges with sandpaper to form the cockbeads. Glue the cockbeads in position on each side of the pilaster strips and after the glue has set, sand down the sides with wet and dry paper flush with the adjacent veneer surfaces of the cheekboards and the opening in the faceboard. Grain fill and sand down. Set the whole assembly to one side.

DOOR VENEERING, GLAZING & HANGING

Next take the door assembly and veneer the whole of the outer cut edges. Check against the opening in the faceboard to ensure that a good fit has been obtained. Veneer the cut edges round the glazing openings in the door. Veneer with cross-banding the outer surface of the door assembly with

neatly mitred corners as shown on the plan. Sand down all veneered surfaces of the door with 150 grit garnet paper and 240 grit wet and dry paper. Grain fill and sand down as before.

Mark out the positions of the hinges on the right-hand edge of the door and cut out recesses to suit the full depth of the closed hinges using a fretsaw or coping saw. There is no need to cut a recess on the side of the opening in the faceboard.

Before glazing the door, all surfaces of door and case should be stained, sealed and polished. Alternatively, a varnished finish could be applied but this will not give a quality of finish suitable for this particular clock.

Glaze the upper and lower opening of the door with 2mm clear glass cut to fit the opening with about 0.5mm clearance all round. Fit hardwood glazing beads cut from surplus coping strips and fix these in position with moulding pins — do not use adhesive on the glazing beads.

Next, screw the door hinges into place on the door, and hang to your satisfaction. Fix the small brass door knob in position.

FINAL ASSEMBLY

Glue the dial in position on the dial-board using a contact adhesive checking that the hole in the dial co-incides exactly with the hole previously drilled in the dial-board.

Take the movement and fix in position behind the dial-board in the manner described in the instructions accompanying the movement. Fix the hands to the movement spindle as directed.

Take the pendulum rod and after carefully measuring the length required on the plan and checking this against the movement as installed in the case, cut off with a hacksaw the surplus length of rod. Neatly clean up the cut edge with a fine grade metal file, fit the bob to the rod and hang the whole assembly to the pendulum suspension hook on the movement.

BRACKET VERSION

The Shepherdess clock case has been designed for use as a shelf or mantel clock, as a bracket clock or as a wall clock. In the latter two cases it is suggested that a small brass mirror plate be screwed in place at the centre of the rear of the topboard.

If it is decided to build the bracket clock version of the Shepherdess, a shelf and brackets are shown on the plan.

These should be constructed of veneered 12mm/½″ plywood and screwed to the lower surfaces of the faceboard and cheekboards before veneering the under surface of the shelf. The bracket clock version should be hung on the wall by means of the brass mirror plate in exactly the same manner as the wall clock version.

Cutting list

COMPONENT	QUANTITY	SECTION	LENGTH
Topboard	1	12 × 78	202
	1	½″ × 3⅛″	8″
Bottomboard	1	6 × 54	178
	1	¼″ × 2⅛″	7″
Backboard	1	6 × 178	325
	1	¼″ × 7″	12⅞″
Faceboard	1	12 × 202	325
	1	½″ × 8″	12⅞″
Cheekboards	2	12 × 60	337
	2	½″ × 2⅜″	13⅜″
Packing Pieces (Total Length)	1	6 × 38	250 minimum
	1	¼″ × 1½″	10″ minimum
Plinth (Total Length)	1	12 × 25	394 minimum
	1	½″ × 1″	15¾″ minimum
Pilasters	2	12 × 18	293
	2	½″ × ¾″	11⅝″
Cock Beads	4	3 × 15	293
	4	⅛″ × ⅝″	11⅝″
Dial-board	1	3 × 140	178
	1	⅛″ × 5½″	7″
Inner Layer of Door	1	12 × 151	287
	1	½″ × 6″	11⅜″
Outer Layer of Door	1	6 × 151	287
	1	¼″ × 6″	11⅜″
Triangular Glueblocks	1	9 × 9	930
	1	⅜″ × ⅜″	36¾″
Square Softwood Bearers (Total Length)	1	9 × 9	458
	1	⅜″ × ⅜″	18″
Scotia (Total Length)	1	9 × 9	908 minimum
	1	⅜″ × ⅜″	36½″ minimum
Coping Bead (Total Length)	1	6 × 22	930 minimum
	1	¼″ × ⅞″	37⅜″ minimum
Glazing Beads (Total Length)	1	5 × 8	1178 surplus
	1	3/16″ × 5/16″	46¾″ surplus

Clock Components and Hardware (excluding screws and pins)

CLOCK MOVEMENT — OPTIONS:
- Quartz pendulum Movements:
- Pendulum length from centres of handshaft to pendulum bob: 155m (6⅛".
- Maximum pendulum swing: 165mm/6½".
- Chiming/melody movements also available.
- Handshaft/fixing nut length: to suit 3–5mm/⅛" – ³⁄₁₆" dial-board and dial thickness (adjust thickness of dial-board if necessary).

CLOCK DIAL — OPTIONS:
- 127 × 127mm/5" × 5" square dial; brass, aluminium or card.

CLOCK HANDS:
- Bushed to suit chosen quartz movement.
- Length to suit dial size.
- Pattern to suit individual choice.

BRASSWARE:
- Hinges: one pair of 25mm/1" butt hinges.
- Door lock: two 6mm/¼" butt hinges.
- Door knob: 9mm/⅜" diameter.

GLASS:
- Two panes to suit door.
- Note: the lower pane can accommodate decorative paintwork.

7. *19th Century Lancet Clock*

Although many of the lancet clocks produced were plain in appearance, this early 19th century example shows how a basic shape may be elaborated with the imaginative use of mouldings, inlaid cross banded veneers, motifs and stringings.

The movement, dial and bezel are all easily obtainable. Mechanical strike or non-strike movements or easy fit quartz movements may be used.

Overall dimensions: 260 wide × 154 deep × 520mm high
10¼″ wide × 6³⁄₁₆″ deep × 20½″ high

Skill level * * *

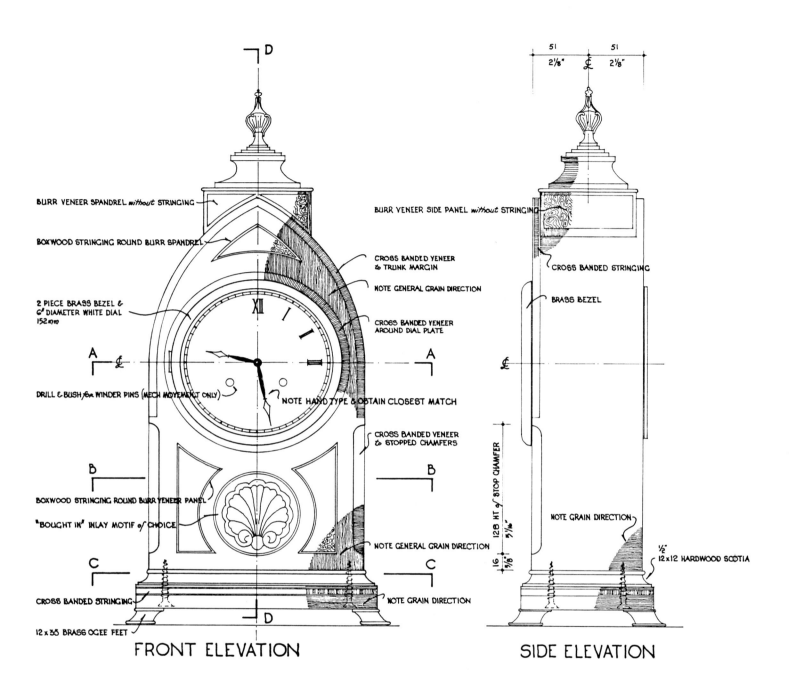

BURR VENEER SPANDREL *without* STRINGING

BOXWOOD STRINGING ROUND BURR SPANDREL

2 PIECE BRASS BEZEL &
6" DIAMETER WHITE DIAL
152 mm

XII

DRILL & BUSH *for* WINDER PINS (MECH MOVEMENT ONLY)

A

B

BOXWOOD STRINGING ROUND BURR VENEER PANEL

"BOUGHT IN" INLAY MOTIF *of* CHOICE

C

CROSS BANDED STRINGING

12 x 33 BRASS OGEE FEET

FRONT ELEVATION

BURR VENEER SIDE PANEL *without* STRINGING

CROSS BANDED VENEER
to TRUNK MARGIN

NOTE GENERAL GRAIN DIRECTION

CROSS BANDED VENEER
AROUND DIAL PLATE

CROSS BANDED VENEER
to STOPPED CHAMFERS

NOTE HAND TYPE & OBTAIN CLOSEST MATCH

NOTE GENERAL GRAIN DIRECTION

NOTE GRAIN DIRECTION

51   51
2⅛"   2⅛"

CROSS BANDED STRINGING

BRASS BEZEL

128 HT *of* STOP CHAMFER
5 1/16"

16   ⅝"

NOTE GRAIN DIRECTION

½"
12 x 12 HARDWOOD SCOTIA

SIDE ELEVATION

D
208 | 8¾₁₆" O/A

140 | 5½" DIAM.

25 mm BRASS HINGE

MECH MOVEMENT

DRILL *for* SPINDLE

2 PIECE BRASS BEZEL

6" DIAM WHITE DIAL

PLAN *at* A-A

102 O/A TRUNK LAMINATES   4¼"
90 O/A SUB FINIAL BASE   3¾"
75 O/A FINIAL MOULDING

48   1⅞"

208 O/A TRUNK LAMINATES
8¾₁₆"

BRASS FINIAL SHEWN DOTTED

18
28
38

¾"
1⅛"
1½"

GENERAL PLAN

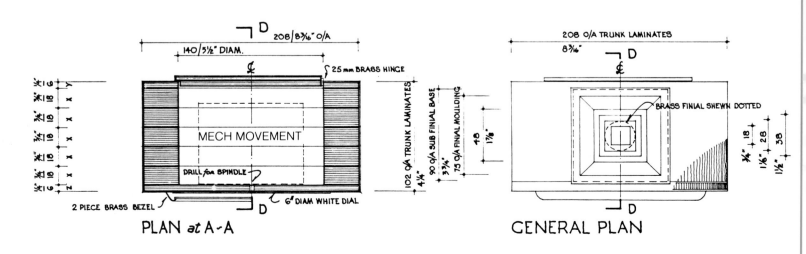

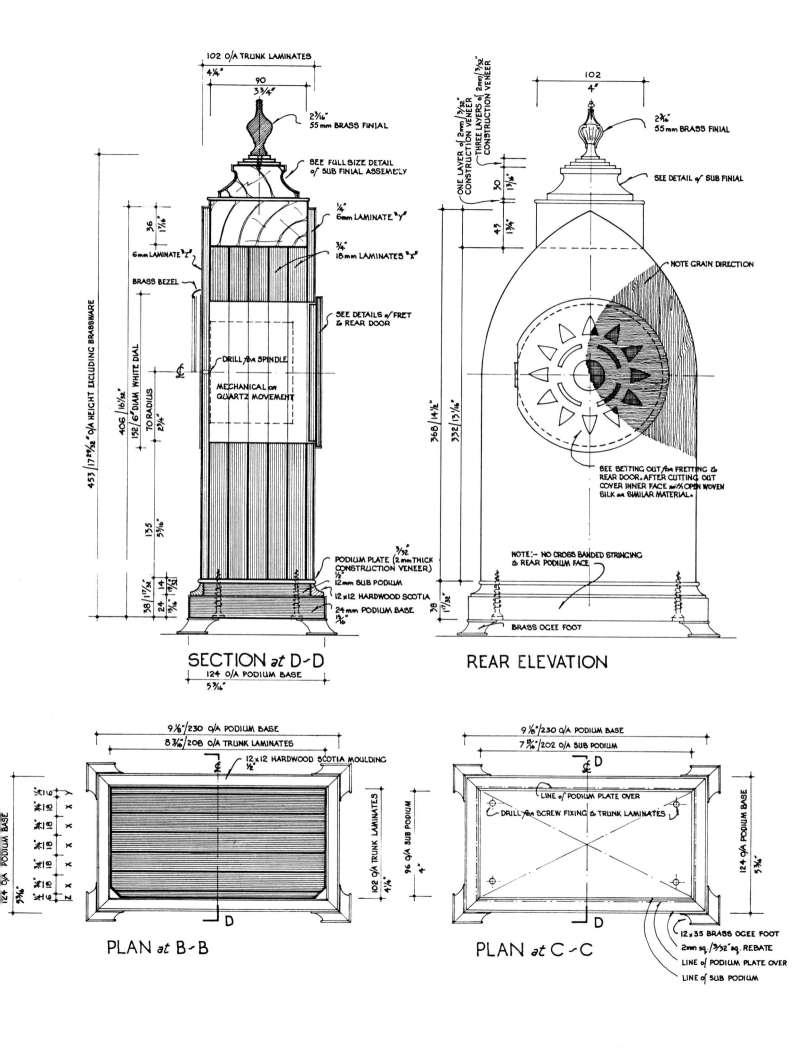

SECTION at D-D

102 O/A TRUNK LAMINATES
4¼"
90
3¾"

2³/₁₆"
55mm BRASS FINIAL

SEE FULL SIZE DETAIL of SUB FINIAL ASSEMBLY

36   1⁷/₁₆"
¼"
6mm LAMINATE "Y"
6mm LAMINATE "Z"
¾"
18mm LAMINATES "X"

BRASS BEZEL

SEE DETAILS of FRET & REAR DOOR

406 16¹/₃₂"
152/6" DIAM WHITE DIAL
TO RADIUS 2¾"

457/17²⁹/₃₂" O/A HEIGHT EXCLUDING BRASSWARE

DRILL for SPINDLE

MECHANICAL or QUARTZ MOVEMENT

135 5⁵/₁₆"

PODIUM PLATE (2mm THICK CONSTRUCTION VENEER) ³/₃₂"
12mm SUB PODIUM ½"
12×12 HARDWOOD SCOTIA
24mm PODIUM BASE ¹⁵/₁₆"

38/1¹/₃₂"
24 14 ¹⁹/₃₂"
¹⁵/₁₆"

124 O/A PODIUM BASE
5³/₁₆"

REAR ELEVATION

102
4"

ONE LAYER of 2mm/³/₃₂" CONSTRUCTION VENEER
THREE LAYERS of 2mm/³/₃₂" CONSTRUCTION VENEER

2³/₁₆"
55mm BRASS FINIAL

SEE DETAIL of SUB FINIAL

30 1³/₁₆"
45 1³/₄"

NOTE GRAIN DIRECTION

368/14½"
332/13¹/₁₆"

SEE SETTING OUT for FRETTING & REAR DOOR. AFTER CUTTING OUT COVER INNER FACE with OPEN WOVEN SILK or SIMILAR MATERIAL.

NOTE:- NO CROSS BANDED STRINGING & REAR PODIUM FACE

38/1¹/₃₂"

BRASS OGEE FOOT

PLAN at B-B

9⅛"/230 O/A PODIUM BASE
8³/₁₆"/208 O/A TRUNK LAMINATES
12×12 HARDWOOD SCOTIA MOULDING ½"

102 O/A TRUNK LAMINATES 4¼"

124 O/A PODIUM BASE 5³/₁₆"

¼" ¾" ¾" ¾" ¼" ⁵/₁₆"
6 18 18 18 6
Z X X X Z Y

PLAN at C-C

9⅛"/230 O/A PODIUM BASE
7¹³/₁₆"/202 O/A SUB PODIUM

LINE of PODIUM PLATE OVER

DRILL for SCREW FIXING & TRUNK LAMINATES

96 O/A SUB PODIUM 4"

124 O/A PODIUM BASE 5³/₁₆"

12×35 BRASS OGEE FOOT
2mm sq./³/₃₂" sq. REBATE
LINE of PODIUM PLATE OVER
LINE of SUB PODIUM

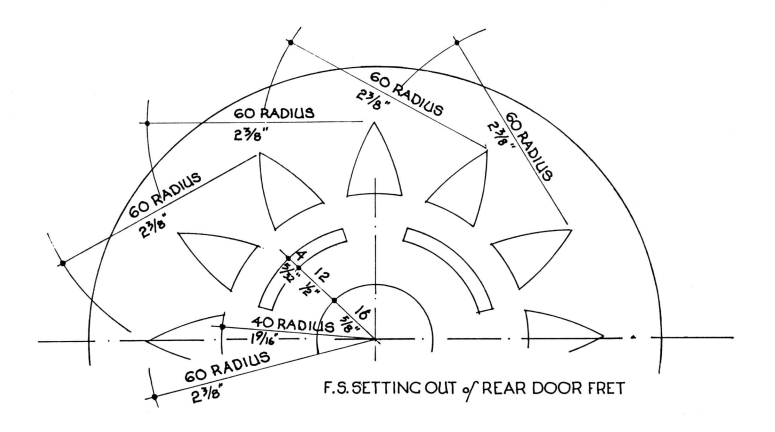

60 RADIUS 2³/₈"
60 RADIUS 2³/₈"
60 RADIUS 2³/₈"
60 RADIUS 2³/₈"

4
5/32" 1/2"
12
16
5/8"

40 RADIUS
1⁹/₁₆"

60 RADIUS
2³/₈"

F.S. SETTING OUT of REAR DOOR FRET

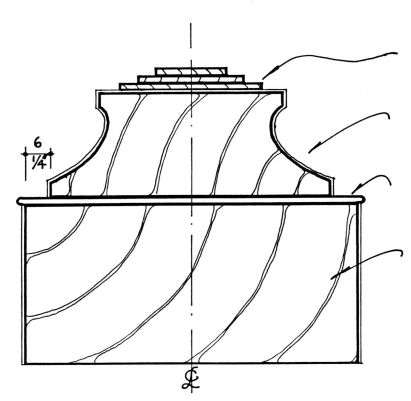

6
1/4

₵L

FINIAL PLATES CUT FROM SCRAP
CONSTRUCTION VENEER. SAND
& FINISH before GLUING in POS'N

3³/₄" x 3¹/₄" x 1³/₁₆"

FINIAL MOULDING OUT OF 90×78×30
SOFTWOOD. SHAPE to PROFILE shewn,
VENEER, SAND and FINISH BEFORE
GLUING in POSITION.

FINIAL PLATE MADE of 2mm CONSTR'N
VENEER. (SAND & FINISH before FIXING)

4" x 3³/₄" x 1³/₄"

SUB FINIAL BASE OUT OF 102×90×45
SOFTWOOD. VENEER as INDICATED ON
ELEVATIONS (SAND & FINISH before FIXING)

F.S. DETAIL of SUB FINIAL

CHECK THIS DIMENSION AGAINST TOP of LAMINATE "X"

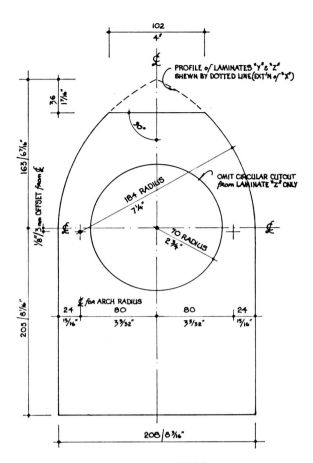

SETTING OUT OF LAMINATE TYPE 'X'

Schedule of Operations

BODY ASSEMBLY & LAMINATES

The shaping and assembly of the laminates forming the main part of the clock case may be done in different ways, depending upon the workshop equipment available.

if you own a bandsaw, it is suggested that the type 'X' laminates are assembled with PVA adhesive and pins before attempting any shaping. Once the adhesive has set hard, carefully mark out the profiles detailed on the plan, including the large diameter hole which will later accept the movement. Attention is drawn to the importance of ensuring that the horizontal edge at the top of the shape is exactly at right angles to the centre line. Working slowly to reduce kerf lines, accurately bandsaw the outer shape. Clean off any kerf marks with a file and sanding block. Cut out the large diameter hole with the bandsaw, cutting through the perimeter at the top centre line. After the central waste wood has been removed, fill the top centre saw cut with a veneer slip using PVA adhesive.

If you do not own a bandsaw, the profiles should be cut out on the individual laminates before assembly, using a coping saw. Take great care in cutting the shapes, ensuring that the saw is held upright. Check each shaped laminate, one against the other, to ensure that you have obtained a good match. Carefully assemble the laminates, using PVA adhesive and pins. Once the adhesive has set hard, clean up the shapes with a file and sanding block.

Carefully mark out for and cut out the shape of laminate 'Y' and fix to the main laminate assembly with PVA adhesive and pins. Clean up saw kerfs with a file and sanding block, paying particular attention to the inside edge of the large diameter hole. Accuracy here will help you later to obtain a good fit to the rear door assembly.

Using the rear of the main laminate assembly as a template, mark out the shape of laminate 'Z'. Accurately draw on the centre lines. After cutting out the outer shape, check the diameter of the movement spindle and drill a hole for this at the intersection of the centre lines. The resultant hole should achieve a 'sloppy' fit with the spindle. Offer up the movement to the *rear* of the laminate and accurately mark the position of the winder pins (front wind mechanical movements only). Drill for the winder pins to a diameter to give a 'sloppy' fit with the winder key. Fix the laminate to the front of the main laminate assembly with PVA adhesive and pins. Clean up saw kerf marks with a file and sanding block.

Check over the whole of the body assembly, punching in the heads of pins. Fill the punch holes and any holes in the cut edges of plywood with stopping compound. Sand off stoppings flush with the surrounding surfaces.

Form the stopped chamfers on the front of the body assembly, using a router or shaping them with a chisel. Clean up the chamfers with a file and/or a sanding block to remove tool marks. Great care should be taken to ensure that they are accurately formed and positioned, one with the other.

SUB FINIAL ASSEMBLY

Make the sub finial base of softwood as shown on the plan, checking that it fits accurately and snugly into the recess at the top of the body assembly. Offer into position at the top of the assembly and mark on the front face the outer profile of laminate 'Z'. Using this profile as a guide, draw in the position of the burr veneer spandrels and side panels. Cut these shapes out of burr veneer and fix in position using a contact adhesive. Veneer the rear face of the sub finial base with the chosen general veneer type and trim off surplus veneer with a sharp craft knife. Next, veneer the sides, accurately fitting around the burr panels and trim off surplus veneer. Repeat the process with the front face. Sand the veneered faces to a final finish, using progressively finer grades of abrasive paper working parallel with the general grain direction.

From 2mm/³⁄₃₂" thick construction veneer cut out the large finial plate to a size giving 1mm projection all round the top of the sub finial base. Round all cut edges as indicated on the plan. Sand to a finish as described.

Make, in softwood, the finial moulding to the shape shown on the plan. It is suggested that the curved profiles are cut with a bandsaw or coping saw, but with a longer block of wood than required. After carefully cleaning up the curved surfaces, cut off any surplus length of wood to obtain the height required. Veneer all surfaces with grain direction as indicated on the plan. Sand to a finish as described.

Make the small finial plates from 2mm/³⁄₃₂" construction veneer to the sizes shown on the plan. Sand to a finish as described.

VENEERING, CROSSBANDINGS & INLAY

Veneer the whole of the rear face of the body assembly with the grain set in the direction indicated on the plan. Trim off any surplus veneer in the manner previously described.

Veneer the whole of the side faces of the body assembly with the grain set in the direction indicated on the plan. Trim off any surplus veneer. Cut out for and insert the cross banded stringing in the positions indicated on the plan.

Veneer the stopped chamfers with the grain set cross banded and trim off any surplus veneer.

Working on a flat cutting board, make a 181mm/7⅛" diameter circle of veneer. Work in small segmental areas so as to give the visual impression of grain radiating out from the centre point of the circle. The segments may be held together with masking tape or cellotape. When the complete disc has been made up trim round the outer perimeter to form an accurate circle.

Take the veneer sheet that is to be used for facing up the front of the body assembly and carefully mark on the centre lines shown on the plan. Place the veneer disc just made accurately upon the centre lines and mark round the perimeter. Remove the disc and cut round the drawn perimeter, removing the centre waste. insert the veneer disc in the centre hole and hold in position with tape.

Repeat the process just described with the inlay motif of your choice, positioning the motif below the disc in the

position shown on the plan. Insert and tape the motif in position.

Take the large sheet of veneer, complete with inserted disc and motif, and lay accurately on the front face of the body assembly using a contact adhesive. Trim off any surplus veneer around the outer edge of the body. Carefully trim round the spindle and winder holes.

Mark out for and accurately cut out for the portion to be occupied by cross banding on the curved edges of the front of the body assembly. Veneer with grain laid cross banded taking care that the grain takes a radial direction. It is best to work in small strips to achieve this. Trim off surplus veneer as described.

Cut out for and insert the burr veneer panels and stringing where shown on the plan. Alternatively, this may be done in the manner described for the inlay motif but in that case difficulty may be experienced in holding the stringing surrounds to the curves shown. If you do decide to adopt this approach it is suggested that you omit the boxwood stringing.

On completion of all veneering work to the body assembly, sand all surfaces to a finish using progressively finer grades of abrasive papers and working parallel with the general grain directions.

REAR DOOR

Cut out the rear door and sub rear door components. Offer up the smaller diameter component to the rear door opening and check for a loose but accurate fit. Clean up the saw kerf marks to all cut edges and glue the two components together. Veneer the cut edges of the larger perimeter and trim off surplus veneer. Veneer the outer face of the door, laying on the veneer with grain in the direction indicated on the plan. Sand down the veneer, but not to a final finish.

On the outer face of the rear door, mark out the fretted pattern to the setting out detail shown on the plan. Accurately cut out the fretted parts with a fine toothed fretsaw. As necessary, clean up the fretted edges with needle files to remove any kerf marks. Sand all surfaces to a final finish.

PODIUM

Make the podium base and sub podium in plywood of the sizes and thicknesses shown on the plan. Veneer the podium base as shown on the plan, including the upper surface. Trim off surplus veneer and sand to a finish as described. Accurately position the sub podium on top of the podium base and fix it with PVA and pins.

Make the podium plate with 2mm/³⁄₃₂″ thick construction veneer and sand to a finish.

Take the hardwood scotia moulding and cut to lengths to fit round the podium, neatly mitring at corners. Glue in positions shown on the plan and sand to a finish.

Glue the podium plate in position on top of the podium assembly and when adhesive has set hard drill the screw fixing clearance holes where indicated on the plan.

FINISHING & FINAL ASSEMBLY

Brush off all sanding dust before applying finishes and work in a dust free environment. Seal all surfaces with a meths based sanding sealer and polish all surfaces with button polish or heavy french polish. When bone dry, flat down the final coat with very fine wire wool and bring back to a gloss with wax polish. Alternatively, after applying the sanding sealer, apply three coats of polyurethane varnish, flatting down each coat when dry and bringing to a final gloss with wax polish.

Screw the podium assembly in position on the base of the body assembly, taking care that it is accurately placed.

Assemble the various parts of the sub finial, gluing each in position accurately. When adhesive has set hard glue the sub finial in position at the top of the body, taking great care with the positioning. Drill for and fix the brass finial.

Screw the brass ogee feet to the underside of the podium.

Fix the dial to the front of the body with small screws or pins. Where winder holes have been formed in the dial for a front wind mechanical movement, neatly bush the holes before fixing the dial. Offer up the brass bezel and fix in position, ensuring it is exactly centred relative to the dial.

Fix the movement to the inner face of the dial-board and fit hands to the main spindle in accordance with the manufacturer's instructions.

Carefully cover the inner face of the rear door with a contrasting colour open weave silk or similar material. A general household adhesive is best for this. Apply the adhesive sparingly to the wood surface only and make sure that the silk is stretched tight without wrinkles.

Fix the brass hinge to the rear door and hang the door in position. If the door is a loose fit in the opening, fit a small brass side hook to retain the door in the closed position.

Note: Since this clock case features an extensive use of veneers, the completed clock should not be placed directly above any heat source.

Cutting list

COMPONENT	QUANTITY	SECTION	LENGTH
Laminate X (Plywood)	5	208 × 18	333
	5	8³⁄₁₆″ × ³⁄₄″	13⅛″
Laminate Y (Plywood)	1	208 × 6	371
	1	8³⁄₁₆″ × ¼″	14⅝″
Laminate Z (Plywood)	1	208 × 6	371
	1	8³⁄₁₆″ × ¼″	14⅝″
Rear Door (Plywood)	1	140 dia × 6	–
	1	5½″ dia × ¼″	–
Sub Rear Door (Plywood)	1	145 dia × 3	–
	1	5¹¹⁄₁₆″ dia × ⅛″	–
Podium Plate (Construction Veneer)	1	106 × 2	212
	1	4³⁄₁₆″ × ³⁄₃₂″	8⅛″
Sub Podium (Plywood)	1	96 × 12	202
	1	4″ × ½″	7¹⁵⁄₁₆″

Podium Base (Plywood)	1	124 × 24	230
	1	5³⁄₁₆″ × ¹⁵⁄₁₆″	9⅛″
Podium Scotia (Hardwood)	1	12 × 12	708 minimum
	1	½″ × ½″	28⅝″ minimum
Sub Finial Base (Softwood)	1	ex 45 × 90	106
	1	ex 1¾″ × 3⁹⁄₁₆″	4³⁄₁₆″
Finial Mould (Softwood)		ex 30 × 76	92
		ex 1³⁄₁₆″ × 3″	3⅝″
Finial Plates (Construction Veneer)	3	Cut to suit	

Clock Components and Hardware (excluding screws and pins)

CLOCK MOVEMENT — OPTIONS:

1. Mechanical Movements.

   Spring driven bracket clock movement without pendulum.

   Front winding or rear winding versions available.

   Overall size of movement, including swing of gong/bell hammers, not to exceed size of 'movement hole' — 140mm dia × 90mm/5½″ dia × 3¾″.

   Handshaft: check length and adjust thickness of dial-board if necessary.

   Compact circular and rectangular movements available.

   Single bell strike and twin bell strike options available.

2. Quartz movements

   Standard or melody movements available.

   Shaft length/fixing nut: to suit 6mm/¼″ dial-board.

CLOCK DIAL — OPTIONS:

- 152mm/6″ diameter.
- Steel dial with enamel paint finish; aluminium dial with sprayed paint finish.
- Note: if front winding mechanical movement is used, drill holes in the dial and bush to accommodate winding keys.

CLOCK HANDS:

- Bushed to suit chosen mechanical or quartz movements.
- Length to suit dial size. Pattern to suit individual choice.

BRASSWARE:

- Bezel: to suit 152mm/6″ dial. All-in-one dial and bezel combinations are also available.
- One 25mm/1″ butt hinge for rear door. One 9mm/⅜″ door latch for rear door.
- One 55mm/2³⁄₁₆″ flame finial. Additional patterns; acorn, pineapple, urn.
- Four ogee/corner feet: 35 × 35 × 12mm/1⅜″ × 1⅜″ × ½″.

INLAYS:

- Inlay motif and stringing: various motif patterns and sizes available. Adjust layout of stringing to suit motif.

GLASS:

- To suit brass bezel.

8. 'Sexton' Bracket Clock

This is a traditionally styled bracket clock which has been developed so that the maker can build up 'apparently complicated' mouldings by stacking a number of layers of simple DIY moulding shapes together. This stacking theme is also used with the two Regulator clocks, the 'Deacon' and Full-Cased Wall clocks, the 'Chorister' and 'Curate' mantel clocks and with the George III Bracket clock which is a larger and more ornate version of the bracket clock design.

   The instructions have presumed the use of a quality timber such as mahogany, incorporating mahogany construction veneers. There is also an ebony and walnut alternative version which could make a very fine result.

Overall dimensions: 190 wide × 104 deep × 253mm high (excluding handle)

                       7½″ wide × 4³⁄₃₂″ deep × 10⅛″ high (excluding handle)

Skill level * * * *

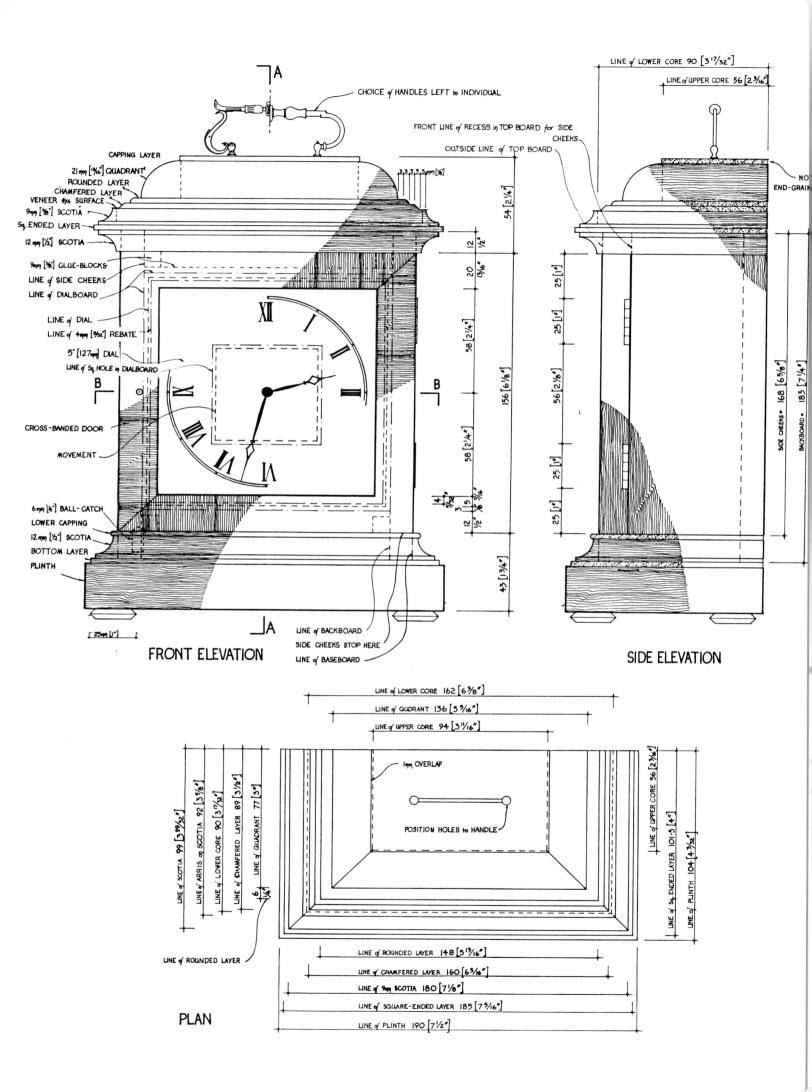

CHOICE of HANDLES left to INDIVIDUAL

LINE of LOWER CORE 90 [3 17/32"]

LINE of UPPER CORE 56 [2 3/16"]

FRONT LINE of RECESS in TOP BOARD for SIDE CHEEKS

OUTSIDE LINE of TOP BOARD

CAPPING LAYER

21 mm [13/16"] QUADRANT
ROUNDED LAYER
CHAMFERED LAYER
VENEER this SURFACE
9mm [3/8"] SCOTIA
Sq. ENDED LAYER

12 mm [1/2"] SCOTIA

9mm [3/8"] GLUE-BLOCKS
LINE of SIDE CHEEKS
LINE of DIALBOARD

LINE of DIAL
LINE of 4mm [5/32"] REBATE

5" [127mm] DIAL
LINE of Sq. HOLE in DIALBOARD

3,3,3,3,3mm [1/8"]

NO END-GRAIN

54 [2 1/4"]

12 [1/2"]
20 [13/16"]

58 [2 1/4"]

156 [6 1/8"]

58 [2 1/4"]

25 [1"]
25 [1"]
56 [2 1/8"]
25 [1"]
25 [1"]

SIDE CHEEKS = 168 [6 5/8"]
BACKBOARD = 183 [7 1/4"]

CROSS-BANDED DOOR

MOVEMENT

XII
I
II
III
IIII
V
VI
VII
VIII
IX

6 mm [1/4"] BALL-CATCH
LOWER CAPPING
12 mm [1/2"] SCOTIA
BOTTOM LAYER
PLINTH

4 [5/32"]
3
5
12 [1/2"] 6 3/16

43 [3/4"]

[25mm [1"]]

FRONT ELEVATION

LINE of BACKBOARD
SIDE CHEEKS STOP HERE
LINE of BASEBOARD

SIDE ELEVATION

LINE of LOWER CORE 162 [6 3/8"]

LINE of QUADRANT 136 [5 5/16"]

LINE of UPPER CORE 94 [3 11/16"]

1mm OVERLAP

POSITION HOLES to HANDLE

LINE of SCOTIA 99 [3 29/32"]
LINE of ARRIS on SCOTIA 92 [3 5/8"]
LINE of LOWER CORE 90 [3 17/32"]
LINE of CHAMFERED LAYER 89 [3 1/2"]
LINE of QUADRANT 77 [3"]

6 [1/4"]

LINE of UPPER CORE 56 [2 3/16"]
LINE of Sq. ENDED LAYER 101·5 [4"]
LINE of PLINTH 104 [4 3/32"]

LINE of ROUNDED LAYER

LINE of ROUNDED LAYER 148 [5 13/16"]

LINE of CHAMFERED LAYER 160 [6 5/16"]

LINE of 9mm SCOTIA 180 [7 1/8"]

LINE of SQUARE-ENDED LAYER 185 [7 5/16"]

LINE of PLINTH 190 [7 1/2"]

PLAN

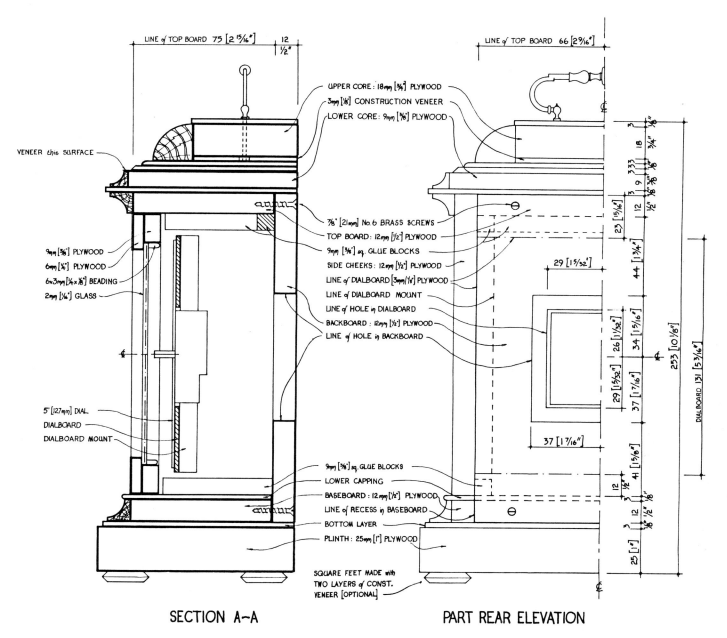

LINE of TOP BOARD 75 [2 15/16"]   12
                                    1/2"

UPPER CORE: 18mm [3/4"] PLYWOOD
3mm [1/8"] CONSTRUCTION VENEER
LOWER CORE: 9mm [3/8"] PLYWOOD

LINE of TOP BOARD 66 [2 9/16"]

VENEER this SURFACE

9mm [3/8"] PLYWOOD
6mm [1/4"] PLYWOOD
6x3mm [1/4 x 1/8"] BEADING
2mm [1/16"] GLASS

7/8" [21mm] No.6 BRASS SCREWS
TOP BOARD: 12mm [1/2"] PLYWOOD
9mm [3/8"] sq. GLUE BLOCKS
SIDE CHEEKS: 12mm [1/2"] PLYWOOD
LINE of DIALBOARD [3mm/1/8"] PLYWOOD
LINE of DIALBOARD MOUNT
LINE of HOLE in DIALBOARD
BACKBOARD: 12mm [1/2"] PLYWOOD
LINE of HOLE in BACKBOARD

5" [127mm] DIAL
DIALBOARD
DIALBOARD MOUNT

9mm [3/8"] sq. GLUE BLOCKS
LOWER CAPPING
BASEBOARD: 12mm [1/2"] PLYWOOD
LINE of RECESS in BASEBOARD
BOTTOM LAYER
PLINTH: 25mm [1"] PLYWOOD

SQUARE FEET MADE with
TWO LAYERS of CONST.
VENEER [OPTIONAL]

29 [1 5/32"]

37 [1 7/16"]

37 [1 7/16"]

SECTION A~A   PART REAR ELEVATION

LINE of RECESS in BASEBOARD [& BACKBOARD] 132 [5 1/8"]

SIDE CHEEKS PINNED to BACKBOARD
VENEER SIDE CHEEKS

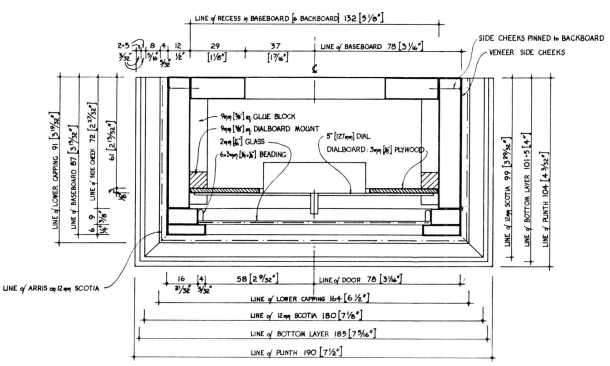

2·5   8   4   12   29   37   LINE of BASEBOARD 78 [3 1/16"]
3/32" 5/16" 5/32" 1/2" [1 1/8"]   [1 7/16"]

9mm [3/8"] sq. GLUE BLOCK
9mm [3/8"] sq. DIALBOARD MOUNT
2mm [1/16"] GLASS
6x3mm [1/4 x 1/8"] BEADING

5" [127mm] DIAL
DIALBOARD: 3mm [1/8"] PLYWOOD

LINE of LOWER CAPPING 91 [3 19/32"]
LINE of BASEBOARD 87 [3 13/32"]
LINE of SIDE CHEEK 72 [2 27/32"]
61 [2 13/32"]
3 [1/8"]
6 9 [1/4" 11/8"]

LINE of 12mm SCOTIA 99 [3 29/32"]
LINE of BOTTOM LAYER 101·5 [4"]
LINE of PLINTH 104 [4 3/32"]

LINE of ARRIS on 12mm SCOTIA

16   4   58 [2 9/32"]   LINE of DOOR 78 [3 1/16"]
21/32" 5/32"

LINE of LOWER CAPPING 164 [6 1/2"]
LINE of 12mm SCOTIA 180 [7 1/8"]
LINE of BOTTOM LAYER 185 [7 5/16"]
LINE of PLINTH 190 [7 1/2"]

SECTION B~B

Schedule of Operations

GENERAL CONSTRUCTION

The 'Sexton' is designed to be built from the base upwards and to suit hand methods of construction.

All the 'layers and cappings' (refer Front Elevation) are single sheets of 3mm/⅛" mahogany construction veneer. The hardwood mouldings are mahogany or ramin and are all mitred.

The centre section of the clock is a box construction comprising a backboard, side cheeks, top and baseboard, door and dial-board. (Refer Section A-A and Part Rear Elevation) and 9mm/⅜" glue blocks aiding assembly.

The top section of the clock is built up in layers as is the base section.

BASE OF THE CLOCK

Begin by accurately cutting and planing the 25mm/1" plinth to size, *minus* 1mm on the overall length and width; this will allow for the thickness of the veneer. Veneer the surfaces of the plinth in the following order: 1. The underneath; 2. The back edge; 3. The side edges; 4. The front edge; 5. The top surface. Using 150 grit wet and dry, carefully sand the complete plinth and finish the *top surface only* with 240 grit wet and dry (the other surfaces will have a final clean up later.)

Mark a 2.5mm/³⁄₃₂" border on the top of the plinth (front and side edges only) to establish the dimensions of the 'Bottom layer' (check with plan). Cut the bottom layer to size and finely sand down to 240 grit wet and dry. Glue and pin to the plinth.

Refer to Section A-A Part Rear Elevation and Section B-B for details of the 'baseboard' and scotia moulding which form the next layer.

Note: Recess in back of baseboard to accommodate backboard.

Mark the position of the 'baseboard' on the 'bottom layer' making sure that the 12mm/½" scotia fits comfortably round it. Accurately cut the baseboard to size. Mark the recess for the backboard onto the baseboard, having checked the thickness of the material to be used for the backboard (allow for thickness of veneer on the backboard). Cut the recess; this will require accurate knife, saw and chisel work. Glue and pin the baseboard to the plinth/bottom layer.

Cut the overall length of the 12mm/½" scotia (leaving room for the cutting of the mitres and a little surplus)

required to fit round the baseboard; sand clean before cutting the mitres. Mark the position of the mitres on the front scotia first, then accurately cut to size. Glue in position (a fast grab PVA glue is very useful for all the mouldings, thus eliminating the need for cramps or taping). Once the front scotia is glued and set the appropriate mitres for the side scotias can be cut (make sure the side scotias are slightly longer than necessary, allowing room for trimming at the back). Offer up the side scotias to the front scotia and check the mitre joints for fit. Make any fine adjustments you think necessary, then glue the side scotias in position. When these have set, trim the back edge flush with the plinth using a sharp chisel.

Measure the overall size of the 'lower capping', allowing yourself a visually neat overlap on top of the arris for the scotia (refer Section B-B and A-A). Cut to size, carefully shape the rounded edges on the front and sides then finely sand these edges. Glue the lower capping to the baseboard and scotia (these should form a flat surface) using positioning pins only where the side cheeks will sit (refer Section B-B), as these pins should not show later. Cramps and stout boards will be necessary to ensure that the complete capping is glued flat to the baseboard.

When the cramps are removed, cut a recess in the 'lower capping'. Accurately line up with the recess cut in the baseboard using a sharp knife (taking light cuts) and a sharp chisel. Sand and clean the top surface of the lower capping with 240 grit wet and dry. Drill hole to accommodate 6mm/¼" ball catch (refer to Front Elevation).

CENTRE SECTION OF THE CLOCK

The backboard acts as the 'keel' for the centre section, so this should be built first. Accurately measure and cut to size, ensuring that it is straight and square, that it fits the recess in the baseboard/lower capping and that it is the correct height.

Mark the position of the rectangular hole in the backboard (for access to the movement) and carefully cut the hole with the coping saw. Veneer the inside surface of the rectangular hole, then veneer the complete back surface of the backboard, carefully trimming in afterwards to the edges of the rectangular hole (use a sharp craft knife and a smooth file). Sand clean with a 150 grit wet and dry.

Position the backboard in the recess that is in the baseboard/lower capping. Establish the position of the fixing screws for the backboard (refer Section A-A and Part Rear Elevation). Centre punch the position of these fixing screws on rear of backboard, accurately cramp the backboard in position, drill the pilot holes for the screws through the backboard into the baseboard, remove backboard and drill the clearance and countersink holes into the backboard, screw the backboard, without glue, into position.

Establish the position of the 9mm/⅜" glue blocks that will sit on the baseboard/lower capping and that will secure the side cheeks (refer Section A-A and Section B-B). Ensure that these glue blocks are slightly shorter than the width of the side cheeks, and that they are in alignment with and square to the edges of the backboard. Check that the gluing surfaces of these blocks are straight, square and flat, sand clean the other surfaces that will show. Accurately pin and glue the blocks in position. Punch home pins and fill holes. Sand clean afterwards.

Mark out the side cheeks and accurately cut to size, ensuring that they are straight and square. When sitting in position they should fit snugly against the glue blocks on the baseboard/lower capping and tightly against the edges of the backboard; the final height of the side cheeks should be in exact alignment with the final height of the backboard.

Carefully veneer the front and back lippings of the side cheeks and trim the veneer edges. Veneer the main outside surface of each side cheek and trim the veneer edges. Sand clean with 150 grit wet and dry.

Sand clean the inside surfaces of the side cheeks and carefully mark the position of the 9mm/⅜" dial-board mounts (refer Section B-B) on these surfaces. Also mark the position of the glue blocks on the side cheeks that will support the top board (refer Section A-A), checking the thickness of the material that will be used for the top board. Ensure that the gluing surfaces of the glue blocks and dial-board mounts are straight, square and flat, and that the surfaces that will show are sanded clean. Accurately glue the blocks and dial-board mounts, using pins, in position. Punch home pins and fill holes. Sand clean afterwards.

Assemble and cramp (without glue) the side cheeks in their final position, checking that they are straight, parallel and square with the other components, and with each other.

The top board can now be measured and cut to fit in situation; you will see that it is necessary to cut out recesses to accommodate the side cheeks on the sides of the top board (refer Side Elevation). Before proceeding with making the top board, check that the inside distance between the top of the side cheeks equals the inside distance between the bottom of the side cheeks. Plane, straight and square, the back edge of the top board, allowing yourself an overlap on the remaining dimensions of the top board. Place the top board on top of the side cheeks with the back edge butting against the inside surface of the backboard; you can then scribe (with a sharp pencil) the position of the recesses for the side cheeks. Mark the lines for recesses with a craft knife; remove the appropriate wood from the recesses with a sharp saw, trim to your knife line with a sharp chisel and file. Place the top board in position, resting on the top glue blocks of the side cheeks. Mark the position of the top glue block on the backboard (refer Section A-A and Rear Elevation) and mark and plane to size the outside line of the top board (refer Side Elevation). Check for fit.

Dismantle the complete box structure. Glue and pin the top glue block on the backboard. Sand clean all the surfaces in the box structure that had previously been sanded with 150 grit wet and dry, this time using 240 grit wet and dry. Glue and cramp the box structure in its final position.

When the glue on the box structure has set, you can then proceed with cutting and fitting the scotia that sits at the top of the box structure. Repeat the procedure laid out for the assembly of the scotia on the baseboard/lower capping, as previously stated. You might find it helpful to tape the front scotia this time and also to work with the clock placed upside down on a flat board.

The door will be made and fitted later.

TOP SECTION OF THE CLOCK

This section is built up in layers like the base section (refer Front Elevation and Section A-A).

Make sure the top of the box structure i.e. the top board and scotia, is flat and straight. Mark out, on mahogany construction veneer, the square-ended layer, this should overlap the top scotia of the box structure by 2.5mm/¹⁄₁₀" on the front and sides, and should be flush with the back of the clock. Accurately cut and plane to size. Sand this layer clean paying careful attention to the edges. Accurately pin and glue in position, making sure the pins miss the joints of the previous scotia and that they do not show in the final result.

With a pencil gauge, establish the position of the lower core (refer Section A-A, Plan and Front Elevation), the distance in from the front edge and side edges of the square-ended layer should be 2.5mm/$\frac{1}{10}$" plus 9mm/$\frac{3}{8}$" scotia), the back of the lower core should finally sit flush with the back of the clock. Accurately mark out the lower core to size, but reduce the measured width (90mm/3$\frac{17}{32}$" on the plan) by the thickness of a veneer; this is to allow for the veneering of the back of the lower core. Accurately cut and plane to size, ensuring that the lower core is straight and square. Veneer the back edge and sand clean with 240 grit wet and dry. Accurately pin and glue in position, again ensuring that you miss the joints of the previous scotia.

Repeat the procedure for the assembly of the 9mm/$\frac{3}{8}$" scotia is flat and straight. Veneer this surface, trim the edges and sand clean with 240 grit wet and dry.

With a pencil gauge, mark the position of the chamfered layer on top of your veneered surface; the line of the chamfered layer should be 3mm/$\frac{1}{8}$" in from the arris on the 9mm/$\frac{3}{8}$" scotia (front and sides) and the back edge should be flush with the back of the clock. Mark out on mahogany construction veneer the overall size of the chamfered layer. Cut and plane to size, leaving the edges square. Check for fit, then mark the line of the chamfer (3mm/$\frac{1}{8}$" in from the square edge) and accurately plane to this line. Carefully sand clean with 240 wet and dry. Glue in position making sure that no pins will show.

Repeat the same process for the round-ended layer, ensuring that the line of this layer is 3mm/$\frac{1}{8}$" in from the top line of the chamfer. The rounding over of this layer has a 3mm/$\frac{1}{8}$" radius.

The next stage is to make the upper core. You should first check that the thickness of the upper core is the same thickness as the 21mm/$\frac{7}{8}$" quadrant; this might involve using 18mm/$\frac{3}{4}$" plywood and 3mm/$\frac{1}{8}$" construction veneer (as shown in Section A-A) or possibly 12mm/$\frac{1}{2}$" and 9mm/$\frac{3}{8}$" plywood; this is left to the discretion of the maker. Glue the layers for the upper core together.

Mark the position of the upper core on the top surface of the round-ended layer with a pencil gauge. Accurately mark on your 21mm/$\frac{7}{8}$" plywood the dimensions of the upper core, but reduce the measured width (56mm/2$\frac{3}{16}$" on the plan) by the thickness of a veneer, this will allow for the veneering of the back edge of the upper core. Accurately cut and plane to size ensuring that the upper core is straight and square. Veneer the back edge and sand clean with 240 grit wet and dry. Position the core with two-sided tape as it will have to be removed later.

The next stage is to assemble the 21mm/$\frac{7}{8}$" quadrant around the upper core. The same procedure is followed as with the assembly of the scotias i.e. front component first etc. Though when gluing it is *very important* that the surface that sits on the round-ended layer is glued and *not* the surfaces that are in contact with the upper core.

When the quadrant has set in position the capping layer can be made. You should first remove the upper core by carefully prizing it apart, possibly with a thin blade, along the line with the two-sided tape. Remove the two-sided tape. Replace the upper core in position to check if the top of it is flush with the top of the quadrant. Mark out the capping layer to size on mahogany construction veneer, allowing for a 1mm overlap (refer to Plan). Cut and plane to size then carefully sand clean with 240 grit wet and dry. Check for fit. Remove upper core and capping layer and carefully glue together, making sure that you have an equal overlap on the front and sides, and that the back edge is flush with the back of the upper core. When the glue has set you can drill the holes for the handle and the recess holes for the fixing nuts for the handle.

Note: The upper core/capping layer unit is not glued in position until the complete clock has had its final polish.

THE DOOR

The construction of the door is based on the principle of laminating a sheet of 6mm/$\frac{1}{4}$" plywood (with a square hole cut into it) to a sheet of 9mm/$\frac{3}{8}$" plywood (with a slightly larger hole cut into it). The difference in dimensions of the two holes forms a rebate in which the glass will sit. In making the door, work in situation to the opening in your clock case as well as with the dimensions of your plan.

Mark and cut a sheet of 9mm/$\frac{3}{8}$" plywood to 156 × 156mm/6$\frac{1}{8}$" × 6$\frac{1}{8}$" *minus* the thickness of two pieces of veneer; this is to allow for a snug fit in the opening, but do double check with the dimensions on your particular case. Mark and cut a sheet of 6mm/$\frac{1}{4}$" plywood to the exact dimensions of the 9mm/$\frac{3}{8}$" plywood.

With a marking gauge, establish the dimensions of the square hole in the 6mm/$\frac{1}{4}$" plywood as shown on the Front Elevation (116mm sq./4$\frac{1}{2}$" sq). Repeat this process on the 9mm/$\frac{3}{8}$" plywood, only increase the dimensions of the hole by 8mm/$\frac{5}{16}$" to allow for a 4mm/$\frac{5}{32}$" rebate all round. Remove the wood with a coping saw. Carefully clean down to your lines with a sharp chisel and file.

Pin and glue the two sheets together making sure of accurate alignment. Punch the pins home, fill and sand clean when the filler is set.

When the glue has set, check the door for fit in the

opening of your case, making allowances for the veneered surfaces.

Veneer the surfaces of the door in the following order: 1. The inside surfaces of the hole in the 6mm/¼″ plywood; 2. The back surface of the door; 3. The top and bottom edges; 4. The side edges; 5. The front surface — this should be cross-banded as shown in the Front Elevation. I find that it is best to secure two *opposing* sides of cross-banding (with the mitres cut) to the door with two-sided tape; the other two sides can then be offered up under the original cross bandings and the appropriate mitres marked and cut; these two pieces can then be glued, and afterwards, the initial two pieces are removed (with the two-sided tape) and then glued in position.

After the door has been veneered, the slots for the hinges can be cut. The door is then sanded clean with 150 and 240 grit wet and dry. Drill for the door handle, check for fit, remove and put to one side. Fit the hinges.

The door can now be initially hung. Once you are satisfied that the door fits correctly, you can then establish the hole to accommodate the ball of the ball-catch. Remove the door for finishing and rehanging later.

The dial-board can now be made. This needs to be accurately cut out of 3mm/⅛″ plywood, to fit in position on the dial-board mounts. Check the position of the movement on the dial-board (refer Part Rear Elevation, Front Elevation, Section A-A and B-B). Note: the spindle of the movement should sit exactly in the centre of the glass door. Cut the rectangular hole out of the dial-board (refer Part Rear Elevation) making sure you have some clearance around the movement. The dial-board is pinned and glued in position after the finishing stage.

There is room for manoeuvre as to the choice of feet for the clock. You could opt for the feet specified in the plan or those shown on the ebony and walnut clock illustrated. Alternatively, you might like to choose turned brass bun feet. Wooden feet are pinned and glued in position after the finishing stage.

FINISHING

There is a very wide range of finishes and polishes on the market and the type of finish used is, ultimately, the individual craftperson's choice.

The following items need finishing and polishing before final assembly (before finishing, check over the whole clock to make sure everything is clean): 1. The main casework; 2. The inside of the case and the dial-board (I suggest using a matt black paint for this); 3. The door; 4. The beadings of the door; 5. The feet; 6. The outside surfaces of the upper core/capping layer unit.

Once you have achieved a finish that you are satisfied with, the final assembly procedure is as follows: 1. glue and pin the dial-board in position; 2. fix the glass in the door with beadings which can be pinned in position; 3. drill clearance holes in the feet and glue and pin in position (you might have to scrape some finish off to provide a gluing surface); 4. place the ball-catch in position and re-hang the door; 5. fix the handle to the upper core/capping layer unit and glue the complete unit in place; 6. fix Quartz movement to the dial and secure the dial-board with either a contact adhesive or two-sided tape. Fix the hands to the movement.

AN EBONY AND WALNUT ALTERNATIVE

This version of the 'Sexton' is, essentially, the same as the mahogany version, except that I have used ebony where mahogany construction veneer was used (i.e. on the capping, rounded, chamfered, square-ended and bottom layers and on the lower capping and on the feet), and have used walnut veneer instead of mahogany veneer. I also made my own mouldings from solid walnut, cove router bits for the scotias and a block plane with careful sanding for the 21mm/⅞″ quadrant.

If you are lucky enough to find some ebony of the same width as required on the various layers and cappings, then you follow the same procedure as laid out for the mahogany version. I found, however, that I had to cut ebony lippings that fitted round a mahogany construction veneer core — it was necessary to mitre all these lippings. The lippings were made by planing my main block of ebony flat and cutting the lippings, slightly thicker than required, on a bandsaw. The planed surfaces were glued to the appropriate surface on the clock around a mahogany construction veneer core (which had previously been fixed in position). Then, when the glue was set, the rough saw-cut surface of the ebony was planed flush with the mahogany core.

Cutting list

COMPONENT	QUANTITY	SECTION	LENGTH
Plinth	1	25 × 104	190
	1	1″ × 4³/₃₂″	7½″
Bottom Layer	1	3 × 101.5	185
	1	⅛″ × 4″	7⁵/₁₆″
Baseboard	1	12 × 87	156
	1	½″ × 3¹⁵/₃₂″	6⅛″
Lower Capping	1	3 × 91	164
	1	⅛″ × 3¹⁹/₃₂″	6½″
Backboard	1	12 × 132	183
	1	½″ × 5⅛″	7¼″
Topboard	1	12 × 75	132
	1	½″ × 2¹⁵/₁₆″	5⅛″
Sidecheeks	2	12 × 72	168
	2	½″ × 2²⁷/₃₂″	6⅝″
Square Ended Layer	1	3 × 101.5	185
	1	⅛″ × 4″	7⁵/₁₆″
Lower Core	1	9 × 90	162
	1	⅜″ × 3¹⁷/₃₂″	6⅜″
Chamfered layer	1	3 × 89	160
	1	⅛″ × 3½″	6⁵/₁₆″
Rounded Layer	1	3 × 83	148
	1	⅛″ × 3¼″	5¹³/₁₆″
Upper Core/Construction Veneer	1	21 × 56	94
	1	⅞″ × 2³/₁₆″	3¹¹/₁₆″
Capping layer	1	3 × 57	96
	1	⅛″ × 2¼″	3¹³/₁₆″
Inner Layer of Door	1	9 × 156	156
	1	⅜″ × 6⅛″	6⅛″
Outer Layer of Door	1	6 × 156	156
	1	¼″ × 6⅛″	6⅛″
Dial-board	1	3 × 132	132
	1	⅛″ × 5⅛″	5⅛″
Dial-board Mounts	2	9 × 9	132
	2	⅜″ × ⅜″	5⅛″
Bottom Layer Scotia (Total Length)	1	12 × 12	378 minimum
	1	½″ × ½″	15¹/₁₆″ minimum
Topboard Scotia (Total Length)	1	12 × 12	330 minimum
	1	½″ × ½″	13″ minimum

Lower Core Scotia (Total Length)	1	9 × 9	378 minimum
	1	⅜″ × ⅜″	14¹⁵⁄₁₆″ minimum
Upper Core Quadrant (Total Length)	1	21 × 21	290 minimum
	1	⅞″ × ⅞″	11⁹⁄₁₆″
Glue Blocks (Total Length)	1	9 × 9	364
	1	⅜″ × ⅜″	14⅜″

Clock Components and Hardware (excluding screws and pins)

CLOCK MOVEMENT — OPTIONS:
- Quartz Clock Movements.
- Standard or melody movements available.
- Shaft length/fixing nut: to suit 3–5mm/⅛″ – ³⁄₁₆″ dial-board and dial thickness (adjust thickness of dial-board, if necessary).
- Note: If the maker wishes to use a mechanical movement, the overall depth of the clock case will need to be increased to accommodate the chosen model. Various small mechanical bracket clock movements are available.

CLOCK DIAL — OPTIONS:
- 127 × 127mm/5″ × 5″ square dial. Brass, aluminium or card.

CLOCK HANDS:
- Bushed to suit chosen mechanical or quartz movements.
- Length to suit dial size.
- Pattern to suit individual choice.

BRASSWARE:
- Hinges: two pairs of 25mm/1″ butts.
- Front door handle: 6mm/¼″ brass knob.
- Front door lock: one 6mm/¼″ ball catch.
- Carrying handle: 75 × 50mm/3″ × 2″ approx). Various patterns available.

GLASS:
- To suit front door.

9/10.
Chorister and Curate Mantel Clocks

The 'Chorister' and 'Curate' are traditionally designed mantel clocks originally designed to suit a mini-pendulum movement and a dial with an appropriate cut-out to display the pendulum. Unfortunately, this dial and mini-pendulum combination is not always easily available on the market though a standard quartz movement can be used effectively with a chapter ring that is fixed to a decorative dial-board. The difference between the two clocks lies in the top mouldings only.

Choosing a suitable timber will determine the 'flavour' of the clock and as the choice of timbers available can be extremely wide, I have narrowed the instructions to suit a complete mahogany version (using mahogany construction veneers). For my 'Chorister' I chose burr mahogany veneers and made my own mouldings, cappings and layers out of solid Indian rosewood.

Overall dimensions: 148 wide × 91 deep × 208mm high
$5^{15}/_{16}$″ wide × $3^{21}/_{22}$″ deep × $8^{5}/_{16}$″ high

Skill level ****

Schedule of Operation

GENERAL CONSTRUCTION

These instructions are designed to suit hand methods of construction and I leave it to the discretion of the maker to use alternative machinery methods if preferred.

The Chorister and the Curate are both designed to be built from the base upwards. The bottom layer, lower scotia/lower core and capping sit on top of the plinth.

The centre section of both clocks is a box construction comprising a veneered backboard (which is housed into the lower core and lower capping), veneered side cheeks, a topboard and a dial-board. A veneered and glazed front and rear door are fitted and the main box construction.

The top section of the Chorister comprises three layers: the upper scotia (which 'wraps' around the centre box section); the torus (which 'wraps' around the upper core); and the capping layer.

THE PLINTH, BOTTOM LAYER, LOWER SCOTIA/CORE, LOWER CAPPING

From a piece of 9mm/⅜" plywood, carefully cut and plane to size the rectangular baseboard (refer section C-C).

Check the height of the plinth. On a piece of 12mm/½" plywood (solid wood can be used on the plinth, if wished) plane a long straight and square edge; you can then mark out, with a marking gauge, the height of the four cheeks of the plinth, which you should be able to get out of a single strip of plywood that is 500 × 25mm/20" × 1", allowing for the surplus in width and length. Accurately plane the complete strip to the correct height.

Mark, cut and plane the rear cheek of the plinth to size, checking for straightness and squareness. Note: The rear cheek should be in exact alignment with the baseboard and square to it. Mark out the 'cut-out' on the rear cheek. Drill holes, large enough to accommodate a coping saw blade and carefully remove the wood. Clean down the sawn surfaces to your final line with files and wet and dry paper. Cut the four baseboard supports to length. Accurately glue and pin the two rear baseboard supports in position on the rear cheek. Glue and pin the rear cheek to the baseboard, checking for alignment and squareness.

The front cheek of the plinth is mitred to the two side cheeks. Deal with the front cheek first. Mark the position of the mitres on the front cheek making sure that they are in exact alignment with the front of the baseboard then cut leaving a little surplus for trimming later. Carefully trim

down to your final line with a sharp chisel. Mark out the cut-out shape on the front cheek of the plinth (refer front elevation). This can be done by copying the shapes on the plan to the wood. Carefully remove the wood for the cut-out, with the coping saw, allowing a little surplus. Clean the sawn surfaces down to your final line with round and triangular files. Glue and pin the front cheek to the baseboard, checking for alignment and squareness. Fix the front two baseboard supports to the front cheek.

Cut the side cheeks approximately 9mm/⅜" oversize (in the length). Mark and cut the mitres on the side cheeks and repeat the process. Trim off any surplus wood at the rear of the side cheeks with a sharp chisel.

Sand clean the complete plinth and check for any defects (fill and sand if necessary). Veneer the surfaces of the plinth in the following order: 1. The rear cheek; 2. The side cheeks; 3. The front cheek; 4. The top of the plinth. Carefully cut/file/sand the veneers to their final surfaces after you have glued each surface. Once the plinth is veneered, sand all the surfaces clean with 150 grit wet and dry paper (these will have a final clean with 240 grit wet and dry prior to final finishing).

With a pencil gauge, mark the position of the bottom layer on the top of the plinth. From a piece of mahogany construction veneer (optional), mark and cut the bottom layer to size, checking that it fits accurately on the plinth. Mark a 3mm/⅛" border on the front and side edges of the bottom layer; carefully plane and sand a quarter round on these edges (working the end grain first). Sand the complete bottom layer clean with 240 grit wet and dry, then glue and pin in position making sure that no pins will be left exposed.

Mark the position of the lower core (refer section C-C), making sure that a 9mm/⅜" scotia will fit accurately round the lower core. From a piece of 9mm/⅜" plywood, mark, cut and plane the overall rectangular lower core to size to fit accurately in position on top of the bottom layer. Mark the position of the recess in the lower core that will accommodate the base of the backboard (refer section C-C) and remove the wood with the coping saw; file down to your final line. Glue and screw the lower core in position.

Measure the overall length of the 9mm/⅜" scotia required to fit around the lower core allowing for mitre cutting and waste. Sand clean the scotia *before* cutting the mitres. Mark the position of the mitres on the front scotia first and cut to size. Check that the mitres on the front scotia are in accurate alignment with the lower core then glue in position with a fast-grab PVA glue. Once the front scotia has been glued and set, the appropriate mitres for the side scotias can be cut (make sure that the side scotias are slightly longer than necessary for trimming at the back).

Measure the overall size of the lower capping, allowing yourself a visually neat overlap on top of the lower scotia. Cut and plane to size, checking that the lower capping is straight and square and that it sits accurately on top of the lower scotia. Shape the front and side edges of the lower capping then sand the complete lower capping clean. Glue the lower capping to the lower core/scotia (these should form a flat surface) using positioning pins and cramps/stout boards.

When the cramps are removed, cut a recess in the lower capping; accurately line up with the recess previously cut in the lower core using a sharp knife and chisel.

Drill the hole for the 6mm/¼″ ballcatch (refer front elevation and section C-C).

CENTRE SECTION OF THE CLOCK

The backboard acts as the 'keel' for the centre section, so this should be built first. Measure and cut to size ensuring that it is straight and square, that it fits the recess in the lower core/lower capping and that it is the correct height.

Mark the position of the rectangular hole in the backboard (to accommodate the rear door) and carefully cut out with the coping saw; file down to your knife cut. Veneer the inside surfaces of the rectangular hole, then veneer the complete back surface of the backboard; trim the edges of the veneers after you have glued each surface. Sand clean with 150 grit wet and dry.

Position the backboard in the recess that is in the lower core/lower capping. Establish the position of the fixing screws for the backboard (refer Section AA and rear elevation). Centre punch the position of these fixing screws on rear of the backboard; accurately cramp the backboard in position; drill the pilot holes for the screws through the backboard into the lower core; remove the backboard; drill the clearance and countersink holes for the screws into the backboard; screw the backboard, without glue, into position.

Establish the position of the 9mm/⅜″ glue blocks that will sit on the lower core/lower capping and that will secure the side cheeks (refer Section A-A and Section B-B).

Check that the gluing surfaces of these blocks are straight, square and flat; sand clean the other surfaces that will show. Cut the glue blocks to length then glue and pin the blocks in position. Punch home pins and fill the holes. Sand clean afterwards.

Mark out the side cheeks and cut and plane to size, straight and square. When sitting in position, the side cheeks should fit snugly against the glue blocks on the lower core/lower capping and tightly against the edges of the backboard; the final height of the side cheeks should be in exact alignment with the final height of the backboard.

Carefully veneer the front and back lippings of the side cheeks and trim the veneer edges. Veneer the main outside surface of each side cheek and trim the veneer edges. Sand clean with 150 grit wet and dry.

Sand clean the inside surfaces of the side cheeks and mark the position of the 9mm/⅜″ dialboard mounts and the rear glue blocks that connect the side cheeks with the backboard. (Refer Section A-A and Section B-B). Also mark the position of the glue blocks on the side cheeks that will support the topboard (refer Section A-A), checking with the thickness of the material that will be used for the topboard. Glue and pin the glue blocks and dial-board mounts in position on the side cheeks. Punch home pins and fill holes. Sand clean afterwards.

Assemble the side cheeks in position with cramps and without glue. Check that the side cheeks are parallel with each other and that they are straight and square with the backboard and with the lower capping.

The topboard can now be measured and cut to fit in situation; you will see that it is necessary to cut out recesses in the sides of the topboard in order to accommodate the side cheeks (refer Side Elevation and full size plan of the Curate). Before proceeding with making the topboard, check that the inside distance between the top of the side cheeks equals the inside distance between the bottom of the side cheeks. Plane the back edge of the topboard, allowing yourself a small overlap on the remaining dimensions of the topboard. Place the topboard on top of the side cheeks with the back edge butting against the inside surface of the backboard; you can then scribe the position of the recesses for the side cheeks. mark the lines for the recesses with a craft knife; remove the appropriate wood for the recesses with a sharp saw; trim to your knife line with a sharp chisel and file. Place the topboard in position, resting on top of the glue blocks of the side cheeks. Check for fit; you should have an overlap at the front of the topboard that will sit over the top of the front door. Check that your complete box structure is straight, square and true.

Repeat the procedure for fitting the fixing screws at the

top of the backboard, as for the base of the backboard.

Dismantle the complete box structure. Sand clean all the surfaces of the box structure (excepting the top and bottom of the side cheeks and backboard) with 240 grit wet and dry. Dismantle, then carefully glue and cramp the box structure in its final position.

When the glue has set, remove the cramps and trim any surplus wood on the topboard to its final position.

TOP SECTION OF THE CLOCK (THE CHORISTER)
The first stage of the top section is to cut and fit the upper scotia. The same procedure is followed as employed in the assembly of the lower scotia. Once the upper scotia is fixed, make sure that the top of it is flush with the top surfaces of the topboard/side cheeks/backboard.

The next layer of the top section is the torus/upper core layer. Measure and cut to size the upper core, making sure that it is straight and square. Veneer the back edge of the upper core and trim the veneer edges. Accurately pin and glue the upper core in position on top of the topboard (you can establish the position of the upper core by running a marking gauge around the upper scotia). The torus moulding should now be made; you can either make the torus from 21 × 9mm/$^{13}/_{16}$″ × $^3/_8$″ stripwood that has been bought in or from stripwood that you have made up yourself. Measure and cut as before the overall length of the torus required and allow a surplus. You should then make a template of the cross section of the torus; this can be done by drawing out the shape of the plan onto a thick piece of card, then cut out with a craft knife. Using your template, mark the torus shape onto both end sections of the stripwood. The stripwood should then be pinned (on the inside edge where the pin holes will not show later) to a board that is fixed to your bench; it should overhang the edge of the board slightly. Plane the stripwood down to the torus lines. Finish shaping the torus with 150 grit wet and dry following this with 240 grit wet and dry and remove from the board that it had been pinned to. When fixing the torus to the top section of the clock, you should follow the same procedure as used for fixing the lower and upper scotias.

The capping layer is made from 3mm/$^1/_8$″ mahogany construction veneer, (optional — on my version of the Chorister, I chose to make the capping layer with a burr mahogany centre panel that had a solid rosewood lipping). Carefully measure and cut the construction veneer to size. Mark a 3mm/$^1/_8$″ border on the top of the capping layer and

on the front and side edges only. Carefully plane a quadrant on the front and side edges. Sand clean the complete capping layer with 150 and 240 grit wet and dry. Cramp and glue the capping layer accurately in position until set (you will need a stout board to bear onto the capping layer, thus ensuring that it is glued flatly and evenly).

TOP SECTION OF THE CLOCK (THE CURATE)
Repeat the procedure for applying the upper scotia as followed on the Chorister.

After applying the upper scotia, a middle layer is applied — this can be made out of 3mm/$^1/_8$″ mahogany construction veneer. Accurately measure and cut to size. Sand clean with 150 and 240 grit wet and dry. Glue and pin in position.

Measure and cut to size the upper core, making sure that it is straight and square. Glue and pin in position.

Repeat the procedure for applying the top scotia as employed with the lower scotia. Ensure the top of the top scotia is flush with the upper core.

Measure and cut to size the capping layer, making sure that you have an even overlap around the top scotia. Round the edges (not the back edge), sand clean. Glue and cramp the capping layer, following the procedure employed on the Chorister.

FRONT DOOR
The construction of this door is based on the principle of laminating a sheet of 6mm/$^1/_4$″ plywood (with a rectangular hole cut into it) to a sheet of 9mm/$^3/_8$″ plywood (with a slightly larger hole cut into it). The difference in dimensions of the two holes forms a rebate in which the glass will sit. In making the door, work in situation to the opening in your clock case as well as to the dimensions on your plan.

Mark and cut a sheet of 9mm/$^3/_8$″ plywood to the overall dimensions of the door *minus* the thickness of a piece of veneer *all* the way round the edges, this will allow for a snug fit in the opening, but do double check the dimensions on your particular clock case. Mark and cut a sheet of 6mm/$^1/_4$″ plywood to the exact dimensions of the 9mm/$^3/_8$″ sheet.

With a marking gauge, establish the dimensions of the rectangular hole in the 6mm/$^1/_4$″ plywood, as shown in the front elevation. Repeat this process on the 9mm/$^3/_8$″ plywood, only increase the dimensions of the hole by 10mm/$^{13}/_{16}$″ to allow for a 5mm/$^3/_{16}$″ rebate all round. Cut the holes by drilling in the corners and removing the wood

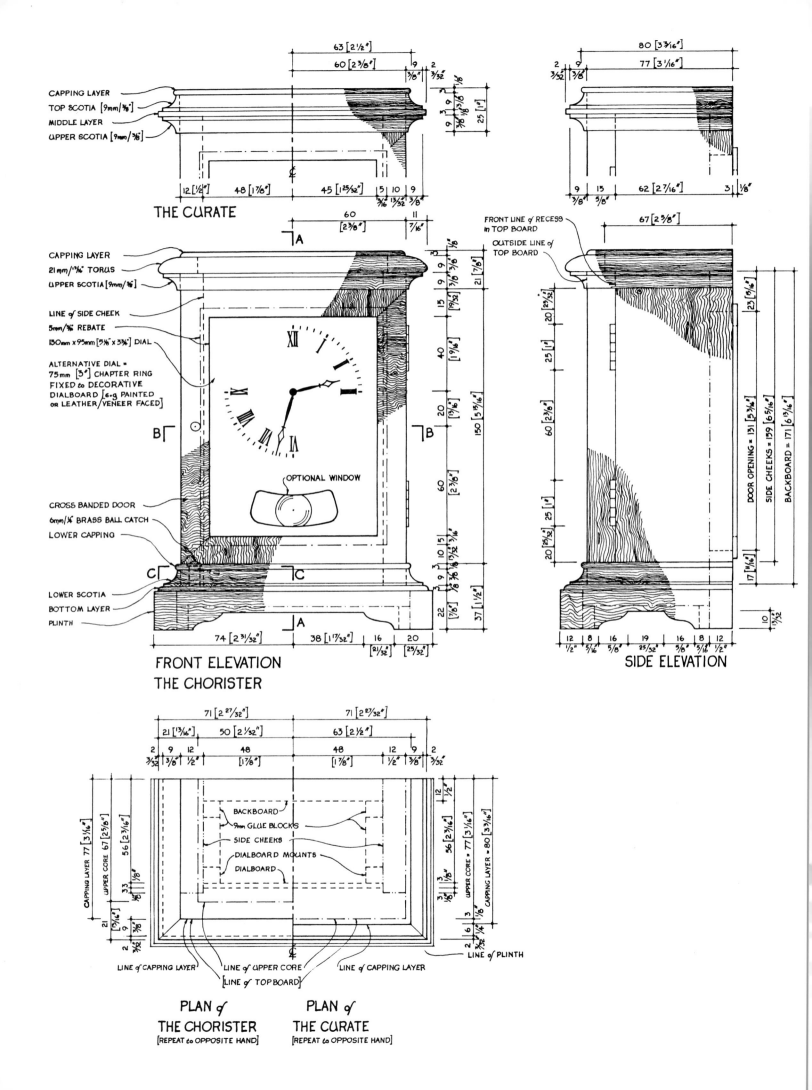

THE CURATE

FRONT ELEVATION
THE CHORISTER

SIDE ELEVATION

PLAN of
THE CHORISTER
[REPEAT to OPPOSITE HAND]

PLAN of
THE CURATE
[REPEAT to OPPOSITE HAND]

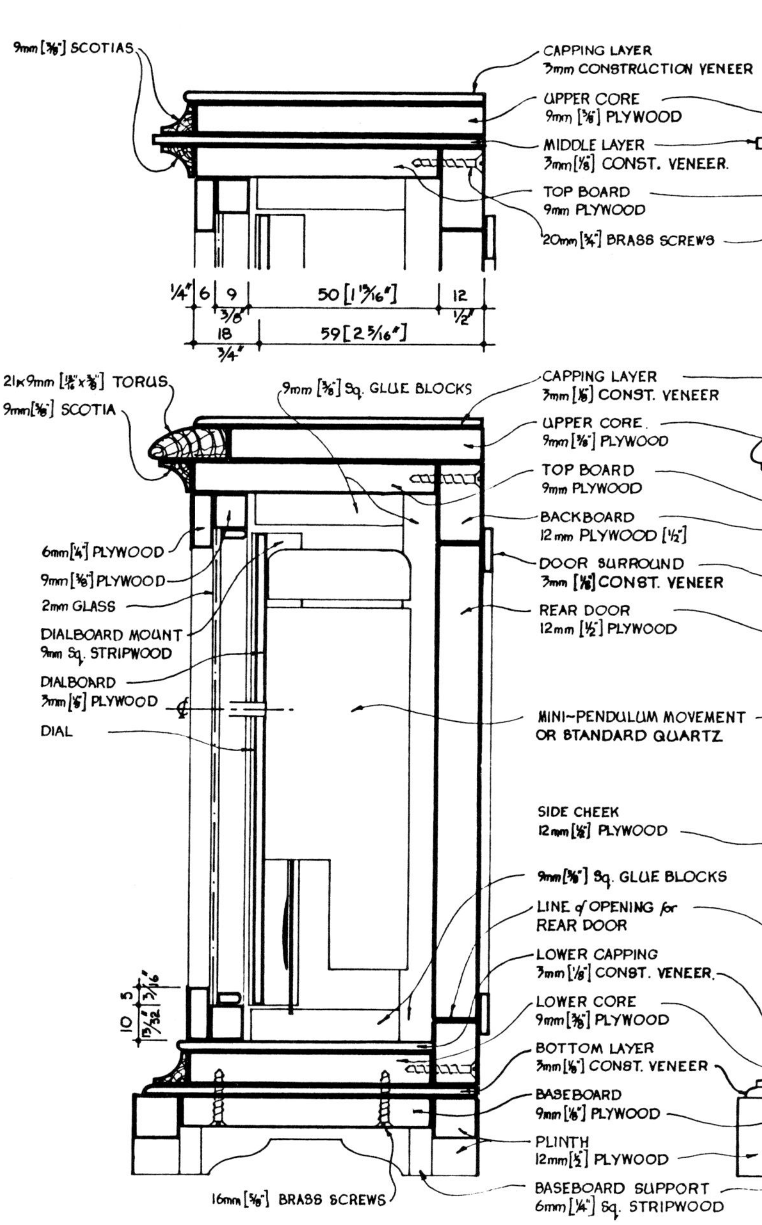
9mm [3/8"] SCOTIAS
CAPPING LAYER 3mm CONSTRUCTION VENEER
UPPER CORE 9mm [3/8"] PLYWOOD
MIDDLE LAYER 3mm [1/8"] CONST. VENEER.
TOP BOARD 9mm PLYWOOD
20mm [3/4"] BRASS SCREWS
1/4" 6 9 3/8" 50 [1 15/16"] 12 1/2"
18 3/4" 59 [2 5/16"]
21x9mm [13/16" x 3/8"] TORUS
9mm [3/8"] SCOTIA
9mm [3/8"] Sq. GLUE BLOCKS
CAPPING LAYER 3mm [1/8"] CONST. VENEER
UPPER CORE 9mm [3/8"] PLYWOOD
TOP BOARD 9mm PLYWOOD
BACKBOARD 12mm PLYWOOD [1/2"]
6mm [1/4"] PLYWOOD
9mm [3/8"] PLYWOOD
2mm GLASS
DOOR SURROUND 3mm [1/8"] CONST. VENEER
REAR DOOR 12mm [1/2"] PLYWOOD
DIALBOARD MOUNT 9mm Sq. STRIPWOOD
DIALBOARD 3mm [1/8"] PLYWOOD
DIAL
MINI-PENDULUM MOVEMENT OR STANDARD QUARTZ
SIDE CHEEK 12mm [1/2"] PLYWOOD
9mm [3/8"] Sq. GLUE BLOCKS
LINE of OPENING for REAR DOOR
LOWER CAPPING 3mm [1/8"] CONST. VENEER.
LOWER CORE 9mm [3/8"] PLYWOOD
BOTTOM LAYER 3mm [1/8"] CONST. VENEER
BASEBOARD 9mm [3/8"] PLYWOOD
PLINTH 12mm [1/2"] PLYWOOD
BASEBOARD SUPPORT 6mm [1/4"] Sq. STRIPWOOD
16mm [5/8"] BRASS SCREWS
10 5 13/32" 3/16"

SECTION A~A

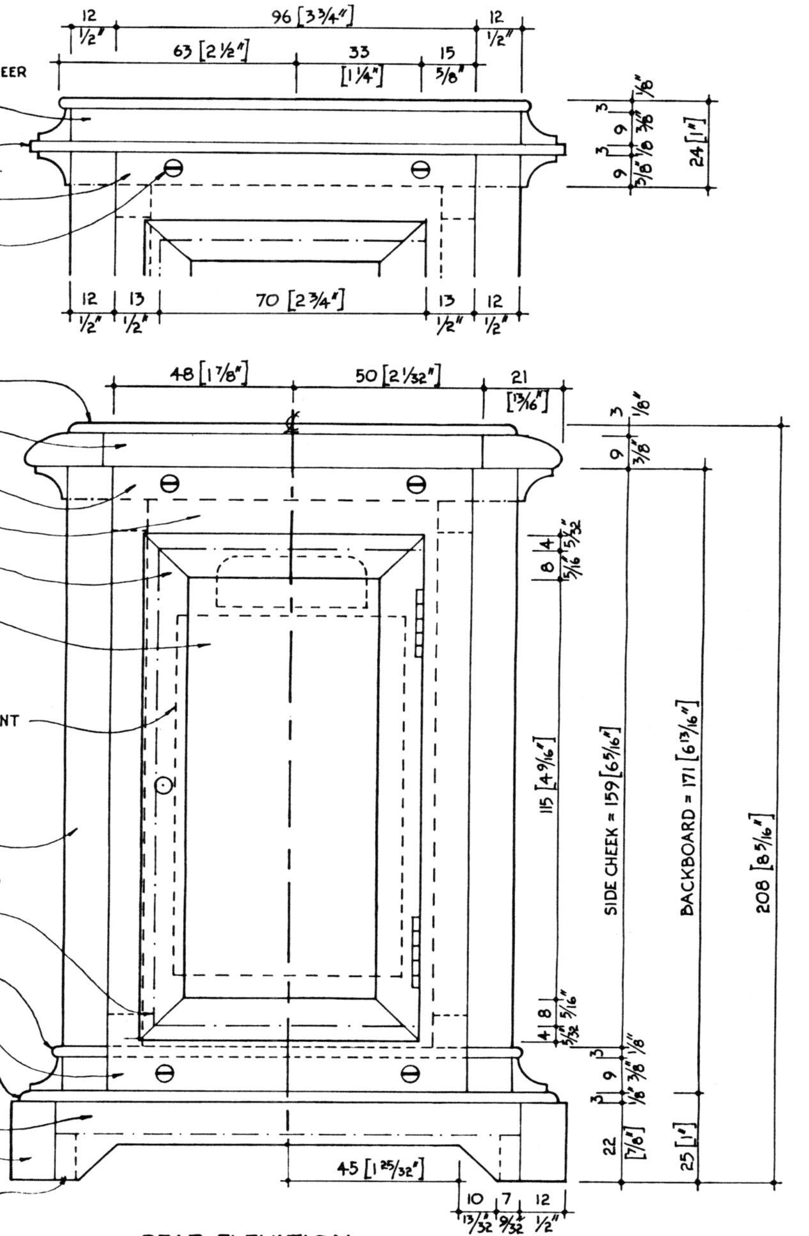
12 1/2" 96 [3 3/4"] 12 1/2"
63 [2 1/2"] 33 [1 1/4"] 15 5/8"
3 1/8" 9 3/8" 3 1/8" 9 3/8" 24 [1"]
12 1/2" 13 1/2" 70 [2 3/4"] 13 1/2" 12 1/2"
48 [1 7/8"] 50 [2 1/32"] 21 [13/16"]
3 1/8" 9 3/8"
4 5/32" 8 5/16"
115 [4 9/16"]
SIDE CHEEK = 159 [6 5/16"]
BACKBOARD = 171 [6 13/16"]
208 [8 5/16"]
8 5/16" 4 5/32"
3 1/8" 9 3/8" 3 1/8"
22 [7/8"] 25 [1"]
45 [1 25/32"]
10 13/32" 7 9/32" 12 1/2"

REAR ELEVATION

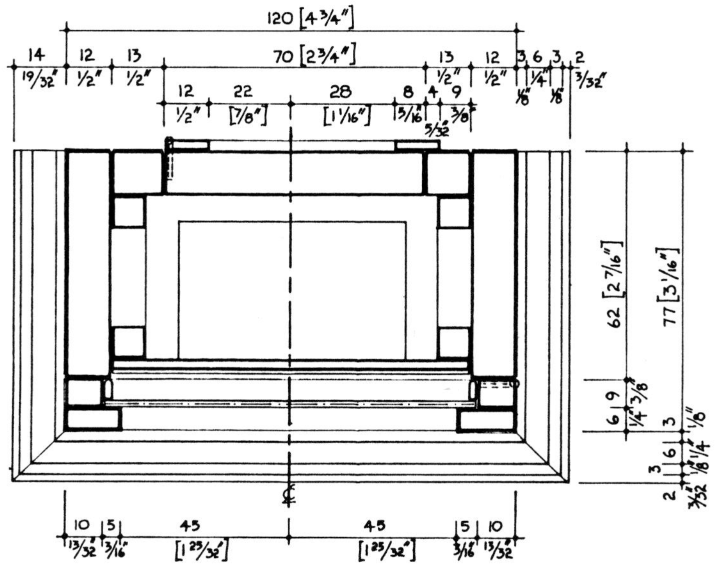
120 [4 3/4"]
14 19/32" 12 1/2" 13 1/2" 70 [2 3/4"] 13 1/2" 12 1/2" 3 1/8" 6 1/4" 3 1/8" 2 3/32"
12 1/2" 22 [7/8"] 28 [1 1/16"] 8 5/16" 4 5/32" 9 3/8"
62 [2 7/16"] 77 [3 1/16"]
6 1/4" 9 3/8" 3 1/8"
3 1/8" 6 1/4"
2 3/32"
10 13/32" 5 3/16" 45 [1 25/32"] 45 [1 25/32"] 5 3/16" 10 13/32"

SECTION B~B

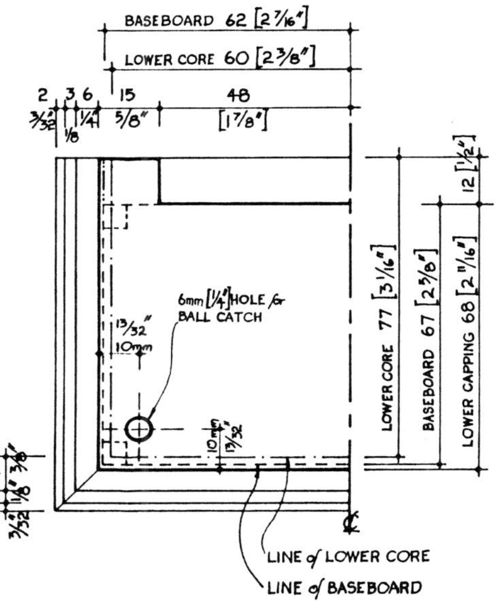
BASEBOARD 62 [2 7/16"]
LOWER CORE 60 [2 3/8"]
2 3/32" 3 1/8" 6 1/4" 15 5/8" 48 [1 7/8"]
6mm [1/4"] HOLE for BALL CATCH
13/32" 10mm
10 13/32"
LOWER CORE 77 [3 1/16"]
BASEBOARD 67 [2 5/8"]
LOWER CAPPING 68 [2 11/16"]
12 [1/2"]
9 3/8" 3 1/8" 2 3/32"
LINE of LOWER CORE
LINE of BASEBOARD

SECTION C~C

with a coping saw. Carefully clean down to your lines with a sharp chisel and file.

Pin and glue the two plywood sheets together, making sure of accurate alignment. Punch the pins home, fill and sand clean when the filler has set.

When the glue has set, check the door for fit in the opening of your case, making allowances for the veneered surfaces.

Veneer the surfaces of the door in the following order: 1. The inside surfaces of the hole in the 6mm/¼" plywood; 2. The back surface of the door; 3. The top and bottom edges; 4. The side edges; 5. The front surface — this can either be veneered out of one sheet of burr veneer (if that is your choice of timber) without any mitre joins, or, it can be cross-banded with a straighter grained timber — as shown in the front elevation — in which case mitre joins should be employed. When cross banding, I find that it is best to secure two *opposing* sides of oversize cross-banding (with the mitres cut) in position on the door with two-sided tape; the other two sides can then be offered up, under the original cross-bandings, and the appropriate mitres cut; these two pieces can then be glued, and afterwards, the initial two pieces are removed (with the two-sided tape) and then glued in position. Trim off surplus veneer at the edges.

After the door has been veneered, the slots for the hinges can be cut. The door is then sanded clean with 150 and 240 grit wet and dry.

The glass is then temporarily placed in position and the 6 × 3mm/¼" × ⅛" beadings (which can be cut out of 3mm/⅛" mahogany construction veneer with a cutting gauge) are fitted, but not fixed, in position. These are then put to one side for finishing later. Remove the glass.

Drill the hole for the door handle, check the handle for fit, remove and put to one side.

The door can now be initially hung. Once you are satisfied that the door fits correctly, you can then establish the hole on the lower edge of the door to accommodate the ball of the ball catch. Remove the door for finishing and re-hanging later.

REAR DOOR

Measure and cut a piece of 12mm/½" plywood to fit the opening in the backboard but be sure to reduce the dimensions of this piece of wood by the thickness of a piece of veneer *all* the way round the edges. Veneer the edges of the plywood but do check that the door will comfortably swing in and out. Veneer the front and back surfaces of the door. Sand clean all the surfaces of the door with 150 and 240 grit wet and dry. From a piece of mahogany construction veneer, cut 12mm/½" strips which will be used for the door surround. Note: These strips will form a rebate on three sides of the door only while the strip on the hinge side will be flush with the edge of the plywood panel. Sand clean the strips before cutting the mitres.

Before you cut and fix the edge strips of the door, be sure to apply a finish (see section on finishing) to the veneered surface first. Once you have done this, you will have to scrape away some of the finish round the edges of the door to provide a gluing surface for the strips.

Measure and cut the mitres for the strip on the hinge side first. Glue in position. Cut the mitres on the top and bottom strips, check for fit with the mitres on the strip on the hinge side, glue in position. Cut the mitres on the remaining strip, check for fit, glue in position. When the glue has set, you can then chop the hinges into the door and fix the handle. Initially hang the door and when it is correct, remove for final finishing and re-hanging later.

DIAL-BOARD

The dial-board can now be made; this needs to be accurately measured and cut to fit the appropriate opening between the two side cheeks. Check the dial-board for fit on the dial-board mounts and drill four fine positioning holes through the dial-board into the mounts. Remove the dial-board.

Fix the dial to the dial-board with two-sided tape and check that the dial is visually in alignment, in its final position, with the front door in its closed position. Scribe the positions of the centre hole and, if using a mini-pendulum movement, the pendulum window on the dial-board, then separate the dial from the dial-board. Drill the centre hole in the dial-board, checking for fit with the fixing nut of your chosen clock movement. Remove the wood for the pendulum window with a coping saw after drilling access holes then carefully file down to your scribed lines.

Glue and pin the dial-board to the dial-board mounts checking for alignment with the previously drilled positioning holes. The dial can be fixed to the dial-board at the final stage of the project.

FINISHING

Before finishing, check over all the components that you

have made, they should all have been sanded clean with 240 grit wet and dry.

The following items need finishing and polishing before final assembly: 1. main casework; 2. inside of the case and the dial-board (I suggest using a matt black paint for this); 3. front door; 4. strips on the rear door; 5. beadings of the front door. Note: The mouldings that are available from DIY shops are usually made from mahogany or ramin, the ramin can easily be stained to match most woods.

Once you have achieved a finish of your choice, the final assembly procedure is as follows: 1. glue and pin the dial-board in position; 2. fix the glass in the door — the beadings can be pinned in position; 3. place the ball catch in position and re-hang the front door; 4. re-hang the rear door — this can be kept in position with a ball catch that is fixed to the door and not to the backboard; 5. fix the dial to the dial-board — this can be done with two-sided tape or with a contact adhesive; 6. fix the movement and hands in position.

Cutting list

COMPONENT	QUANTITY	SECTION	LENGTH
Plinth — back piece	1	12 × 22	124
	1	½″ × ⅞″	4⅞″
Plinth — side pieces	2	12 × 22	91
	2	½″ × ⅞″	3²¹/₃₂″
Plinth — front piece	1	12 × 22	148
	1	½″ × ⅞″	5⅞″
Baseboard	1	9 × 67	148
	1	⅜″ × 2⅝″	5⅞″
Bottom Layer	1	3 × 89	144
	1	⅛″ × 3⁹/₁₆″	5¾″
Lower Core	1	9 × 77	120
	1	⅜″ × 3¹/₁₆″	4¾″
Lower Capping	1	3 × 80	126
	1	⅛″ × 3³/₁₆″	5″
Backboard	1	12 × 90	171
	1	½″ × 3¾″	6¹³/₁₆″
Topboard	1	9 × 65	120
	1	⅜″ × 2⁹/₁₆″	4¾″
Side Cheeks	2	12 × 62	159
	2	½″ × 2⁷/₁₆″	6⁵/₁₆″
Upper Core	1	9 × 67	100
	1	⅜″ × 2⅝″	4¹/₁₆″
Capping Layer	1	3 × 77	120
	1	⅛″ × 3¹/₁₆″	4¾″
Dial-board	1	3 × 96	130
	1	⅛″ × 3¾″	5⅛″
Dial-board Mounts	2	9 × 9	130
	2	⅜″ × ⅜″	5⅛″

Inner Layer of Front Door	1	9 × 120	150
	1	⅜″ × 4¾″	5¹⁵⁄₁₆″
Outer Layer of Front Door	1	6 × 120	150
	1	¼″ × 4¾″	5¹⁵⁄₁₆″
Inner Layer of Rear Door	1	12 × 70	131
	1	½″ × 2¾″	5³⁄₁₆″
Stripwood Surround for Rear Door (Total Length)	1	3 × 12	426 minimum
	1	⅛″ × ½″	16¹³⁄₁₆″
Lower Core Scotia (Total Length)	1	9 × 9	310 minimum
	1	⅜″ × ⅜″	12⅜″ minimum
Topboard Scotia (Total Length)	1	9 × 9	286 minimum
	1	⅜″ × ⅜″	11⅜″ minimum
Upper Core Torus (Total Length)	1	9 × 21	318 minimum
	1	⅜″ × ¹³⁄₁₆″	12⁹⁄₁₆″ minimum
Glazing Beads (Total Length)	1	3 × 5	540 surplus
	1	⅛″ × ³⁄₁₆	21⅜″″ surplus
Glue Blocks (Total Length)	1	9 × 9	380
	1	⅜″ × ⅜″	15″
Baseboard Supports	4	6 × 6	13
	4	¼″ × ¼″	½″

THE CURATE — VARIATIONS

Upper Core	1	9 × 77	120
	1	⅜″ × 3¹⁄₁₆″	4¾″
Capping Layer	1	3 × 80	126
	1	⅛″ × 3³⁄₁₆″	5″
Upper Core Scotia (Total Length)	1	9 × 9	286 minimum
	1	⅜″ × ⅜″	11⅜″ minimum

Clock Components and Hardware (excluding screws and pins)

Note: This clock case was originally designed to suit a 'Kienzle 715/660' mini-pendulum movement and a 130 × 95mm/5⅛″ × 3¾″ 'carriage clock dial' with a cut-out aperture to display the swinging pendulum. Both the movement and dial are now difficult to obtain, even so, this clock case has been included in the book as it is the only design in the 'carriage clock' category. Standard quartz movements may be used and dial options are given using generally available carriage clock dials — adjust the size of your clock case to accommodate your chosen dial.

CLOCK MOVEMENT — OPTIONS: STANDARD QUARTZ MOVEMENT.
- Hand shaft/fixing nut length: to suit 3–5mm/⅛″ – ³∕₁₆″ dial-board and dial thickness. Adjust thickness of dial-board, if necessary.

CARRIAGE CLOCK DIALS — OPTIONS GENERALLY AVAILABLE:
- 130 × 95mm/5⅛″ × 3¾″ (original dial size)
- 137 × 90mm/5¹³∕₃₂″ × 3⁹∕₁₆″
- 127 × 89mm/5″ × 3½″
- 140 × 90mm/5½″ × 3⁹∕₁₆″
- 120 × 75mm/4¾″ × 3″
- 95 × 75mm/3¾″ × 3″
- 85mm/3⅜″ diameter chapter ring fixed to decorative dial-board.
- Note: Some carriage clock dials available are integral with a movement and hands and with moonphase, world time and date/calendar displays.

CLOCK HANDS:
- Bushed to suit chosen.
- Length to suit dial size.
- Pattern to suit individual choice.

BRASSWARE:
- Hinges:
  front door — one pair of 25mm/1″ butts
  rear door — one pair of 18mm/¾″ butts.
- Door knob: front door — one 9mm/⅜″ diameter knob.
- Door lock:
  front door — one 6mm/¼″ ball catch
  rear door — one 9mm/⅜″ latch.

GLASS:
- To suit front door.

11/12.
'Carter' and 'Ostler' Mantel Clocks

Carter

Ostler

These two designs follow the same laminating, veneering and moulding themes of the 'Coachman' and 'Groom' clocks though they have been developed for use as mantel clocks, again with 'flat cornice' and 'gabled cornice' options. The choice of veneers will determine the flavour of the clock as will the finishes. With the Ostler, you might like to consider gilding or painting the columns gold. There is also an option for increasing the overall thickness of the Ostler with an extra laminate at the rear of the case.

Overall dimensions: 174 wide × 45 deep × 199mm high
6⅞″ wide × 1⅞″ deep × 7⅞″ high
188 wide × 66 deep × 238mm high
7½″ wide × 2¾″ deep × 9⅜″ high

Skill level *

'Carter'

Schedule of Operations

BACKBOARD & FACEBOARD

Take the 18mm/¾″ thick sheet of plywood and carefully mark out the shape of the clock as shown on the Front Elevation, including the shaped portion at the 'eaves'. At this stage ignore the plinth or skirting and the scotia mouldings which are to be applied later. Cut out a similar shape to the first.

Accurately mark the position of the 60mm/2⅜″ hole, (check this measurement against the actual movement being used) which will later accept the rear body of the insertion movement, on both pieces of plywood. Drill starter holes and with a coping saw or fretsaw cut out the holes. Accuracy here is important if the insertion movement is to fit snugly after final assembly.

Cut out the outside shape of both pieces, paying particular attention to the shaped 'eaves'. lay one piece on the other to ensure that the shapes are identical and fix together using PVA adhesive and panel pins.

Check that all edges are at right angles to the front face of the assembly and correct any minor errors using a file or shaper plane, which may also be used to remove any saw marks or minor protrusions of panel pin heads.

Sand down the front, back and edges of the assembly to ensure a perfectly flat surface ready for veneering. Be careful not to round over any edges or corners when sanding.

VENEERING

Note the direction of veneer grain as shown on the plan and then glue veneer with contact adhesive to the sides of the assembly, including the area to be covered by the plinth or skirting, and also along the shaped 'eaves', but at this stage *not* on the 'roof'. Trim off surplus veneer. Glue veneer to the front face of the assembly and trim off surplus veneer as before, including the surplus covering the area of the movement insertion hole.

Sand down all surfaces with 'wet and dry' paper on a sanding block. Always sand in the direction of the grain and don't oversand.

SKIRTING

Place the assembly to one side and using 12mm/½″ thick plywood cut out the components for the 25mm/1″ high skirting to the lengths shown on the plan.

Check that the sides of the skirting are parallel and square to each other and correct any minor errors and remove any saw marks with a file and sandpaper block. Ensure that the top surface of the skirting is flat enough to receive veneer since it will not be possible to sand down after fixing.

Using PVA adhesive and panel pins fix the side skirting members to the edges of the main assembly. Ensure that they are accurately placed. Fix the front skirting member to the front of the main assembly in the same manner and make certain that the top of the member is level with the top of the side members previously fixed and has no 'steps'.

Sand down the vertical faces of the skirting perfectly flat, ready to receive veneer. Apply veneer to the top surface of the skirting. Trim off surplus veneer and sand down with a sanding block ensuring that no scratches are made on the vertical veneer face of the main assembly. Veneer the vertical surfaces of the skirting and sand down carefully, working with the grain of the veneer. Place the whole of the assembly to one side.

MOULDINGS

Take the 9mm/⅜″ hardwood scotia moulding and sand down for the full length, using a sanding block on upper and lower square edges and sandpaper wrapped around a short length of dowel for the concave surface.

Take the main assembly and measure along the front upper surface of the skirting and cut a suitable length from the scotia moulding. Mitre each end of this length of scotia. Check this for accuracy against the main assembly and fix in position using PVA adhesive and, if necessary, moulding pins. cut lengths from the scotia moulding at least 25mm/1″ greater than required for the side skirtings. cut mitre at one end of each member and offer up to the already fixed front scotia moulding. Fix in position and cut off any surplus projection at the rear of the moulding.

Re-sand the moulding, paying particular attention to the mitred corners, using sandpaper wrapped around a short length of dowel.

Take the remaining portion of the hardwood scotia moulding and cut off two lengths that are greater than the front rake of the 'gable' of the main assembly. Form a 'bastard mitre' where the two lengths of gable scotia are to intersect at the peak of the gable. Check for accuracy against the main assembly. Accurately mark off against the main assembly where these members are to intersect the

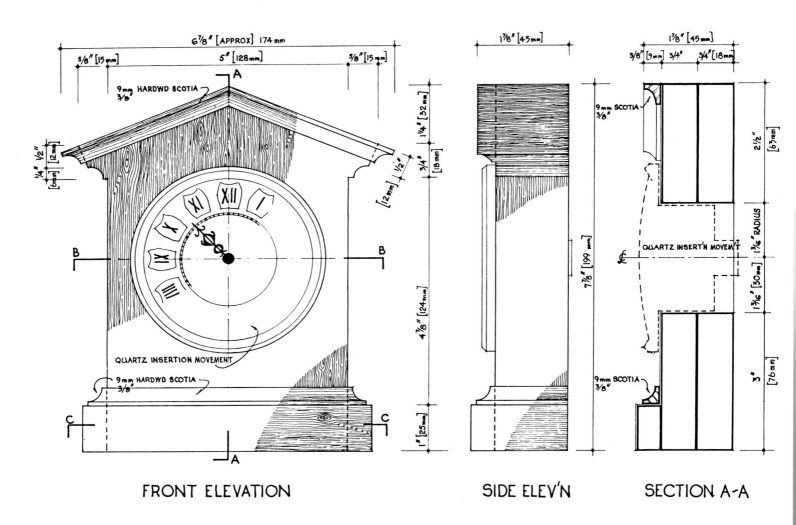

FRONT ELEVATION   SIDE ELEV'N   SECTION A-A

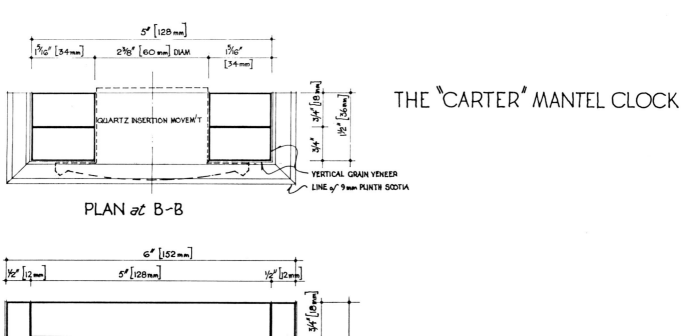

PLAN at B-B

THE "CARTER" MANTEL CLOCK

PLAN at C-C

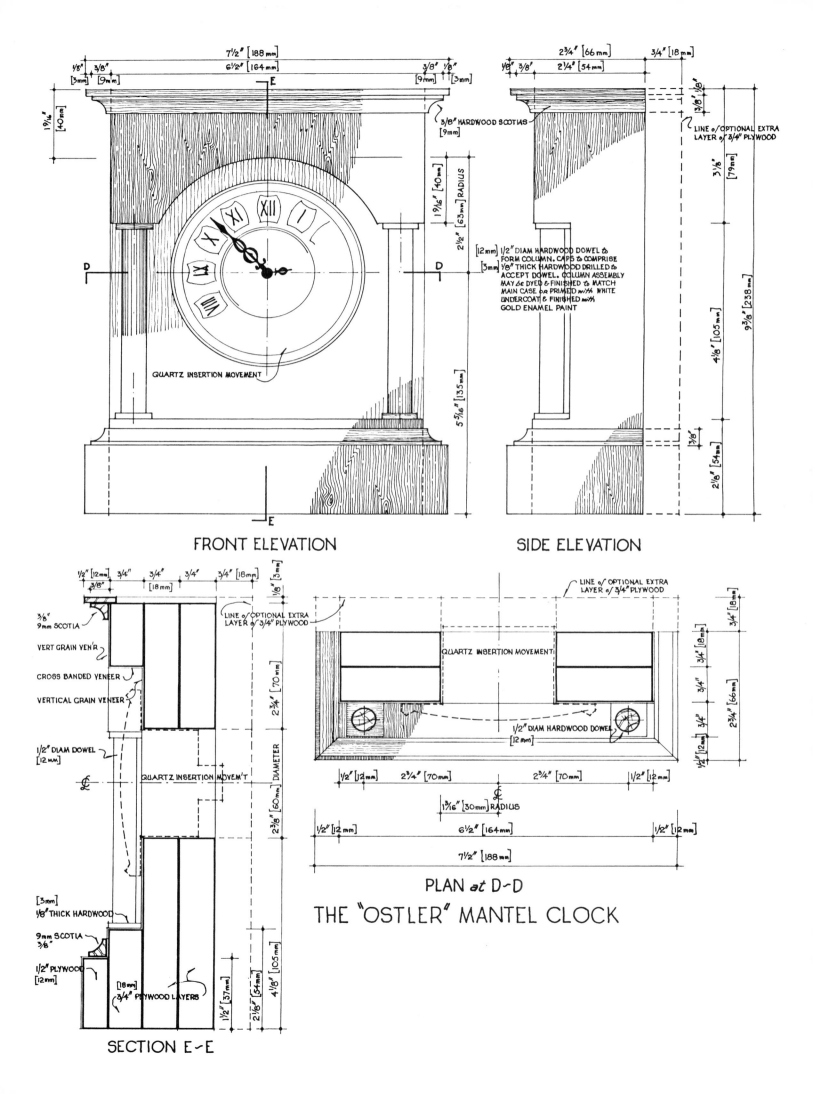

FRONT ELEVATION

SIDE ELEVATION

PLAN at D-D

THE "OSTLER" MANTEL CLOCK

SECTION E-E

side members at the eaves and cut mitres at those points. Fix the front gable scotias to the main assembly with PVA adhesive and moulding pins. Cut lengths of scotia moulding for the sides, working in a manner similar to that described for the skirting scotia mouldings. Mitre the ends to fit the ends of the gable scotia already fixed and fix in position with PVA and moulding pins. Cut off any surplus length of side scotia at the rear. Sand down the whole of the gable scotia.

ROOF VENEER

Check that the top of the gable scotia does not project above the line of the roof, removing any such projection with a file and sandpaper block. Sand over the whole of the roof area ready to receive veneer. Glue veneer over the whole of the roof surface, including the top of the scotia moulds, and neatly trim off any surplus veneer in the manner previously described. Sand the roof, working in the direction of the grain.

FINISHING & FINAL ASSEMBLY

Check back over all the fixed scotia mouldings and punch in any protruding heads of moulding pins, where used. Fill with matching filler and sand down when dry.

Next take the insertion movement and insert into the hole in the face of the assembly to ensure a good fit.

Remove the movement and put to one side until finishes for the case have been completed. Check over the whole of the case for blemishes, finger marks etc. Select and apply the method of preferred finish.

Green baize of felt may be glued to the base of the clock to prevent any scratches to polished surfaces.

Finally, push the insertion movement into place.

'Ostler'

Schedule of Operations

BODY LAMINATES

It will be noted that the plan shows an optional additional layer of 18mm/¾″ thick plywood to the main body of the clock. It will be necessary at this stage to decide which version to select.

Take the 18mm/¾″ thick piece of plywood and mark out the two (or three) layers forming the main body of the clock. At this stage also mark out the arched hood member, making sure that the arch itself is accurately marked out.

Cut out the arched hood member and the two (or three) layers forming the main body.

Mark out with care the position of the 60mm/2⅜″ holes (check this measurement against the actual movement being used) which will later accept the insertion movement on all layers of the main body. Drill starter holes and with a coping saw or fretsaw cut out the holes. Accuracy here is important if the insertion movement is to fit snugly after final assembly.

Lay the two (or three) pieces of the main body on top of each other to ensure that the shapes are identical and fix together using PVA adhesive and panel pins.

Lay the arched hood member on top of the now assembled main body of the clock to ensure that it is of the correct shape and will fit accurately on the main assembly. Do *not* fix the arched member at this stage.

Check that all edges on the main assembly and the arched hood are at right angles to the front face of the assembly and correct any minor errors. Put the arched member to one side for later fixing.

Sand down the front, back and edges of the main assembly to a perfectly flat surface ready for veneering. Be careful not to round over any edges or corners when sanding.

VENEERING

Note the direction of the veneer grain as shown on the plan and then cut out with a craft knife pieces of veneer of the general shapes required, but a little larger than required. Put these pieces of veneer to one side for use later.

Sand down the front, sides and underside of the arched member, paying particular attention to the underside of the arch itself. Veneer the underside of the arch with cross banded veneer. Do *not* at this stage veneer any other parts of the arched member, which should be put to one side for future fixing.

Take the main assembly and veneer the front face *only* covering the areas to be later covered by the arched member and skirting.

Trim off surplus veneer including the area covering the insertion movement hole. Sand down to a finished surface the whole of the front veneered face of the main assembly.

Next, mark and cut out the 37mm/1½″ high, 18mm/¾″ thick lower column platform. Check that sides are parallel and square to each other and check for accuracy against the lower front face of the main assembly. Correct any minor errors and sand the upper surface ready to accept veneer. Veneer the top surface of the column platform with cross banded veneer, trim off surplus veneer and sand to a finished surface.

Fix the column platform to the lower part of the front of the main assembly with PVA and panel pins, making sure that it accurately positioned.

Take the arched member and fix to the top of the front face of the main assembly with PVA and panel pins.

Check that the sides of the total assembly are at right angles to the front face and sand ready to receive veneer. Do not round over any edges or corners while sanding.

Veneer the sides of the total assembly including the areas to be covered by the side skirtings. Trim off surplus veneer.

Veneer the front of the arched member and the front of the column platform. Trim off surplus veneer and sand all surfaces to a finish.

SKIRTING
Using 12mm/½" thick plywood, cut out the 37mm/1½" high skirting members to the lengths shown on the plan. Check that sides are parallel and square to each other. Sand the top surfaces level to receive veneer.

Fix the front skirting member to the lower front face of the total assembly with PVA and panel pins making sure that it is accurately positioned. Fix the side skirting members to the sides of the total assembly with PVA and panel pins. Ensure that the top surfaces are level with the top surface of the front skirting member. Sand down all vertical surfaces of the skirting ready to receive veneer.

Veneer the top surfaces of the skirting with cross banded veneer, cut with a mitre at intersections with side skirting. Trim off surplus veneer and sand to a finish taking care that the abrasive paper does not scratch adjoining veneers.

Veneer the side vertical faces of the skirting, trim off surplus veneer in the usual manner and then veneer the vertical face of the front skirting. Trim off surplus veneer and sand the whole of the vertical surfaces to a finish. Place the whole of the assembly thus far completed to one side.

MOULDINGS
Take the 9mm/⅜" hardwood scotia moulding and sand down for the full length.

Take the main assembly and accurately measure along

the front upper surface of the skirting and then cut a suitable length from the scotia moulding and mitre at each end of this length. Fix in position using PVA adhesive and, if necessary, moulding pins. Cut lengths from the scotia moulding at least 25mm/1" greater than required for each of the side skirtings. Cut mitre at one end of each and offer up to the already fixed front scotia moulding. Fix in position in the same manner as the front scotia and neatly cut off any surplus at the rear of the side moulding.

Carefully re-sand the now fixed skirting moulding, paying particular attention to the mitred corners.

Take the remainder of the hardwood scotia moulding and form the cornice moulding at the top of the main assembly, working in a manner similar to that described for the skirting scotia.

Check over all fixed scotia mouldings and neatly punch in any pins, and fill; sand down when dry.

FINISHING & FINAL ASSEMBLY
Next, take the insertion movement and insert into the hole in the face of the assembly ensuring a good fit.

Remove the movement and put to one side until finishes for the case have been completed. Check over the whole of the case for blemishes and finger marks etc. Apply the finish of your choice; see Chapter 5 for guidance.

After finishes have been carried out on the case generally, take the 12mm/½" diameter dowel and sand down by hand the full circumference for the full length. Measure off against the completed case the lengths required for the columns. It should be noted that the length of each column should include the thickness of the column caps. Check that the cut length is a snug fit into the available space.

Take a short length of 38mm/1½" wide hardwood lath and drill 12mm/½" diameter holes to accept the ends of the columns as a tight fit. After drilling the holes in the lath, sand down over the whole length and mark out the column caps accurately to the sizes required. Cut out with a fret saw and sand down the cut edges. Glue the caps to each end of the columns with PVA adhesive. Check that the assembled column and caps are still a tight fit in the available space on the main clock case. Remove and finish to match the main case or select the alternative painted method described on the plan. Glue the columns in position on the main case.

Green baize or felt is then glued to the base of the clock to prevent scratches to polished surfaces.

Finally, push the insertion movement into place.

'Carter' Cutting List

COMPONENT	QUANTITY	SECTION	LENGTH
Backboard Laminate	1	18 × 128	199
	1	¾″ × 5″	7⅞″
Middle Laminate	1	18 × 128	199
	1	¾″ × 5″	7⅞″
Plinth Laminates — side pieces	2	18 × 25	36
	2	¾″ × 1″	1½″
Plinth Laminate — front piece	1	18 × 25	152
	1	¾″ × 1″	6″
Gable Scotia (Total Length)	1	9 × 9	282 minimum
	1	⅜″ × ⅜″	11¼″ minimum
Plinth Scotia (Total Length)	1	9 × 9	236 minimum
	1	⅜″ × ⅜″	9½″ minimum

Ostler' Cutting List

COMPONENT	QUANTITY	SECTION	LENGTH
Backboard laminate	1	18 × 164	235
	1	¾″ × 6½″	9¼″
Middle Laminate	1	18 × 164	235
	1	¾″ × 6½″	9¼″
Faceboard laminate — top piece	1	18 × 164	76
	1	¾″ × 6½″	3″
Faceboard Laminate — bottom piece	1	18 × 164	105
	1	¾″ × 6½″	4⅛″
Plinth Laminate — side pieces	2	18 × 37	54
	2	¾″ × 1½″	2¼″
Plinth laminate — front piece	1	18 × 37	188
	1	¾″ × 1½″	7½″
Scotia (Total Length)	1	9 × 9	640 minimum
	1	⅜″ × ⅜″	26″
Pillars/dowels	2	12 dia	105
	2	½″ dia	4⅛″
Pillar Caps	4	3 × 18	18
	4	⅛″ × ¾″	¾″
Optional Extra Laminate	1	18 × 164	235
(additional lengths of scotia & side piece	1	¾″ × 6½″	9¼″
Plinth laminates will be needed)			

Clock Components and Hardware (excluding screws and pins)

CLOCK MOVEMENTS — OPTIONS:
- 'Insertion Movement' (all-in-one movement/dial/bezel/glass/hands combination); 102mm/ 4″ outside diameter.
- Various designs and models available.

13.
Traditional Full Cased Wall Clock

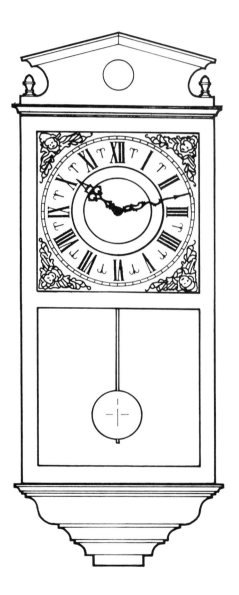

Most early wall clocks were uncased but it soon became obvious that movements should be protected from dust and pendulums from inquisitive fingers. Thus the full cased design emerged.

The design detailed here is typical of that period. Construction is easy and includes a method for building the door without joints or rebates.

A quartz pendulum movement may be used with a brass dial.

Overall dimensions: 225 wide × 100 deep × 630mm high
8⅞″ wide × 4″ deep × 24¾″ high.

Skill level ***

Schedule of Operations

CONSTRUCTION

Because this clock case has glass in the bottom of the door, a procedure is outlined below on the assumption that construction will be carried out in prefinished sub-assemblies.

Cut out the various plywood items in the Cutting List. Do not try to saw these to final sizes since some splintering will be encountered on sawn edges.

Carefully mark out on each rough component the final sizes given on the drawing and plane to those sizes. It is suggested that the two cheekboards are planed as a pair to ensure identical dimensions.

SHAPING CRESTBOARD

Refer to the profile on the plan and draw out the crestboard.

After cutting the straight edges with a tenon or similar saw, cut out the profiles with a fret saw, using a fine toothed blade. If a hand saw is used, take great care to ensure that the saw is held perfectly upright.

Clean the cut edges with a sanding block and abrasive paper, just sufficiently to remove any saw kerfs.

TOP AND BOTTOM BOARDS

Mark out and plane to final size the top and bottom boards. Check the lengths of the boards, one against the other to ensure they are identical.

The top board is not veneered as all surfaces are either hidden or are covered with moulding.

Veneer the top (inside) surface of the bottom board with decorative veneer and trim off surplus veneer. The other surfaces of the bottom board are not veneered at this stage. Sand the inner face to finish with a sanding block and progressively finer abrasive paper and set to one side for the later application of finishes.

VENEERING CHEEKBOARDS

Take the cheekboards which you have already planed to final size and veneer the inner faces only with a matching decorative veneer and trim off surplus veneer. Veneer the rear cut edges with a balancing veneer and trim off surplus. Sand to a finish as described and set aside for later use.

The outer faces and the front cut edge of the cheekboards are to be veneered *after* assembly and the upper and lower edges remain unveneered.

BACKBOARD

Mark out the height of the backboard on the rough sawn component to the dimension given on the drawing. The width of the backboard should be taken as the length of the bottom board less the thickness of the two cheekboards. It is as well to check this carefully against the actual components that you have already made. Having done this, plane the backboard to size.

Veneer the rear face of the backboard with a balancing veneer and trim off surplus. Veneer the front face of the backboard with decorative veneer (Note: a vertical book match would look well here). Trim off surplus and sand to a finish. Note that it is not necessary to veneer the edges of the backboard but veneer to the cut edges of the access hole in the upper centre of the backboard would look well.

FINISHING CASE COMPONENTS

The best finish to use is french polish but pleasing results may be obtained with varnish, cellulose or polyurethane finishes. Before applying finishes to the case components carefully mark out the areas which will accept glue in the final assembly and cover these with cellotape before applying finish.

CARCASS ASSEMBLY

Using the backboard as a 'keel' place it flat on a clean bench surface and offer up the cheekboards and the top and bottom boards 'dry' to check for squareness.

Carefully mark out for and drill the screw holes and clearance holes for attachment of the top and bottom boards to the cheekboards.

Making sure that you have screws and glueblocks to hand, glue and screw the cheekboards to the top and bottom boards without tightening the screws finally home. It is suggested that PVA adhesive is the best for this. Glue the edges of the backboard and insert in position. Tighten up the screws and glue and place in position the glue blocks to the backboard. Set the whole assembly to one side for the adhesive to harden, preferably overnight.

DIAL-BOARD

Carefully measure inside the case assembly to ascertain the size needed for the dial-board and plane to size. Mark out on the dial-board the exact position that the spindle of the movement will take up. Note: This will be central left to right but not top to bottom. Ascertain the diameter of the fixing bush of the movement and drill a hole of that size.

In the case assembly mark the position to be taken by the dial-board and insert glue blocks. When these are set hard offer up the dial-board and fix to the glueblocks with PVA.

It should be noted that the margins of the dial-board will project beyond the edges of the brass dial and those margins should be painted matt black before fixing the dial-board.

VENEER OUTSIDE CASE ASSEMBLY

Veneer the under surface of the bottom board and trim off surplus. Note that although the majority of this will be covered by the pendant base, it is best to use decorative veneer here.

Veneer the front edge of bottom board with decorative veneer set cross banded and trim off surplus.

Veneer the front edge of cheekboards with decorative veneer and trim off surplus.

Veneer the sides of the cheekboards with matched grain decorative veneers. Trim off surplus and sand all surfaces to a finish.

DOOR

Use the assembled case to measure the size required for the door members and mark those dimensions on to both the plywood door layers and plane as a pair to those dimensions. Mark out on each layer the size of the apertures for glazing and cut these accurately with a fret saw.

Glue and cramp the two components together. Clean up any surplus glue and leave to set hard before veneering.

Veneer the outer and inner cut edges of the door sub-assembly with decorative veneer. Trim off surplus and veneer the front and inside faces with decorative veneer. Trim off and sand the whole of the door sub-assembly to a finish.

Apply finishes to the door before marking out for and chopping in the brass hinges. Also chop in the hinges to the case assembly. Remove the hinges before glazing the door.

VENEERING CRESTBOARD

Clean up as necessary cut edges of the crestboard and apply a common veneer to the rear face. Trim off surplus veneer and apply decorative veneer crossbanded to the cut edges. Trim off surplus and then apply decorative veneer bookmatched to the front face. Trim off surplus and sand all faces to a finish.

Apply finishes to all veneered surfaces, except where moulding is to be glued, and to the rest of the case.

SCOTIA MOULDINGS

The scotia mouldings specified are standard DIY type mouldings. If you are unable to get these in a matching timber to the wood chosen for the veneers it will be necessary to stain the scotias to a similar colour.

Pre-sand the scotias in long lengths, staining them if necessary. It is best to apply finishes to the total lengths of scotia before cutting.

Cut the pre-finished scotias to the lengths required, mitring at intersections. Glue in position on the crestboard and, where indicated on the drawings, to the bottom and topboards.

PENDANT BASE

The pendant base is built as a separate assembly, pre-finished and fixed to the main case with dowels and glue.

Mark out and plane to size the baseboards for the pendant base checking each one against the relevant moulding for thickness.

Working face down on the bench, fix baseboard B to baseboard A with adhesive and 25mm/ 1″ panel pins. Fix baseboard C to baseboard B and baseboard D to baseboard C in a similar manner.

Cut the mouldings to length with neat mitres at intersections. Fix to the edges of baseboards with adhesive and pins neatly punched home. Fill the resultant holes with proprietary filler. Sand down and ensure that there is a good junction where scotia and quadrant meet.

Where scotia and quadrant meet veneer as indicated on the drawing starting with the side faces and ending with the front face.

Mark out for, drill for and glue in position the fixing dowels as shown on the drawings.

Sand all surfaces to a finish and apply final finishes before attaching to the base of the main case.

BRASSWARE

Carefully mark out for and drill pilot holes in the crestboard to accept the decorative brass finials.

Fix the dial in position on the dial-board and fix the body of the quartz movement by means of the fixing bush and fit the hands.

Screw in position the brass plate which is to act as a suspension hook.

Hang the door after cleaning the glass on both sides.

Screw the brass finials in position. Hang the pendulum and set up the clock in its final position.

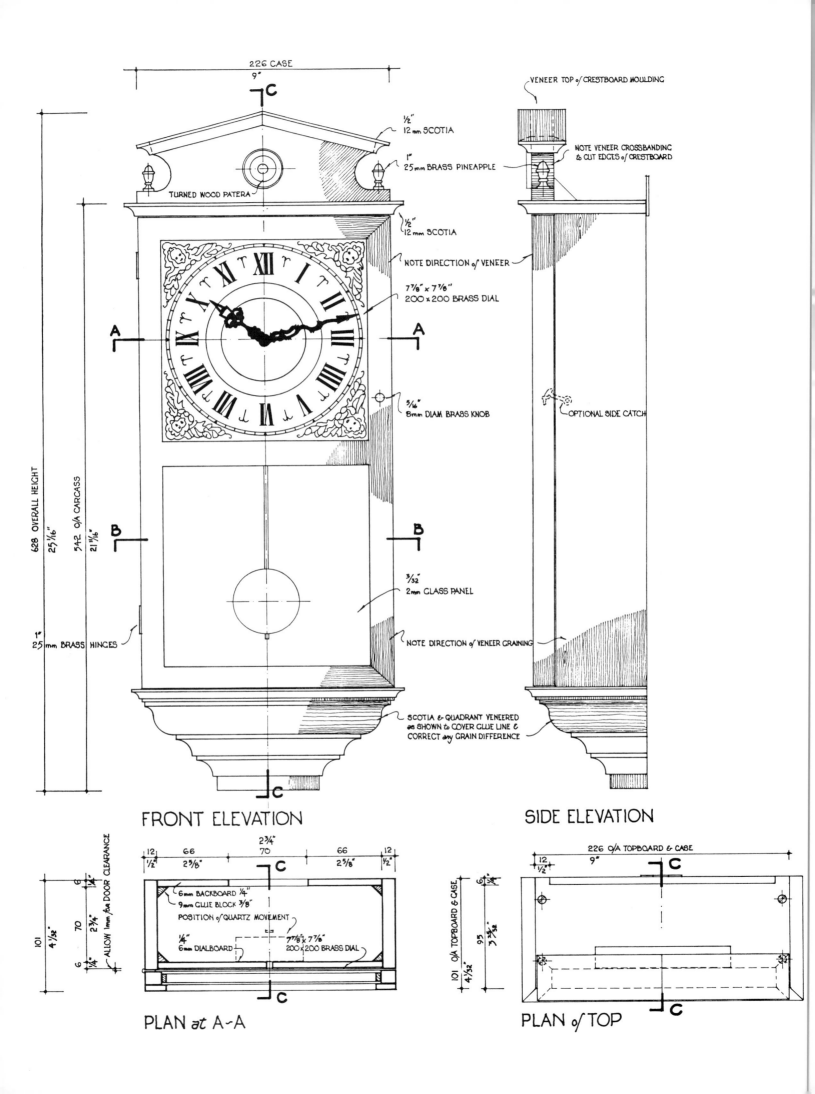

226 CASE
9"

½"
12 mm SCOTIA

1"
25mm BRASS PINEAPPLE

TURNED WOOD PATERA

NOTE VENEER TOP of CRESTBOARD MOULDING

NOTE VENEER CROSSBANDING
to CUT EDGES of CRESTBOARD

½"
12 mm SCOTIA

NOTE DIRECTION of VENEER

7⅞" x 7⅞"
200 x 200 BRASS DIAL

5/16"
8mm DIAM BRASS KNOB

OPTIONAL SIDE CATCH

3/32"
2mm GLASS PANEL

628 OVERALL HEIGHT
25 5/16"

542 O/A CARCASS
21 11/16"

1"
25mm BRASS HINGES

NOTE DIRECTION of VENEER GRAINING

SCOTIA & QUADRANT VENEERED
as SHOWN to COVER GLUE LINE &
CORRECT any GRAIN DIFFERENCE

FRONT ELEVATION

SIDE ELEVATION

2¾"
70

12   66   66   12
½"   2⅝"   2⅝" ½"

101
4⅛"

70
2¾"

6
¼"

6
¼"

ALLOW 1mm for DOOR CLEARANCE

6mm BACKBOARD ¼"
9mm GLUE BLOCK 3/8"

POSITION of QUARTZ MOVEMENT

¼"
6mm DIALBOARD

7⅞" x 7⅞"
200 x 200 BRASS DIAL

PLAN at A-A

226 O/A TOPBOARD & CASE
9"

12 ½"

101 O/A TOPBOARD & CASE
4⅛"

95
3 23/32"

6
¼"

PLAN of TOP

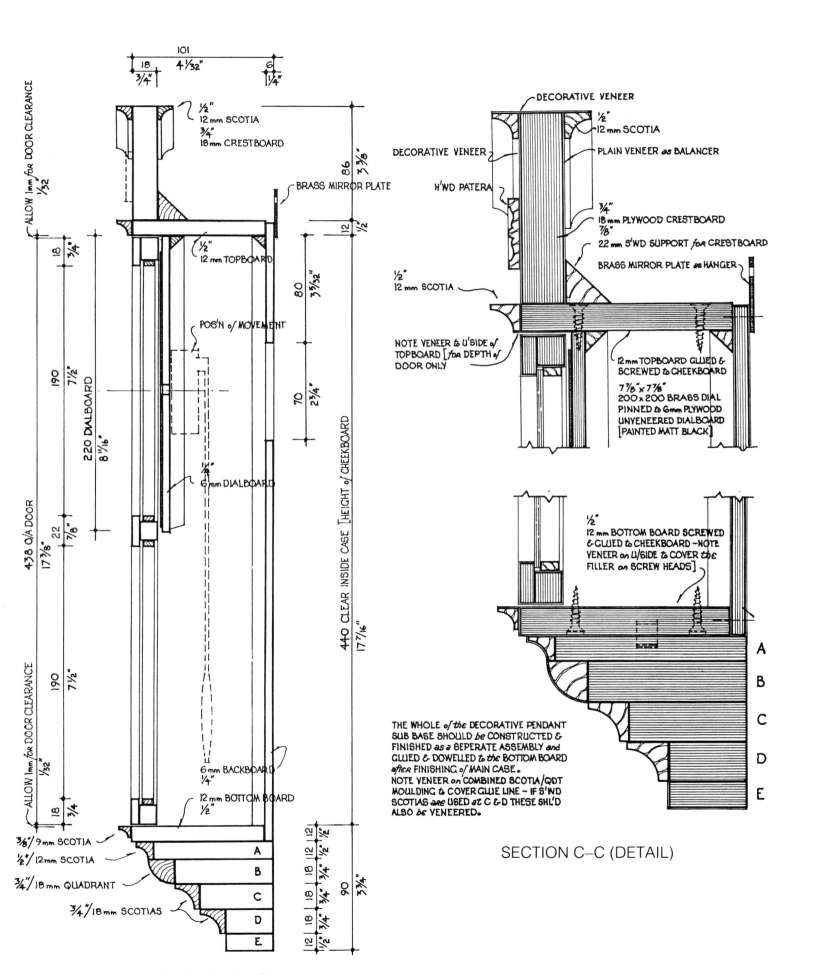

SECTION C-C

101
18 — ¾"
4 1/32"
6 — ¼"

½" 12mm SCOTIA
¾" 18mm CRESTBOARD

BRASS MIRROR PLATE

86 — 3⅜"

ALLOW 1mm for DOOR CLEARANCE 1/32"

18 — ¾"

½" 12mm TOPBOARD

12 — ½"

80 — 3 5/32"

190 — 7½"

POS'N of MOVEMENT

70 — 2¾"

220 DIALBOARD — 8 11/16"

¼" 6mm DIALBOARD

440 CLEAR INSIDE CASE [HEIGHT of CHEEKBOARD] 17 7/16"

438 O/A DOOR — 17⅜"

22 — ⅞"

190 — 7½"

¼" 6mm BACKBOARD

ALLOW 1mm for DOOR CLEARANCE 1/32"

12mm BOTTOM BOARD ½"

18 — ¾"

⅜" / 9mm SCOTIA
½" / 12mm SCOTIA
¾" / 18mm QUADRANT
¾" / 18mm SCOTIAS

A
B
C
D
E

12 — ½"
12 — ½"
18 — ¾"
18 — ¾"
18 — ¾"
12 — ½"

90 — 3¾"

SECTION C-C (DETAIL)

DECORATIVE VENEER

½" 12mm SCOTIA

DECORATIVE VENEER

PLAIN VENEER as BALANCER

H'WD PATERA

¾" 18mm PLYWOOD CRESTBOARD

⅞" 22mm S'WD SUPPORT for CRESTBOARD

BRASS MIRROR PLATE as HANGER

½" 12mm SCOTIA

NOTE VENEER to U'SIDE of TOPBOARD [for DEPTH of DOOR ONLY]

12mm TOPBOARD GLUED & SCREWED to CHEEKBOARD

7⅞" x 7⅞"
200 x 200 BRASS DIAL PINNED to 6mm PLYWOOD UNVENEERED DIALBOARD [PAINTED MATT BLACK]

½" 12mm BOTTOM BOARD SCREWED & GLUED to CHEEKBOARD — NOTE VENEER on U/SIDE to COVER the FILLER on SCREW HEADS]

A
B
C
D
E

THE WHOLE of the DECORATIVE PENDANT SUB BASE SHOULD be CONSTRUCTED & FINISHED as a SEPERATE ASSEMBLY and GLUED & DOWELLED to the BOTTOM BOARD after FINISHING of MAIN CASE.
NOTE VENEER on COMBINED SCOTIA/QDT MOULDING to COVER GLUE LINE — IF S'WD SCOTIAS are USED at C & D THESE SHL'D ALSO be VENEERED.

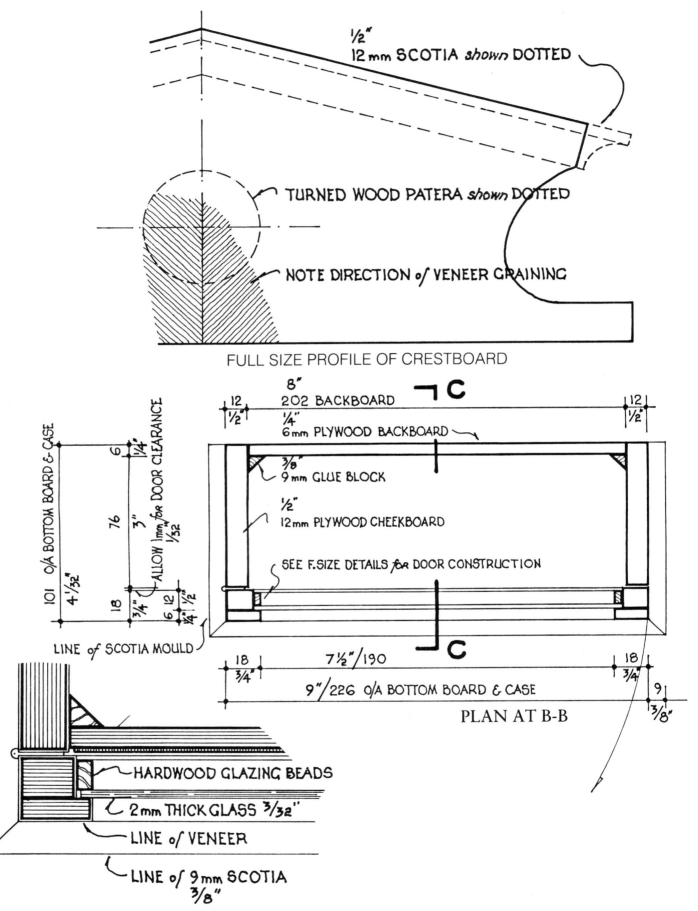

½"
12 mm SCOTIA *shown* DOTTED

TURNED WOOD PATERA *shown* DOTTED

NOTE DIRECTION *of* VENEER GRAINING

FULL SIZE PROFILE OF CRESTBOARD

8"
202 BACKBOARD

12
½"

12
½"

¬C

¼"
6 mm PLYWOOD BACKBOARD

⅜"
9 mm GLUE BLOCK

½"
12 mm PLYWOOD CHEEKBOARD

SEE F.SIZE DETAILS *for* DOOR CONSTRUCTION

O/A BOTTOM BOARD & CASE

6
¼"

76
3"

ALLOW 1 mm *for* DOOR CLEARANCE
1/32

101   O/A BOTTOM BOARD & CASE
4 1/32"

18
¾"

6 12
¼" ½"

LINE *of* SCOTIA MOULD

└C

18
¾"

7½"/190

18
¾"

9
⅜"

9"/226 O/A BOTTOM BOARD & CASE

PLAN AT B-B

HARDWOOD GLAZING BEADS

2 mm THICK GLASS 3/32"

LINE *of* VENEER

LINE *of* 9 mm SCOTIA
⅜"

FULL SIZE PLAN AT A–A (DETAIL FOR DOOR CONSTRUCTION)

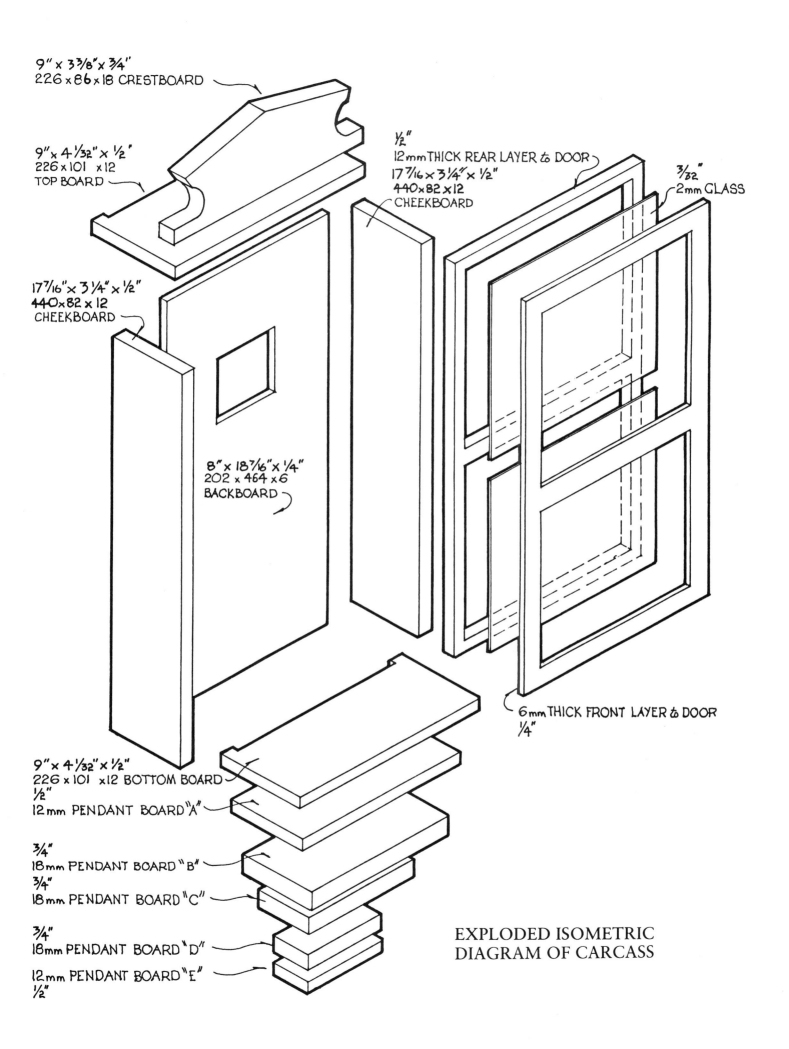

9" x 3 3/8" x 3/4"
226 x 86 x 18 CRESTBOARD

9" x 4 1/32" x 1/2"
226 x 101 x 12
TOP BOARD

1/2"
12mm THICK REAR LAYER to DOOR
17 7/16" x 3 1/4" x 1/2"
440 x 82 x 12
CHEEKBOARD

3/32"
2mm GLASS

17 7/16" x 3 1/4" x 1/2"
440 x 82 x 12
CHEEKBOARD

8" x 18 7/16" x 1/4"
202 x 464 x 6
BACKBOARD

6mm THICK FRONT LAYER to DOOR
1/4"

9" x 4 1/32" x 1/2"
226 x 101 x 12 BOTTOM BOARD
1/2"
12mm PENDANT BOARD "A"

3/4"
18mm PENDANT BOARD "B"
3/4"
18mm PENDANT BOARD "C"

3/4"
18mm PENDANT BOARD "D"

12mm PENDANT BOARD "E"
1/2"

EXPLODED ISOMETRIC
DIAGRAM OF CARCASS

Cutting list

COMPONENT	QUANTITY	SECTION	LENGTH
Top Board	1	12 × 101	226
	1	½″ × 4¹⁄₃₂″	9″
Bottom Board	1	12 × 101	226
	1	½″ × 4¹⁄₃₂″	9″
Cheekboards	2	12 × 82	440
	2	½″ × 3¼″	17⁷⁄₁₆″
Backboard	1	6 × 202	464
	1	¼″ × 8″	18⁷⁄₁₆″
Dial-board	1	6 × 202	220
	1	¼″ × 8″	8¹¹⁄₁₆″
Inner Layer of Door	1	12 × 226	438
	1	½″ × 9″	17³⁄₈″
Outer Layer of Door	1	6 × 226	438
	1	¼″ × 9″	17³⁄₈″
Crestboard	1	18 × 86	226
	1	¾″ × 3³⁄₈″	9″
Pendant Board A	1	12 × 86	196
	1	½″ × 3⁷⁄₁₆″	7¾″
Pendant Base B	1	18 × 71	166
	1	¾″ × 2¹³⁄₁₆″	6½″
Pendant Board C	1	18 × 53	130
	1	¾″ × 2¹⁄₁₆″	5″
Pendant Board D	1	18 × 35	94
	1	¾″ × 1⁵⁄₁₆″	3½″
Pendant Board E	1	12 × 35	94
	1	½″ × 1⁵⁄₁₆″	3½″
Crestboard Scotia (Total Length)	1	12 × 12	564 minimum
	1	½″ × ½″	22½″ minimum
Top Board Scotia (Total Length)	1	12 × 12	476 minimum
	1	½″ × ½″	19¹⁄₁₆″ minimum
Bottom Board Scotia (Total Length)	1	12 × 12	476 minimum
	1	½″ × ½″	19¹⁄₁₆″ minimum
Pendant Board A Scotia (Total Length)	1	12 × 12	416 minimum
	1	½″ × ½″	16⁵⁄₈″ minimum
Pendant Board B Quadrant (Total Length)	1	18 × 18	380 minimum
	1	¾″ × ¾″	15¹⁄₈″
Pendant Board C Scotia (Total Length)	1	18 × 18	308 minimum
	1	¾″ × ¾″	12¹⁄₈″ minimum
Pendant Board D Scotia (Total Length)	1	18 × 18	236 minimum
	1	¾″ × ¾″	9¹⁄₈″ minimum

Glue Block Triangles	1	9 × 9	1730
	1	⅜″ × ⅜″	68⅛″
Glazing Beads	1	3 × 8	1328
	1	⅛″ × ⁵⁄₁₆″	52¾″
Turned Patera	1	5 × 22 dia	—
	1	³⁄₁₆″ × ⅞″ dia	—

Clock Components and Hardware (excluding screws and pins)

CLOCK MOVEMENT — OPTIONS:

1. Mechanical movements.
   Spring Driven.
   Maximum length from centres of handshaft to pendulum bob: 245mm/ 9⅝″.
   Maximum pendulum swing: 190mm/ 7½″.
   Maximum 'plate size' (front face of movement): 165 × 165mm/ 6½″ × 6½″.
   Depth of movement: variable according to make — adjust depth of box if necessary.
   Handshaft: check length and adjust thickness of dial-board, if necessary.

2. Quartz Pendulum Movements:
   Pendulum length from centres of handshaft to pendulum bob: 245mm/ 9⅝″.
   Maximum pendulum swing: 190mm/ 7½″.
   Chime/melody movements also available.
   Handshaft/fixing nut length: to suit 6–8mm/ ¼″ – ⁵⁄₁₆″ dial-board and dial thickness.

CLOCK DIAL — OPTIONS:

- 200 × 200mm/ 7⅞″ × 7⅞″ square dial.
- Solid brass, alloy, aluminium and hand painted models available.
- Note: If front winding mechanical movement is used, drill holes in the dial and bush to accommodate winding keys.

CLOCK HANDS:

- Bushed to suit chosen mechanical or quartz movement.
- Length to suit dial size.
- Pattern to suit individual choice.

BRASSWARE:

- Hinges: one pair of 25mm/ 1″ butt hinges.
- Door Lock: one hook and eye or one concealed bullet catch.
- Door knob 8 or 9mm/ ⁵⁄₁₆″ or ⅜″ diameter.
- Two 25mm/ 1″ pineapple finials. Additional patterns: acorn, flame and urn.
- One mirror plate.

GLASS:

- Two panes to suit door.

14.
Traditional Half Cased Wall Clock

This traditionally designed half-cased wall clock has the advantage of protecting the modern quartz movement from dust while, at the same time, leaving the pendulum free as a 'wag on the wall' conversation piece. The swinging pendulum cannot be put out of adjustment by accident or intent.

Construction is simple and uses standard DIY mouldings and plain veneers of your choice.

Overall dimensions: 225 wide × 100 deep × 553mm high
8⅞″ wide ×   4″ deep × 21¾″ high.

Skill level ***

Schedule of Operations

PREPARATION

Cut out the various plywood items to size. Do not try to saw these to final sizes since some splintering will be encountered on sawn edges.

Carefully mark out on each rough component the final sizes given on the drawing and plane to those sizes. It is suggested that the two cheekboards are planed as a pair to ensure identical dimensions.

SHAPING CASE MEMBERS

Refer to the profiles on the drawing for the backboard and the cheekboards and mark these out on to the components.

Cut out the profiles with a fret saw. If a hand saw is being used take great care to ensure that the saw is held perfectly upright. Clean the cut edges with medium abrasive paper just sufficiently to remove any saw kerfs.

VENEERING IN GENERAL

For a comparatively small sized project such as this, it is suggested that the best adhesive to use with the veneers is a contact adhesive applied in accordance with the maker's instructions.

Inspect your sheets of veneer and select areas of matching grain where this is obviously important — Eg the inside faces of the cheekboards.

When cutting areas of veneer from a larger sheet always cut oversize and trim back after gluing in position. Use a craft knife with a new blade and a steel straight edge or ruler. Make a number of light cuts, in particular when cutting across the grain.

Do not apply veneer to any plywood surface without using a balancing veneer on the opposite surface. Any common veneer will serve that purpose.

TOP AND BOTTOM BOARDS

Mark out and plane to final size the top and bottom boards. Check the length of each board, one against the other to ensure they are identical.

Measure the quartz movement and find the exact position that the pendulum rod will take. To the bottom board mark that position and cut out a slot.

Veneer the front and side sawn edges only of the top board with decorative veneer laid cross banded. Trim off and sand to a finish.

Veneer the front edge only of the bottom board with decorative veneer and trim off surplus veneer.

Veneer the top face of the bottom board with common veneer and trim off surplus.

Carefully veneer the underside of the bottom board with decorative veneer and trim off.

Sand off all veneered surfaces and set aside for finishing.

VENEERING BACKBOARD

Sand the rear and front faces of the backboard with a medium abrasive paper sufficiently to achieve a smooth bed for the veneers.

With common veneer, face up the rear of the backboard using a contact adhesive.

Trim the surplus veneer back to the sawn edge of the backboard with a craft knife. A fine file may be used to remove any minor projections of veneer.

Veneer the sawn edges of the back board with decorative veneer laid as a cross banding, as previously described.

Veneer the front face of the back board with decorative veneer. When you trim off surplus veneer make sure that the cross banding on the edges is not damaged.

Sand all veneered surfaces to a finish, using progressively finer grades of abrasive paper and a sanding block. Work only in the direction of the grain. Set aside for later finish.

VENEERING CHEEKBOARDS

Veneer the rear cut edges of the cheekboards with common veneer and trim off as described previously.

Using decorative matching veneers veneer the inside faces of the cheekboards and trim off as described.

Using decorative matching veneers veneer the outer faces of the cheekboards and trim off.

Veneer the whole of the front edges of the cheekboards with decorative veneer laid as cross banding and take particular care with the shaped areas. Trim off surplus veneer.

As described for the backboard, sand all faces and set aside for later finishes.

FINISHING CASE COMPONENTS

The best finish to use is french polish but pleasing results may be obtained with varnish, cellulose or polyurethane finishes. In the latter cases, grain fill the wood before you apply the initial coat (which should be flowed on rather than brushed in). When this first coat has dried hard flat

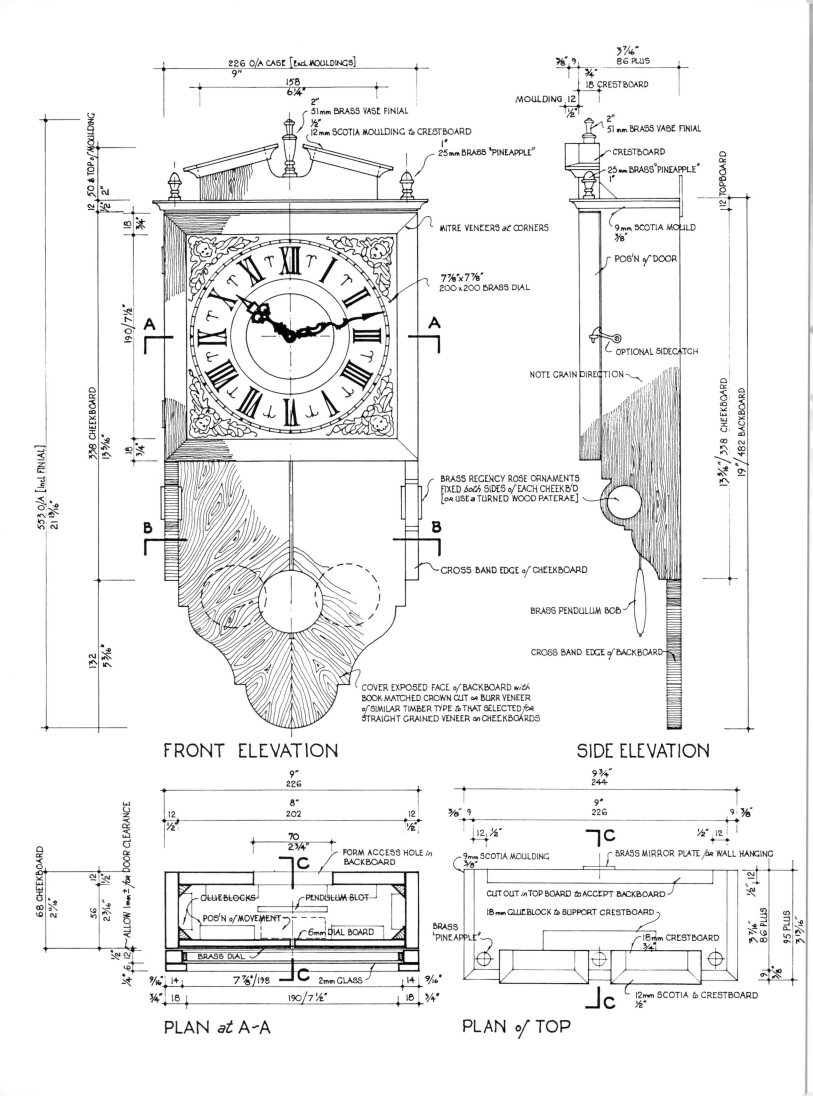

226 O/A CASE [excl MOULDINGS]
9"
158
6¼"

2"
51mm BRASS VASE FINIAL
½"
12mm SCOTIA MOULDING to CRESTBOARD
1"
25mm BRASS "PINEAPPLE"

3⁷⁄₁₆"
86 PLUS
⅜" 9
¾"
18 CRESTBOARD
MOULDING 12
½"

2"
51mm BRASS VASE FINIAL
CRESTBOARD
25mm BRASS "PINEAPPLE"
1"
12 TOPBOARD

50 to TOP o/ MOULDING
12 ½" 2"
18 ¾"

MITRE VENEERS at CORNERS

9mm SCOTIA MOULD
⅜"

POS'N o/ DOOR

7⅞"x7⅞"
200 x 200 BRASS DIAL

190/7½"

A ⊣ ⊢ A

OPTIONAL SIDECATCH

NOTE GRAIN DIRECTION

18 ¾"

BRASS REGENCY ROSE ORNAMENTS
FIXED both SIDES o/ EACH CHEEKB'D
[or USE a TURNED WOOD PATERAE]

B ⊣ ⊢ B

CROSS BAND EDGE o/ CHEEKBOARD

338 CHEEKBOARD
13⁵⁄₁₆"

13⁵⁄₁₆"/338 CHEEKBOARD
19"/482 BACKBOARD

553 O/A [incl FINIAL]
21¹³⁄₁₆"

BRASS PENDULUM BOB

CROSS BAND EDGE o/ BACKBOARD

132
5³⁄₁₆"

COVER EXPOSED FACE o/ BACKBOARD with
BOOK MATCHED CROWN CUT or BURR VENEER
o/ SIMILAR TIMBER TYPE to THAT SELECTED for
STRAIGHT GRAINED VENEER on CHEEKBOARDS

FRONT ELEVATION

SIDE ELEVATION

9"
226
8"
202
12 ½"   12 ½"

70
2¾"

FORM ACCESS HOLE in
BACKBOARD

9¾"
244
9"
226
⅜" 9   9 ⅜"
12 ½"   ½" 12

9mm SCOTIA MOULDING
⅜"
BRASS MIRROR PLATE for WALL HANGING

CUT OUT in TOP BOARD to ACCEPT BACKBOARD

18mm GLUEBLOCK to SUPPORT CRESTBOARD

68 CHEEKBOARD
2¹¹⁄₁₆"

12 ½"
56
2³⁄₁₆"

ALLOW 1mm ± for DOOR CLEARANCE

GLUEBLOCKS
PENDULUM SLOT
POS'N o/ MOVEMENT
6mm DIAL BOARD
BRASS DIAL

½" 12
¼" 6

9⁄₁₆" 14   14 9⁄₁₆"
¾" 18   7⅞"/198   18 ¾"
190/7½"

2mm GLASS

BRASS
"PINEAPPLE"

18mm CRESTBOARD
¾"

12mm SCOTIA to CRESTBOARD
½"

½" 12
3⁷⁄₁₆"
86 PLUS
95 PLUS
3¹³⁄₁₆"
9 ⅜"

PLAN at A-A

PLAN o/ TOP

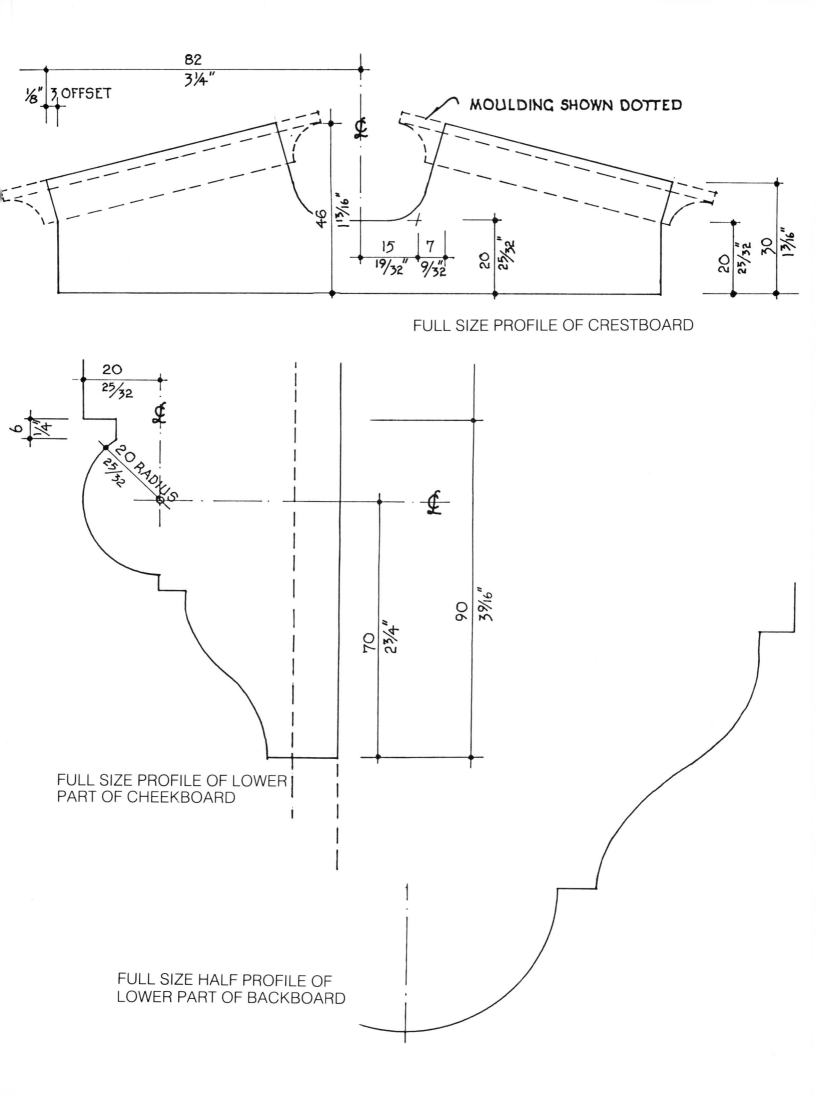

82
3¼"

⅛" 3 OFFSET

MOULDING SHOWN DOTTED

46
1¹⁵/₁₆"

15
19/32"

7
9/32"

20
25/32"

20
25/32"

30
1³/₁₆"

FULL SIZE PROFILE OF CRESTBOARD

20
25/32"

6
¼"

20 RADIUS
25/32

70
2³/₄"

90
3⁹/₁₆"

FULL SIZE PROFILE OF LOWER
PART OF CHEEKBOARD

FULL SIZE HALF PROFILE OF
LOWER PART OF BACKBOARD

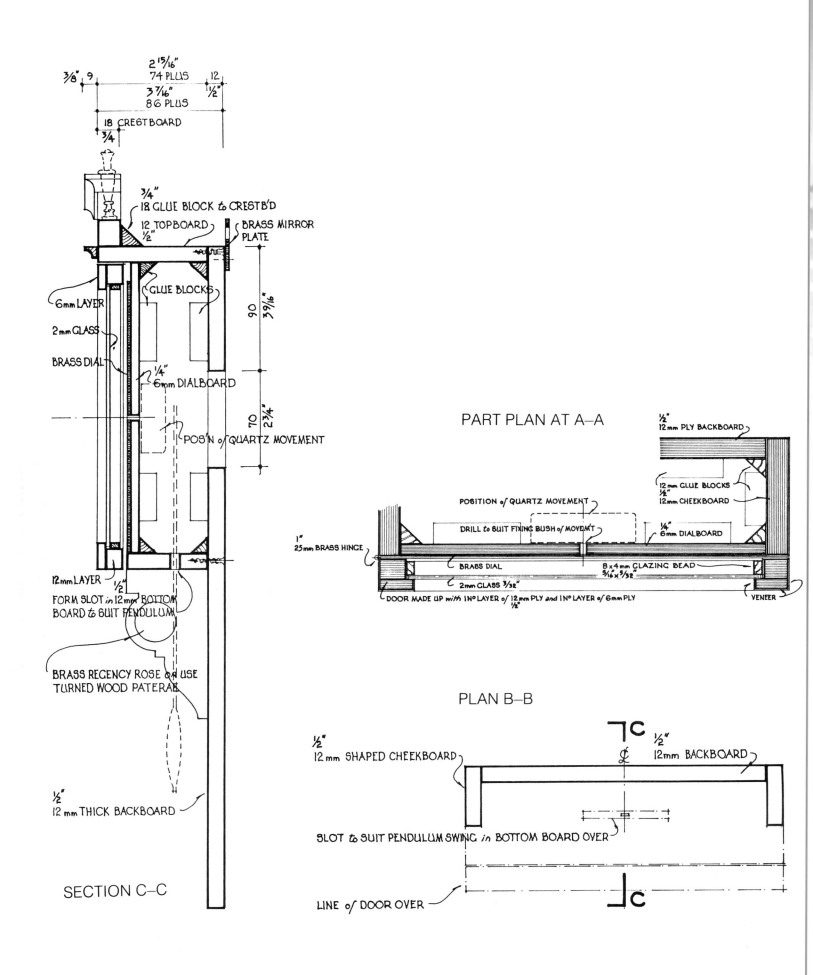

2 15/16"
74 PLUS

12
1/2"

3/8" 9

3 7/16"
86 PLUS

18 CRESTBOARD
3/4"

3/4"
18 GLUE BLOCK to CRESTB'D

12 TOPBOARD
1/2"

BRASS MIRROR PLATE

GLUE BLOCKS

6mm LAYER

2mm GLASS

BRASS DIAL

1/4"
6mm DIALBOARD

90
3 9/16"

70
2 3/4"

POS'N of QUARTZ MOVEMENT

12mm LAYER
1/2"

FORM SLOT in 12mm BOTTOM BOARD to SUIT PENDULUM

BRASS REGENCY ROSE or USE TURNED WOOD PATERAE

1/2"
12mm THICK BACKBOARD

SECTION C–C

PART PLAN AT A–A

1/2"
12mm PLY BACKBOARD

POSITION of QUARTZ MOVEMENT

12 mm GLUE BLOCKS
1/2"
12mm CHEEKBOARD

DRILL to SUIT FIXING BUSH of MOVEM'T

1/4"
6mm DIALBOARD

1"
25mm BRASS HINGE

BRASS DIAL

8 x 4mm GLAZING BEAD
5/16" x 5/32"

2mm GLASS 3/32"

DOOR MADE UP with 1No LAYER of 12mm PLY and 1No LAYER of 6mm PLY
1/2"

VENEER

PLAN B–B

1/2"
12mm SHAPED CHEEKBOARD

C

₵

1/2"
12mm BACKBOARD

SLOT to SUIT PENDULUM SWING in BOTTOM BOARD OVER

LINE of DOOR OVER

C

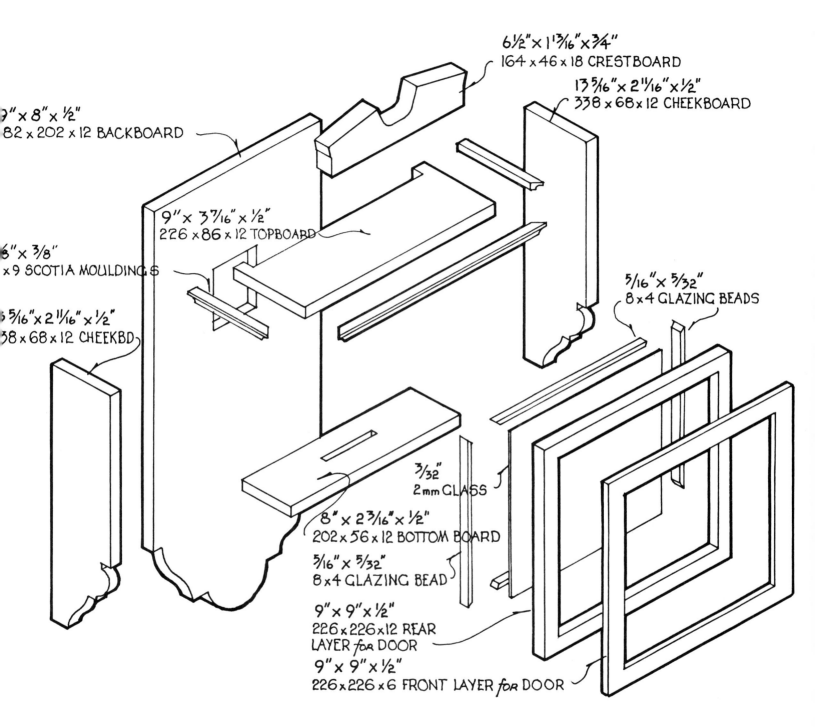

6½" × 1¹³⁄₁₆" × ¾"
164 x 46 x 18 CRESTBOARD

13⁵⁄₁₆" × 2¹¹⁄₁₆" × ½"
338 x 68 x 12 CHEEKBOARD

9" × 8" × ½"
82 x 202 x 12 BACKBOARD

9" × 3⁷⁄₁₆" × ½"
226 x 86 x 12 TOPBOARD

6" × ⅜"
x 9 SCOTIA MOULDINGS

⁵⁄₁₆" × 2¹¹⁄₁₆" × ½"
38 x 68 x 12 CHEEKBD

⁵⁄₁₆" × ⁵⁄₃₂"
8 x 4 GLAZING BEADS

3⁄32"
2mm GLASS

8" × 2³⁄₁₆" × ½"
202 x 56 x 12 BOTTOM BOARD

⁵⁄₁₆" × ⁵⁄₃₂"
8 x 4 GLAZING BEAD

9" × 9" × ½"
226 x 226 x 12 REAR
LAYER for DOOR

9" × 9" × ½"
226 x 226 x 6 FRONT LAYER for DOOR

EXPLODED ISOMETRIC DIAGRAM
[NOTE:- GLUE BLOCKS, CREST MOULDINGS & DIALBOARD OMITTED FOR CLARITY

down with grade 0000 wire wool, working in the direction of the grain. Repeat the process until satisfactory results are obtained. Flat down the final coat and apply solid wax polish to obtain a final gloss.

Before applying finishes to the case components carefully mark out the portions which will accept glue in the final assembly process and cover these with cellotape before applying finish.

CARCASS ASSEMBLY

Using the backboard as the 'keel' place it flat on a clean bench surface and offer up the top and bottom boards and the cheekboards 'dry' for a trial assembly. The glue blocks should be ready at hand.

When you are satisfied that the case is truly square in the dry trial, take the assembly apart. Using a PVA adhesive glue the cheekboards and the relevant glue blocks to the backboard. Before these members have set glue the top-board and bottomboard in position and cramp up the whole to set hard.

DIAL-BOARD

Carefully measure inside the case assembly to ascertain the size needed for the dial-board and plane component size. Mark out on the dial-board the exact position that the spindle of the movement will take up. Note: This will be central left to right but shouldn't be central top to bottom — refer to the drawing for this. Ascertain the diameter of the fixing bush of the quartz movement and drill a hole of that size.

In the case assembly mark out the position to be taken by the dial-board and insert glue blocks. when these are set hard offer up the dial-board and fix to the glue blocks with PVA.

It should be noted that the margins of the dial-board will project beyond the edges of the brass dial and those margins are best painted black before fixing the dial-board.

DOOR

Use the assembled case to measure the size required for the door. Mark out for this overall size on both the component door layers and plane as a pair to that size. Mark out on each layer the size of the apertures for glazing and cut these accurately with a fret saw.

Glue and cramp the two components together. Clean up any surplus glue and leave to set hard before veneering.

Veneer the outer and inner cut edges of the door sub-assembly with decorative veneer. Trim off surplus veneer and veneer the front and inside faces with decorative veneer. Trim off surplus veneer and sand the whole of the door assembly to a finish.

Apply finishes to the door before marking out for and chopping in the brass hinges. Also chop in these hinges to the case assembly. Remove the hinges before glazing the door.

CRESTBOARD

Refer to the plan and draw out the profiles on to the crestboard and plane to size before fretting the shapes. Clean up the cut edges and apply common veneer to the rear face. Trim off surplus veneer and apply the decorative veneer crossbanded to cut edges. Trim off surplus and apply decorative veneer to front face. Sand all veneer to a finish.

Apply finishes to all veneered surfaces except where scotia moulding is to be glued.

SCOTIA MOULDINGS

The scotia moulds specified are standard DIY type mouldings. If you are unable to get these in a matching timber to the wood chosen for the veneers it will be necessary to stain the scotias to a similar colour.

Pre-sand the scotias in long lengths and if necessary apply stain. It is best to apply finishes to the total lengths of scotia before cutting.

Cut the pre-finished scotias to the lengths required, mitring at intersections. Glue in position on the top board and crestboard.

BRASSWARE

Carefully mark out and drill pilot holes in the assembled case to accept the decorative items of brassware shown on the drawings.

Fix the dial in position on the dial-board and fix the body of the quartz movement by means of the fixing bush and fit the hands.

Screw in position the brass plate which is to act as a suspension hook.

Hang the door after cleaning the glass on both sides.

Screw all items of decorative brassware in position and set up the clock in its final position.

Cutting list

COMPONENT	QUANTITY	SECTION	LENGTH
Topboard	1	12 × 86	226
	1	½″ × 3⁷⁄₁₆″	9″
Bottomboard	1	12 × 56	202
	1	½″ × 2³⁄₁₆″	8″
Backboard	1	12 × 202	482
	1	½″ × 8″	19″
Cheekboards	2	12 × 68	338
	2	½″ × 2¹¹⁄₁₆″	13⁵⁄₁₆″
Crestboard	1	18 × 46	164
	1	¾″ × 1¹³⁄₁₆″	6½″
Inner Layer of Door	1	12 × 226	226
	1	½″ × 9″	9″
Outer Layer of Door	1	6 × 226	226
	1	¼″ × 9″	9″
Crestboard Scotia (Total Length)	1	12 × 12	300 minimum
	1	½″ × ½″	12″
Topboard Scotia (Total Length)	1	9 × 9	434 minimum
	1	⅜″ × ⅜″	17⅜″
Paterae	4	5 × 30 dia	–
	4	³⁄₁₆″ × 1³⁄₁₆″ dia	–

Clock Components and Hardware (excluding screws and pins)

CLOCK MOVEMENT — Options:

1. Mechanical movements.
   Spring Driven.
   Pendulum length from centres of handshaft to pendulum bob: 245mm/ 9⁵⁄₈″.
   Maximum pendulum swing: 190mm/ 7½″.
   Maximum 'plate size' (front face of movement): 165 × 165mm/ 6½″ × 6½″.
   Depth of movement: variable according to make — adjust depth of box and side profile, if necessary.
   Handshaft: check length and adjust thickness of dial-board, if necessary.

2. Quartz Pendulum Movements.
   Pendulum length from centres of handshaft to pendulum bob: 245mm/ 9⁵⁄₈″.
   Maximum pendulum swing: 190mm/ 7½″.
   Chiming/melody movements also available.
   Handshaft/fixing nut length: to suit 6–8mm/ ¼″ – ⁵⁄₁₆″ dial-board and dial thickness.

CLOCK DIAL — Options:

- 200 × 200mm/ 7⅞″ × 7⅞″ square dial.
- Drill holes in dial for front winding mechanical movement.
- Solid brass, alloy, aluminium and hand painted models.

BRASSWARE:

- Hinges: one pair of 25mm/ 1″ butt hinges.
- Door Lock: one hook and eye or one concealed bullet catch.

GLASS:

- To suit door.

CLOCK HANDS:

- Bushed to suit mechanical or quartz movement.
- Length to suit dial size.
- Pattern to suit individual choice.

- Two 25mm/ 1″ pineapple finials. Additional patterns: acorn, flame and urn. One 51mm/ 2″ vase finial.
- One mirror plate.

15. Vienna Regulator Clock

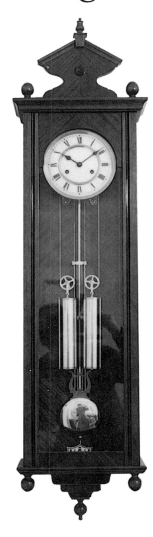

The Vienna Regulator clock is well known for its accurate time keeping and the originals are much in demand.

Well engineered replicas of original movements are freely available from retail horological suppliers. The drawings have been devised to suit no fewer than five movement types.

This plan faithfully reproduces the elegantly slim lines of the early regulator cases, but utilises only standard DIY wood mouldings. It is now possible for a replica of these famous clocks to be built by most woodworkers.

The clock may be constructed in mahogany or walnut.

Overall dimensions: 338 wide × 156 mm deep
13¼″ wide × 4⅛″ deep
(Height varies to suit movement)

Skill level ＊＊＊＊

Schedule of Operations

You will note from the drawings that this design is suitable for use with various sizes and makes of Vienna regulator movements. It will obviously be necessary at an early stage to decide which of these movements you intend to use and to adjust on the drawings any minor differences in dimensions. It is recommended that you obtain your movement before commencing any work on construction. Manufacturers do, from time to time, alter the specification of their products or even decide to withdraw a model from the market. They also use differing methods to calculate pendulum lengths. Always check dimensions against the actual movement before starting work.

CONSTRUCTION

The procedures outlined below are based on the assumption that construction is completed in sub-assemblies, all of which are prefinished before final assembly.

The recommended timber shown on the drawings is mahogany, but original Vienna clocks were often built in walnut. If you should opt for the latter timber, the standard mouldings may be treated with ferrous sulphate solution to colour the wood to tone in with walnut. This chemical is obtainable from most chemists in crystal form. Make up a weak solution with clean water and brush on to a test area of sanded scrap moulding to check for depth of colour. Allow the test area to dry and rinse with clean water. After drying, apply the finish you anticipate using on the completed case. it may be necessary to carry out several such tests before deciding on the final strength of the ferrous sulphate solution.

Cut out the various components, except mouldings, to the various sizes given in the cutting list. The sizes stated are actual finished sizes and allowance should be made for planing etc.

SIDELIGHTS

Take the sidelight components and plane to the cross sections required, working in pairs to ensure that the members are identical.

Form the rebates and stopped rebates as shown on the drawings.

Form the tenons at the extremities of the members, working in pairs to ensure they are identical, and then cut the mortices in the stiles to accept the tenons of the sidelight rails. Check the joints for tightness of fit and assemble dry to check for squareness of the two sub-assemblies.

Glue up and cramp the members of each sub-assembly using PVA adhesive. Any excess adhesive should be cleaned off immediately with a damp cloth. Put the sub-assemblies to one side for the adhesive to set hard, preferably overnight.

Sand down the sidelight sub-assemblies on all surfaces which will be exposed to view in the completed clock case, using progressively finer abrasive paper. Clean off all sanding dust and apply the finish of your choice. It is suggested that the best finish to use is french polish, but pleasing results may be obtained with varnish, polyurethane or cellulose finishes. In the latter cases, grain fill the timber before applying the initial coat which should be 'flowed on' rather than brushed in. Do not overwork the finish. When the first coat has dried hard, flat down with 0000 wire wool, working in the direction of the grain. Repeat the process until a satisfactory finish has been achieved. Flat down the final coat and apply a solid wax polish to obtain a final gloss. Carefully set aside the completed sidelights until required.

TOP & BOTTOM BOARDS

Take the top and bottom board components and check for size and squareness before carefully marking and forming the recesses at the rear of the boards which will later accept the backboard component. Sand down the top and bottom boards before applying veneers.

Veneers may be applied in the traditional manner using hot glue and a veneer hammer or, alternatively, by using an impact adhesive. Attention is particularly drawn to the grain directions that are indicated on the drawings for the surfaces which will be exposed to view in the completed clock case.

Veneer the upper surface of the bottom board with book matched veneer and trim off surplus veneer all round. Veneer the under surface of the bottom board in a similar manner. The whole of this latter surface should be veneered, notwithstanding the fact that a large portion of the veneer will ultimately by covered by the pendant sub-assembly. Veneer the edge of the bottom board with veneer set vertically as cross banding.

Veneer the under surface of the top board in a similar manner to the bottom board and cross band the edge.

Sand down the veneered surfaces at the top and bottom boards and carefully mark out for and form the mortices to accept the tenons of the sidelight sub-assemblies. Mark out for and form on the underside of the bottom board the blind holes to accept the dowel fixing of the pendant sub-assembly. Mark out for and form the recess on the top of the top board to accept the supporting strut of the crest board sub-assembly.

Cut to size and glue in position the packing pieces on the upper surface of the top board. These are best butt jointed rather than mitred at the intersections.

Apply finishes to the top and bottom boards in the manner used for the sidelight sub-assemblies and set to one side for later use.

BACK BOARD

Take the plywood component for the back board and check for size and squareness. Sand down before applying veneers. Veneer the rear surface of the back board with plain veneer to act as a balancer. Veneer the front surface of the back board with quarter matched veneers. (Note that the intersection of these veneers is not at the precise half height point of the back board.) Mark out for and drill the screw fixing holes and sand to a finish. Apply finish to the front face of the back board in the manner previously described.

CASE ASSEMBLY

Dry-assemble the sidelights and the top and bottom boards to check for squareness. Glue and cramp these members together. If necessary, pin temporary battens diagonally across the back of the members to hold them square while the glue is setting overnight.

After removing cramps, screw the back board in position and set the whole case assembly to one side.

DOOR

Take the frame components for the door and plane to size. Form the rebates and stopped rebates as shown on the drawings. form the through grooves on the face of the stiles.

Form the tenons at the ends of the top and bottom rails and mark out for and form the mortices in the stiles to accept the tenons just made. Assemble dry and check for squareness and size by offering up to the case assembly.

Carefully cut out the shape of the dial mask and, after sanding, veneer the rear face of the mask with plain veneer to act as a balancer. Veneer the front face of the mask with book matched veneer. Sand down and finish as previously described.

Offer up the dial mask to the dry assembled door framing and carefully mark out the additional width required in the stile glazing rebates to accommodate the thickness of the dial mask. Cut the increased rebate width required.

Glue up and cramp together the stiles and rails of the door but do not attempt to fix the dial mask at this stage. Check for squareness and set aside for the adhesive to set hard.

Sand down the stile/rail sub-assembly. Veneer the top return surface of the bottom rail, trim and then veneer the front face of the rail with book matched veneer. Veneer the vertical return faces of the stiles and trim off. Veneer the vertical front faces of the stiles and trim off. Clean up the trimmed edge of the front veneer where it abutts the vertical half round grooves in the stiles by the use of abrasive paper wrapped round a short length of dowel of suitable diameter. Sand all veneered surfaces and apply finishes as previously described. It will be noted that on the drawings the vertical grooves are described as being painted black. It is suggested that the black paint used is a flat paint applied after the application of the first coat of finish. In this way, any surplus paint which has trespassed onto the flat veneer surfaces may be wiped off without staining the wood surface. The subsequent coats of finish may then be carried across the painted surface.

On completion of the finishes to the stile/rail sub-assembly, position the dial mask in the widened glazing rebate and glue to the front face of the top rail.

Offer up the door sub-assembly to the case assembly and carefully mark out for the door hinges on the inside face of the stiles and the outer face of the sidelights. Chop out for the hinges, taking care to protect the finished surfaces of the two assemblies. The use of a piece of old blanket on the top of your work bench will be helpful here.

GLAZING

Carefully measure the sizes of glass required for the sidelights and the door, not forgetting to allow a little off the opening sizes to allow the glass to slide in without pressure. 2mm picture glass has been shown on the drawings since a thicker glass would look a little clumsy on the finished clock case.

Take the 6mm glazing bead lengths and cut to size to suit the openings, neatly mitring the intersections. Sand the beads to a finish and apply finish as last. Place the glass in position and fix the glazing beads with small brads, panel pins or veneer pins.

Screw the hinges in position and fix the brass side hook to the case, checking that the door hangs well. Remove the door and put it to one side until final assembly.

MOULDINGS & PENDANT SUB-ASSEMBLY

Take the lengths of solid mahogany moulding for the bottom board and cut to the lengths required, forming neat mitres at the intersections. Sand to a finish and apply finish as previously described. Fix in position with impact adhesive.

Take the lengths of softwood moulding for the top board and cut to size with neat mitres at the intersections. Sand as required and veneer the surfaces of the mouldings, sanding and finishing before fixing in position with impact adhesive. Set the whole of the case assembly to one side.

Take the components for the baseboard parts of the pendant sub-assembly and sand down. Check the sizes of the baseboards against the actual sections of the mouldings. It is essential that the sizes of baseboards A and B are such that an accurate marry is obtained between the coved and half-round mouldings. Working face down on the bench fix base board B to baseboard A with adhesive and 25mm/ 1″ panel pins. Fix baseboard C to baseboard B and baseboard D to baseboard C in a similar manner. After the adhesive has had time to set cut the softwood mouldings to length with neat mitres at the intersections. Fix into positions at the edges of the baseboards as shown on drawings using adhesive and veneer pins. Punch home pin heads and fill any resultant holes with a proprietory filler. Sand down, paying particular attention to the junction between the coved and half-round mouldings. The coved moulds are best sanded with abrasive paper wrapped round a dowel of suitable diameter.

Veneer the exposed edges of baseboard C with cross banded veneer. Veneer the faces of the coved and half-round mouldings with veneer laid lengthwise, starting with the side mouldings and finishing with the front mouldings, paying particular attention to the mitred edges of the mouldings. Make the solid mahogany pendant baseplate, sand it to a finish and glue to the underside of baseboard D, being careful to wipe off any excess glue with a damp cloth.

Drill for and glue in position the fixing dowels to baseboard A.

Sand to a finish all visible surfaces of the pendant sub-assembly and apply finishes as previously described.

CRESTBOARD

Take the plywood component for the crestboard and mark out the profile, working from the detail on the drawings. Carefully cut out the profile with a fret saw, coping saw or band saw and neatly clean up the cut edges with abrasive.

To the cut edges of the crestboard profile, carefully veneer to form cross banding. Trim off excess veneer and veneer the face with book matched veneer.

From scrap wood, make the supporting strut for the crestboard and glue and screw in position at the back of the crestboard.

Sand all veneer to a finish on the crestboard and apply finishes as previously.

Make the keyston, sand to a finish and apply finishes. From scrap mahogany, make the keyston cap, sand to a finish, apply finishes and glue in position on the top of the keyston. Glue the keyston in position on the crestboard and allow glue to set.

Cut the crestboard mouldings to length with neat mitres at intersections. Sand to a finish and apply finishes before fixing with impact adhesive.

FINIALS & PATERA

On the lathe faceplate make the turned crestboard patera in mahogany to any decorative concentric pattern of your choice. Whilst still on the faceplate, sand to a finish and apply finishes with the lathe running at a slow speed. Remove the patera on completion and fix in position on the crestboard with impact adhesive.

On the lathe, turn the onion finials to the profile shown on the drawings. It is best to make a plywood template of the profile to ensure that each finial is a match for the others. With the finials still mounted, sand to a finish and apply finishes with the lathe running at a slow speed. it is necessary to ensure that the spigots of the finials are of a diameter to suit the diameters of the drill bits which will be used to drill the finial fixing holes in the case assembly. It is best to go for a tight fit for the spigots since, traditionally, the finials of a regulator clock case were not glued in place but were retained in position by a friction fit only. This is, of course, not essential, since a loose fitting finial can always be glued in position.

On the lathe, make the pendant finial to the profile shown in the drawings. Sand and finish as described for the onion finials. On completion, offer up to the pendant baseplate and carefully mark for and cut the flattened portion at the rear of the finial.

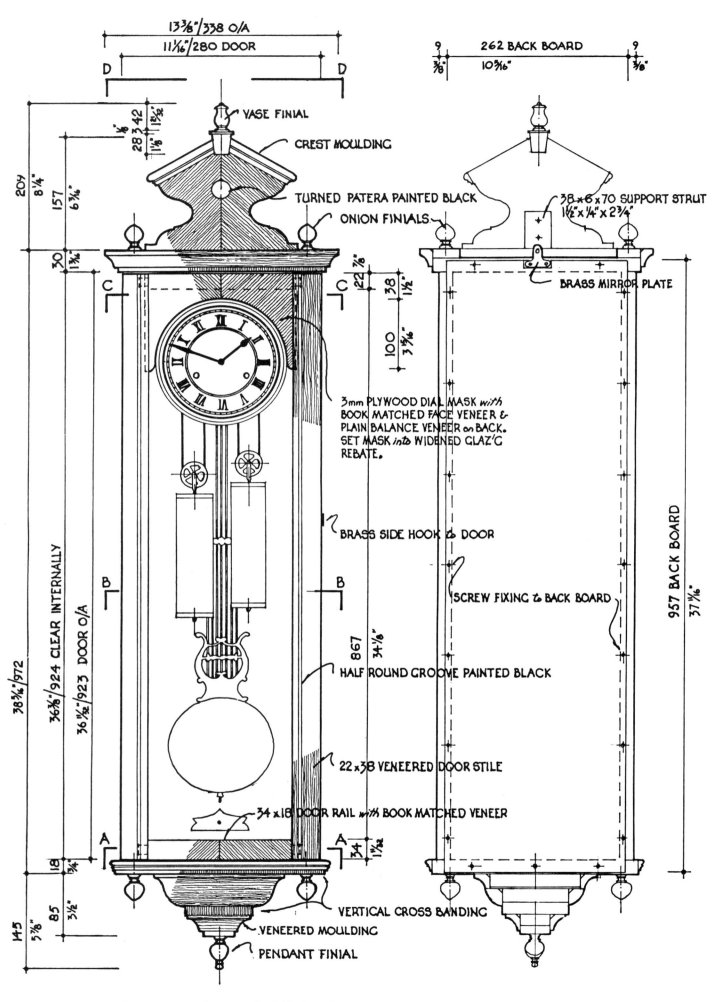

13⅜"/338 O/A
11¹⁄₁₆"/280 DOOR

262 BACK BOARD
9 · ³⁄₈"
10³⁄₁₆"
9 · ³⁄₈"

D · D

VASE FINIAL

CREST MOULDING

28 3 42
1⅛" ¹⁄₈" 1¹⁄₃₂"

157
6¾"

209
8¼"

TURNED PATERA PAINTED BLACK

ONION FINIALS

38 × 6 × 70 SUPPORT STRUT
1½" × ¼" × 2¾"

30
1³⁄₁₆"

C · C

22 ⅞"

38 1½"
100 3⁹⁄₁₆"

BRASS MIRROR PLATE

3mm PLYWOOD DIAL MASK with
BOOK MATCHED FACE VENEER &
PLAIN BALANCE VENEER on BACK.
SET MASK into WIDENED GLAZ'G
REBATE.

36⅜"/924 CLEAR INTERNALLY

36¹¹⁄₃₂"/923 DOOR O/A

B · B

BRASS SIDE HOOK to DOOR

SCREW FIXING to BACK BOARD

957 BACK BOARD
37⅝"

38⅛"/972

867 34⅛"

HALF ROUND GROOVE PAINTED BLACK

22 × 38 VENEERED DOOR STILE

A · A

34 1¹⁄₃₂"

34 × 18 DOOR RAIL with BOOK MATCHED VENEER

18 ¾"

85 3½"

145 5⅝"

VERTICAL CROSS BANDING

VENEERED MOULDING

PENDANT FINIAL

FRONT ELEVATION   BACK ELEVATION

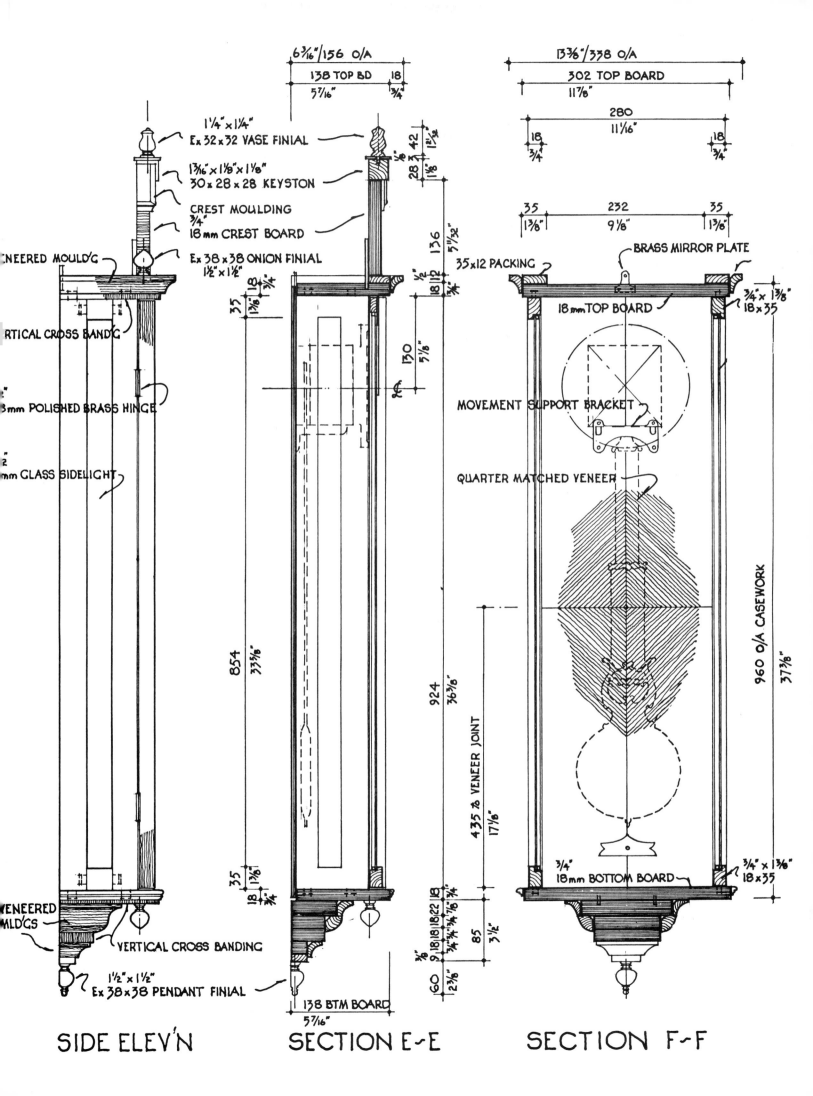

6³/₁₆"/156 O/A
138 TOP BD | 18
5⁷/₁₆" | ³/₄"

13³/₈"/338 O/A
302 TOP BOARD
11⁷/₈"

280
11¹/₁₆"

18 | 18
³/₄" | ³/₄"

35 | 232 | 35
1³/₈" | 9⅛" | 1³/₈"

1¼" × 1¼"
Ex 32×32 VASE FINIAL

1³/₁₆" × 1⅛" × 1⅛"
30 × 28 × 28 KEYSTON

CREST MOULDING
³/₄"
18mm CREST BOARD

Ex 38 × 38 ONION FINIAL
1½" × 1½"

VENEERED MOULD'G

RTICAL CROSS BAND'G

mm POLISHED BRASS HINGE

mm GLASS SIDELIGHT

28⅜ | 42
1¹/₁₆" | 1¹⁵/₃₂
1⅛"
⅛"

136
5¹¹/₃₂"

18 | 12 | ½"
³/₄"

35
1³/₈"

130
5⅛"

₵

854
33⅝"

924
36⅜"

435 ℄ VENEER JOINT
17⅛"

BRASS MIRROR PLATE

35×12 PACKING

18mm TOP BOARD

³/₄" × 1³/₈"
18 × 35

MOVEMENT SUPPORT BRACKET

QUARTER MATCHED VENEER

960 O/A CASEWORK
37⅞"

35
1³/₈"

18 | ³/₄"
1³/₆"

VENEERED
MLD'GS

VERTICAL CROSS BANDING

1½" × 1½"
Ex 38 × 38 PENDANT FINIAL

9 |18|18|22| 18
⅜" | ³/₄"³/₄"⁷/₈" | ³/₄"

85
3½"

60
2³/₈"

138 BTM BOARD
5⁷/₁₆"

³/₄"
18mm BOTTOM BOARD

³/₄" × 1³/₈"
18 × 35

SIDE ELEV'N   SECTION E~E   SECTION F~F

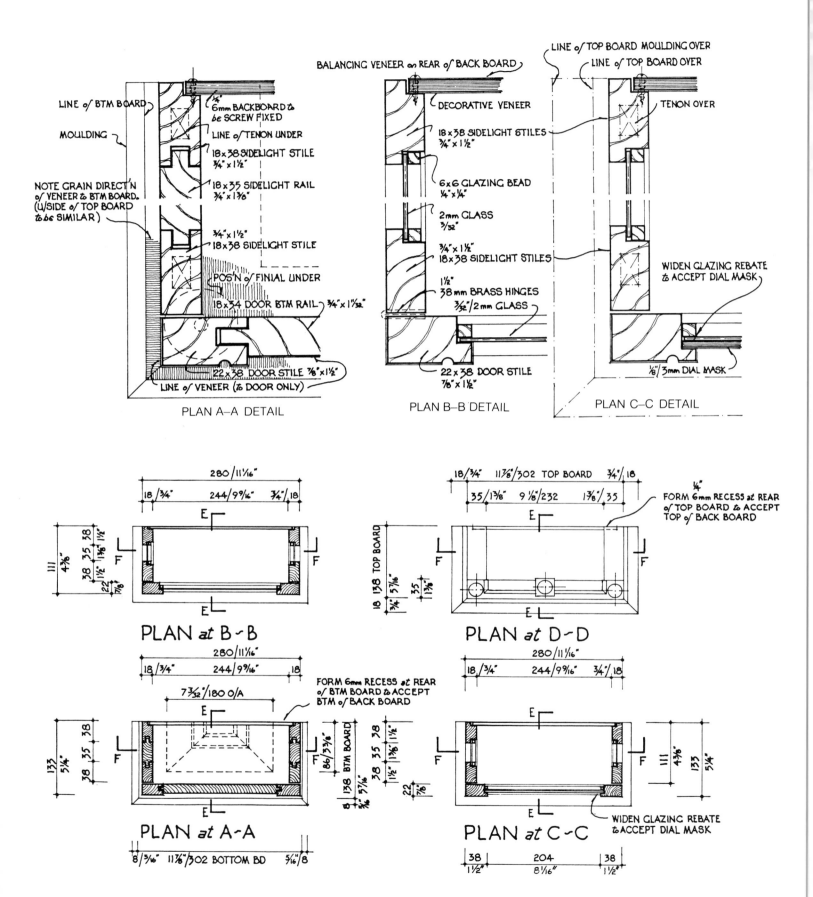

PLAN A–A DETAIL

LINE of BTM BOARD

MOULDING

NOTE GRAIN DIRECT'N of VENEER to BTM BOARD. (U/SIDE of TOP BOARD to be SIMILAR)

¼" 6mm BACKBOARD to be SCREW FIXED
LINE of TENON UNDER
18 x 38 SIDELIGHT STILE ¾" x 1½"
18 x 35 SIDELIGHT RAIL ¾" x 1⅜"
¾" x 1½"
18 x 38 SIDELIGHT STILE
POS'N of FINIAL UNDER
18 x 34 DOOR BTM RAIL ¾" x 1½₂"
22 x 38 DOOR STILE ⅞" x 1½"
LINE of VENEER (to DOOR ONLY)

PLAN B–B DETAIL

BALANCING VENEER on REAR of BACK BOARD

DECORATIVE VENEER
18 x 38 SIDELIGHT STILES ¾" x 1½"
6 x 6 GLAZING BEAD ¼" x ¼"
2mm GLASS ³⁄₃₂"
¾" x 1½"
18 x 38 SIDELIGHT STILES
1½"
38 mm BRASS HINGES ³⁄₃₂" / 2mm GLASS
22 x 38 DOOR STILE ⅞" x 1½"

PLAN C–C DETAIL

LINE of TOP BOARD MOULDING OVER
LINE of TOP BOARD OVER
TENON OVER
WIDEN GLAZING REBATE to ACCEPT DIAL MASK
⅛" / 3mm DIAL MASK

PLAN at B–B

280 / 11⅛"
18 / ¾"   244 / 9⁹⁄₁₆"   ¾" / 18
111 4⅜"
38 35 38
1½ 1⅜ 1½
38 1½
22 ⅞

PLAN at D–D

18 / ¾"   11⅞" / 302 TOP BOARD   ¾" / 18
35 / 1⅜"   9⅛" / 232   1⅜" / 35
¼" FORM 6mm RECESS at REAR of TOP BOARD to ACCEPT TOP of BACK BOARD
18 138 TOP BOARD
¾ 5⅜"
35 1⅜"

PLAN at A–A

280 / 11⅛"
18 / ¾"   244 / 9⁹⁄₁₆"   18
7³⁄₃₂" / 180 O/A
132 5¼"
38 35 38
FORM 6mm RECESS at REAR of BTM BOARD to ACCEPT BTM of BACK BOARD
86 / 3⅜"
8 138 BTM BOARD
5" 5⅜"
22 ⅞
8 / ⁵⁄₁₆"   11⅞" / 302 BOTTOM BD   ⁵⁄₁₆" / 8

PLAN at C–C

280 / 11⅛"
18 / ¾"   244 / 9⁹⁄₁₆"   ¾" / 18
111 4⅜"
135 5¼"
WIDEN GLAZING REBATE to ACCEPT DIAL MASK
38 1½"   204 8⅛₆"   38 1½"

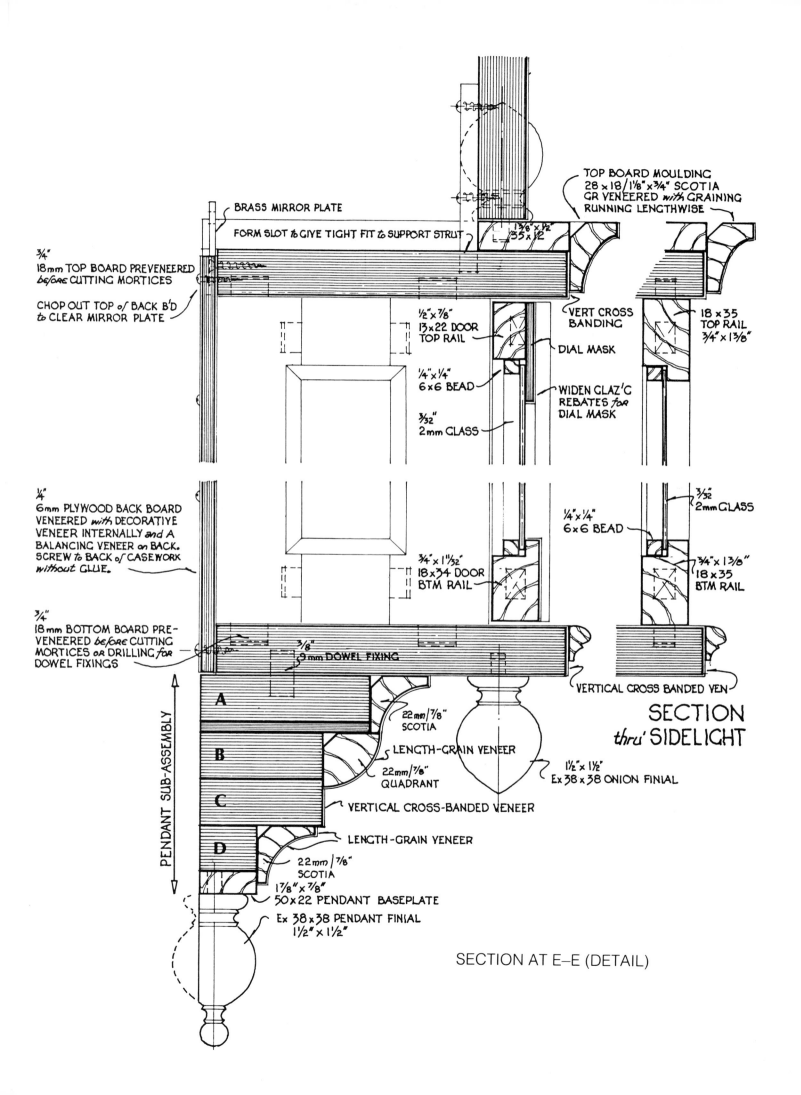

BRASS MIRROR PLATE

FORM SLOT to GIVE TIGHT FIT to SUPPORT STRUT

3/4"
18mm TOP BOARD PREVENEERED *before* CUTTING MORTICES

CHOP OUT TOP of BACK B'D to CLEAR MIRROR PLATE

TOP BOARD MOULDING
28 × 18/1 1/8" × 3/4" SCOTIA
GR VENEERED *with* GRAINING
RUNNING LENGTHWISE

1 3/8" × 1/2"
35 × 12

VERT CROSS BANDING

DIAL MASK

1/2" × 7/8"
13 × 22 DOOR TOP RAIL

1/4" × 1/4"
6 × 6 BEAD

3/32"
2mm GLASS

WIDEN GLAZ'G REBATES *for* DIAL MASK

18 × 35
TOP RAIL
3/4" × 1 3/8"

1/4"
6mm PLYWOOD BACK BOARD VENEERED *with* DECORATIVE VENEER INTERNALLY *and* A BALANCING VENEER on BACK. SCREW to BACK of CASEWORK *without* GLUE.

3/32"
2mm GLASS

1/4" × 1/4"
6 × 6 BEAD

3/4" × 1 1/32"
18 × 34 DOOR BTM RAIL

3/4" × 1 3/8"
18 × 35
BTM RAIL

3/4"
18mm BOTTOM BOARD PRE-VENEERED *before* CUTTING MORTICES *or* DRILLING *for* DOWEL FIXINGS

3/8"
9mm DOWEL FIXING

VERTICAL CROSS BANDED VEN

PENDANT SUB-ASSEMBLY

A
B
C
D

22mm/7/8"
SCOTIA

LENGTH-GRAIN VENEER

22mm/7/8"
QUADRANT

VERTICAL CROSS-BANDED VENEER

LENGTH-GRAIN VENEER

22mm/7/8"
SCOTIA

1 7/8" × 7/8"
50 × 22 PENDANT BASEPLATE

Ex 38 × 38 PENDANT FINIAL
1 1/2" × 1 1/2"

1 1/2" × 1 1/2"
Ex 38 × 38 ONION FINIAL

SECTION
thru' SIDELIGHT

SECTION AT E–E (DETAIL)

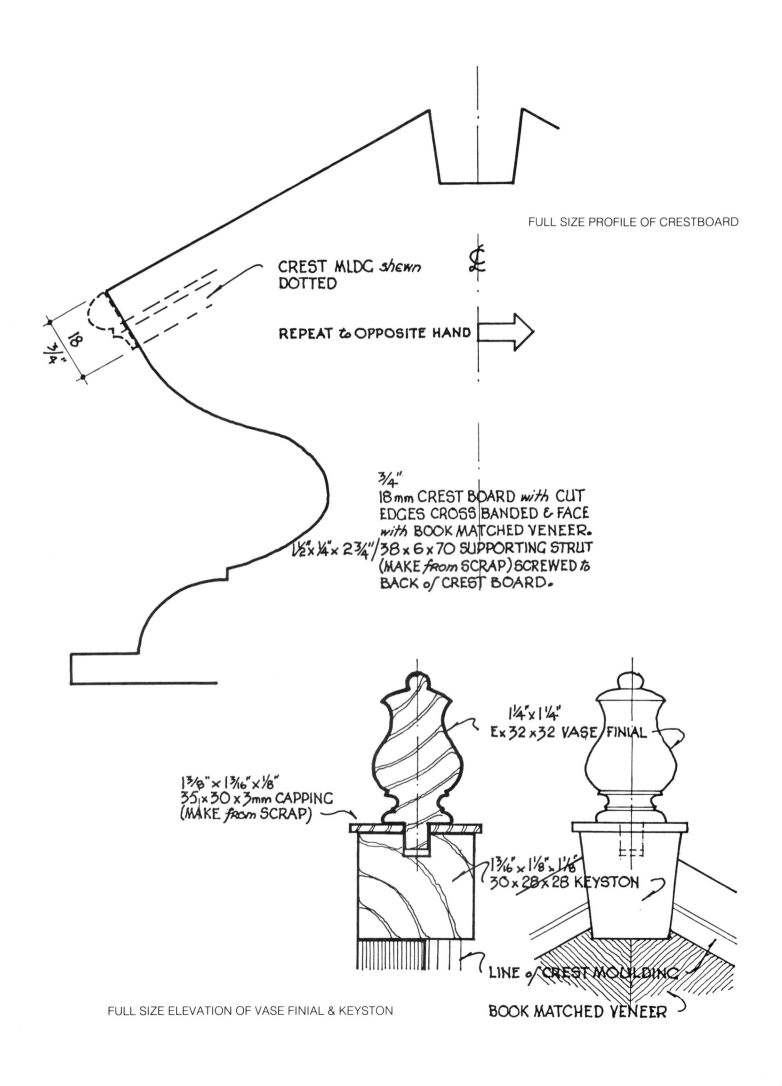

FULL SIZE PROFILE OF CRESTBOARD

CREST MLDG shewn
DOTTED

℄

REPEAT to OPPOSITE HAND →

¾"
18mm CREST BOARD with CUT
EDGES CROSS BANDED & FACE
with BOOK MATCHED VENEER.
1½"x ¼"x 2¾"/38 x 6 x 70 SUPPORTING STRUT
(MAKE from SCRAP) SCREWED to
BACK of CREST BOARD.

18

¾"

1¼"x 1¼"
Ex 32 x 32 VASE FINIAL

1⅜" x 1³⁄₁₆" x ⅛"
35 x 30 x 3mm CAPPING
(MAKE from SCRAP)

1³⁄₁₆" x 1⅛" x 1⅛"
30 x 28 x 28 KEYSTON

LINE of CREST MOULDING

FULL SIZE ELEVATION OF VASE FINIAL & KEYSTON

BOOK MATCHED VENEER

To the case assembly, carefully mark out for and drill the spigot holes for the finials.

FINAL ASSEMBLY & MOVEMENT INSTALLATION

Offer up the pendant sub-assembly to the bottom of the case assembly and ensure that there is a good 'marry' between the two assemblies before gluing. It is as well to make a small groove in the side of the dowels so that excess adhesive can be squeezed out without the need to exert excessive pressure. Put the completed case to one side for the adhesive to set hard, preferably overnight.

Screw the brass mirror plate exactly in the centre of the rear of the top board.

Refer now to the manufacturer's fixing instructions for the movement and carefully mark on the backboard the position of the movement supporting bracket. Lay the clock case on its back on the bench. Bolt the movement to the supporting bracket and lay it in position where you have marked the backboard. Carefully close the door of the case and ensure that the outer rim of the clock dial marries up with the edge of the dial mask. Adjust the marked position of the bracket as necessary to obtain this relationship. When you are satisfied with the positioning of the movement, unbolt the bracket and screw it to the backboard. Re-hang the glazed door.

Hang the clock case on the wall and re-bolt the movement to the bracket and hang the pendulum in position. On the backboard, mark the required position of the pendulum indicator and screw it to the backboard.

With the clock still on the wall, carefully fix the finials in position and place the crestboard in position with the supporting strut sitting in the slot on the top of the topboard. Like the finials, the crestboard was not glued in position on the original clocks.

Hang the weights in position as recommended by the manufacturer and start the movement as instructed.

Cutting list

COMPONENT	QUANTITY	SECTION	LENGTH
Sidelight Stiles incl tenons	4	18 × 38	942
	4	¾″ × 1½″	37⅛″
Sidelight Rails incl tenons	4	18 × 35	53
	4	¾″ × 1⅜″	2⅛″
Door Stiles	2	22 × 38	923
	2	⅞″ × 1½″	26¹¹/₃₂″
Bottom Door Rail incl tenons	1	18 × 34	228
	1	¾″ × 1¹¹/₃₂″	9¹/₁₆″
Top Door Rail incl tenons	1	12 × 22	228
	1	½″ × ⅞″	9¹/₁₆″
Door Dial Mask (Ply)	1	3 × 138	216
	1	⅛″ × 5⁷/₁₆″	8⁹/₁₆″

Top Board (Ply)	1	18 × 138	302
	1	¾″ × 5⁷⁄₁₆″	11⁷⁄₈″
Top Board Packing (Total)	1	12 × 35	508
	1	½″ × 1⅜″	20″
Top Board Moulding (Total)	1	18 × 28	650 minimum
	1	¾″ × 1⅛″	25¾″ minimum
Crest Board (Ply)	1	18 × 157	216
	1	¾″ × 6³⁄₁₆″	8⁹⁄₁₆″
Keyston	1	28 × 28	30
	1	1⅛″ × 1⅛″	1³⁄₁₆″
Bottom Board (Ply)	1	18 × 138	302
	1	¾″ × 5⁷⁄₁₆″	11⁷⁄₈″
Bottom Board Moulding (Total)	1	18 × 9	614 minimum
	1	¾″ × ⅜″	24¼″ minimum
Backboard (Ply)	1	6 × 262	957
	1	¼″ × 10⁵⁄₁₆″	37¹¹⁄₁₆″
Vase Finial incl spigot	1	ex 32 × 32	51
	1	ex 1¼″ × 1¼″	2″
Onion Finials incl spigot	4	ex 38 × 38	54
	4	ex 1½″ × 1½″	2⅛″
Pendant Finial incl spigot	1	ex 38 × 38	68
	1	ex 1½″ × 1½″	2¹¹⁄₁₆″
Baseboard A (Composite Ply)	1	22 × 65	136
	1	⅞″ × 2⅝″	5⅜″
Baseboard A Moulding (Total)	1	22 × 22	354 minimum
	1	⅞″ × ⅞″	14⅛″ minimum
Baseboard B (Ply)	1	18 × 47	100
	1	¾″ × 1⅞″	3⅞″
Baseboard B Moulding (Total)	1	22 × 22	282 minimum
	1	⅞″ × ⅞″	11⅛″
Baseboard C (Ply)	1	18 × 47	100
	1	¾″ × 1⅞″	3⅞″
Baseboard D (Ply)	1	18 × 22	50
	1	¾″ × ⅞″	1⅞″
Baseboard D Moulding (Total)	1	22 × 22	182 minimum
	1	⅞″ × ⅞″	7⅛″ minimum
Pendant Baseplate	1	9 × 22	50
	1	⅜″ × ⅞″	1⅞″
Glazing Beads (Surplus)	7	6 × 6	1 metre lengths
	7	¼″ × ¼″	1 yard lengths
Crest Board Moulding (Total)	1	18 × 9	280 minimum
	1	¾″ × ⅜″	11″ minimum

Clock Components and Hardware (excluding screws and pins)

CLOCK MOVEMENT/DIAL COMBINATIONS — OPTIONS:

  1. Hermle/mechanical.
     Weight driven.
     180mm/ 7⅛″ diameter dial.
     750mm/ 29½″ length pendulum.
     Note: Clear internal length of case: 924mm/ 36⅛″.

  2. Hermle/mechanical.
     Weight driven.
     180mm/ 7⅛″ diameter dial.
     660mm/ 26″ length pendulum.
     Note: clear internal length of case: 889mm/ 35″.

  3. Kieninger/mechanical.
     Weight driven.
     180mm/ 7⅛″ diameter dial.
     650mm/ 25⅝″ length pendulum.
     Note: clear internal length of case: 825mm/ 32½″.

  4. Other mechanical movements.
     Check pendulum length and adjust internal length of case accordingly.
     1 to 4:
     Maximum pendulum swing: 229mm/ 9″. Adjust case width if necessary.
     Maximum movement/dial depth: 102mm/ 4″. Adjust case depth if necessary.

  5. Quartz movements.
     Not available in regulator format.

PENDULUM — OPTIONS:
  – Wooden pendulum, lyre pendulum, grid-iron pendulum.

CLOCK DIAL:
  – Integral with movement.

CLOCK HANDS:
  – Bushed to suit movement.
  – Length to suit dial.
  – Pattern to suit individual choice.

BRASSWARE:
  – Hinges: One pair of 38mm/ 1½″ butt hinges.
  – Door Locks:
    One hook and eye (fixed to door and right hand sidelight style), OR
    One pair of ball catches (fixed to interior of top and bottom boards.

GLASS:
  – To suit door.
  – To suit sidelight stiles.

16. *Small Vienna Regulator Clock*

The Vienna Regulator clock is famous for its accurate time keeping and the originals are always in demand. This is a smaller and slightly simpler version of the previous plan.

Well engineered replicas of original movements are obtainable from most horological suppliers and these, together with drawings faithfully illustrating the elegance of the traditional cases, mean that the making of a replica is now within the reach of most woodworkers.

Original regulators were usually built in walnut, but any close grained hardwood will give a pleasing result.

Overall dimensions: 274 wide × 160 deep × 807mm high
                              10¼″ wide × 6¼″ deep × 31¾″ high.

Skill level * * *

Schedule of Operations

CONSTRUCTION

The procedures outlined below are based on the assumption that construction is completed in sub-assemblies, all of which are prefinished before final assembly.

Cut out the various components, except mouldings, to the sizes given in the cutting list. The sizes stated are finished sizes and allowance should be made for planing etc.

SIDELIGHTS

Take the sidelight components and plane to the cross sections required, working in pairs to ensure they are identical.

Form the rebates and stopped rebates as shown on the drawings.

Form the tenons at the extremities of the members and then mark for and cut the mortices in the stiles to accept the tenons of the sidelight rails. It should be noted that the outer face of the rails is set back from that of the stiles. Check the joints for tightness of fit and assemble dry to check for squareness.

Glue and cramp the members of each sub-assembly using PVA adhesive. Any excess adhesive should be wiped off immediately with a damp cloth. Leave overnight to set hard.

Sand down to a finish all surfaces which will be exposed to view in the completed clock case, using progressively finer abrasive paper. Clean off all sanding dust and apply the finish of your choice.

The best finish to use is french polish, but pleasing results may be obtained with varnish, polyurethane or cellulose finishes. In the latter cases grain fill the wood before applying the initial coat which should be flowed on rather than bruhed in. When the first coat has dried hard, flat down with 0000 wire wool, working in the direction of the grain. Repeat the process until a satisfactory result has been achieved. Flat down the final coat and apply a solid wax polish to obtain a final gloss.

TOP & BOTTOM BOARDS

Take the top and bottom board components and check for size and squareness before marking for and forming the recesses at the rear which will later accept the back board.

To the bottom board, carefully mark and cut out the shaped front using the profile shape on the drawings.

Sand down the boards and clean off all sanding dust before applying the veneers with hot glue and a veneering hammer or by using an impact adhesive.

Sand down all veneered surfaces to a finish with progressively finer grades of paper.

Form the mortices to accept the end tenons of the sidelight sub assemblies. Mark out and drill the blind holes on the underside of the bottom board to accept the dowel fixing of the pendant sub-assembly. Mark out for and form the slot on the upper surface of the top board to accept the crestboard sub-assembly.

Apply finishes to the boards and set aside for later use.

BACKBOARD

Take the plywood component for the backboard and check for squareness and size. Sand down all surfaces and apply any common veneer to the rear face to act as a balancer. Veneer the front face and edges with the decorative veneer of your choice. Drill the screw fixing holes and sand the veneers to a finish. Dust off all surfaces and apply finishes.

CASE ASSEMBLY

Dry assemble the top and bottom boards and the sidelight sub-assemblies to check for squareness. Glue and cramp together, again checking for squareness. If necessary, pin temporary battens diagonally across the back of the members to hold square while the glue is setting overnight.

After removing cramps and temporary battens, screw the backboard in position and set the whole case to one side.

DOOR

Take the frame components for the door and plane to size. Form rebates and stopped rebates as shown on drawings.

Form the tenons at the ends of the top and bottom rails and form the mortices in the stiles to accept the tenons just made. Assemble dry and offer up to the case assembly to check for squareness and size.

Carefully cut out the dial mask from 3mm/⅛″ plywood and, after sanding, veneer the rear face with common veneer as a balancer. Cross band the cut edge of the arch and veneer the front of the mask with book matched veneers as shown on the drawings. Sand down and finish as previously described.

Offer up the dial mask to the dry assembled door members and carefully mark on the stile the additional width needed to the glazing rebates to accept the dial mask. Cut the increased rebate width required.

Glue up and cramp the door members but do not fix the dial mask at this stage. Check for squareness and set aside for glue to set.

Sand down the door members to a finish. Veneer cross banding to the top of the bottom rail and veneer the front face of the bottom rail with book matched veneer. Sand veneered surfaces to a finish.

Offer up the dial mask into the widened glazing rebate and glue to the front face of the top rail.

Set aside for later finishing.

SPLIT COLUMNS

Take the two members for the 'split spindle' columns and plane to size. Since the two members will be turned together on the lathe it is essential that a good 'marry' is obtained between them. Glue paper along the length of one of the members and then glue the second member to the paper. You will now have a square section divided down the centre by the paper. When the glue has set hard bind the ends of the workpiece with twine as a precaution against premature separation and place in the lathe. Make sure that the teeth of the drive centre are set across the end grain before tightening the tailstock. Turn to the profile shown on the drawing.

On completion, sand to a finish on the lathe, clean off all dust and apply finishes with the lathe on slow speed.

After finishes have been completed, remove the column from the lathe and split into two along the line of the paper. Clean off all traces of paper from the rear of the two halves and glue into position on the face of the door stiles.

Apply finishes to the rest of the door.

HINGING

Offer up the door to the case assembly and carefully mark and cut out recesses on the front of the sidelight stile and the rear of the door stile to accept the hinges. Screw the hinges in position and mark out for and fix the brass sidehook where indicated on the drawings.

GLAZING

Carefully measure the size of glass required for the sidelights and the door, not forgetting to allow a little off the measured sizes so that the glass will slide into position without pressure. Obtain 2mm/³⁄₃₂″ thick picture glass from your local merchant.

Take the glazing bead lengths and cut to sizes required, allowing for neat mitres at intersections. Sand the beads and apply finishes and fix in position with panel pins or veneer pins.

PENDANT BASE

Take the plywood components for the baseboards in the pendant base. Check for size and squareness and check thickness against the relevant mouldings. It is essential that the thickness of baseboards B and C are such that an accurate 'marry' is obtained between the coved and quarter round mouldings.

Working face down on the bench fix baseboard B to baseboard A with adhesive and 25mm/1″ panel pins. Fix baseboard C to baseboard B and baseboard D to baseboard C in a similar manner.

Cut the softwood mouldings to length with neat mitres at intersections. Fix to the edges of the baseboards with adhesive and pins and neatly punch in the pin heads and fill resultant holes with proprietary filler. Sand down and ensure that you have a good junction where cove and quadrant meet.

Veneer the exposed edges of baseboards A and D with cross banded veneer. Veneer the faces of the coved and quadrant mouldings with veneer laid lengthwise, starting with the side mouldings and finishing with the front mouldings. Pay particular attention to the mitred areas.

Mark out for, drill for and glue into position the fixing dowels to baseboard A.

Sand to a finish all surfaces of the pendant base and apply finishes and set aside for future assembly.

CRESTBOARD

Take the plywood component for the crestboard and mark out the profile shown on the drawing. Cut out with a fret saw or coping saw. Clean up the cut edge with a file and abrasive paper to remove saw kerfs.

Veneer the cut edges to form cross banding. Trim off excess and veneer the face with book matched veneer.

From scrap wood make the supporting strut for the crestboard and glue and screw into position.

Sand all veneer to a finish and apply finishes as previously.

Make the keyston, sand and apply finishes. From scrap hardwood make the keyston capping, sand and finish. Glue with its capping into position and allow glue to set.

Cut the crestboard mouldings to lengths with neat mitres at intersections, sand and finish as previously described. Fix in position on the crest using impact adhesive.

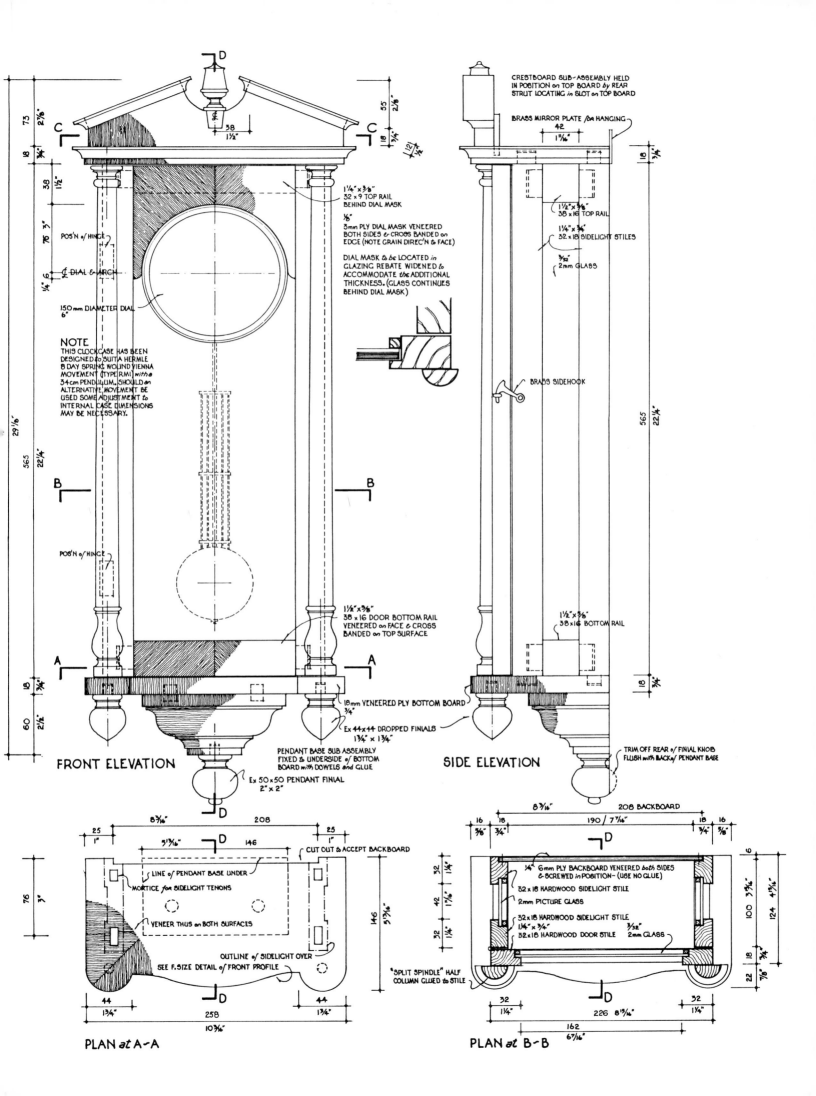

FRONT ELEVATION

NOTE
THIS CLOCKCASE HAS BEEN
DESIGNED to SUIT a HERMLE
8 DAY SPRING WOUND VIENNA
MOVEMENT (TYPE RM) with a
34cm PENDULUM. SHOULD an
ALTERNATIVE MOVEMENT BE
USED SOME ADJUSTMENT to
INTERNAL CASE DIMENSIONS
MAY BE NECESSARY.

150 mm DIAMETER DIAL
6"

POS'N of HINGE

C DIAL & ARCH

POS'N of HINGE

1¼" × ⅜"
32 × 9 TOP RAIL
BEHIND DIAL MASK

⅛"
3mm PLY DIAL MASK VENEERED
BOTH SIDES & CROSS BANDED on
EDGE (NOTE GRAIN DIREC'N & FACE)

DIAL MASK to be LOCATED in
GLAZING REBATE WIDENED to
ACCOMMODATE the ADDITIONAL
THICKNESS. (GLASS CONTINUES
BEHIND DIAL MASK)

1½" × ⅜"
38 × 16 DOOR BOTTOM RAIL
VENEERED on FACE & CROSS
BANDED on TOP SURFACE

18mm VENEERED PLY BOTTOM BOARD
¾"

Ex 44×44 DROPPED FINIALS
1¾" × 1¾"

PENDANT BASE SUB ASSEMBLY
FIXED to UNDERSIDE of BOTTOM
BOARD with DOWELS and GLUE

Ex 50×50 PENDANT FINIAL
2" × 2"

SIDE ELEVATION

CRESTBOARD SUB-ASSEMBLY HELD
IN POSITION on TOP BOARD by REAR
STRUT LOCATING in SLOT on TOP BOARD

BRASS MIRROR PLATE for HANGING
42
1 11/16"

1½" × ⅜"
38 × 16 TOP RAIL

1¼" × ¾"
32 × 18 SIDELIGHT STILES

3/32"
2mm GLASS

BRASS SIDEHOOK

1½" × ⅜"
38 × 16 BOTTOM RAIL

TRIM OFF REAR of FINIAL KNOB
FLUSH with BACK of PENDANT BASE

PLAN at A-A

CUT OUT to ACCEPT BACKBOARD

LINE of PENDANT BASE UNDER

MORTICE for SIDELIGHT TENONS

VENEER THUS on BOTH SURFACES

OUTLINE of SIDELIGHT OVER

SEE F. SIZE DETAIL of FRONT PROFILE

PLAN at B-B

208 BACKBOARD

190 / 7 7/16"

6mm PLY BACKBOARD VENEERED both SIDES
& SCREWED in POSITION- (USE NO GLUE)

32 × 18 HARDWOOD SIDELIGHT STILE

2mm PICTURE GLASS

32 × 18 HARDWOOD SIDELIGHT STILE

32 × 18 HARDWOOD DOOR STILE   2mm GLASS

"SPLIT SPINDLE" HALF
COLUMN GLUED to STILE

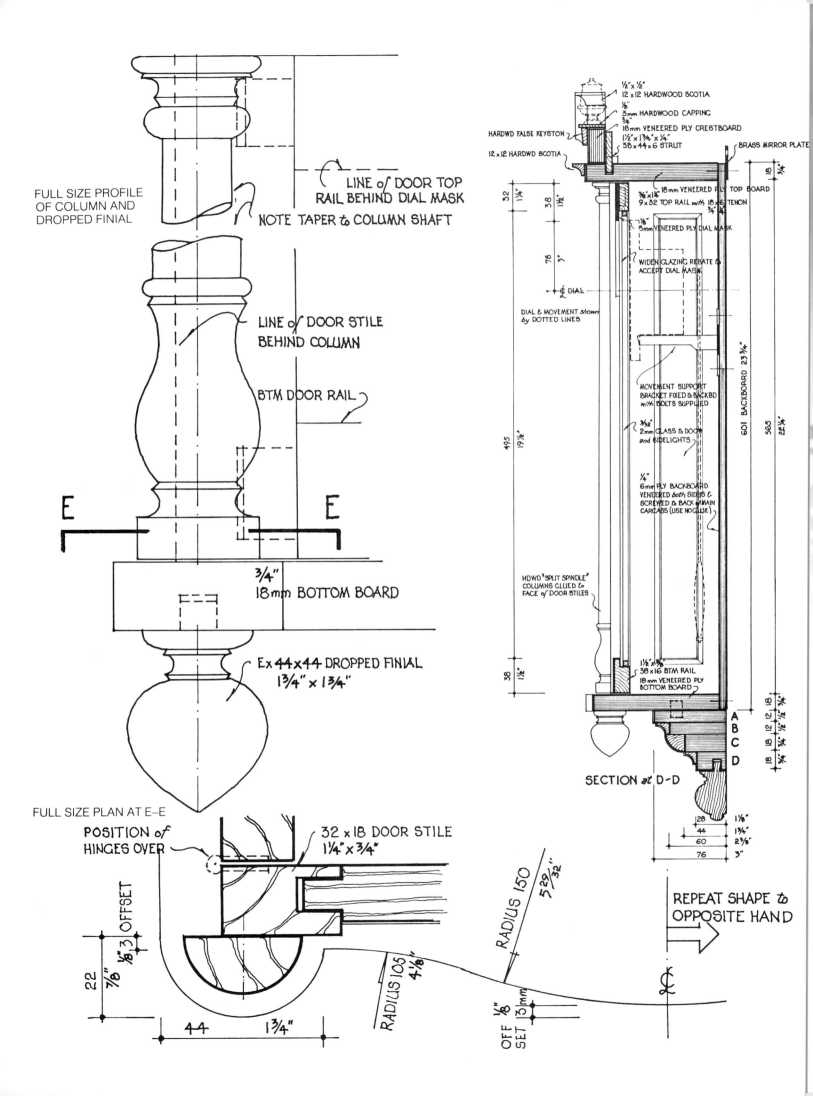

FULL SIZE PROFILE
OF COLUMN AND
DROPPED FINIAL

NOTE TAPER to COLUMN SHAFT

LINE of DOOR TOP
RAIL BEHIND DIAL MASK

LINE of DOOR STILE
BEHIND COLUMN

BTM DOOR RAIL

3/4"
18mm BOTTOM BOARD

Ex 44x44 DROPPED FINIAL
1 3/4" x 1 3/4"

FULL SIZE PLAN AT E–E

POSITION of
HINGES OVER

32 x 18 DOOR STILE
1 1/4" x 3/4"

22 7/8" 3 1/8" OFFSET

44   1 3/4"

RADIUS 105 4 1/8"

RADIUS 150 5 29/32"

OFF SET 1/8" 3mm

1/2" x 1/2"
12 x 12 HARDWOOD SCOTIA

1/8"
3mm HARDWOOD CAPPING

3/4"
18mm VENEERED PLY CRESTBOARD

1 1/2" x 1 3/4" x 1/4"
38 x 44 x 6 STRUT

HARDWD FALSE KEYSTON

12 x 12 HARDWD SCOTIA

BRASS MIRROR PLATE

18 3/4"

3/8" x 1 1/4"
18mm VENEERED PLY TOP BOARD

9 x 32 TOP RAIL with 18 x 6 TENON

3/4" 1/4"

1/8"
5mm VENEERED PLY DIAL MASK

WIDEN GLAZING REBATE to
ACCEPT DIAL MASK

32 1 1/4"

38 1 1/2"

76 3"

¢ DIAL

DIAL & MOVEMENT shown
by DOTTED LINES

601 BACKBOARD 23 3/4"

565 22 1/4"

MOVEMENT SUPPORT
BRACKET FIXED to BACKBD
with BOLTS SUPPLIED

3/32"
2mm GLASS to DOOR
and SIDELIGHTS

1/4"
6mm PLY BACKBOARD
VENEERED both SIDES &
SCREWED to BACK of MAIN
CARCASS (USE NO GLUE)

495 19 1/2"

HDWD "SPLIT SPINDLE"
COLUMNS GLUED to
FACE of DOOR STILES

1 1/2" x 5/8"
38 x 16 BTM RAIL

18 mm VENEERED PLY
BOTTOM BOARD

38 1 1/2"

A
B
C
D

18 3/4"
12 1/2"
18 3/4"

SECTION at D–D

128 1 1/8"
44 1 3/4"
60 2 3/8"
76 3"

REPEAT SHAPE to
OPPOSITE HAND

¢

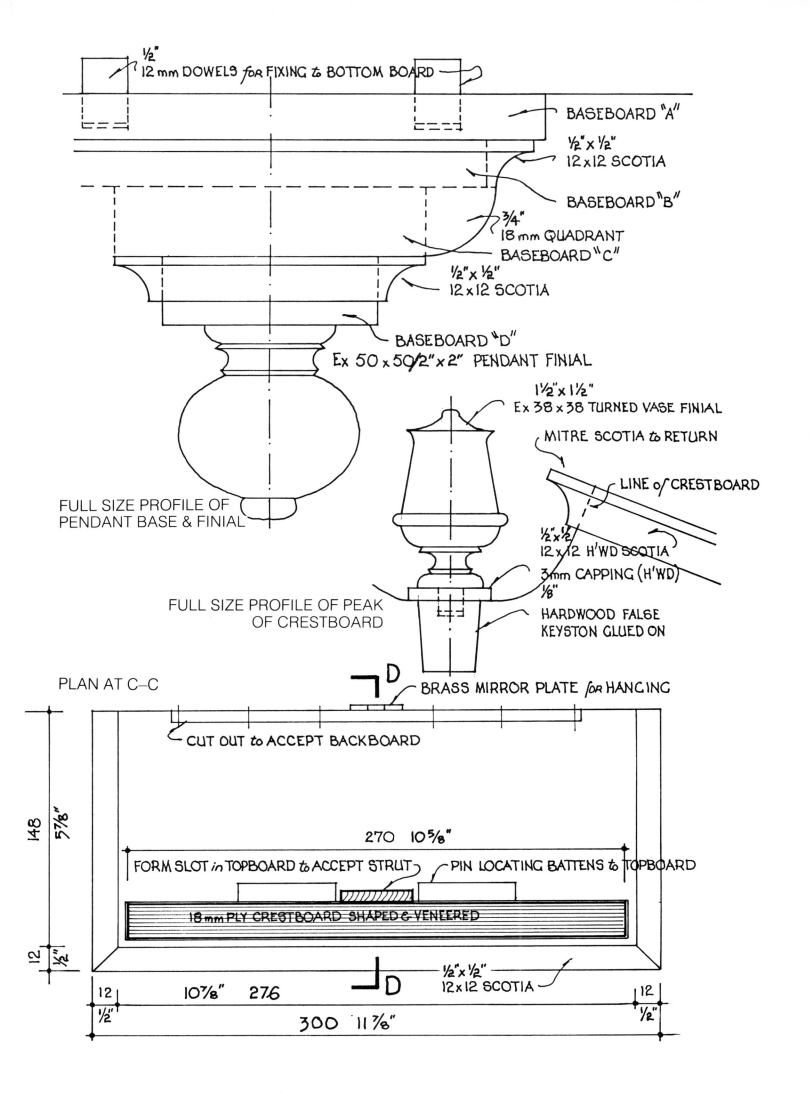

½"
12 mm DOWELS *for* FIXING *to* BOTTOM BOARD

BASEBOARD "A"

½" x ½"
12 x 12 SCOTIA

BASEBOARD "B"

¾"
18 mm QUADRANT
BASEBOARD "C"

½" x ½"
12 x 12 SCOTIA

BASEBOARD "D"
Ex 50 x 50/2" x 2" PENDANT FINIAL

FULL SIZE PROFILE OF
PENDANT BASE & FINIAL

1½" x 1½"
Ex 38 x 38 TURNED VASE FINIAL

MITRE SCOTIA *to* RETURN

LINE *of* CRESTBOARD

½" x ½"
12 x 12 H'WD SCOTIA

3 mm CAPPING (H'WD)
⅛"

HARDWOOD FALSE
KEYSTON GLUED ON

FULL SIZE PROFILE OF PEAK
OF CRESTBOARD

BRASS MIRROR PLATE *for* HANGING

PLAN AT C–C

CUT OUT *to* ACCEPT BACKBOARD

148   5⅞"

270   10⅝"

FORM SLOT *in* TOPBOARD *to* ACCEPT STRUT   PIN LOCATING BATTENS *to* TOPBOARD

18 mm PLY CRESTBOARD SHAPED & VENEERED

12   ½"

12   10⅞"   276   ½" x ½"
12 x 12 SCOTIA

½"

12   ½"

300   11⅞"

FINIALS

On the lathe, turn the finials to the profiles shown on the drawing. With the finials still mounted sand to a finish and apply the finishes with the lathe running at a slow speed.

It is necessary to ensure that the spigot diameters of the finials suit the diameter of drills used in making the fixing holes in the case assembly.

To the underside of the case and pendant base and to the top of the crestboard, carefully mark out for and drill the finial fixing holes.

FINAL ASSEMBLY

Take the moulding for the edge of the top board, cut to lengths with neat mitres at intersections. Sand to a finish and apply finishes as previously. When finishes are dry glue in position on the edge of the top board with impact adhesive.

Offer up the pendant base sub-assembly to the underside of the case and ensure that there is a good marry between the two sub-assemblies before you glue them together. Put the completed clock case to one side for the adhesive to set hard, preferably overnight.

Screw the brass mirror plate into position at the centre of the top of the backboard.

MOVEMENT INSTALLATION

Following the manufacturer's instructions bolt the movement to the cantilever support bracket.

Lay the completed case on its back on the bench with the door open. Lay the movement on its back on the face of the backboard and close the case door to check that the dial perimeter exactly coincides with the rim of the arch in the dial mask. When you are satisfied with that relationship carefully mark on the backboard the positions of the bracket screw holes, drill the holes for the bolts and bolt the bracket firmly in position.

Take the coiled strike gong and lay in position so that the strike hammer touches. Mark, drill for and screw the gong in position. Flick back the strike hammer a few times to ensure a good sounding strike and adjust the hammer as necessary.

Hang the clock on the wall and hang the pendulum in position. The pendulum at rest should coincide with the centre of the backboard if the clock is hanging properly perpendicular. Mark the required position of the pendulum indicator and screw it to the backboard.

With the clock still on the wall, place the crestboard and finials in position. In original Vienna Regulators the crestboard and finials were friction fitted only.

Clock Components and Hardware (excluding screws and pins)

CLOCK MOVEMENT/DIAL COMBINATIONS — OPTIONS:

1. Mechanical Movements.
   Spring driven.
   150mm/5^{29}/$_{32}$" diameter dial
   Pendulum length from centres of handshaft to pendulum bob: 340mm/13$\frac{3}{8}$".
   Maximum pendulum swing: 180mm/7$\frac{1}{8}$". Adjust width of case if necessary.
   Maximum depth of movement/dial: 100mm/3^{15}/$_{16}$". Adjust depth of case if necessary.

2. Quartz Movements.
   Not available in regulator format.

PENDULUM OPTIONS:

– Wooden pendulum, lyre pendulum, grid-iron pendulum.

CLOCK DIAL:

– Integral with mechanical movement.

CLOCK HANDS:

– Bushed to suit movement.
– Length to suit dial.
– Pattern to suit individual choice.

BRASSWARE:

– Hinges: one pair of 38mm/1$\frac{1}{2}$" butts.
– Door lock: one hook and eye or concealed bullet catch.
– One mirror plate.

GLASS:

– To suit door.
– To suit sidelights.

Cutting list

COMPONENT	QUANTITY	SECTION	LENGTH
Sidelight Stiles incl tenons	4	18 × 32	589
	4	3/4" × 1 1/2"	2 15/16"
Sidelight Rails incl tenons	4	16 × 38	74
	4	5/8" × 1 1/2"	2 15/16"
Door Stiles	2	18 × 32	565
	2	3/4" × 1 1/4"	22 1/4"
Door Top Rail incl tenons	1	9 × 32	192
	1	3/8" × 1 1/4"	7 11/16"
Door Bottom Rail incl tenons	1	16 × 38	192
	1	5/8" × 1 1/2"	7 11/16"
Dropped Finials incl spigots	2	ex 44 × 44	60
	2	ex 1 3/4" × 1 3/4"	1 3/8"
Pendant Finial incl spigot	1	ex 50 × 50	70
	1	ex 2" × 2"	2 3/4"
Crest Finial incl spigot	1	ex 38 × 38	60
	1	ex 1 1/2" × 1 1/2"	1 3/8"
Split Columns	2	ex 40 × 20	565
	2	ex 1 9/16" × 25/32"	22 1/4"
Back Board (Ply)	1	3 × 208	601
	1	1/8" × 8 3/16"	23 3/4"
Top Board (Ply)	1	18 × 148	276
	1	3/4" × 5 7/8"	10 7/8"
Bottom Board (Ply)	1	18 × 146	258
	1	3/4" × 5 13/16"	10 3/16"
Pendant Baseboard A (Ply)	1	12 × 76	146
	1	1/2" × 3"	5 13/16"
Pendant Baseboard B (Ply)	1	12 × 60	114
	1	1/2" × 1 3/8"	4 1/2"
Pendant Baseboard C (Ply)	1	18 × 44	82
	1	3/4" × 1 3/4"	3 1/4"
Pendant Baseboard D (Ply)	1	18 × 28	58
	1	3/4" × 1 1/8"	2 5/16"
Crest Board (Ply)	1	18 × 73	270
	1	3/4" × 2 7/8"	10 5/8"
Scotia Moulding (Total Length)	1	12 × 12	1500
	1	1/2" × 1/2"	59"
Quadrant Moulding (Total Length)	1	18 × 18	254
	1	3/4" × 3/4"	10"

17/18.
'Coachman' and 'Groom' Wall Clocks

Coachman

Groom

These two wall clocks employ a simple laminating technique using layers of shaped plywood that can be veneered and embellished with mouldings to give a traditional feel. The main difference between the two clocks is with the use of either a 'flat cornice' or a 'gabled cornice'. Both designs utilise 'all-in-one' movement, bezel and dial combinations (insertion movements).

Overall dimensions: 188 wide × 60 deep × 298mm high
7½″ wide × 2½″ deep × 11⅞″ high
140 wide × 63 deep × 240mm high
5½″ wide × 2⅝″ deep × 9½″ high

Skill level *

'Coachman' Wall Clock

Schedule of Operations

FACEBOARD & BACKBOARD

First, take the 18mm/¾" thick sheet of plywood and accurately mark out the backboard to a size 140 × 298mm/5½" × 11⅞". Cut out this portion, ensuring that all sides are cut and are at right angles to the face of the board. Clean up the sides with a file or shaper plane and remove all saw or file marks with the sanding block. Copy the shape at the bottom of the plan and transfer it carefully to the board. The backboard shaped portion can be reproduced simply by photocopying the half-size scale plan on a zoom lens copier, increasing the image by 100%. Cut out the shape with a coping saw or fretsaw, being sure that the cut is kept close to the line and at right angles to the face of the board. Clean up the shaped edge with a file and sandpaper block and sandpaper wrapped dowel.

Put the backboard to one side and take the remaining piece of 18mm/¾" plywood and mark carefully and cut out a piece, size 194 × 140mm/7¾" × 5½", to form the faceboard. Clean up edges as described above.

To both backboard and faceboard accurately mark out the position of the 60mm/2⅜" hole which will later accept the rear body of the insertion movement. Check this measurement against actual movement being used. Drill starter holes and with a coping saw or fretsaw cut out the holes. Accuracy here is important if the insertion movement is to fit snugly after final assembly.

Offer up the faceboard on top of the backboard and mark with a pencil and trysquare the precise relationship of each board to the other. Ensure that the bottom edge of the faceboard is at right angles to the side edge of the backboard and that the projections of the faceboard beyond the edge of the backboard are both equal. Fix the faceboard to the backboard using PVA adhesive and panel pins.

CORNICE FRIEZE

Take the 6mm/¼" thick piece of plywood and cut a strip 33mm/1⅛" wide for the full length to form the cornice frieze. Ensure that the edges are parallel and clean up the cut surfaces with a file or shaper plane and a sandpaper block. From this full length cut a piece just over 152mm/6" long and fix to the top of the faceboard with PVA and veneer pins, ensuring that the lower edge of the strip is at right angles to the side of the faceboard and that the upper edge coincides accurately with the top of the faceboard. Cut the remaining portion of the frieze strip into two pieces and fix with PVA and veneer pins to the top sides of the faceboard/backboard assembly being certain that the lower edges coincide with the lower edge of the front frieze and that the upper edges coincide with the top of the assembly. Check over the whole of the assembly, sand all surfaces ready for veneering, ensuring that no edges or corners are rounded over in the sanding process.

VENEERING

Cut long strips of veneer for covering the vertical sides of the backboard, noting the direction of veneer grain shown on the plan. After fixing in position trim off the surplus veneer. Next, crossband with veneer the cut edges of the ornamental shapes at the bottom of the backboard and trim off any surplus veneer. Carefully sand to a finish the portions already veneered before proceeding to the next stage.

Noting the direction of grain indicated on the plan, veneer the lower front face of the backboard, trim off surplus veneer and sand to a finish.

Next veneer the whole of the cornice frieze, including the area to be covered later by the cornice moulding with the veneer set vertical grained as shown on the plan. Trim off surplus veneer and sand to a finish.

The next stage is to lay cross banded veneer around the edges of the faceboard, including the lower horizontal edge where it intersects with the already veneered front face of the backboard. Trim off surplus veneer and sand to a finish.

Take the remainder of the sheet of veneer and cut out four pieces with the grain set diagonally as shown on the drawings. Take pains to ensure that the edges of the veneer are accurately cut where they are to meet each other on the front of the faceboard since the relationship of the diagonal grain is an important feature of the design. Lay the four pieces of veneer with a contact adhesive ensuring that the meeting edges are a snug fit one with the other. Trim off surplus veneer including that covering the movement insertion hole and sand to finish.

MOULDINGS

Take the 9mm/⅜" hardwood scotia moulding and sand down for the full length, using a sanding block on the upper and lower square edges and sandpaper wrapped round a short length of dowel for the concave surface.

Take the main assembly and carefully measure along the intersection of the lower portion of the faceboard and the exposed upper face of the backboard and then cut a suitable length from the scotia moulding. Using the mitre box, neatly saw mitre cuts at each end of this length of scotia. Check this for accuracy against the main assembly and fix in position using PVA adhesive and, if necessary, veneer or moulding pins. Cut lengths from the scotia moulding at least 25mm/1″ greater than required for the side mouldings at this position. Cut mitre at one end of each member and offer up to the already fixed front scotia moulding. Fix in position in the same manner as the front scotia and neatly cut off any surplus projection at the rear of the side mouldings.

Carefully re-sand the now fixed lower scotia moulding, paying particular attention to the mitred corners, using sandpaper wrapped around a short length of dowel.

Take the remaining portion of the 9mm/⅜″ scotia moulding and repeat the process just described to form the scotia just below the cornice frieze.

Next, take the 18mm/¾″ scotia moulding and form the cornice above the frieze in the same manner described for the lower scotia mouldings, ensuring that the upper surface of the cornice is flush with the top of the main assembly.

Check back over all the fixed scotia mouldings and neatly punch in any protruding heads of moulding pins, where used, using a 25mm/1″ panel pin as a punch. Fill in any resultant holes with filler and sand down when dry.

FINISHING & ASSEMBLY

Next, take the insertion movement and insert into the hole in the face of the assembly to ensure that a snug fit is obtained. Remove any projections in the hole as required.

Remove the movement and put to one side until finishes for the case have been completed. Drill a small hole in the back of the backboard at exact upper centre for hanging the completed clock on the wall or, alternatively, a small brass mirror plate may be screwed into the same position to serve the same purpose.

Check over the whole of the clockcase to ensure that there are no blemishes and remove any finger marks by the gentle use of a pencil eraser. Select the method of finishing preferred. Chapter 5 describes the options and methods used.

Finally, push the Insertion Movement into place.

'Groom' Wall Clock

Schedule of Operation

BACKBOARD & FACEBOARD

Take the 18mm/¾″ thick plywood and accurately mark out a piece 177 × 134mm/7″ × 5¼″ which is to form the backboard. Before cutting mark out the shape of the 'roof' as shown on the plan together with the 2 scalloped shapes at the lower corners of the backboard. Cut out the shape ensuring that the sawn edges are at an exact right angle to the front face. Correct any minor errors with a file and clean up with a sandpaper block. Now put the backboard to one side. (Photocopy the shaped area as described in para.1 of 'The Coachman'.)

Using the 18mm/¾″ thick plywood mark out a piece, size 134 × 240mm/5¼″ × 9½″, to form the faceboard. Before cutting mark out the shape of the 'roof', which should be identical to the roof already formed at the top of the backboard. Draw out the ornamental shape for the lower portion of the faceboard as shown on the plan and transfer this to the faceboard. Check that the 2 scalloped shapes are in fact identical to those already formed at the lower part of the backboard. Cut out the straight line portions of the faceboard with a tenon saw ensuring that the sawn edges are at right angles to the face of the faceboard. Cut out the ornamental shapes with a coping saw or fretsaw, again ensuring that the cut surfaces are at right angles to the face of the faceboard. Clean up all sawn edges with a file and sandpaper block or sandpaper wrapped dowel for the ornamental shapes.

Take both the backboard and the faceboard and on each mark out the position of the 60mm/2⅜″ diameter hole which will later accept the rear body of the insertion movement. Drill starter holes and with a coping saw or fretsaw carefully cut out the holes. Accuracy is important if the insertion movement is to fit snugly after final assembly. Check this measurement against actual movement being used.

Take the faceboard and place it face down on table or benchtop and offer up the backboard to it to check that the 'roof' lines and sides coincide precisely. Fix the two boards together with PVA adhesive and panel pins and after fixing correct any minor errors with a file and sandpaper block. Sand the face of the faceboard ready to accept veneers later and be sure that no edges or corners are rounded over in the sanding process. Place the now joined boards aside.

ARCHED HOOD

It will now be time to form the arched hood member. Take the remainder of the 18mm/¾" plywood and draw out the shape of the arched hood shown on the plan. Check that the slope of the roof coincides with that already formed on the now assembled face and backboards.

Cut out the various shapes of the arched hood with a coping saw or fretsaw taking great care to be sure that the cut edges are at right angles to the face of the member. Particular accuracy is required in cutting the actual arch since any wandering from the line of the curve will spoil the completed clock's appearance. Clean up all cut edges with a file and sandpaper block and with a sandpaper wrapped dowel in the case of the curved portions. Put the arched member to one side.

VENEERING

Take the assembled back and faceboards and cut suitably sized strips of veneer for the vertically grained sides of the assembly. Fix the veneers in position and trim off any surplus veneer. Next cut long strips of veneer across the grain to veneer the cross banded edges of the assembly. Fix in position and trim off any surplus veneer as before. Sand down the sides to a finish.

Veneer the face of the faceboard with vertically grained veneer including the area which will later be covered by the arched hood member. Trim off surplus veneer and sand down to a finish. At this stage do *not* attempt to veneer any part of the roof of the assembly. Place the partially veneered assembly to one side.

Take the arched hood member and cross band all cut edges with veneer apart from the roof. Trim off any surplus veneer and sand to a finish. At this stage do not attempt to veneer the face of the arched hood member but offer up the member to the assembled face and backboards and fix in position using PVA and panel pins. Ensure that the small projection beyond each side of the main assembly are in fact equal and that the line of the roof coincides with that of the main assembly. Sand down the face of the arched hood member ready to receive veneer. Veneer the face with horizontally grained veneer, trim off any surplus and sand to finish.

MOULDINGS

Take the length of 9mm/⅜" scotia moulding and sand down for the full length using a sanding block on the upper and lower edges and a sandpaper wrapped dowel for the concave surface.

Cut off two lengths of scotia that are greater than the front rake of the roof of the main assembly. Form a 'bastard mitre' where the two lengths of scotia are to intersect at the peak of the roof. Check for accuracy against the main assembly and correct or re-cut as necessary. Mark off against the main assembly where these members are to intersect the side members of the eaves and cut mitres in the scotia at these points. Fix the front gable scotias in position with PVA adhesive and, where necessary, moulding pins. Ensure that the top of the gable scotia coincides with the top line of the roof.

From the remainder of the length of scotia moulding cut two lengths at least 25mm/1" greater than the length required for the side eaves of the roof. Mitre each end and offer up to the already fixed front gable scotia moulding. Fix the side members in position with PVA adhesive and, if necessary, moulding pins. Make sure that the upper part of the side scotia members coincides with the line of the roof.

FINISHING & ASSEMBLY

Next sand down the whole of the roof area including the upper surfaces of the scotia moulds ready to receive veneer. Veneer the whole of the roof surface, including the upper part of the scotia moulding, with horizontally grained veneer. Trim off any surplus veneer and sand down the whole area to a finish.

Check back over the fixed scotia mouldings and neatly punch in any protruding heads of moulding pins, where used, using a 25mm/1" panel pin as a punch. Fill in any resultant holes with matching filler and sand down when dry.

Take the insertion movement and insert into the hole in the face of the assembly to check that a snug fit is obtained. Remove any minor projections in the hole as required.

Remove the movement and put to one side until finishes for the case have been completed. Drill a small hole in the back of the backboard at upper centre for hanging the completed clock on the wall or, alternatively, a small brass mirror plate may be screwed into the same position to serve the same purpose.

Check over the whole of the completed clock case to ensure that there are no blemishes and remove any finger marks by the gentle use of a pencil eraser. Select the method of finishing preferred as previously described.

Finally, push the Insertion Movement into place.

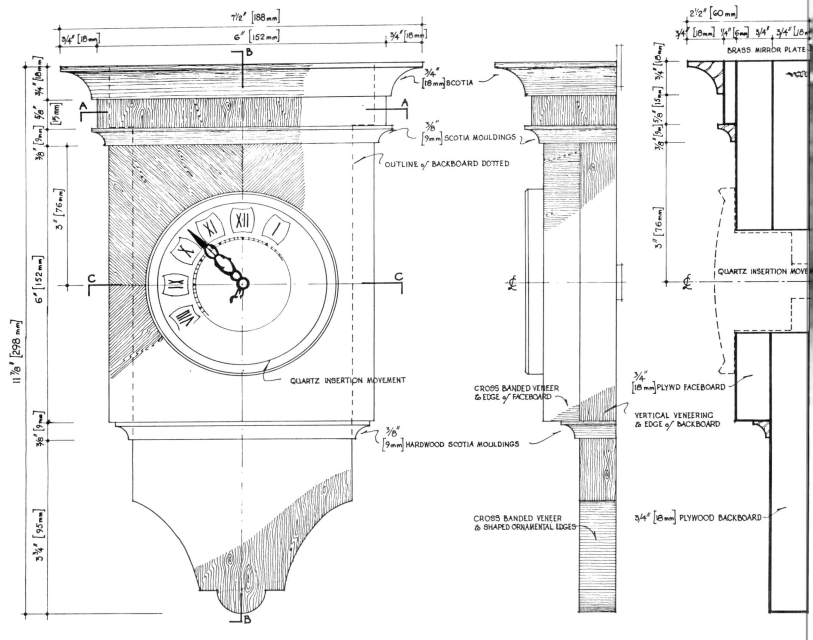

7½" [188mm]

6" [152mm]

¾" [18mm]

¾" [18mm]

B

¾" [18mm]

¾" [18mm] SCOTIA

A — A

⅝" [15mm]

⅜" [9mm]

3" [76mm]

6" [152mm]

11⅞" [298mm]

⅜" [9mm]

3¾" [95mm]

C ——— C

B

⅜" [9mm] SCOTIA MOULDINGS

OUTLINE of BACKBOARD DOTTED

XI   XII   I

X

IX

VIII

QUARTZ INSERTION MOVEMENT

⅜" [9mm] HARDWOOD SCOTIA MOULDINGS

½ FULL SIZE FRONT ELEVATION

CROSS BANDED VENEER to EDGE of FACEBOARD

CROSS BANDED VENEER to SHAPED ORNAMENTAL EDGES

½ F.S. SIDE ELEVATION

2½" [60mm]

¾" [18mm]   ¼" [6mm]   ¾"   ¾" [18mm]

BRASS MIRROR PLATE

⅜" [9mm]   ⅝" [15mm]   ¾" [18mm]

3" [76mm]

QUARTZ INSERTION MOVE'T

¾" [18mm] PLYWD FACEBOARD

VERTICAL VENEERING to EDGE of BACKBOARD

¾" [18mm] PLYWOOD BACKBOARD

½ F.S. SECTION B—

THE "COACHMAN" WALLCLOCK

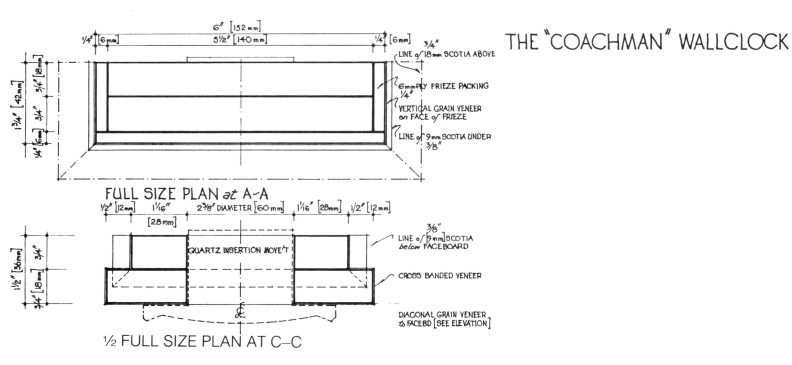

6" [152mm]

5½" [140mm]

¼" [6mm]   ¼" [6mm]

¾" [18mm]

¾" [18mm]

1¾" [42mm]

¾"

¼" [6mm]

¼" [6mm]

LINE of 18mm SCOTIA ABOVE

6mm PLY FRIEZE PACKING

VERTICAL GRAIN VENEER on FACE of FRIEZE

LINE of 9mm SCOTIA UNDER ⅜"

FULL SIZE PLAN at A-A

½" [12mm]   1 1/16" [28mm]   2⅜" DIAMETER [60mm]   1 1/16" [28mm]   ½" [12mm]

1½" [36mm]   ¾"

¾" [18mm]

QUARTZ INSERTION MOVE'T

LINE of ⅜" [9mm] SCOTIA below FACEBOARD

CROSS BANDED VENEER

DIAGONAL GRAIN VENEER to FACEBD [SEE ELEVATION]

½ FULL SIZE PLAN AT C—C

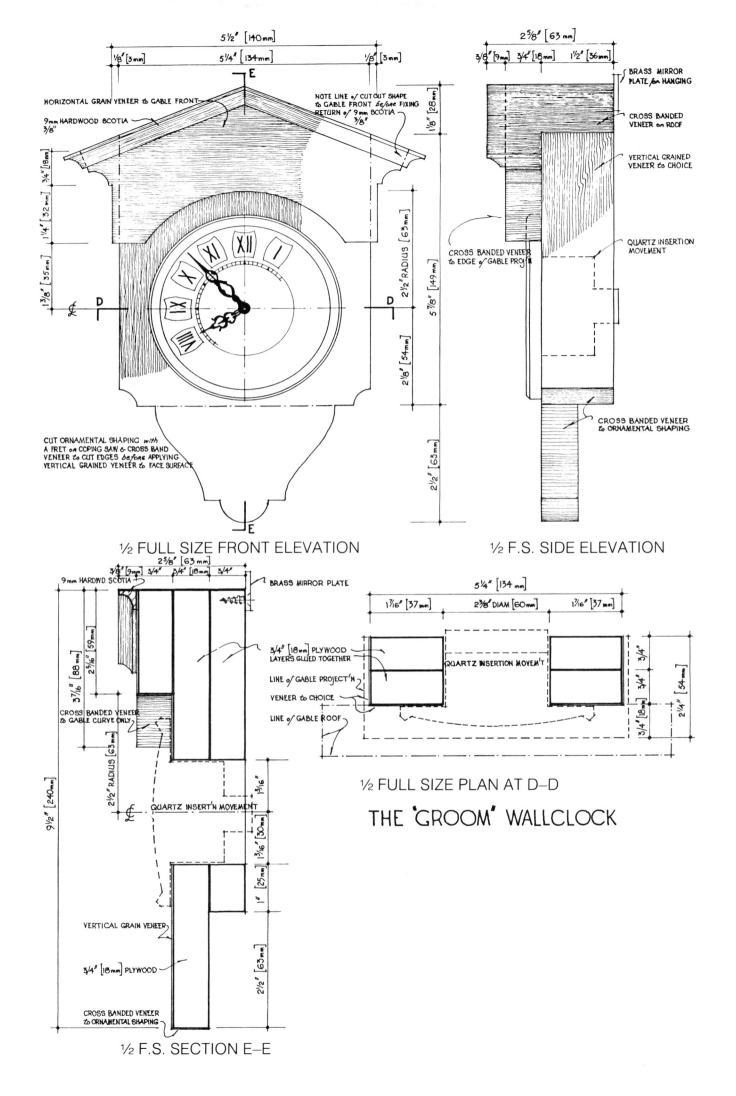

5½" [140mm]

5¼" [134mm]

⅛" [3mm]   ⅛" [3mm]

E

HORIZONTAL GRAIN VENEER to GABLE FRONT

9mm HARDWOOD SCOTIA
⅜"

NOTE LINE of CUT OUT SHAPE
to GABLE FRONT before FIXING
RETURN of 9mm SCOTIA
⅜"

¾" [18mm]

1¼" [32mm]

1⅜" [35mm]

D   D

XI XII I
X
IX
VIII

2½" RADIUS [63mm]

5⅝" [149mm]

2⅛" [54mm]

CUT ORNAMENTAL SHAPING with
A FRET on COPING SAW & CROSS BAND
VENEER to CUT EDGES before APPLYING
VERTICAL GRAINED VENEER to FACE SURFACE

2½" [63mm]

E

½ FULL SIZE FRONT ELEVATION

2⅝" [63mm]

⅜" [9mm] ¾" [18mm] 1½" [36mm]

BRASS MIRROR
PLATE for HANGING

CROSS BANDED
VENEER on ROOF

VERTICAL GRAINED
VENEER to CHOICE

1⅛" [28mm]

CROSS BANDED VENEER
to EDGE of GABLE PROJ'N

QUARTZ INSERTION
MOVEMENT

CROSS BANDED VENEER
to ORNAMENTAL SHAPING

½ F.S. SIDE ELEVATION

2⅝" [63mm]

⅜" [9mm] ¾" [18mm] ¾"

9mm HARDWD SCOTIA

BRASS MIRROR PLATE

3¾¼?

2⁵⁄₁₆" [59mm]

3⁷⁄₁₆" [88mm]

CROSS BANDED VENEER
to GABLE CURVE ONLY

2½" RADIUS [63mm]

9½" [240mm]

QUARTZ INSERT'N MOVEMENT

³⁄₁₆"

³⁄₁₆"

1" [25mm]

VERTICAL GRAIN VENEER

¾" [18mm] PLYWOOD

CROSS BANDED VENEER
to ORNAMENTAL SHAPING

2½" [63mm]

½ F.S. SECTION E–E

¾" [18mm] PLYWOOD
LAYERS GLUED TOGETHER

LINE of GABLE PROJECT'N

VENEER to CHOICE

LINE of GABLE ROOF

5¼" [134mm]

1⁷⁄₁₆" [37mm]   2⅜" DIAM [60mm]   1⁷⁄₁₆" [37mm]

QUARTZ INSERTION MOVEM'T

¾"
¾" [18mm]
¾"
2¼" [54mm]

½ FULL SIZE PLAN AT D–D

THE 'GROOM' WALLCLOCK

'Coachman' Cutting List

COMPONENT	QUANTITY	SECTION	LENGTH
Backboard Laminate	1	18 × 116	298
	1	¾″ × 4½″	11⅞″
Faceboard Laminate	1	18 × 140	194
	1	¾″ × 5½″	7¾″
Frieze — Side Pieces	2	6 × 33	36
	2	¼″ × 1⅜″	1½″
Frieze — Front Piece	1	6 × 33	152
	1	¼″ × 1⅜″	6″
Lower Scotia (Total Length)	1	9 × 9	188
	1	⅜″ × ⅜″	7½″
Middle Scotia (Total Length)	1	9 × 9	248 minimum
	1	⅜″ × ⅜″	10″ minimum
Top Scotia (Total Length)	1	18 × 18	308 minimum
	1	¾″ × ¾″	12½″ minimum

'Groom' Cutting List

COMPONENT	QUANTITY	SECTION	LENGTH
Backboard Laminate	1	18 × 134	177
	1	¾″ × 5¼″	7″
Middle Laminate	1	18 × 134	240
	1	¾″ × 5¼″	9½″
Faceboard Laminate (Gable)	1	18 × 88	184
	1	¾″ × 3 7/16″	7¼″
Scotia (Total Length)	1	9 × 9	264 minimum
	1	⅜″ × ⅜″	10½″ minimum

Clock Components and Hardware (excluding screws and pins)

CLOCK MOVEMENT — OPTIONS:

– 'Insertion Movement' (all-in-one movement/dial/bezel/glass/hands combination): 102mm/4″ outside diameter.
– Various designs and models available.

BRASSWARE:

– One mirror plate.

19.   'Huntsman' Wall Clock

The two main themes of this clock are the simple cabinet construction and the display
of the pendulum movement. The 'Minor' version of the Huntsman has a glazed door
whilst the 'Major' has a decorative panelled door that allows the viewer to glimpse the
pendulum through a fretwork design. The veneered, fretted panel offers the scope for
the use of decorative timbers.

Overall dimensions: 268 wide × 132 deep × 640mm high
10¹¹⁄₁₆″ wide × 5¼″ deep × 25⁵⁄₁₆″ high   Skill level ***

Schedule of Operations

The Huntsman 'Minor' and 'Major' wall clocks are constructed in virtually the same manner, the difference being that the 'Major' has a veneered and fretted panel in the door. Both clocks are designed to accommodate a quartz pendulum movement.

The Huntsman is basically a veneered box carcass (with an applied scotia and beading at the top) that has a laminated and veneered door with glass or wood panels set into it.

CARCASS CONSTRUCTION

The box carcass is built up from the backboard.

From your sheet of 12mm/½" plywood, accurately mark, cut and plane to size, ensuring that everything is straight and square. An access opening for the movement will have to be cut into the backboard (refer Front Elevation Door Partly Removed), mark the opening, first with a pencil and then with a knife-cut, then drill holes in the corner of the opening; the wood is then removed with a fret or coping saw, accurately file down to your knife cut. Sand clean the inside surface of the backboard with 150 grit and then 240 grit wet and dry.

Glue blocks should then be fixed all around the backboard. First, you should check that one of the gluing surfaces on each glue block is straight and flat and that the two surfaces which will eventually show on each glue block are sanded clean. Glue and pin (you might have to drill clearance holes for the pins) the straight and flat surfaces of each glue block to the main inside surface of the backboard, leaving the remaining gluing surface of the glue block projecting slightly beyond the planed edges of the backboard. When the glue has set, these remaining gluing surfaces can be planed flush and square with the planed edges of the backboard.

The side cheeks should now be made (refer Interior Elevation of Left Side Cheek and rest of plan). You should first plane the back edge of each side cheek, making sure that it is straight and square. From this back edge mark out the remaining outside lines of each side cheek; check that the dimensions of the two side cheeks are identical and the same length as the backboard. Cut out the side cheeks, ensuring that the front edges are accurately planed to their final line and that the top and bottom edges are two or three millimeters *oversize* from their final line (these will be

planed flush with the top and bottom boards after the complete box carcass has been assembled). Transfer the lines for the top and bottom edges from the main surface, square onto the back edge. Mark the 'cut-outs' for the front frieze and remove the wood with a tenon saw; accurately file to your final lines, checking for straightness and squareness.

Sand clean the inside surfaces of the side cheeks.

The top and bottom boards should now be made (refer Section A-A and Front Elevation Door Party Removed). The length of these boards should equal the width of the backboard. The width of the bottom board should equal the width of the side cheeks, and the width of the top board should stop at the back of the front frieze (refer Section A-A and Interior Elevation Left Side Cheek). Accurately mark out these boards on your sheet of 12mm/½" plywood; cut and plane to size, making sure that they are straight and square and that they relate to the other members of the box structure.

It will now be necessary to apply a balancing veneer to the inside surfaces of the side cheeks and the bottom board (the backboard and topboard are not veneered at all). A non-decorative veneer can be used for this purpose. Make sure that the inside surfaces of the side cheeks and bottom board (and the veneer) are dust-free before applying your adhesive, and that the edges of the veneer are neatly trimmed to the edges of the plywood after the veneer has been stuck down.

Sand clean the veneers after they have been applied.

The lines for the top and bottom edges of the side cheeks, which had previously been transferred from the main surface to the back edges, should now be transferred back to the main surface, onto the veneers. The position of the glue blocks for the top and bottom boards (refer Interior Elevation Side Cheek) can now be marked in relation to the top and bottom edges of the side cheeks. You should also mark the front line of the dial-board mount and its final fixing position.

The glue blocks and dial-board mounts can now be fixed. Check that the gluing surfaces of these members are straight, flat and square to each other, and that the remaining two surfaces of these members are sanded clean. Glue and pin the glue blocks and dial-board mounts in position.

The front frieze should now be made (refer Section A-A and Front Elevation Door Partly Removed). You need to plane the bottom edge of the frieze only, leaving the other three sides slightly oversize for planing down, after the complete box structure has been assembled and glued.

ASSEMBLING THE CARCASS

The box structure can be assembled with either glue and sash-cramps or with glue and pins. You should first do a test run by assembling the structure dry (without glue), around the backboard — this should be placed flat on a horizontal surface. At this stage, you can hold the structure together either with sash-cramps and blocks of wood to protect the sides of the box, or with 25mm/1″ panel pins that have not been fully hammered home. Check the following: that the sides are square to the backboard and to each other (a set square is useful for this); that the diagonal dimensions of the main opening of the box, i.e. where the door sits, are equal (checking the diagonals is the most reliable way of ensuring that a square or rectangle is geometrically correct; that the front frieze will sit accurately in position.

Once you are satisfied you can glue up using a PVA glue along all necessary surfaces. If you are using panel pins, these should be punched home with a nail punch and the holes filled and sanded later. If you are using sash-cramps, make sure that they are tight enough without distorting the sides. Any surplus glue should be cleaned with a damp rag.

After the glue has set, you should then plane off any projections around the carcass, Eg the ends of the front frieze and side cheeks. Check that the front edges of the side cheeks and bottom board, and the front surface of the front frieze, are all straight and flat in relation to each other. The complete box is then sanded clean using 150 grit wet and dry and made dust free.

VENEERING THE BOX

Veneer the outside surfaces of the box structure in the following order: 1. The bottom board; 2. The side cheeks; 3. The front edge of the bottom board (veneer this oversize in the length and cut back to the final lines once the veneer has been stuck down); 4. The front frieze; 5. The front edges of the side cheeks. If you wish, you can veneer the complete frieze and, later, the front surface of the door in a contrasting timber or contrasting 'figure' of the same timber.

DIAL-BOARD

The dial-board should now be made from your sheet of 6mm/¼″ plywood. Make sure that it accurately fits in position and drill the appropriate holes for the fixing screws. Put the dial-board to one side for sanding and finishing later.

DOOR CONSTRUCTION

The construction of the main door is based on the principle of laminating a sheet of 6mm/¼″ plywood (with a square and rectangular hole cut into it), to a sheet of 12mm/½″ plywood (with a slightly larger square and rectangular hole cut into it). The difference in dimensions of the respective holes will form a rebate in which the glass or the veneered and fretted panel will sit. In making the door, work in situation to the opening in your clock case as well as to the dimensions of your plan.

From your sheet of 12mm/½″ plywood, mark and cut out a panel to the dimensions of your opening *minus* the thickness of a piece of veneer all the way round; the edges of the door will have to be veneered all the way round, so you will have to make allowances for this if you want the door to have a snug fit in the opening of your box structure. Mark and cut a sheet of 6mm/¼″ plywood to the exact dimensions of the 12mm/½″ plywood.

With a marking gauge, establish the dimensions of the square and rectangular holes in the 6mm/¼″ plywood (refer Front Elevation 'Huntsman Major'). Repeat this process on the 12mm/½″ plywood panel, only increase the dimensions of the holes by 10mm/⅜″ to allow for a 5mm/³⁄₁₆″ rebate all the way round (refer Front Elevation Door Partly Removed). Cut out the holes by drilling in the corners and removing the wood with a coping saw. Carefully clean down to your marks with a sharp chisel and file.

Pin and glue the two sheets together making sure of accurate alignment. Punch the pins home, fill and sand clean when the filler is set.

When the glue has set, check the door for fit in the opening of your case, making allowances for the veneered edges of the door.

Sand clean the door with 150 grit wet and dry. The door should then be made dust free.

VENEERING THE DOOR

Veneer the surfaces of the door in the following order: 1. The inside surfaces of the holes in the 6mm/¼″ plywood (it is best if these are cross-banded); 2. The back surface of the door, (veneer the rails first and then the stiles); 3. The top and bottom edges of the door; 4. The side edges of the door; 5. The front surface of the door — this should be

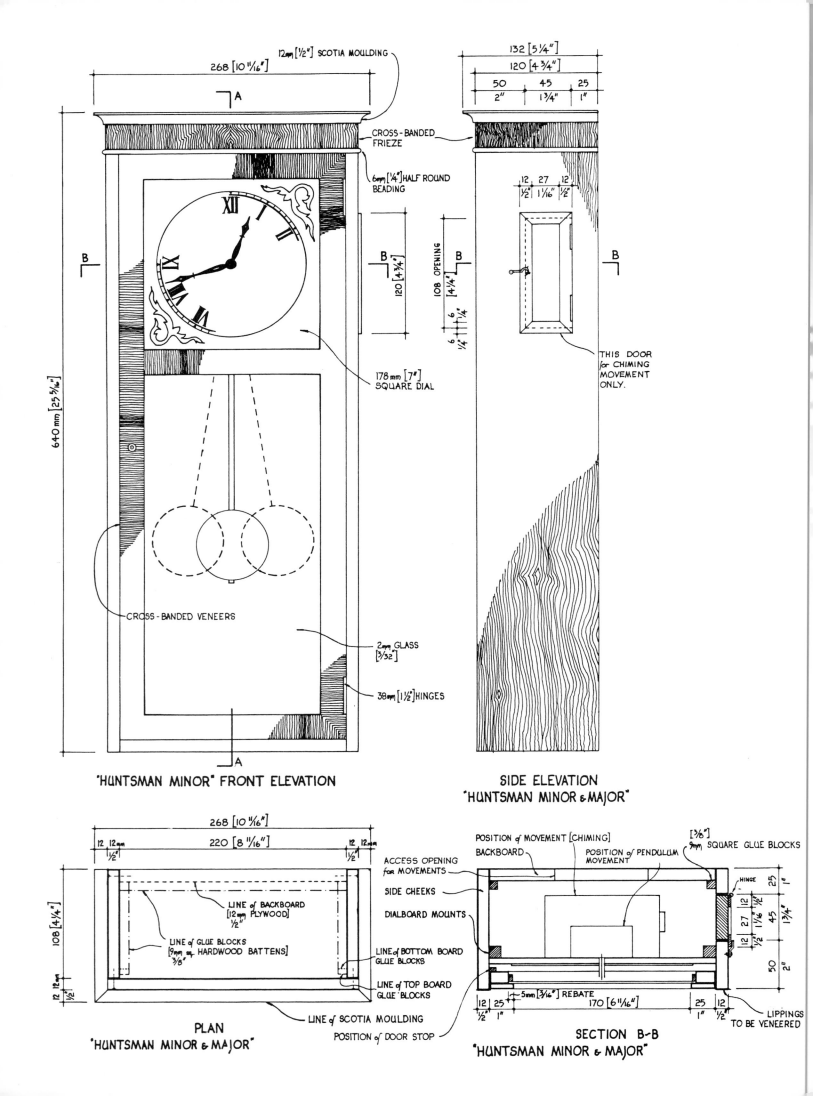

268 [10 11/16"]

12mm [½"] SCOTIA MOULDING

A

CROSS-BANDED
FRIEZE

6mm [¼"] HALF ROUND
BEADING

XII

120 [4¾"]

178mm [7"]
SQUARE DIAL

640 mm [25 5/16"]

B

CROSS-BANDED VENEERS

2mm GLASS
[3/32"]

38mm [1½"] HINGES

A

"HUNTSMAN MINOR" FRONT ELEVATION

---

132 [5¼"]
120 [4¾"]

| 50 | 45 | 25 |
| 2" | 1¾" | 1" |

CROSS-BANDED FRIEZE

| 12 | 27 | 12 |
| ½" | 1 1/16" | ½" |

108 OPENING

B

THIS DOOR
for CHIMING
MOVEMENT
ONLY.

**SIDE ELEVATION
"HUNTSMAN MINOR & MAJOR"**

---

268 [10 11/16"]
220 [8 11/16"]

12 | 12mm | | 12 | 12mm
½" | | | ½"

108 [4¼"]

LINE of BACKBOARD
[12mm PLYWOOD]
½"

LINE of GLUE BLOCKS
[9mm sq. HARDWOOD BATTENS]
3/8"

LINE of BOTTOM BOARD
GLUE BLOCKS

LINE of TOP BOARD
GLUE BLOCKS

12 | 12mm
½"

LINE of SCOTIA MOULDING

**PLAN
"HUNTSMAN MINOR & MAJOR"**

POSITION of MOVEMENT [CHIMING]

BACKBOARD

[3/8"]
9mm SQUARE GLUE BLOCKS

POSITION of PENDULUM
MOVEMENT

ACCESS OPENING
for MOVEMENTS

SIDE CHEEKS

DIALBOARD MOUNTS

HINGE

25	1"
12	½"
27	1 1/16"
45	1¾"
12	½"
50	2"

LINE of BOTTOM BOARD
GLUE BLOCKS

LINE of TOP BOARD
GLUE BLOCKS

5mm [3/16"] REBATE

12 | 25 | | 170 [6 11/16"] | | 25 | 12
½" | 1" | | | | 1" | ½"

POSITION of DOOR STOP

LIPPINGS
TO BE VENEERED

**SECTION B-B
"HUNTSMAN MINOR & MAJOR"**

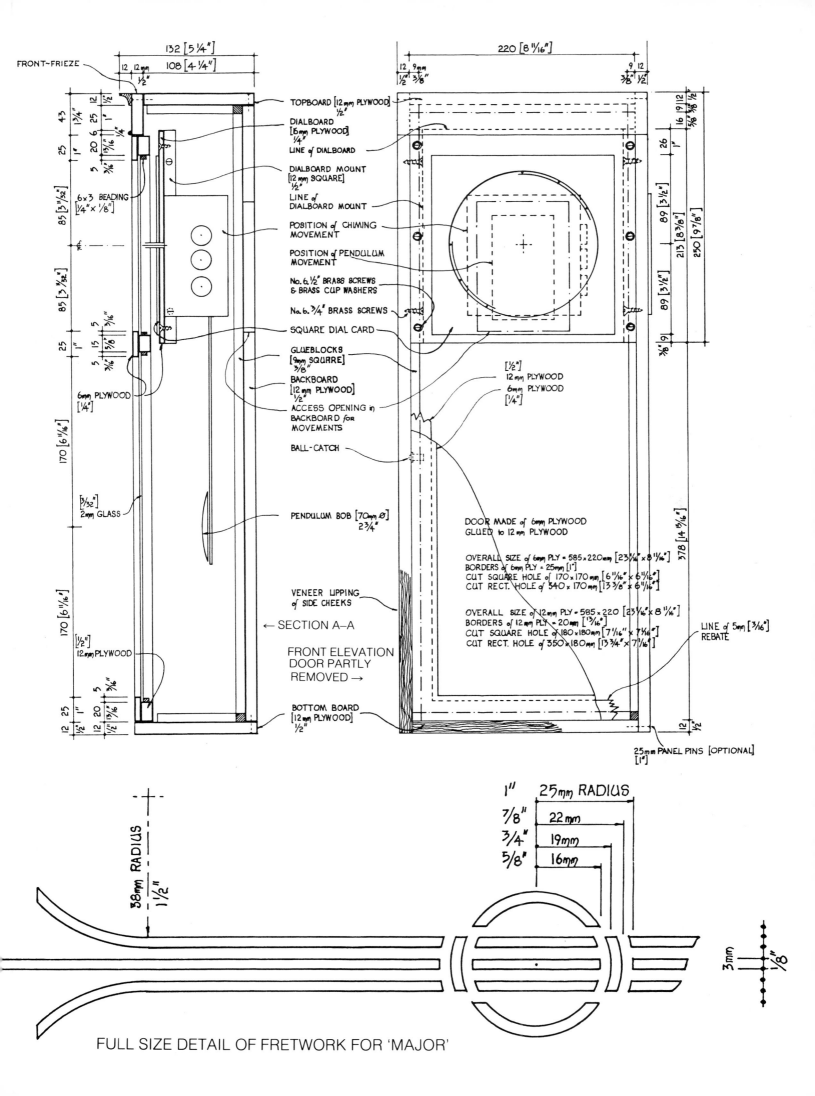

FRONT~FRIEZE

132 [5¼"]
12 12mm
½"
108 [4¼"]

220 [8¹¹⁄₁₆"]
12 9mm
½" ⅜"
9 12
⅜" ½"

16 [9⁄16]12
⅝" ½"

43 [1¾"] 25 [1"] 12 ½"
25 [1"] 20 6 ⅝" ¼"
5 ⁵⁄₁₆"

26 [1"]

85 [3³²⁄"] 6×3 BEADING [¼" × ⅛"]

89 [3½"]

85 [3³²⁄"]

213 [8⅜"]

250 [9⅞"]

25 [1"] 5 15 ⅝"
5 ⁵⁄₁₆"

89 [3½"]

6mm PLYWOOD [¼"]

9 [⅜"]

170 [6¹¹⁄₁₆"]

[½"]
12mm PLYWOOD
6mm PLYWOOD
[¼"]

[3³²⁄"]
2mm GLASS

170 [6¹¹⁄₁₆"]

378 [14¹⁵⁄₁₆"]

[½"]
12mm PLYWOOD

170 [6¹¹⁄₁₆"]

12 25 [1"] 5 ⁵⁄₁₆"
20 [¹³⁄₁₆"]
12 ½"

TOPBOARD [12mm PLYWOOD] ½"

DIALBOARD [6mm PLYWOOD] ¼"

LINE of DIALBOARD

DIALBOARD MOUNT [12mm SQUARE] ½"

LINE of DIALBOARD MOUNT

POSITION of CHIMING MOVEMENT

POSITION of PENDULUM MOVEMENT

No. 6. ½" BRASS SCREWS & BRASS CUP WASHERS

No. 6. ¾" BRASS SCREWS

SQUARE DIAL CARD

GLUEBLOCKS [9mm SQUARE] ⅜"

BACKBOARD [12mm PLYWOOD] ½"

ACCESS OPENING in BACKBOARD for MOVEMENTS

BALL-CATCH

PENDULUM BOB [70mm Ø] 2¾"

VENEER LIPPING of SIDE CHEEKS

← SECTION A–A

FRONT ELEVATION DOOR PARTLY REMOVED →

BOTTOM BOARD [12mm PLYWOOD] ½"

[½"]
12mm PLYWOOD
6mm PLYWOOD
[¼"]

DOOR MADE of 6mm PLYWOOD GLUED to 12mm PLYWOOD

OVERALL SIZE of 6mm PLY = 585×220mm [23¹⁄₁₆" × 8¹¹⁄₁₆"]
BORDERS of 6mm PLY = 25mm [1"]
CUT SQUARE HOLE of 170×170mm [6¹¹⁄₁₆" × 6¹¹⁄₁₆"]
CUT RECT. HOLE of 340×170mm [13⅜" × 6¹¹⁄₁₆"]

OVERALL SIZE of 12mm PLY = 585×220 [23¹⁄₁₆" × 8¹¹⁄₁₆"]
BORDERS of 12mm PLY = 20mm [¹³⁄₁₆"]
CUT SQUARE HOLE of 180×180mm [7¹⁄₁₆" × 7¹⁄₁₆"]
CUT RECT. HOLE of 350×180mm [13¾" × 7¹⁄₁₆"]

LINE of 5mm [³⁄₁₆"] REBATE

12 ½"

25mm PANEL PINS [OPTIONAL] [1"]

38mm RADIUS
1½"

1" 25mm RADIUS
⅞" 22mm
¾" 19mm
⅝" 16mm

3mm
⅛"

FULL SIZE DETAIL OF FRETWORK FOR 'MAJOR'

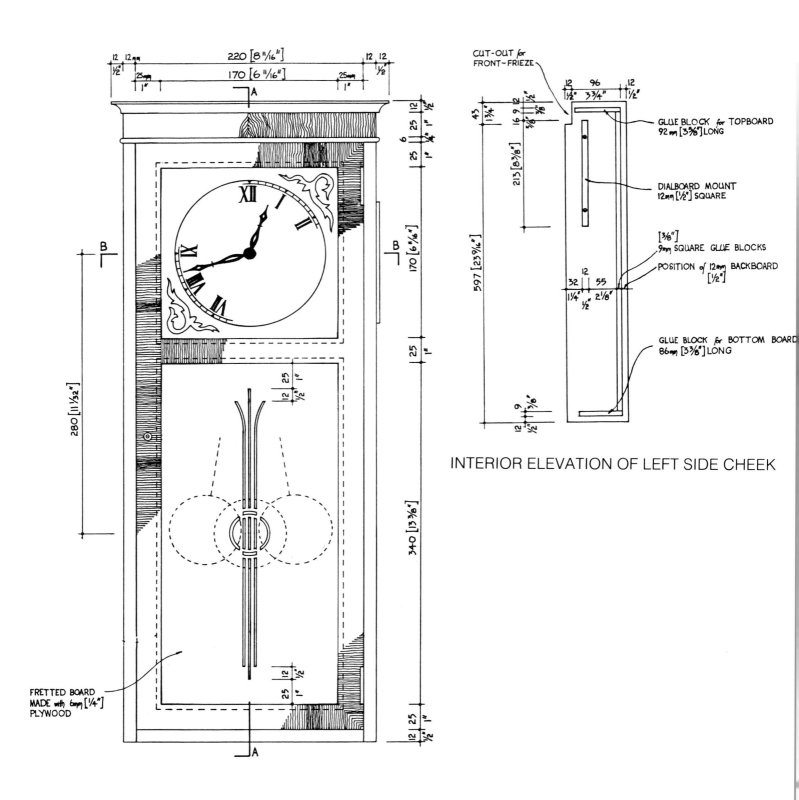

FRONT ELEVATION 'HUNTSMAN MAJOR'

INTERIOR ELEVATION OF LEFT SIDE CHEEK

CUT-OUT for
FRONT-FRIEZE

GLUE BLOCK for TOPBOARD
92mm [3⅝"] LONG

DIALBOARD MOUNT
12mm [½"] SQUARE

[⅜"]
9mm SQUARE GLUE BLOCKS

POSITION of 12mm BACKBOARD
[½"]

GLUE BLOCK for BOTTOM BOARD
86mm [3⅜"] LONG

FRETTED BOARD
MADE with 6mm [¼"]
PLYWOOD

cross-banded as shown in the Front Elevation. When cross-banding the door, I find that it is best to do it in the following manner: a) the centre rail; b) veneer the stiles, stopping short of the mitres by approx 30mm/1³/₁₆"; c) cut out the remaining cross-banding for the stiles (including the mitres) and butt them in position, only fix them to the door with two-sided tape; d) cut out the cross-banding for the top and bottom rails, place in position with them underlapping the cross-banding that has been fixed to the stiles with two-sided tape — you can then mark the mitres for the cross-banding on the rails; e) cut the mitres on the rails, cross-banding, check for accuracy, and glue in position; f) remove the cross-banding on the stiles that had been fixed with two-sided tape, clean off tape, then glue the cross-bandings back into position. Make sure that all the veneer edges are trimmed into the door frame as you go along.

After the door has been veneered the slots for the hinges can be cut.

Sand carefully all the newly veneered surfaces on the box carcass and the main door. If you are going to use grain filler it should be done at this stage.

FINISHING

The type of finish used is, ultimately, the individual craftperson's choice. I suggest that you paint the following surfaces with a matt black paint (*Eg* blackboard paint) — the complete interior of the box carcass, the backboard, the top of the topboard (do this after the 12mm/½" scotia moulding has been applied), and the dial-board. Apply the stains and finishes of your choice (excluding the final wax polish) to the rest of the case before going onto the next stage.

After finishing the carcass and door, the 12mm/½" scotia and 6mm/¼" half round beading should then be fitted. The same procedure for marking, cutting, fixing and finishing is applied to both the beading and scotia. I shall use the scotia as an example.

Measure the overall length of the scotia (leaving room for the cutting of the mitres and a little surplus) required to fit around the top of the box carcass. Cut to *overall* length and sand clean *before* cutting the mitres. Mark the position of the mitres on the front scotia first, then *accurately* cut to size. Tape this moulding in position. Cut the mitres for the appropriate side scotias and check that they fit the front scotia. Note here that you should leave yourself a slight overlap at the back of the side scotias for trimming after they have been glued in position. Once you are satisfied

that the scotias (or the beadings) fit accurately together, you should then untape the front scotia and apply the finish of your choice to all three scotias (or beadings).

When the finish is dry, the scotias can be glued in position using a fast grab glue (you might have to scrape off some of the existing finish on the box carcass to provide a gluing surface for the scotias). Glue the front scotia first and position accurately — allow the glue to set; apply glue to a side scotia, position, allow the glue to set; repeat for the other side scotia; trim off surplus at the back of the scotias. Repeat gluing procedure for the beadings.

Apply blackboard paint to the top of the topboard/scotias. Wax polish the complete box structure.

FINAL ASSEMBLY

The glass (or fretted panel — see later) can now be fitted to the main door. Place in position and measure the size of the fixing beadings required — these can be made from 3mm/⅛" construction veneer. Cut to their appropriate lengths, put them to one side and apply the finish of your choice. Remove the glass and wax polish the door. Replace the glass and fix the beadings in position; these can either be pinned in position (clearance holes should be drilled for the pins) or lightly glued.

Fix backboard in position (this should have a hole drilled in it to accommodate the clock movement — the hole should be in the exact centre of the dial/upper window).

Drill a hole/s for the ball catch (refer Front Elevation Door Partly Removed) and fit in position.

Secure the hinges to the door and hang the door to your satisfaction.

Fix one or two mirror plates to the top of the backboard.

Fix the brass knob to the door.

Fix the dial to the backboard with either contact adhesive or with two-sided tape.

Fix the movement in position and fix the hands onto the movement.

FRETTED PANEL FOR THE 'HUNTSMAN MAJOR'

Cut a panel of 6mm/¼" plywood to fit the lower opening in the main door. Check the plywood for defects and correct if necessary. Sand the front surface clean with 150 grit wet and dry, remove dust. Veneer the front surface with your chosen decorative timber. Mark out the design for the fretwork by taking measurements from the detail on the plan. With a sharp craft knife, cut through the veneer along your markings; on the curved details you should make very light guiding marks with the knife and *gradually* increase the depth of your cuts. Drill holes at the end of each slot and carefully remove the wood with a fretsaw. File accurately down to your final line.

Check the back surface for any defects and fill if necessary. Sand clean with 150 grit wet and dry. Veneer the back surface with a non-decorative balancing veneer. Cramp the panel to a flat surface with the front surface showing upwards. With a sharp craft knife, carefully remove the balancing veneer at the back of the fretwork by cutting *through* the fretwork. Sand and clean the fretwork where necessary.

Sand clean both sides of the panel with 150 and 240 grit wet and dry. Apply the finish of your choice. You might like to apply blackboard paint to the inside surfaces of the fretwork, though this should be done after the main finish has been applied so any surplus can be wiped off the main surfaces.

Fit the panel in the same manner as the glass, though you will need beadings of a smaller width.

It is worth noting that the fretwork can be made with an electric router if you have one.

Cutting list

COMPONENT	QUANTITY	SECTION	LENGTH
Topboard	1	12 × 108	220
	1	½″ × 4¼″	8¹¹⁄₁₆″
Bottomboard	1	12 × 120	220
	1	½″ × 4¾″	8¹¹⁄₁₆″
Backboard	1	12 × 220	616
	1	½″ × 8¹¹⁄₁₆″	24⁵⁄₁₆″
Sidecheeks	2	12 × 120	640
	2	½″ × 4¾″	25⁵⁄₁₆″
Front Frieze	1	12 × 43	268
	1	½″ × 1¾″	10¹¹⁄₁₆″
Dial-board	1	6 × 213	220
	1	¼″ × 8⅜″	8¹¹⁄₁₆″
Dial-board Mounts	2	12 × 12	213
	2	½″ × ½″	8⅜″
Inner Layer of Front Door	1	12 × 220	585
	1	½″ × 8¹¹⁄₁₆″	23¹⁄₁₆″
Outer Layer of Front Door	1	6 × 220	585
	1	¼″ × 8¹¹⁄₁₆″	23¹⁄₁₆″
Inner Layer of Side Door	1	12 × 45	108
	1	½″ × 1¾″	4¼″
Stripwood Surround for Side Door	1	3 × 12	342 minimum
(Total Length)	1	⅛″ × ½″	13⁹⁄₁₆″ minimum
Square Glue Blocks (Total Length)	1	12 × 12	1616 minimum
	1	½″ × ½″	63⅝″
Glazing Beads (Total Length for	1	3 × 6	2050 surplus
Minor — adjust for Major)	1	⅛″ × ¼″	80⅞″ surplus
Huntsman Major — Fretted Door Panel	1	6 × 180	350
	1	¼″ × 7¹⁄₁₆″	13¾″

Scotia (Total Length)	1	12 × 12	532 minimum
	1	½″ × ½″	21³⁄₁₆″ minimum
Half Round Beading (Total Length)	1	6 × 3	496 minimum
	1	¼″ × ⅛″	19¹¹⁄₁₆″

Clock Components and Hardware (excluding screws and pins)

CLOCK MOVEMENT — OPTIONS:

1. Mechanical movements.
   Spring Driven.
   Pendulum length from centres of handshaft to pendulum bob: 280mm/11″.
   Maximum pendulum swing: 203mm/8″.
   Maximum 'plate size' (front face of movement: 165 × 165mm/6½″ × 6½″.
   Depth of movement: variable according to make — adjust depth of box if necessary.
   Handshaft: check length and adjust thickness of dial-board, if necessary.

2. Quartz Pendulum Movements.
   Pendulum length from centres of handshaft to pendulum bob: 280mm/11″.
   Maximum pendulum swing: 203mm/8″.
   Chiming/melody movements also available.
   Handshaft/fixing nut length: to suit 6–8mm/¼″ – ⁵⁄₁₆″ dial-board and dial thickness.

CLOCK DIAL — OPTIONS:

- 170 × 170mm/7″ × 7″ square dial: brass, aluminium or card (drill holes in dial for front winding mechanical movement).
- OR 160mm/6⁵⁄₁₆″ diameter chapter ring fixed to decorative dial-board.
- Note: If front winding mechnaical movement is used, drill holes in the dial and bush to accommodate winding keys.

CLOCK HANDS:

- Bushed to suit chosen mechanical or quartz movement.
- Length to suit dial size.
- Pattern to suit individual choice.

BRASSWARE:

- Hinges:
  One pair of 38mm/1½″ butt hinges (front door);
  One pair of 25mm/1″ butt hinges (side door/optional).
- Door locks:
  Two 6mm/¼″ ball catches (front door);
  One hook and eye (side door/optional).
- Door knob: 8 or 9mm/⁵⁄₁₆″ or ⅜″ diameter.
- One mirror plate.

GLASS:

- Two panes to suit door (Minor).
- One pane to suit door (Major).

20. 'Deacon' Clock

This design was a forerunner to the Full Case Wall Clock employing a double glazed door hung onto a simple box carcass with a decorative crestboard and 'stacked and moulded' pendant base. The main differences between the two designs lie with the decorative details, the size, and the manner in which the door relates to the main carcass.

Overall dimensions: 182 wide × 88 deep × 439mm high
7¼" wide × 3½" deep × 17½" high

Skill level **

Schedule of Operations

BOX CARCASS ASSEMBLY

The design of this clock case is based on the principle of a box carcass constructed with simple butt joints and glue blocks with the base shape and crest added.

Take the sheet of 12mm/½" plywood and carefully mark out the overall sizes of the side cheek boards and the top and bottom boards. At this stage note that the topboard differs in size from the bottom board. Cut out the shapes and check that they are square at all corners. Check the side cheek boards to ensure that they are identical. Clean up the cut edges with a block plane and sanding block, using 150 grit garnet paper, and ensure that the cut edges are square with the face.

Take the sheet of 12mm/½" plywood and mark and cut out the overall size of the rear member of the door. Check for squareness and clean up the cut edges in the manner already described. Place to one side for future use.

Take the sheet of 6mm/¼" plywood and mark and cut out the overall size of the front member of the door. Check for squareness and clean up the cut edges as before. Also place this member to one side for future use.

From the remainder of the sheet of 6mm/¼" plywood mark and cut out the overall size of the dial-board and the backboard. Check both components for squareness and clean up the cut edges as before. Place the dial-board to one side for future use.

Take the backboard just made and offer up the side cheek boards and the top and bottom boards to the backboard to ensure that all are a snug fit one with the other. At this stage it is suggested that the whole of the box carcass be assembled dry (i.e. without glue), by means of veneer pins lightly tacked in place in order to ensure that all the components fit well with each other and are square and parallel. After you are sure that all parts fit well, remove the temporary veneer pins and break down the temporary assembly into its component parts.

Note from the plan the lengths of glue blocks needed at the junction of the backboard and the side cheek boards and cut these lengths from the triangular section ramin strip. Glue these lengths of glue block in position on the backboard using PVA adhesive and veneer pins. Wipe off any excess adhesive with a damp rag and after the glue has had time to set (usually about 1 hour) check that the exposed face of the block which will ultimately be glued to the cheek boards is truly square to the face of the back-

board. *This is most important.* Correct the squareness as necessary using the block plane.

Before gluing the side cheek boards in position carefully mark out on the backboard the position of the access hole for the movement. Drill for and cut out with a fretsaw or coping saw this access hole and clean up the cut edges with a sanding block and garnet paper.

Take the side cheek boards and glue and pin in position on the backboard making sure that the top and bottom edges of the cheek boards coincide precisely with the top and bottom of the backboard. Wipe off any surplus adhesive. When the glue on this part of the assembly has had time to set, lightly spread adhesive on the edges of the top and bottom boards and insert in position into the assembly and secure with veneer pins. After this, place the now completed carcass to one side.

DOOR

Take the already cut out rear member of the door assembly and carefully mark on the positions of the 126mm/5" square glazing holes. Drill for and cut out the holes with a fretsaw or coping saw and clean up the cut edges with a sanding block and garnet paper. Set this rear member to one side and next take the cut out front member of the door assembly. Mark out the 114mm/4½" square glazing holes and drill for and cut out carefully with a fretsaw or coping saw and clean up the cut edges with a sandpaper block and garnet paper, making sure that the cut edges of the holes are kept square with the front face without rounding over in the sanding process.

Take the rear member of the door assembly and place face up on the bench and spread a thin layer of PVA adhesive all over the face. Place the front member down on to the glued face, position so that the outer cut edges coincide with all outer edges of the rear member, securing in position with veneer pins. After the door assembly has dried check the assembly of the combined outer cut edges for squareness with the front face and correct with a block plane as required.

BASE SHAPE ASSEMBLY

The next stage in your project will be to build the base shape using 18mm/¾" scotia moulding and 12mm/½" quadrant, together with 18mm/¾" and 12mm/½" plywood backing pieces. First, cut out a rectangular piece of 18mm/¾" plywood size 108 × 59mm/4¼" × 2⅜", making sure that the corners are square and that the cut surfaces are at right angles to the face. Clean up the cut surfaces with a sanding block. Next take the box carcass assembly already completed and fix the 18mm/¾" plywood backing piece to the underside of the bottom board of the box with PVA adhesive making certain that it is accurately positioned 25mm/1" each side from the side of the baseboard and 25mm/1" back from the front of the baseboard. The back of the packing piece should be flush with the back of the box carcass. Take the length of 18mm/¾" scotia moulding and cut lengths to suit the perimeter of the packing piece just fixed, forming accurate mitres at the points of intersection and leaving a projecting portion at the rear of the side lengths. Glue and pin the scotia mouldings in position and after the glue has set, cut off the projecting parts of the side mouldings flush with the back of the box carcass.

Take the 12mm/½" quadrant and cut off suitable lengths to place in position below the 18mm/¾" scotia just fixed in position. At this stage it is important to note that the front of the quadrant should be flush with the lower front edge of the scotia so that the two together will form the large 'ogee' shape shown on the plan. Neatly mitre the intersecting corners of the quadrant and glue and pin in position to the underside of the 18mm/¾" packing pieces, leaving a projection at the rear of the side quadrants which will be cut off at the rear of the box carcass in the same manner as the scotia. Carefully measure the space behind the mouldings and cut out a 12mm/½" plywood packing piece to accurately fit the space. Glue this into position with PVA adhesive.

Next take the remainder of the 18mm/¾" scotia and cut lengths to fit below the quadrant just fixed. Mitre the corners and glue and pin in position to the underside of the 12mm/½" packing piece just fixed. Cut out and fit an 18mm/¾" packing piece in the manner previously described. Repeat the process with the lower 12mm/½" quadrant, again forming a packing piece. On completion of the assembly of the base shape, check over the whole of the base shape and sand down the mouldings. Trim off any surplus projections at the rear of the packing pieces with a block plane.

DIAL-BOARD

Take the previously cut out dial-board and, after marking the exact centre point, drill a 10mm/⅜" hole for the movement fixing nut. Then take the dial-board and fix in position in the upper part of the box carcass with glue blocks. Care should be exercised to ensure that the dial-board is accurately positioned and that allowance is made for the thickness of the chosen dial type which will be fixed later.

CREST

The next step is to form the crest shape for the top of the clock case. Take the remainder of the 12mm/½" plywood and draw out the shape shown on the plan. Cut out the shape with a fretsaw or coping saw ensuring that the saw is kept upright. Clean up the shaped edges with a medium grade half round file and a sanding block. Place the crest shape to one side.

VENEERING

The next process is to undertake veneering of the various parts and assemblies already made.

Take the door assembly and cut a piece of vertically grained veneer to cover the back of the assembly, allowing about 3mm/⅛" over the edges. Trim for the glazing holes about 3mm/⅛" smaller than the holes required. Put the veneer taken from the holes to one side for use as cross-banding later. Veneer the back of the door assembly making sure that it is well rolled down with a roller or a short length of dowel and trim off excess veneer. Cut out narrow strips of veneer from the glazing hole surplus and cross-band the door edges and the edges of the glazing holes and trim off surplus veneer as before. Next, cross-band the whole of the door front forming neat mitre cuts at the corners as shown on the plan. Trim off surplus veneer and then sand down the whole of the door to a finish using 240 grit wet and dry paper used dry on a sanding block. Work with the grain of the veneer only. Place the now veneered door to one side to await final fitting.

Take the crest shape and veneer cross-banding on all the cut edges and trim off surplus veneer. Accurately mark on the face of the crest shape a centre line at exact right angles to the lower edge of the crest and then veneer the face in the manner shown on the plans. Trim off surplus veneer and sand to a finish with 240 grit paper as before. Paper wrapped round a dowel is best for finishing the curved shapes. Place the crest to one side for later fixing.

Take the box carcass assembly and cut out strips of horizontally grained veneer to suit the base shape which should be veneered first. Commence with the sides of the base shape, ensuring that the veneer is well rolled down on the curves and trim off surplus veneer. Next veneer the front of the base shape, trimming off surplus with great care at the mitred corners of the shape.

Veneer the front edges of the box carcass next, using vertical and horizontally grained veneer neatly mitred at the corners and trim off surplus. Veneer the side cheek boards using vertically grained veneer. Trim off surplus and sand the whole of the box carcass to a finish with 240 grit paper and a sanding block, taking care to work with the grain.

DOOR HANGING

Accurately mark on the back of the door the position of the brass hinges and screw the hinges in position. There is no need with this particular design of clock case to cut any recesses in the door for the hinges. Offer up the door to the box carcass and carefully mark the position of the hinges on the front of the right hand cheekboard. Cut out recesses in the front of the cheekboard to accept the hinges when the door is fixed at a later time. The depth of hinge recess should be slightly less than the thickness of the hinge in the *closed* position. Place the door assembly to one side.

FINISHING & ASSEMBLY

At this stage it will be necessary to select the method of finishing desired. If you decide to opt for a traditional type of finish (i.e. grain fill, stain, seal and polish) the finishes should be carried out before fixing the 9mm/⅜″ scotia mouldings. Should you decide upon a varnished finish then those scotia moulds should be fixed now. Proceed in the manner described for the 18mm/¾″ scotias with neatly mitred corners and a projection at the rear of the side mouldings to be cut off after fixing. If these moulds have been fixed with veneer pins in addition to the adhesive then the heads of the pins should be neatly punched in and filled with filling of a colour to match the natural wood of the mouldings. After the filling has dried, sand down to a finish with 240 grit paper.

Carefully glue and fix the crest in position at the top of the clock case using a short length of glue block at the rear of the crest. Check over the whole of the completed case and door and remove any dirty marks with a pencil eraser and well brush off any sanding dust. When all is clean and dust free, apply the varnish as recommended by the manufacturer. Once all varnish has thoroughly dried offer up the door and screw the hinges to the front of the right-hand cheek in the recesses previously formed. Fix the small brass

door-pull in position and fix a small brass hook and eye to the left-hand cheekboard as shown on the plan.

Glaze the two glazing holes in the door with clear glass before hanging the door and hold the panels in position with glazing beads formed from 6mm/¼″ ramin strip fixed with veneer pins.

Next, glue in position with a contact adhesive the clock dial of your choice and fix the movement in position with the centre fixing nut supplied with the movement. Check the length of the pendulum rod supplied with the movement and remove any surplus length using a junior hacksaw. The length of the pendulum rod should be such that the pendulum bob, when fitted, should be positioned in the centre of the lower glass panel. slide the bob into position at the end of the pendulum rod and fit the hands selected to go with the dial into position on the spindle of the movement.

Should you have decided to select the traditional type of finish, then proceed with the finish before fixing the scotia moulds in position. This will enable the finish to be carried out without any annoyance from the projections of the scotias. Before applying any wax to the clock case as a whole, the scotias should be cut to length, mitred, sanded to a finish with 240 grit paper and have a finish applied before fixing in position. In this case the completed scotias should be fixed in position with a contact adhesive and *not* PVA adhesive. After assembly of the scotias, wax polish the whole of the case and proceed with the installation of the dial movement etc. as described above.

Should you have decided to follow the alternative dial suggestion contained on page 192, then the coloured felt or velvet should be glued to the dial-board with a contact adhesive. In this particular case the glue should be applied to the surface of the dial-board only and the felt or velvet applied while the adhesive is still wet. If using a chapter ring without a self-adhesive backing, it should be stuck to the face of the felt or velvet with contact adhesive applied in a narrow band about 12mm/½″ wide along the centre line of the ring. This will obviate any risk of excess adhesive spoiling the surface of the velvet. The movement etc. should then be installed as described above.

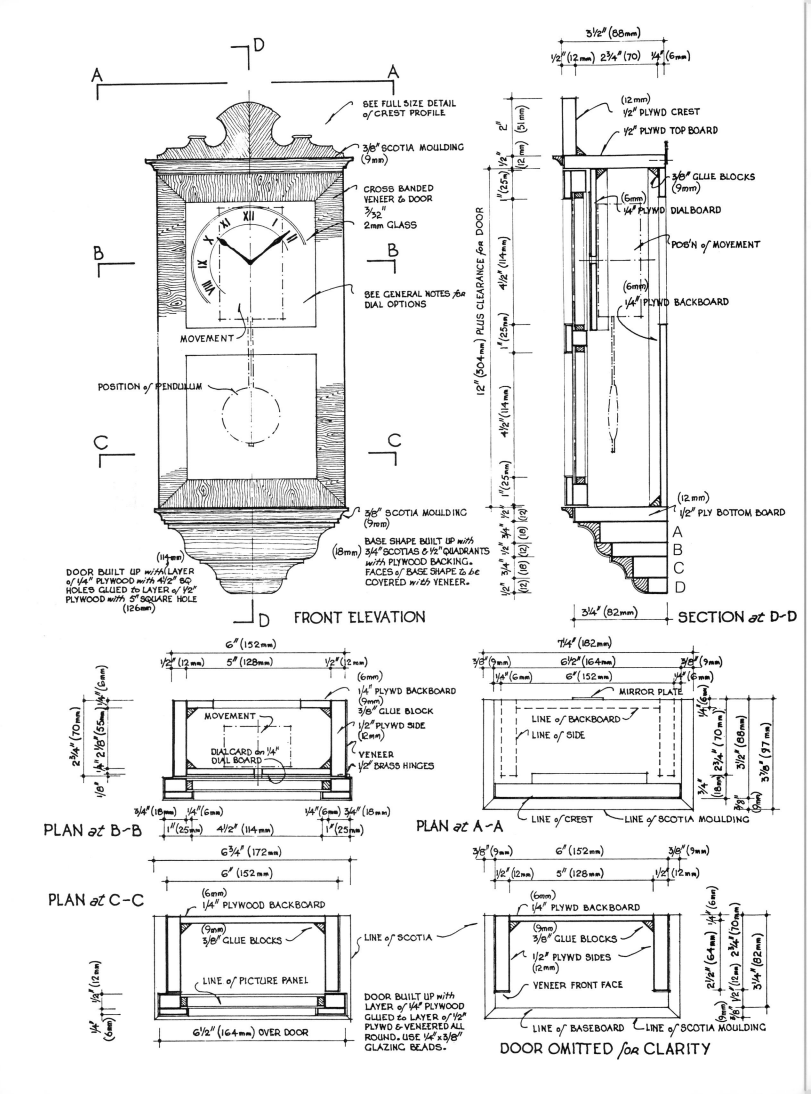

SEE FULL SIZE DETAIL
of CREST PROFILE

3/8" SCOTIA MOULDING
(9mm)

CROSS BANDED
VENEER to DOOR
3/32"
2mm GLASS

SEE GENERAL NOTES for
DIAL OPTIONS

MOVEMENT

POSITION of PENDULUM

3/8" SCOTIA MOULDING
(9mm)

BASE SHAPE BUILT UP with
(18mm) 3/4" SCOTIAS & 1/2" QUADRANTS
with PLYWOOD BACKING.
FACES of BASE SHAPE to be
COVERED with VENEER.

(114mm)
DOOR BUILT UP WITH LAYER
of 1/4" PLYWOOD with 4 1/2" SQ
HOLES GLUED TO LAYER of 1/2"
PLYWOOD with 5" SQUARE HOLE
(126mm)

FRONT ELEVATION

3 1/2" (88mm)
1/2"(12mm) 2 3/4"(70) 1/4"(6mm)

2" (51mm)

(12mm)
1/2" PLYWD CREST
1/2" PLYWD TOP BOARD

1/2" (12mm)
1"(25mm)

4 1/2"(114mm)

12" (304mm) PLUS CLEARANCE for DOOR

3/8" GLUE BLOCKS
(9mm)

(6mm)
1/4" PLYWD DIALBOARD

POS'N of MOVEMENT

(6mm)
1/4" PLYWD BACKBOARD

1"(25mm)

4 1/2"(114mm)

1"(25mm)

1/2" (12)
3/4" (18)
1/2" (12)
1/2" (12)

(12mm)
1/2" PLY BOTTOM BOARD

A
B
C
D

3 1/4" (82mm)

SECTION at D-D

6" (152mm)
1/2" (12mm) 5" (128mm) 1/2" (12mm)

(6mm)
1/4" PLYWD BACKBOARD
3/8" GLUE BLOCK
1/2" PLYWD SIDE
(12mm)

2 3/4" (70mm) 1/4"(6mm)
1"(25) 2 1/8"(55mm)

MOVEMENT

DIALCARD on 1/4"
DIAL BOARD

VENEER
1/2" BRASS HINGES

1/8"

3/4" (18mm) 1/4" (6mm)   1/4" (6mm) 3/4" (18mm)
1"(25mm)   4 1/2" (114mm)   1"(25mm)

PLAN at B-B

7 1/4" (182mm)
3/8"(9mm) 6 1/2" (164mm) 3/8"(9mm)
1/4"(6mm) 6" (152mm) 1/4"(6mm)

MIRROR PLATE

1/4"(6mm)

LINE of BACKBOARD

LINE of SIDE

2 3/4" (70mm)
3 1/2" (88mm)
3 5/8" (97mm)

3/4" (18mm)
3/8" (9mm)

LINE of CREST   LINE of SCOTIA MOULDING

PLAN at A-A

6 3/4" (172mm)
6" (152mm)

PLAN at C-C

(6mm)
1/4" PLYWOOD BACKBOARD

(9mm)
3/8" GLUE BLOCKS

LINE of SCOTIA

LINE of PICTURE PANEL

1/2" (12mm)

1/4" (6mm)

6 1/2" (164mm) OVER DOOR

DOOR BUILT UP with
LAYER of 1/4" PLYWOOD
GLUED to LAYER of 1/2"
PLYWD & VENEERED ALL
ROUND. USE 1/4" x 3/8"
GLAZING BEADS.

3/8"(9mm) 6" (152mm) 3/8"(9mm)
1/2" (12mm) 5" (128mm) 1/2" (12mm)

(6mm)
1/4" PLYWD BACKBOARD

(9mm)
3/8" GLUE BLOCKS

1/2" PLYWD SIDES
(12mm)

VENEER FRONT FACE

LINE of BASEBOARD   LINE of SCOTIA MOULDING

1/4"(6mm)
2 1/2" (64mm) 2 3/4" (70mm)
1/2" (12mm)
3/4" (82mm)
5/8" (9mm)

DOOR OMITTED for CLARITY

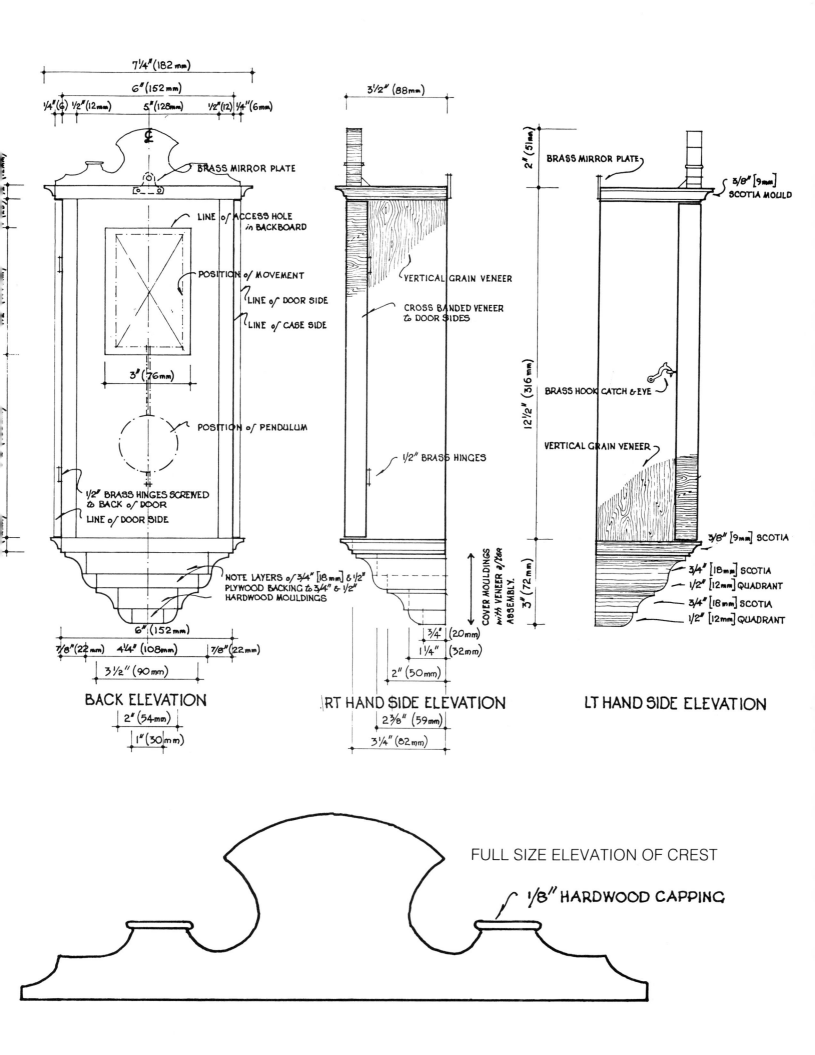

7¼" (182 mm)
6" (152 mm)
¼" (6) ½" (12 mm) 5" (128 mm) ½" (12) ¼" (6 mm)

BRASS MIRROR PLATE

LINE of ACCESS HOLE
in BACKBOARD

POSITION of MOVEMENT

LINE of DOOR SIDE

LINE of CASE SIDE

3" (76 mm)

POSITION of PENDULUM

½" BRASS HINGES SCREWED
to BACK of DOOR
LINE of DOOR SIDE

NOTE LAYERS of 3/4" [18 mm] & 1/2"
PLYWOOD BACKING to 3/4" & 1/2"
HARDWOOD MOULDINGS

6" (152 mm)
7/8" (22 mm)   4¼" (108 mm)   7/8" (22 mm)
3½" (90 mm)

BACK ELEVATION

2" (54 mm)
1" (30 mm)

3½" (88mm)

VERTICAL GRAIN VENEER

CROSS BANDED VENEER
to DOOR SIDES

½" BRASS HINGES

COVER MOULDINGS
with VENEER a/26R
ASSEMBLY.

¾" (20 mm)
1¼" (32mm)
2" (50 mm)

RT HAND SIDE ELEVATION

2 3/8" (59 mm)
3¼" (82 mm)

2" (51mm)

BRASS MIRROR PLATE

3/8" [9mm]
SCOTIA MOULD

12½" (316 mm)

BRASS HOOK CATCH & EYE

VERTICAL GRAIN VENEER

3/8" [9mm] SCOTIA

3" (72 mm)

¾" [18mm] SCOTIA
½" [12mm] QUADRANT
¾" [18mm] SCOTIA
½" [12mm] QUADRANT

LT HAND SIDE ELEVATION

FULL SIZE ELEVATION OF CREST

1/8" HARDWOOD CAPPING

Clock Components and Hardware (excluding screws and pins)

CLOCK MOVEMENT — OPTIONS:

1. Quartz Pendulum Movements.
   Pendulum length from centres of handshaft to pendulum bob: 140mm/5½".
   Maximum pendulum swing: 120mm/4¾".
   Chiming/melody movements also available.
   Handshaft/fixing nut length: to suit 6–8mm/¼" – ⁵⁄₁₆" dial-board and dial thickness. Adjust thickness of dial-board, if necessary.

CLOCK DIAL — OPTIONS:

   – 127 × 127mm/5" × 5" square dial: brass, aluminium or card. (The dial suggested is a 5" square, brass finish. Alternatively, a brass finish chapter ring may be used with a velvet covering on the dial-board.)

CLOCK HANDS:

   – Bushed to suit chosen mechanical or quartz movement.
   – Length to suit dial size.
   – Pattern to suit individual choice.

BRASSWARE:

   – Hinges: one pair of 12mm/½" butt hinges.
   – Door locks: one hook and eye or one concealed bullet catch.
   – Door knob: 8 or 9mm/⁵⁄₁₆" or ⅜" diameter.
   – One mirror plate.

GLASS:

   – Two panes to suit door.
   – Note: The lower pane can accommodate decorative paintwork.

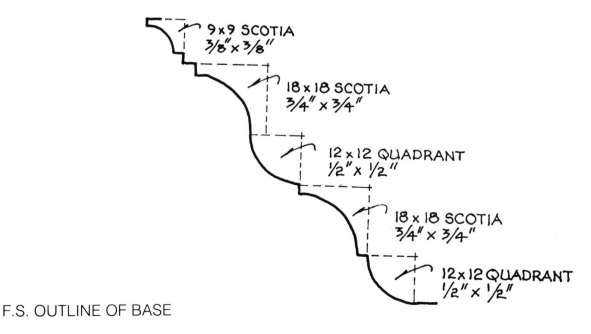

9 x 9 SCOTIA
⅜" x ⅜"

18 x 18 SCOTIA
¾" x ¾"

12 x 12 QUADRANT
½" x ½"

18 x 18 SCOTIA
¾" x ¾"

12 x 12 QUADRANT
½" x ½"

F.S. OUTLINE OF BASE

Cutting list

COMPONENT	QUANTITY	SECTION	LENGTH
Topboard	1	12 × 88	164
	1	½″ × 3½″	6½″
Bottomboard	1	12 × 88	152
	1	½″ × 3½″	6″
Backboard	1	6 × 128	304
	1	¼″ × 5″	12″
Sidecheeks	2	12 × 70	304
	2	½″ × 2¾″	12″
Crestboard	1	12 × 51	164
	1	½″ × 2″	6½″
Dial-board	1	6 × 128	146
	1	¼″ × 5″	5¾″
Pendant Layer A	1	18 × 82	108
	1	¾″ × 3¼″	4¼″
Pendant Layer B	1	12 × 59	90
	1	½″ × 2⅜″	3½″
Pendant Layer C	1	18 × 50	54
	1	¾″ × 2″	2″
Pendant Layer D	1	12 × 20	30
	1	½″ × ¾″	1″
Pendant Layer A Scotia	1	18 × 18	344 minimum
(Total Length)	1	¾″ × ¾″	13¾″ minimum
Pendant Layer B Quadrant	1	12 × 12	256 minimum
(Total Length)	1	½″ × ½″	10¼″ minimum
Pendant Layer C Scotia	1	18 × 18	226 minimum
(Total Length)	1	¾″ × ¾″	9″ minimum
Pendant Layer D Quadrant	1	12 × 12	118 minimum
(Total Length)	1	½″ × ½″	4½″ minimum
Inner Layer of Door	1	12 × 164	304 minus
	1	¼″ × 6½″	12″ minus
Outer Layer of Door	1	6 × 164	304 minus
	1	¼″ × 6½″	12″ minus
Glazing Beads (Total Length)	1	3 × 6	1200 surplus
	1	⅛″ × ¼″	48″ surplus
Triangular Glue Blocks	1	9 × 9	1500 surplus
	1	⅜″ × ⅜″	59″ surplus

21/22.
'Yeoman Minor' and 'Major' Clocks

These two wall clock designs are designed around a pendulum clock movement and display the movement of the pendulum as a major feature. The 'Minor' version has an open-cased construction whilst the 'Major' employs a glazed door similar to the 'Half Case Wall Clock' which is a larger, more decorative example of this type of clock case.

Overall dimensions: 202 wide × 89 deep × 545mm high
8″ wide × 3½″ deep × 21½″ high

Skill level *

Schedule of Operations

CARCASS COMPONENTS

The basis of the construction of this design of clock is the backboard, from which other components are built up.

After carefully studying the plan and these detailed instructions take the sheet of 12mm/½" plywood and mark out the overall sizes of the main components (i.e. backboard, side cheeks, topboard and bottom board). Refer to the plan to check the direction required for the grain of the wood.

Cut out the overall sizes of each main component. Cut out the large slot at the top of the backboard using a tenon saw and coping saw. Cut out the pendulum slot in the bottom board using a coping saw. Check all the components for squareness with a try square and similarly check all edges for squareness to the adjacent main surfaces. Correct where necessary using a plane, shaper plane or file. Check the side cheeks against each other to ensure that they are in fact identical.

Mark out the decorative shapes onto the backboard and side cheeks and carefully cut out using a fret saw or a coping saw. Clean up the decorative edges with a half round file.

Working on a table or bench top, lay the backboard flat and in turn hold the side cheeks in position ensuring that the surfaces which will later be glued marry closely and then, using a trysquare, check that the side cheeks are at right angles to the backboard.

Repeat this checking process for the topboard and bottom board against both the backboard and the side cheeks.

Veneer all exposed cut edges with cross banded veneer. Clean up the veneer and sand down all the main components to a fine finish, using both garnet paper and wet and dry paper. Final assembly of the carcass of the clock case may now commence.

CARCASS ASSEMBLY

Study the plan and using the 9mm/⅜" ramin triangular section cut glue blocks to the various lengths required.

Place the backboard flat on a table or bench top. Pin and glue the glue blocks in place at the edges of the backboard and allow the glue to set hard. Be certain to clean off any excess glue that may have crept onto adjacent surfaces.

While the glue blocks are setting on the backboard lay each side cheek flat on the table top and pin glue blocks to the top and intermediate positions ready to take the top and bottom boards. Allow the glue to set hard, as before. Don't forget to clean off any excess adhesive.

When all the glue blocks have set hard check with a trysquare that the unglued surface of each block is at right angles to the adjacent surfaces. Correct with plane, shaper plane or file as necessary.

Lay the left-hand side cheek flat on the bench top and hold the backboard at right angles to it. Lightly tap in moulding pins to the sides of the glue blocks on the backboard but don't tap them home at this stage. Remove the backboard and thinly spread adhesive on the left-hand cut edge and the glue blocks. Offer up the backboard again to the left-hand side cheek and tap home the moulding pins. Repeat this whole process for the right-hand side cheek. Clean off excess adhesive.

Spread adhesive thinly and evenly on the side edges of the bottom board and place in position between the side cheeks and press home firmly against the previously glued blocks on the cheeks. Clean off excess glue. Repeat the foregoing process for the topboard and set the whole assembly to one side to harden and set.

DIAL-BOARD

After studying the plan mark out carefully the position of the glue blocks required to support the dial-board and glue and pin them into position.

Cut out the dial-board to fit exactly into the space bounded by the side cheeks and the top and bottom boards. Mark the exact centre of the dial-board by drawing diagonal lines from each corner and drill the centre hole.

Spread adhesive evenly over the surface of the dial-board glue blocks and firmly press the dial-board into position. Clean off any excess glue and set the whole assembly to one side to harden.

CREST & MOULDINGS

Mark out the decorative shape for the crest onto 12mm/½" plywood. Cut out the shape carefully with a fret saw or a coping saw. Clean up the decorative cut edge with a file and sandpaper and veneer as for other decorative cut edges. Sand down the whole of the crest with garnet paper and wet and dry paper to a fine finish. Pin and glue a glue block in the position shown on the plan and fix in position on top of the case assembly, ensuring that it is accurately centred above the dial board.

Take the scotia moulding and pin, glue and neatly mitre into position at the top of the case. Punch in any exposed pin heads and fill. Carefully sand down with wet and dry paper all over the surface of the scotia moulding, paying particular attention to the mitre join.

Check over the whole of the assembled case and remove with wet and dry paper any dirty marks or excess glue that may have escaped earlier attention. Apply your chosen finish (see Chapter 5).

Fit the dial and movement.

'Yeoman Major'

The Yeoman Major clock case is basically the same as the Minor clock case but with the addition of a glazed door to cover the dial front.

In general proceed as described for the Minor clock case, but it is suggested that it is better to construct the door before starting on cutting out the main components.

DOOR

From the large sheet of 12mm/½" plywood cut a square 202 × 202mm/8" × 8". Check with a trysquare and check cut edges for squareness with the adjacent surfaces. Carefully mark out a square hole of the size shown on the plan and cut out with a fret saw or coping saw and clean up the cut edges as previously described using a file. Put the resultant frame to one side.

Cut a square 202 × 202mm/8" × 8" from the sheet of 3mm/⅛" plywood and check against the square of 12mm/½" plywood previously cut. Carefully mark out a square hole of the size shown on the plan and cut out with a fret saw or coping saw. Clean up the cut surfaces with a file as previously described.

Coat one surface of the 12mm/½" thick frame with adhesive spread evenly and to this surface offer up the 3mm/⅛" thick frame taking care that the two surfaces to be glued together have the grain of the surface wood at right angles to each other. Clean off excess glue and place the frames together under a heavy weight taking care that they do not slip when the weight is applied. Alternatively, the two frames may be glued and pinned together. In the latter case the heads of the pins should be punched in, filled and rubbed down with wet and dry paper before veneering commences.

When the adhesive joining the two frames has set hard the exposed surfaces may be veneered. First veneer the inside edge of the outer frame and then the outer edge of the whole frame. The face of the frame is veneered last.

Now proceed with the cutting out and assembly of the main carcass of the clockcase in the manner described for the Minor clock case. However, an amendment must be made to the front of each of the side cheeks to take the dial door. Reference to the plan will give an indication of the requirements in this regard, but do not measure from the drawing. Take your measurements to be cut out from the side cheeks from the dial door just constructed.

On completion of the clock case and before final sanding of the surfaces to a finish, mark out the exact position of the hinges on the front cut edge of the right-hand side cheek. Cut out for these hinges with a fret saw or coping saw, allowing a depth of cut a little less than the total thickness of the hinge when closed. There is no need to cut any recess on the inner face of the dial door.

Complete the finishing of the case before fitting the glass to the door by means of 5mm/³⁄₁₆" beading and moulding pins. Finally, install the dial and movement.

'Yeoman Minor' Cutting List

COMPONENT	QUANTITY	SECTION	LENGTH
Topboard	1	12 × 89	178
	1	½″ × 3½″	7″
Bottom Board	1	12 × 89	178
	1	½″ × 3½″	7″
Backboard	1	12 × 178	476
	1	½″ × 7″	18¾″
Side Cheeks	2	12 × 89	374
	2	½″ × 3½″	14¾″
Crestboard	1	12 × 45	178
	1	½″ × 1¾″	7″
Dial-board	1	12 × 178	178
	1	½″ × 7″	7″
Triangular Glue Blocks	1	9 × 9	1068
	1	⅜″ × ⅜″	42″
Topboard Scotia	1	9 × 9	416 minimum
(Total Length)	1	⅜″ × ⅜″	16½″

'Yeoman Major' Cutting List

COMPONENT	QUANTITY	SECTION	LENGTH
Topboard	1	12 × 89	178
	1	½″ × 3½″	7″
Bottom Board	1	12 × 89	178
	1	½″ × 3½″	7″
Backboard	1	12 × 178	488
	1	½″ × 7″	19¼″
Side Cheeks	2	12 × 89	386
	2	½″ × 3½″	15¼″
Crestboard	1	12 × 45	178
	1	½″ × 1¾″	7″
Dial-board	1	12 × 178	190
	1	½″ × 7″	7½″
Triangular Glue Blocks	1	9 × 9	1116
	1	⅜″ × ⅜″	44″
Topboard Scotia	1	9 × 9	416 minimum
	1	⅜″ × ⅜″	16½″ minimum
Inner Layer of Door (ply)	1	12 × 202	202
	1	½″ × 8″	8″
Outer Layer of Door (ply)	1	6 × 202	202
	1	¼″ × 8″	8″

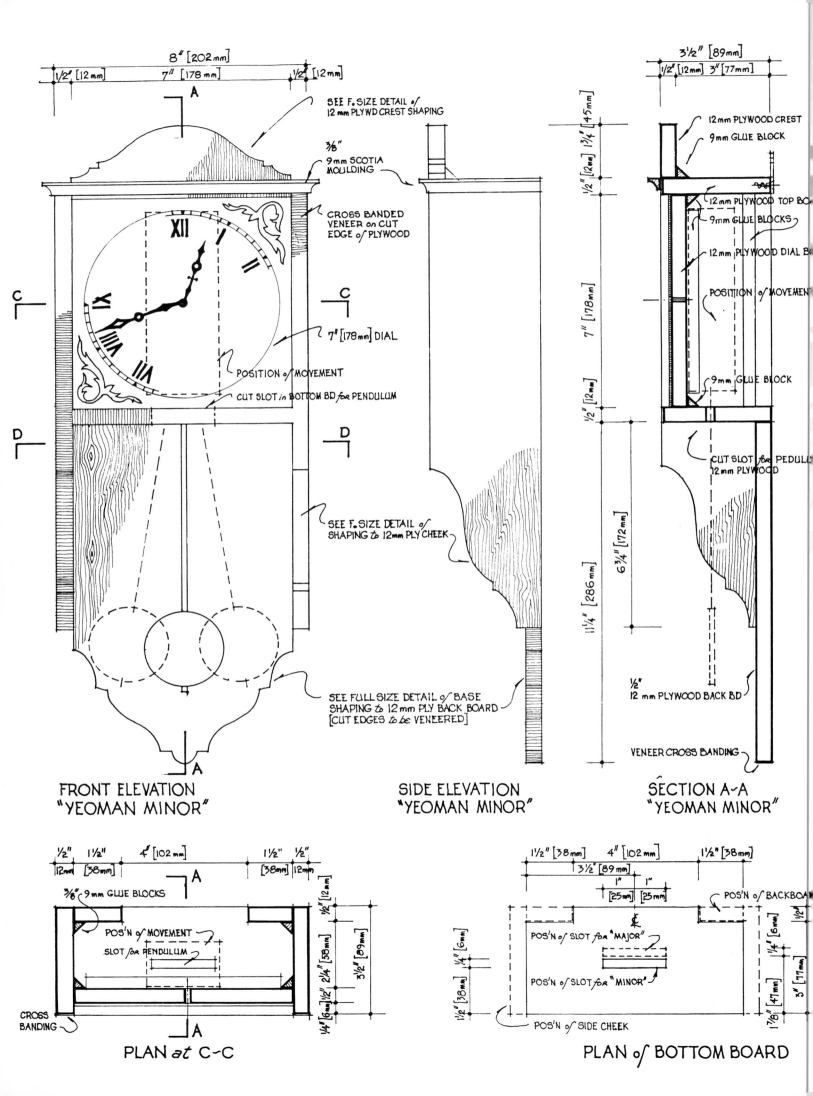

8" [202mm]
1/2" [12mm]   7" [178 mm]   1/2" [12mm]

A

SEE F. SIZE DETAIL of
12 mm PLYWD CREST SHAPING

3/8"
9mm SCOTIA
MOULDING

CROSS BANDED
VENEER on CUT
EDGE of PLYWOOD

XII

C ——— C

7" [178mm] DIAL

POSITION of MOVEMENT

CUT SLOT in BOTTOM BD for PENDULUM

D ——— D

SEE F. SIZE DETAIL of
SHAPING to 12mm PLY CHEEK

SEE FULL SIZE DETAIL of BASE
SHAPING to 12mm PLY BACK BOARD
[CUT EDGES to be VENEERED]

A

FRONT ELEVATION
"YEOMAN MINOR"

SIDE ELEVATION
"YEOMAN MINOR"

3 1/2" [89mm]
1/2" [12mm] 3" [77mm]

12mm PLYWOOD CREST
9mm GLUE BLOCK

1 3/4" [45mm]
1/2" [12mm]

12mm PLYWOOD TOP BO
9mm GLUE BLOCKS
12mm PLYWOOD DIAL B
POSITION of MOVEMEN

7" [178mm]

9mm GLUE BLOCK

1/2" [12mm]

CUT SLOT for PEDULU
12mm PLYWOOD

6 3/4" [172mm]

11 1/4" [286mm]

1/2"
12 mm PLYWOOD BACK BD

VENEER CROSS BANDING

SECTION A~A
"YEOMAN MINOR"

1/2"   1 1/2"   4" [102mm]   1 1/2"   1/2"
12mm   [38mm]   [38mm]   12mm

A

3/8" 9mm GLUE BLOCKS

1/2" [12mm]

POS'N of MOVEMENT

2 1/4" [58mm]   3 1/2" [89mm]

SLOT for PENDULUM

1/2"
1/4" [6mm] 1/2"

CROSS
BANDING

A

PLAN at C-C

1 1/2" [38mm]   4" [102mm]   1 1/2" [38mm]
3 1/2" [89mm]
1" 1"
[25mm] [25mm]

POS'N of BACKBOA

POS'N of SLOT for "MAJOR"

1/4" [6mm]
1/2"

POS'N of SLOT for "MINOR"

1/2" [38mm]
1/4" [6mm]

3" [77mm]

1 3/4" [47mm]

1/2"

POS'N of SIDE CHEEK

PLAN of BOTTOM BOARD

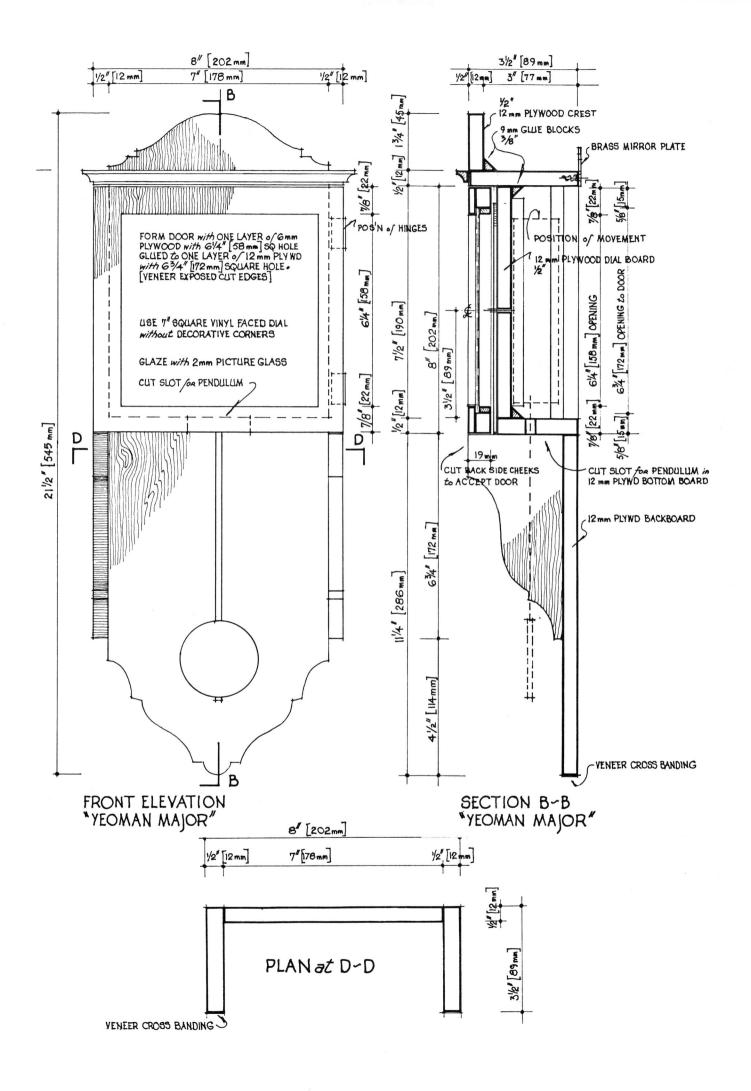

**FRONT ELEVATION
"YEOMAN MAJOR"**

**SECTION B~B
"YEOMAN MAJOR"**

PLAN at D~D

8" [202mm]
1/2" [12mm]
7" [178mm]
1/2" [12mm]

3 1/2" [89mm]
1/2" [12mm]
3" [77mm]

FORM DOOR with ONE LAYER of 6mm PLYWOOD with 6 1/4" [58mm] SQ HOLE GLUED to ONE LAYER of 12mm PLYWD with 6 3/4" [172mm] SQUARE HOLE. [VENEER EXPOSED CUT EDGES]

USE 7" SQUARE VINYL FACED DIAL without DECORATIVE CORNERS

GLAZE with 2mm PICTURE GLASS

CUT SLOT for PENDULUM

POS'N of HINGES

1/2" 12mm PLYWOOD CREST

9mm GLUE BLOCKS
3/8"

BRASS MIRROR PLATE

POSITION of MOVEMENT

12mm PLYWOOD DIAL BOARD
1/2"

CUT BACK SIDE CHEEKS to ACCEPT DOOR

CUT SLOT for PENDULUM in 12mm PLYWD BOTTOM BOARD

12mm PLYWD BACKBOARD

VENEER CROSS BANDING

VENEER CROSS BANDING

21 1/2" [545mm]

2 1/4" [22mm]
7/8"
6 1/4" [58mm]
7 1/2" [190mm]
7/8" [22mm]

1 3/4" [45mm]
1/2" [12mm]
8" [202mm]
3 1/2" [89mm]
1/2" [12mm]

6 3/4" [172mm]
11 1/4" [286mm]
4 1/2" [114mm]

7/8" [22mm]
5/8" [15mm]
6 1/4" [158mm] OPENING
6 3/4" [172mm] OPENING to DOOR

19mm

8" [202mm]
1/2" [12mm]
7" [178mm]
1/2" [12mm]

1/2" [12mm]
3 1/2" [89mm]

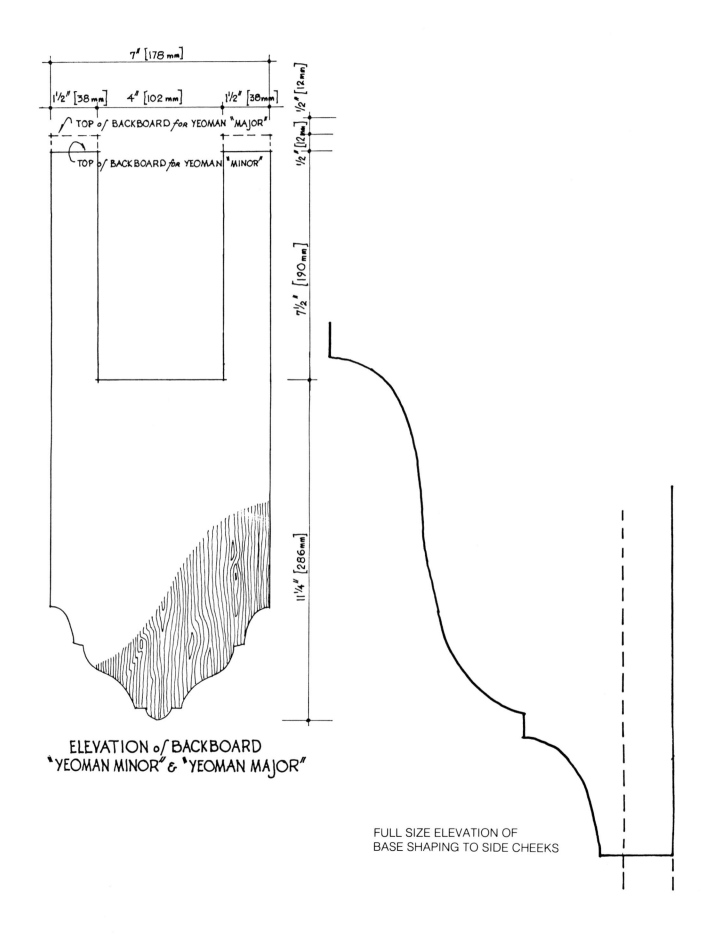

ELEVATION of BACKBOARD
"YEOMAN MINOR" & "YEOMAN MAJOR"

FULL SIZE ELEVATION OF
BASE SHAPING TO SIDE CHEEKS

Clock Components and Hardware (excluding screws and pins)

CLOCK MOVEMENT — OPTIONS:

1. Quartz Pendulum Movements.
   Pendulum length from centres of handshaft to pendulum bob: 292mm/11½″.
   Maximum pendulum swing: 165mm/6½″.
   Chiming/melody movements also available.
   Handshaft/fixing nut length: to suit 12–14mm/½″ – ¹³⁄₁₆″ dial-board and dial thickness. Adjust thickness of dial-board, if necessary.

CLOCK DIAL — OPTIONS:

- 178 × 178mm/7″ × 7″ square dial: brass, aluminium or card;
- OR 150mm/6″ diameter chapter ring fixed to decorative backboard.

CLOCK HANDS:

- Bushed to suit chosen mechanical or quartz movement.
- Length to suit dial size.
- Pattern to suit individual choice.

BRASSWARE:

- Hinges: One pair of 25mm/1″ butt hinges (for Major only);
- Door lock: one hook and eye or one concealed bullet catch (for Major only).
- One mirror plate.

GLASS:

- To suit door (for Major only).

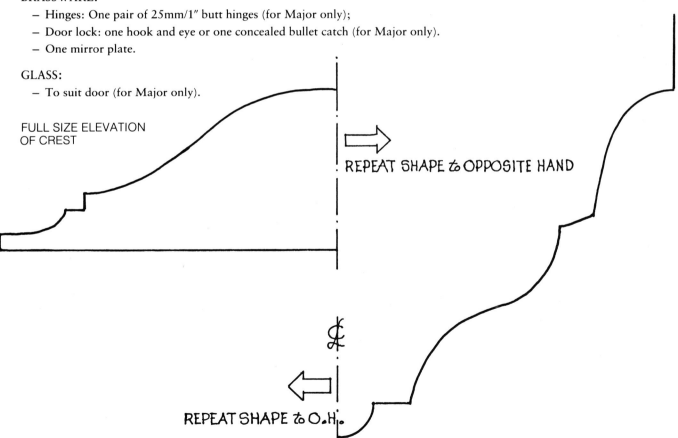

FULL SIZE ELEVATION
OF CREST

REPEAT SHAPE to OPPOSITE HAND

REPEAT SHAPE to O.H.

FULL SIZE ELEVATION OF BASE
SHAPING TO BACK BOARD

23. *English Drop Dial Clock*

This plan features a pattern of wall clock popular in the first half of the 19th century. The bezel surround is of turned mahogany with solid mahogany carved ears. The trunk is of veneered mahogany with inlaid brass stringing.

The design incorporates an easy to obtain dial and bezel and the movement may be striking or non-striking, mechanical or easy to fit quartz.

Overall dimensions: 380 wide × 146 deep × 513mm high
14¹⁵⁄₁₆″ wide × 5¾″ deep × 20³⁄₁₆″ high.

Skill level ✳ ✳ ✳

Schedule of Operations

BOX ASSEMBLY & DOORS

Cut out the board components for the box assembly to the sizes given in the cutting list, making due allowance for planing, etc. Shape the bottom of the front panel and the backboard to the radius shown on the plan. Cut out the check at the front of the cheekboards where the front panel is to be fixed. Carefully mark out for and cut out the door opening in the right-hand cheekboard and set aside the waste from this for future use as the door. Check that all sides of these components are parallel and at right angles. Offer up the components one to the other and make any minor adjustments to ensure a good fit, but do not fix them together at this stage.

Carefully mark out for and cut out the pendulum window in the front panel to the shape shown on the drawing, using a coping saw held at an angle of sixty degrees. Clean up the resultant chamfers with a chisel and a file. Great care is essential at this stage.

Fix all the board components together as shown on the plan, using PVA adhesive and glue blocks.

Take the softwood block to be used for making the curved box base and drop door. Carefully cut to length, measuring against the open bottom of the box assembly. Mark out the curves to the radius given on the plan, using a plywood template, and carefully bandsaw to shape. Check the shape against the curved lower edges of the front panel and backboard. Cut out the opening for the drop door, setting aside the waste for later use as the door itself. Fix the two resultant curved base components to the bottom of the box assembly with PVA adhesive and glue blocks.

Clean up the whole of the box assembly, using a block plane set fine to remove any minor projections etc. Sand to a general, but not final, finish.

Veneer the whole of the front panel with straight grained mahogany veneer using a contact adhesive. Trim off surplus veneer round the edges of the front panel and the pendulum window opening. Cut out for and insert the brass stringing and rings, using soft brass wire and sections cut from the end of a suitable diameter brass tube. Fix the brasswork with a contact adhesive. Once the adhesive has set hard, preferably overnight, file off any brass standing proud of the veneer face, taking care to avoid damage.

From soft brass sheet cut out small strips to the shapes required to face up the chamfered surfaces of the pendulum window. Check for a good fit between the strips and fix in position with an epoxy resin adhesive. File off any surplus brass as last described.

If it is so wished, the inlay brasswork and brass lining to the pendulum window may be omitted. In this case, it is suggested that the chamfered surround to the pendulum window is faced with veneer to form a colour contrast with the adjacent mahogany veneer.

Veneer the curved bottom of the box assembly with straight grained mahogany veneer, cutting out a central panel of veneer to face the drop door. This will ensure continuity of grain on the whole of the base.

Sand the whole of the box assembly to a finish, using progressively finer abrasive paper, working parallel with the grain direction.

Check that the drop door is a reasonable fit, clean off the lower surface with sandpaper and veneer the soft wood shape on all surfaces. Sand to a finish as last described.

Make the side door in the manner shown on the plan, using the waste wood cut from the door opening in the right-hand cheekboard. Sand this waste wood to a finish before gluing the door surround strips into position. Sand the surround strips to a finish.

DIAL-BOARD & BEARERS

Take the dial-board component and fix to the lathe faceplate. Turn the movement recess on the inner face. The size of the recess may vary to suit the size of the movement purchased. Turn the perimeter of the dial-board and then form the centre hole to accept the movement spindle.

Remove the dial-board from the faceplate and refix to work on the outer face. Offer up the clock dial to the outer face and mark the position of the small lug shown on the plan. Remove the dial and offer up the brass bezel to mark the outer face of the lug. Against the bezel check the depth required for the lug. Remove the bezel and turn the lug and dial recess. Turn the outer shape to the profile shown on the plan. Sand to a finish with progressively finer abrasives and burnish with a handful of wood shavings. It is suggested that the finish of your choice, i.e. button polish, french polish etc, is applied and then brought to a final gloss before removing the dial-board from the lathe.

Make the mahogany bearers and screw to the rear of the dial-board, checking the distance between them against the width of the box assembly and ensuring that they are parallel. The dial-board should be an easy sliding fit to the box. Carefully position the dial-board to the box in the position shown on the plan, mark the position of the top

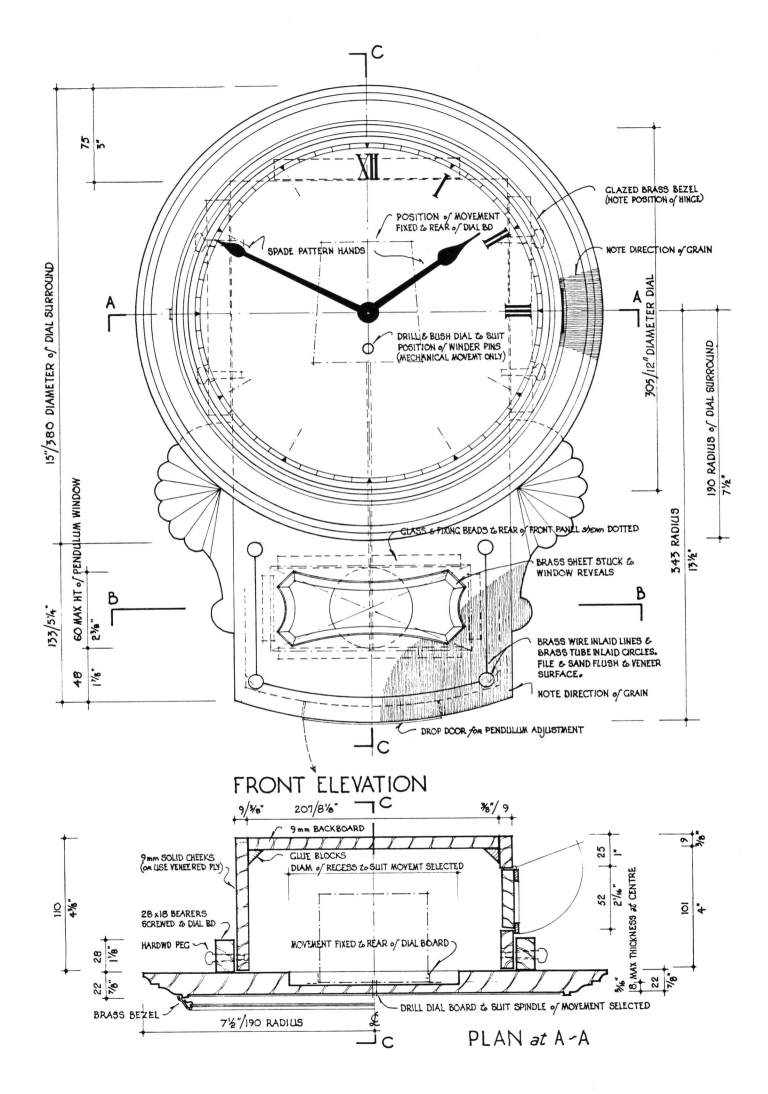

FRONT ELEVATION

PLAN at A-A

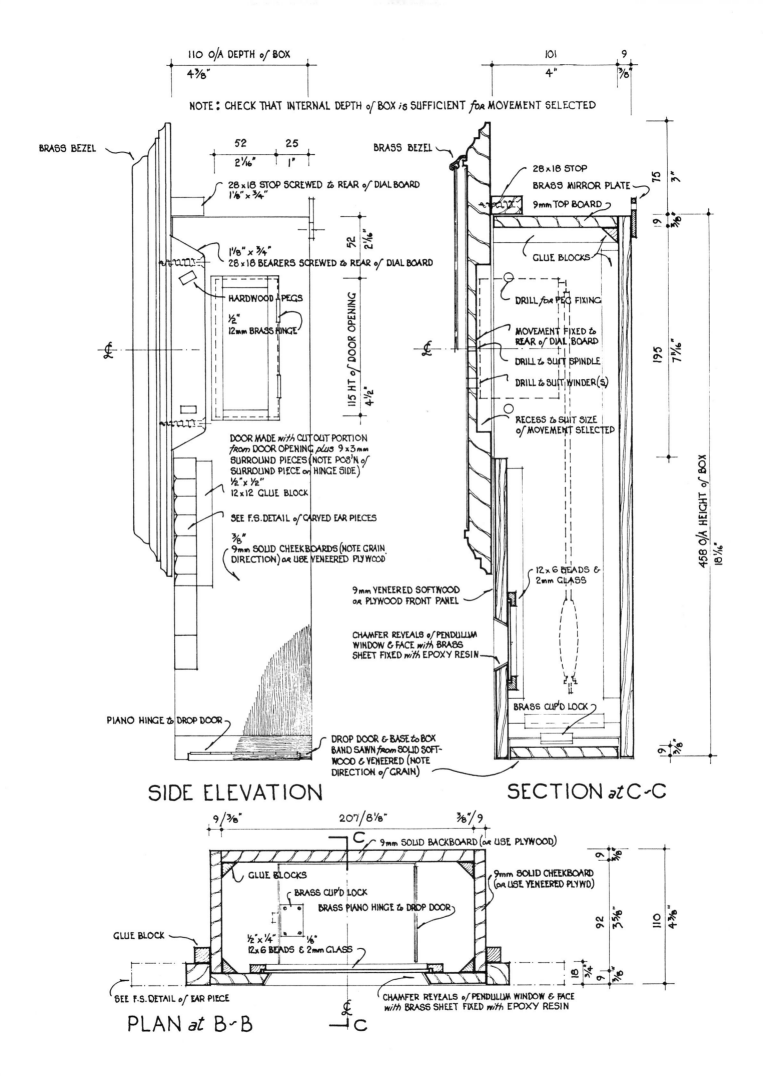

110 O/A DEPTH of BOX
4³/₈"

101   9
4"   ³/₈"

NOTE: CHECK THAT INTERNAL DEPTH of BOX is SUFFICIENT for MOVEMENT SELECTED

BRASS BEZEL

52   25
2¹/₁₆"   1"

28 × 18 STOP SCREWED to REAR of DIAL BOARD
1¹/₈" × ³/₄"

1¹/₈" × ³/₄"
28 × 18 BEARERS SCREWED to REAR of DIAL BOARD

52
2¹/₁₆"

HARDWOOD PEGS
½"
12mm BRASS HINGE

115 HT of DOOR OPENING
4½"

DOOR MADE with CUT OUT PORTION
from DOOR OPENING plus 9 × 3mm
SURROUND PIECES (NOTE POS'N of
SURROUND PIECE on HINGE SIDE)
½" × ½"
12 × 12 GLUE BLOCK

SEE F.S. DETAIL of CARVED EAR PIECES

³/₈"
9mm SOLID CHEEKBOARDS (NOTE GRAIN
DIRECTION) or USE VENEERED PLYWOOD

PIANO HINGE to DROP DOOR

DROP DOOR & BASE to BOX
BAND SAWN from SOLID SOFT-
WOOD & VENEERED (NOTE
DIRECTION of GRAIN)

SIDE ELEVATION

BRASS BEZEL

28 × 18 STOP
BRASS MIRROR PLATE
9mm TOP BOARD

75   3"

GLUE BLOCKS

19   ³/₈"

DRILL for PEG FIXING

MOVEMENT FIXED to
REAR of DIAL BOARD
DRILL to SUIT SPINDLE
DRILL to SUIT WINDER(S)

195   7¹¹/₁₆"

RECESS to SUIT SIZE
of MOVEMENT SELECTED

9mm VENEERED SOFTWOOD
or PLYWOOD FRONT PANEL

12 × 6 BEADS &
2mm GLASS

CHAMFER REVEALS of PENDULUM
WINDOW & FACE with BRASS
SHEET FIXED with EPOXY RESIN

BRASS CUP'D LOCK

458 O/A HEIGHT of BOX
18¹/₁₆"

9   ³/₈"

SECTION at C-C

9/³/₈"   20⁷/8⅛"   ³/₈"/9

9mm SOLID BACKBOARD (or USE PLYWOOD)

C

GLUE BLOCKS

9mm SOLID CHEEKBOARD
(or USE VENEERED PLYWD)

9   ³/₈"

BRASS CUP'D LOCK
BRASS PIANO HINGE to DROP DOOR

92   3⁵/₈"   110   4³/₈"

GLUE BLOCK

½" × ¼"   ⅛"
12 × 6 BEADS & 2mm GLASS

18   ¾"
9   ³/₈"

SEE F.S. DETAIL of EAR PIECE

CHAMFER REVEALS of PENDULUM WINDOW & FACE
with BRASS SHEET FIXED with EPOXY RESIN

PLAN at B-B

C

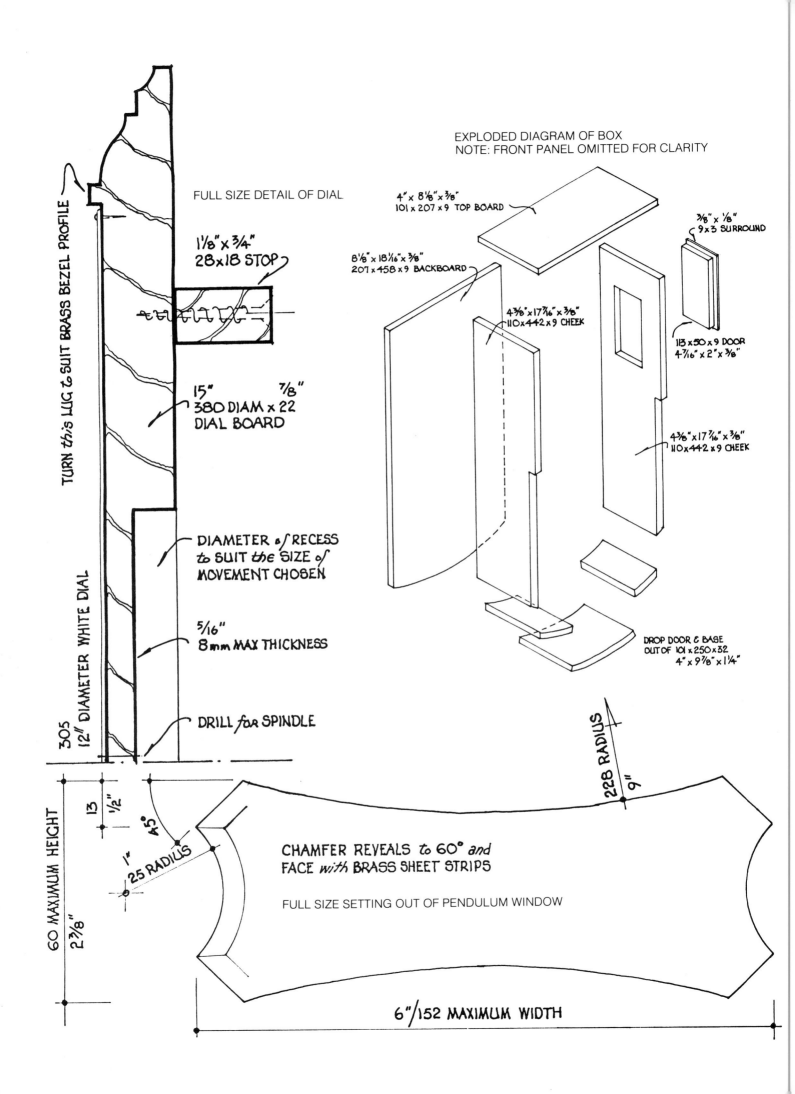

FULL SIZE DETAIL OF DIAL

TURN *this* LUG *to* SUIT BRASS BEZEL PROFILE

1⅛" x ¾"
28 x 18 STOP

15"   ⅞"
380 DIAM x 22
DIAL BOARD

DIAMETER *of* RECESS
to SUIT *the* SIZE *of*
MOVEMENT CHOSEN

5/16"
8mm MAX THICKNESS

DRILL *for* SPINDLE

305
12" DIAMETER WHITE DIAL

EXPLODED DIAGRAM OF BOX
NOTE: FRONT PANEL OMITTED FOR CLARITY

4" x 8⅛" x ⅜"
101 x 207 x 9 TOP BOARD

⅜" x ⅛"
9 x 3 SURROUND

8⅛" x 18 1/16" x ⅜"
207 x 458 x 9 BACKBOARD

4⅜" x 17 7/16" x ⅜"
110 x 442 x 9 CHEEK

113 x 50 x 9 DOOR
4 7/16" x 2" x ⅜"

4⅜" x 17 7/16" x ⅜"
110 x 442 x 9 CHEEK

DROP DOOR & BASE
OUT OF 101 x 250 x 32
4" x 9⅞" x 1¼"

228 RADIUS   9"

60 MAXIMUM HEIGHT
2⅜"

13   ½"

45°

1"
25 RADIUS

CHAMFER REVEALS *to* 60° *and*
FACE *with* BRASS SHEET STRIPS

FULL SIZE SETTING OUT OF PENDULUM WINDOW

6"/152 MAXIMUM WIDTH

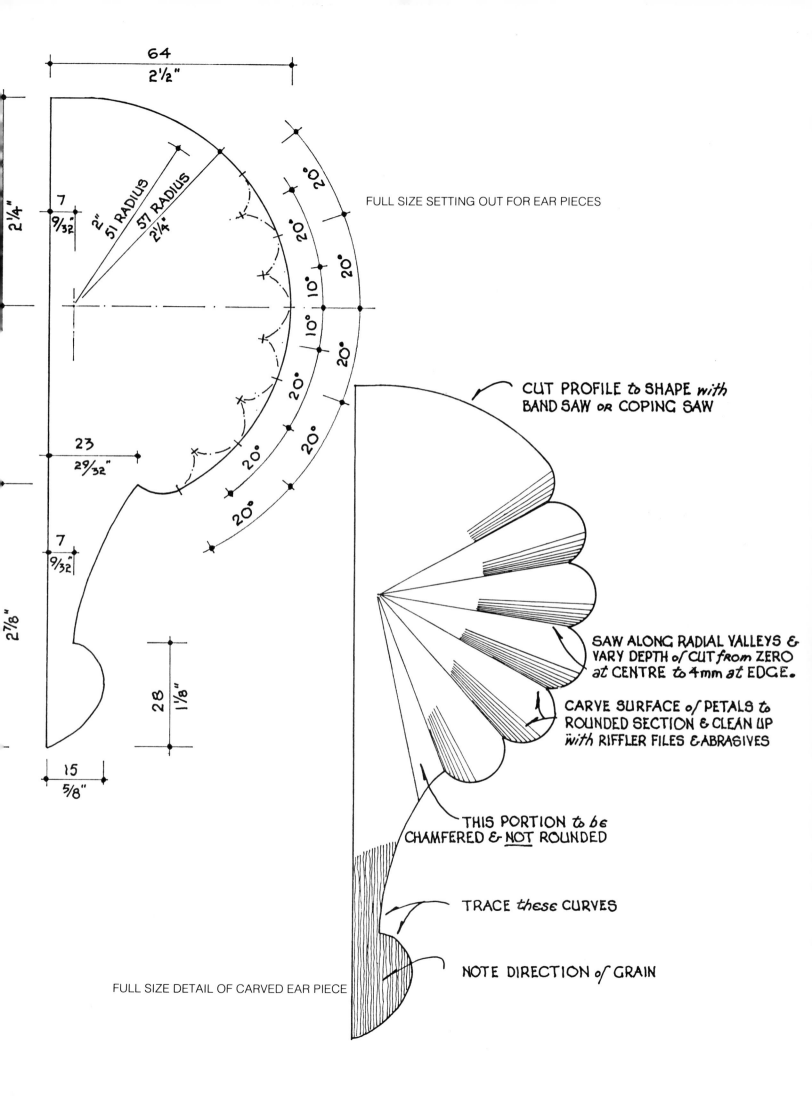

FULL SIZE SETTING OUT FOR EAR PIECES

64
2½"

2¼"

7
9/32"

2" 51 RADIUS
2¼" 57 RADIUS

20°
20°
20°
10° 10°
10°
10°
20°
20°
20°
20°
20°
20°
20°

23
29/32"

7
9/32"

2⅛"

28
1⅛"

15
5/8"

CUT PROFILE to SHAPE with
BAND SAW or COPING SAW

SAW ALONG RADIAL VALLEYS &
VARY DEPTH of CUT from ZERO
at CENTRE to 4mm at EDGE.

CARVE SURFACE of PETALS to
ROUNDED SECTION & CLEAN UP
with RIFFLER FILES & ABRASIVES

THIS PORTION to be
CHAMFERED & NOT ROUNDED

TRACE these CURVES

NOTE DIRECTION of GRAIN

FULL SIZE DETAIL OF CARVED EAR PIECE

stop batten and screw it to the rear of the dial-board.

With the dial-board still in position, mark out for and drill the holes in the bearers and box sides to accept the fixing pegs. Make the fixing pegs from waste scrapwood, carefully tapering to form a tight fit in the holes. Remove the dial-board from the box assembly.

EAR PIECES

Take the components for the ear pieces and carefully mark out the setting out lines and shapes shown on the plan. Accurately cut out the shapes and carefully make the sloping saw cuts in the radial valleys. With a sharp bevel chisel round the surfaces of the petals between the valleys. Clean up the rounded surfaces with a file and abrasives. Sand all surfaces to a finish as previously described, paying particular attention to end grain on the shaped edges.

FINISHING & FINAL ASSEMBLY

Brush off all sanding dust before applying finishes and work in a dust free environment. Seal all surfaces with a meths based sanding sealer and polish all exposed surfaces with button polish or a heavy french polish. When bone dry, flat down the final coat with very fine wire wool and bring back to a gloss with wax polish. Alternatively, after applying the sanding sealer, apply three coats of polyurethane varnish, flatting down each coat when dry and bringing final coat to a gloss with wax polish.

Fix the glass to the pendulum window using 12 × 6mm/½″ × ¼″ glazing beads made from scrap material and secured in position with short veneer pins. Hang the side door with 12mm/½″ brass hinges as shown on the plan. If the door is a loose fit secure with a small brass side hook.

To the inner face of the drop door, fix in position a small brass cupboard lock, carefully cutting out the keyhole shape. Ideally, this should have a brass keyhole liner. Hang the drop door in position with a length of piano hinge.

Fix a brass mirror plate top centre of the backboard.

Fix the ear pieces in position on the sides of the box assembly, using glue blocks. Make sure that the surfaces of the ear pieces are exactly flush with the surface of the front panel and that their relationship with the rim of the dial-board is as shown on the plan.

Fix the dial to the dial-board with small screws or pins. Offer up the brass bezel and fix in position, making sure that it is exactly central relative to the dial.

Fix the movement in position at the rear of the dialboard, having previously drilled the dial and board to take the winder pins and key (mechanical movements only). Neatly bush the winder hole(s) in the dial. Fit the hands in position in accordance with the maker's instructions.

Hang the completed case on the wall and, using the side door, hang the pendulum and bob from the suspension point on the movement. With all mechanical movements the pendulum should only be hung *after* the clock has been positioned on the wall, otherwise damage may occur to the suspension spring. With mechanical movements the time keeping of the clock may be varied by screwing up or down the retaining screw to the bob; generally screw UP to speed UP and DOWN to slow DOWN. With quartz movements the time keeping is not affected by the length of the pendulum rod or the position of the bob.

Cutting list

COMPONENT	QUANTITY	SECTION	LENGTH
Backboard (softwood or Ply)	1	207 × 9	458
	1	8⅛″ × ⅜″	18¹/₁₆″
Cheekboards incl side doors	2	110 × 9	442
(Hardwood)	2	4⅜″ × ⅜″	17⁷/₁₆″
Top Board (Softwood)	1	101 × 9	207
	1	4″ × ⅜″	8⅛″
Drop Door & Box Base (Softwood)	1	101 × 32	250
(Bandsaw to shape out of 1 piece)	1	4″ × 1¾″	9⅞″
Front Panel	1	225 × 9	250
(Veneered Softwood or Ply)	1	8⅞″ × ⅜″	9⅞″

Dial-board (Hardwood)	1	22 thick	380 diameter
	1	⅞″ thick	15″ diameter
Stop (Softwood)	1	22 × 18	152
	1	⅞″ × ¾″	6″
Bearers (Hardwood)	2	22 × 18	180
	2	⅞″ × ¾″	7⅛″
Ear Pieces (Hardwood)	2	64 × 18	178
	2	2½″ × ¾″	7″
Glazing Beads, Fixing Pegs, Door Surrounds, Glue Blocks	Out of waste scraps		

Clock Components and Hardware (excluding screws and pins)

CLOCK MOVEMENT — OPTIONS:

1. Mechanical movements.

   Spring Driven.

   Pendulum length from centres of handshaft to pendulum bob: 245mm/9⅝″.

   Maximum pendulum swing: 203mm/8″.

   Depth of movement: variable according to make — adjust depth of box if necessary.

   Handshaft: check length and adjust thickness of dial-board, if necessary.

2. Quartz Pendulum Movements.

   Pendulum length from centres of handshaft to pendulum bob: 245mm/9⅝″.

   Maximum pendulum swing: 203mm/8″.

   Chiming/melody movements also available.

   Handshaft/fixing nut length: to suit 8–10mm/5⁄16″–⅜″ dial-board and dial thickness.

   Note: If position of pendulum of quartz movement fouls the rear of the turned dial-board, some material from the dial-board might need to be removed.

CLOCK DIAL — OPTIONS:

– 305mm/12″ diameter.

– Steel dial with enamel paint finish; aluminium dial with sprayed paint finish.

CLOCK HANDS:

– Bushed to suit chosen mechanical or quartz movement.

– Length to suit dial size.

– Pattern to suit individual choice.

BRASSWARE:

– Bezel: diameter to suit 305mm/12″ diameter dial.

– Hinges: Side door — one pair of 12mm/½″ butt hinges;   Drop door — piano hinge cut to suit door width.

– Door locks:

   Side door: one latch (various patterns available);

   Drop door: one cupboard lock 50 × 12mm (2″ × ½″ to pin) maximum (smaller locks will provide a neater result).

– Key escutcheon for drop door: to suit size of keyhole.

– Brass strip and inlay: Brass wire to inlay front face of box (optional); Brass tube (or rod) to inlay front face of box (optional); Brass sheet/strip to fix on pendulum window surround (optional).

GLASS:

– To suit diameter of brass bezel.

– To suit pendulum window.

Appendix I — Product Guide

Ashby Design Workshop — Plans, Products and Publications

Clock Planpacks

The 23 clock designs in this book are based on original working drawings from the Ashby Design Workshop collection of Planpacks. Ashby Planpacks comprise 'Schedules of Operations' and large dyeline/blueprint sheets which are the metric A1 size (840mm × 594mm or 33¹/₁₆″ × 23⅜″) that consequently accommodate full size profiles and details which would not be possible to print in a book or a magazine.

The reduced plans in this book will enable you, the reader, to build any of the clock designs, though you might prefer to work from the full A1 size working drawings in your workshop environment. The larger illustrations and the full size profiles will give you a good visual perspective of your project and the drawing sheets are more suited to the physical rigours of the workshop, allowing you to scribble notes along the way without damaging your valued book.

The A1 size Clock Planpacks, with the exception of drawing numbers ADW201–ADW208 are available in the UK from the stockists entered in the 'Product & Supplier Charts' in Appendix II. All the Clock Planpacks, including ADW201–ADW208, are, however, available from the publishers of this book, Stobart Davies Ltd., and from UK woodworking magazines.

At the time of writing, Ashby Design Workshop has not established a stockist network in the USA though, in the first instance, the Clock Planpacks will be available from the American publishers of the book, Linden Publishing Co, Fresno, California; many of the USA clock component suppliers in Appendix II will hopefully carry stocks of the Clock Planpacks in due course.

The Clock Planpacks will also be available, in due course, through distributors in other countries in Europe and Australasia.

Clock Kits

The 'Product & Supplier Charts' are designed to enable the maker to track down all the items he or she requires for a successful woodworking project, though this could be a time consuming exercise in its own right. Should demand emerge for complete kits with all the project components in one pack, Ashby Design Workshop will give details of their availability with printed inserts in this book and the Ashby 'Catalogue & Sourcebook', and through its stockist network and the woodworking press.

Furniture Planpacks

In addition to clock designs, Ashby Design Workshop also publishes furniture designs and Planpacks, many of which are based on English antiques that passed through our Somerset workshop during the 1980s. These Planpacks are also based around large A1 size dyeline/blueprint sheets with complete project information.

The collection of Ashby Design Workshop Planpacks, at the time of writing, is listed opposite and those that have asterisks (*) besides them have both metric and imperial dimensions. It is anticipated that all the Planpacks will have dual metric and imperial dimensions by 1993 to suit woodworkers in the USA and the rest of the world. Also listed are new Planpack designs that are due to be published in 1992 and a few furniture plans are illustrated to whet your appetite!

ASHBY DESIGN WORKSHOP: PLAN LIST

* ADW 101/2 Regency Davenport Desk
  ADW 103 18th c. Gateleg Table
  ADW 104 Spice Racks
  ADW 105 Victorian Sewing Box
* ADW 106/7 17th c. Longcase Clock
  ADW 108 Workbenches
  ADW 109 Workshop Accessories
  ADW 110 Nursery Play Table
  ADW 111a/b Bunk Beds with Storage
  ADW 112 Coffee Table with Storage
  ADW 113 Traditional Console Table
  ADW 114 Storage Stool & Plant Trough
  ADW 115 Lap or Table Desk
  ADW 116 Magazine Racks
  ADW 117 Coffee Tables
  ADW 118 Corner Display Shelves
  ADW 119 Kitchen Accessories
  ADW 120 Six Traditional Tripod Stools
  ADW 121 Child's Chair & Settle
  ADW 122 Patio Chair & Bench
  ADW 123 Victorian Corner Whatnot
  ADW 124 Traditional Rocking Cradle
  ADW 125 Wall Desk with Display
  ADW 126 Jacobean Oak Coffer
  ADW 127/8 Welsh Kitchen Dresser
  ADW 129 Jacobean Joynt Stool/Bench
* ADW 130 English Drop Dial Clock
* ADW 131 19th c. Lancet Clock
* ADW 132 18th c. Balloon Clock
  ADW 133 Victorian Canterbury Whatnot
* ADW 134 Vienna Regulator
* ADW 135 Grand-daughter Clocks
* ADW 136 Small Vienna Regulator
  ADW 137 Sheraton Half Round Card Table
  ADW 138 19th c. Fireplace Surround
  ADW 139 19th c. Dressing Table
* ADW 140 'The Navigator' Clock/Barometer
* ADW 141 19th c. French Mantel Clock
* ADW142 George III Period Bracket Clock
* ADW 143 Traditional Full Cased Wall Clock
* ADW 144 Traditional Half Cased Wall Clock
  ADW 145 Traditional Corner Cupboards
  ADW 146 Hanging Shelves/Display Units (1992)
  ADW 147 Bird Frames (1992)
  ADW148 Bird Fences (1992)
  ADW 149 Victorian Writing Slope/s (1992)
  ADW 150 Cassette Storage (1992)
* ADW 201 The Yeoman
* ADW 202 The Huntsman
* ADW 203 The Shepherdess
* ADW 204 The Coachman and Groom
* ADW 205 The Carter and Ostler
* ADW 206 The Sexton
* ADW 207 The Deacon
* ADW 208 The Chorister and Curate
  ADW 401/4 Tapa Dining Chairs
* ADW 501/2 Longleat No. 1 Urn Stand
  ADW 503/6 Longleat No. 2 Universal Desk
* ADW 301/4 Woodturners Portfolio No. 1

SHERATON HALF ROUND CARD TABLE
ADW/137
****

755 × 914 mm (Diameter)

The design of this elegant table is from a measured drawing of an actual antique. Either construct a replica with full veneers and inlays or build a more 'up to date' version using English hardwoods. Alternatively build in beech for painted finishes.

THE LONGLEAT 'UNIVERSAL' DESK
ADW/503/6
****

This extended Planpack has detailed plans of an actual Chippendale Period Desk at Longleat House.
Using a 'deck chair' type prin-cipal, the top may be raised or tilted to over a thousand dif-ferent working positions.
The desk may then be used for reading, writing, or for drawing or as a music stand.

724 × 470 × 740 mm
(Closed)

18th CENTURY GATE-LEG DINING TABLE
ADW/103
***

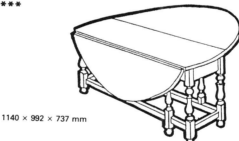

1140 × 992 × 737 mm

The traditional gate-leg table is admirably suited to the home of today. This design, based on an actual antique, features elegant turned legs to a beautifully designed profile. The original table was of brown oak, but it may be built in any English hardwood.

REGENCY PERIOD 'DAVENPORT' DESK
ADW/101–2
****

788 × 484 × 520 mm

This design is based on measured details of an actual antique desk but offers either details of the original construction or of a method more suited to modern techniques. The compact size and large storage capacity make it a useful addition to the home.

VICTORIAN CANTERBURY & WHATNOT
ADW/133

★
★
★
★

568 x 440 x 742mm

The ingenious Victorians devised the Canterbury to store sheet music and sometimes extended it vertically as a Whatnot to display bric a brac. Canterburies are sought after today because of their usefulness as magazine racks. The upper part may be omitted if desired. Construction is a wood turner's delight.

PATIO SEATING
ADW/122 ★ ★

These country pub seats will give your patio that rural look or may be used inside your conservatory or porch.
The simple construction will simulate traditional pegged jointing. Use any hardwood.

560 x 678 x 405mm
1017 x 678 x 405mm

WELSH KITCHEN DRESSER
ADW/127-8

★
★
★
★

1343 x 440 x 1968mm

The "Welsh" kitchen dresser is possibly the most popular piece of traditional furniture in regular use today. This double Planpack reflects the well proportioned sturdy lines of the original "dog-kennel" design. An extra door may be inserted for more storage.

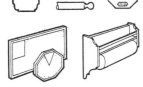

KITCHEN ACCESSORIES
★ ★ ADW/119

This Planpack has easy-build projects for the kitchen including knife blocks, cutting boards, kitchen roll holders & a 4 piece rolling pin set for various pastries.

LAP OR TABLE DESK
ADW/115

★
★

394 x 170 x 115mm

This compact item will be a hot favourite with the family for the writing of letters and doing homework etc. The design offers good storage space for paper, pens and envelopes, stamps etc.

BUNK BED WITH STORAGE (Five Versions)
ADW/111 ★ ★ ★

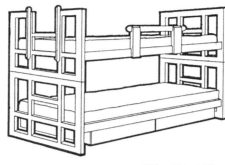

2020 x 1800 x 1020mm

This Planpack contains five pleasing alternative designs for the headboards and footboards of these versatile bunk-beds. The double decker bed may be easily dismantled to form two single beds & the matresses are supported on softwood slats or sheet plywood. A bonus feature is the additional drawer space under the lower bunk.
The construction is based on straight forward mortise and tenon jointing and the use of any English hardwood is recommended.

JACOBEAN PERIOD OAK COFFER
ADW/126

★
★
★
★

★
★
★

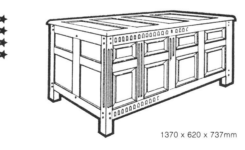

1370 x 620 x 737mm

The Planpack for this project illustrates the finely proportioned panels so typical of this period in history. An unusual feature of the original antique which inspired this design is the use of two rows of panels. Vary to your choice by omission of carving etc.

JACOBEAN PERIOD "Joynt" STOOL (PLUS A FIRESIDE BENCH STOOL
ADW/129

★
★
★

457 x 340 x 520mm
1162 x 340 x 520mm

This typical Period stool has splayed legs at the ends to give a greater stability. Pegged mortise and tenon "joynts" (without use of glue!) would have been used originally. The fireside bench is a longer version with a central stretcher. Carving details are given.

VICTORIAN CORNER WHATNOT
ADW/123

★
★
★

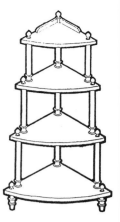

This is a good example of a popular piece of antique furniture used for the display of bric a brac. The original antique had turned walnut columns, finials and feet & solid walnut shelving.
The height may be varied by adjusting the lengths of the columns and the shelves may be made with 16mm plywood & veneers of your choice.

1037 x 636mm wide

19th CENTURY FIREPLACE SURROUND
ADW/138

★
★
★

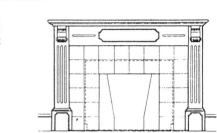

This 19th Century Fireplace Surround has been designed to suit most fireplace openings and enables you to decide whether to continue with open fires or change to electric or gas heating. The plan is dimensioned to suit almost any size of fireplace.

"TAPA" SYSTEM DINING CHAIRS
ADW/401

★
★
★

The dining chair is probably the most used piece of furniture in any home. This extended Planpack shows a similar method of construction for each of FOUR chair designs, but fully details each type. The "mystique" so often surrounding chair building is well and truly exploded in this comprehensive Planpack.
The projects are suitable for all woodworkers except, perhaps, the outright beginner. Virtually any timber may be used but "home-grown" hardwoods are probably best.

Catalogue & Sourcebook

For those readers wishing to find out more about Ashby Design Workshop's plans, products and publications, the company's UK 'Catalogue & Sourcebook' gives the following information:

* Illustrations of all the current Ashby Planpacks.
* Current price lists and ordering details.
* A booklet giving sources for ideas and useful woodworking information.
* Ten 'Product & Supplier Charts' covering the following areas:
  1. Ashby Plan Stockists; 2. Clock/Case Components; 3. Finishes and Polishes; 4. Fixtures and Fittings; 5a/5b. Hand Tools; 6. Machinery; 7. Publications; 8. Timber; 9. Woodturning.
* The 'Future Antiques Roadshow' — a prototype television script.

The 'Folder Format' of the 'Catalogue & Sourcebook' also allows readers to gather information on new Ashby Design Workshop products without having to purchase a replacement annual catalogue.

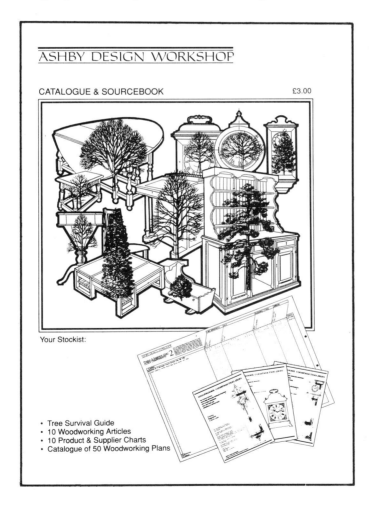

ASHBY DESIGN WORKSHOP

CATALOGUE & SOURCEBOOK   £3.00

Your Stockist:

* Tree Survival Guide
* 10 Woodworking Articles
* 10 Product & Supplier Charts
* Catalogue of 50 Woodworking Plans

The 'Catalogue & Sourcebook' is available from Ashby Stockists in the UK and from Stobart Davies Ltd in the UK. A North American version will also be published in due course.

Appendix II — Sources of Supply

ASHBY DESIGN WORKSHOP

Product & Suppliers Chart — 1
Ashby Plan Stockists

Within this Chart, you will see that stockists of Ashby Design Workshop Planpacks provide a wide range of services and products which will aid you in the creation and completion of your projects. The Chart gives you an "at-a-glance" understanding of a stockist's specialities, though talking to and visiting your stockist will give "in-depth" knowledge and will be an enjoyable activity.

COMPANY, Address	Hardwoods	Softwoods	Sheet Materials	Veneers and Bandings	Mouldings – Standard	Mouldings – Custom	Hand Tools	Machinery – Portable	Machinery – Fixed	Machine Tooling	Safety Equipment
ASP LTD., Argus House, Boundary Way, Hemel Hempsted, Herts HP2 7ST											
PRACTICAL WOODWORKING, c/o Stobart Davies Ltd, Priory House, Priory St., Hertford, Herts SG14 1RN											
CHARLTONS TIMBER CENTRE, Frome Road, Radstock, Nr. Bath, Avon BA3 3PT	●	●	●	●	●	●	●	●	●	●	●
ART VENEERS CO. LTD., Industrial Estate, Mildenhall, Suffolk IP28 7AY				●			●				
FYLDE WOODTURNING SUPPLIES, Unit 126 Oyston Mill, Strand Road, Preston, Lancs. PR1 8UJ	●	●							●		●
THE WOODCRAFT CENTRE, Vauxhall Street, Longton, Stoke-on-Trent ST3 1PL	●		●	●			●	●			●
SEVERN PLYWOOD LTD., Gloucester Road, Stonehouse, Glos.			●								
L. H. TURTE LTD., 6-12 Park St., Croydon, Surrey CR0 1YE							●	●		●	●
JANIK ENTERPRISES LTD., Brickfield Lane, Ruthin, Clwyd LL15 2TN											
JEAN BURHOUSE FURNITURE, The Old Saw Mill, Inver, Dunkeld, Perth PH8 0JR	●	●	●	●		●	●				●
H.S. WALSH & SONS LTD., 243 Beckenham Rd, Beckenham, Kent, BR3 4TS							●				
JOHN BODDY'S FWTS LTD., Riverside Sawmills, Boroughbridge, N.Yorks. YO5 9LJ	●			●	●		●	●			●
WALKER & ANDERSON (KL) LTD., Windsor Rd, King's Lynn, Norfolk, PE30 5PL							●	●		●	●

ASHBY DESIGN WORKSHOP

Product & Suppliers Chart — 2
Clock/Case Components

Whilst each Ashby Clock Plan specifies the clock components required for a project, there are, in reality, many varieties and styles of clock movements, dials, hands and accessories available. This Chart will enable you to get acquainted with various suppliers' specialities and will help you to locate the items you require. It will also further your knowledge of this fascinating craft.

	COMPANY, Address	Barometers	Electric	Hygrometers	Insertion	LCD	Mechanical – Hermle	Mechanical – Keininger	Mechanical – Urgos	Quartz	Thermometers	Aluminium	Arched	Bracket
MS	PARK CLOCKS, 13 Oakfield Court, Damory Street, Blandford Forum, Dorset DT11 7HF													
MS	TIMECRAFT, Unit 19, Sefton Lane, Ind. Estate, Maghull, Liverpool L31 8BX					V	V	V	V			V	V	V
MS	MARTIN H. DUNN, Glebe Farm, Clarkes Road, North Killingholme				●		●	●		●		●	●	
ST	CHARLTONS TIMBER CENTRE, Frome Road, Radstock, Nr. Bath, Avon BA3 3PT	●		●	●		●	●		●	●			
ST	ART VENEERS CO. LTD., Industrial Estate, Mildenhall, Suffolk IP28 7AY	●	●	●				●		●				●
ST	THE WOODCRAFT CENTRE LTD., Vauxhall Street, Stoke-on-Trent ST3 1PL	●			●			●		●	●			
ST	H.S. WALSH & SONS LTD., 243 Beckenham Rd, Beckenham, Kent, BR3 4TS	●	●	●	●	●				●	●			
ST	JOHN BODDY'S FWTS LTD., Riverside Sawmills, Boroughbridge, N.Yorks. YO5 9LJ	●	●	●	●	●				●	●	●		

MF: Manufacturer   ST: Stockist
MS: Manufacturer Stockist
V: Various Models/Sizes/Patterns

Table 1

	SPECIALIST SUPPLIES																						SERVICES		PUBLICATIONS				ORDERING											
	Adhesives & Abrasives	Antique Restoration	Cabinet Making	Carpentry & Joinery	Carving	Chair Making	Clock/Case Components	Craft Accessories	Finishes & Polishes	Fixtures & Fittings	Fretwork	Gilding	Marquetry & Inlay	Models & Miniatures	Pyrography	Skiver Leathers	Upholstery	Woodcuts/Engraving	Woodturning	Machining – Blanks	Machining – Boards	Machining – Cutting Lists	Tool Sharpening	Courses & Demonstrations	Books	Magazines	Plans	Videos	Literature – Company Cat.	Literature – Product Specs.	Literature – Stockist List	Sales – Credit Cards	Sales – Counter	Sales – Direct to Customer	Sales – Mail Order/Carriers	Sales – Self Selection	Sales – Trade Accounts	Sales – Through Stockists	Sales – Saver Schemes	Telephone
																								●	●	●	●		●	●		●			●		●	●		0442 66551
																							●	●	●	●	●		●		●	●		●	●	●			0992 501518
●						●	●	●	●		●	●					●	●	●	●	●		●	●	●	●			●		●	●	●	●		●	●		0761 436229
●	●	●				●	●			●			●			●								●				●			●	●	●	●		●	●		0638 712550
●																		●	●					●															0772 732322
●	●	●	●	●		●	●	●	●	●	●	●		●					●	●	●		●	●	●	●		●			●	●	●	●		●	●		0782 599911
																												●			●	●	●	●		●	●		0453 82 6886
●										●			●	●	●		●						●	●							●			●		●	●		071-688-5513
						●								●																		●		●			●		082 42 2096
●	●	●	●			●	●			●		●	●		●		●		●				●	●				●			●	●	●	●		●	●		0350 2723
								●																●	●		●		●		●	●	●	●	●	●	●	●	081 778 7061
●	●	●	●		●	●	●	●	●	●	●	●	●	●	●	●	●	●	●	●	●		●	●	●	●		●			●	●	●	●	●	●	●		0423 322370
●		●	●					●											●			●	●	●	●	●	●		●	●			●			●			0553 772443

Table 2

															ACCESSORIES & FITTINGS												ORDERING											
	brass	Card	Carriage	Ceramic	Chapter Rings	Circular	Dial/bezel combi.	Hand Painted	Longcase	Numerals	Plastic	Round	Specialist	Square	Steel/enamel	Vienna	Bezels	Carrying Handles	Clock Books	Door Fittings – Various	Feet – Various	Finials Spires & Paterae	Fretwork & Spandrels	Hands	Horological Supplies	Kits	Pillar Bases/Capitals	Plans	Literature – Company Cat.	Literature – Product Specs.	Literature – Stockist List	Sales – Credit Cards	Sales – Counter	Sales – Direct to Customer	Sales – Mail Order/Carriers	Sales – Self Selection	Sales – Trade Accounts	Sales – Through Stockists	Sales – Saver Schemes	Telephone
																									●			●	●								●			0258 480488
		V		V	V	V		V	V	V			V		V	V	V			●	●	●	●	V	●	●	●			●			●	●	●		●		051 526 2516
			●	●	●	●	●	●			●		●		●		●		●	●	●	●	●	●	●	●	●		●	●	●	●	●	●	●	●		●	0469 540 901
		●	●	●	●				●		●		●				●																						0761 436229
																								●		●		●				●	●						0638 712550
●	●	●	●	●	●	●	●	●	●	●	●		●		●		●		●	●	●	●	●	●	●		●			●	●	●	●	●	●		●		0782 599911
●	●	●	●	●	●	●	●	●	●	●	●	●	●	●	●	●	●	●	●	●	●	●	●	●	●	●	●		●	●	●	●	●	●	●	●	●		081 778 7061
	●		●	●	●	●			●		●				●		●		●	●	●	●	●	●		●			●	●	●	●	●	●	●	●			0423 322370

US Suppliers

Adams Brown Co.
26 N. Main
Cranbury, NJ 08512
609–655–8269
Books only

Albert Constantine & Son
2050 Eastchester Rd
Bronx, NY 10461
212–792–1600
General Woodworking Supply

American Clockmaker
PO Box 326
Clintonville, WI 64929
715–823–5101

American Reprints Co.
PO Box 379
Modesto, CA 95353
209–667–2906
Books only

Arlington Book Co.
2706 Elsmore
Fairfax, VA 22031
703–280–2005

Cas-Ker Co.
PO Box 14069
Cincinnati, OH 45214
513–241–7073

Craftsman Wood Service Co.
1735 W. Cortland Ct.
Addison, IL 60101
312–629–3100
General Woodworking Catalog

Emperor Clock Co.
Emperor Industrial Park
Fairhope, AL 36532
205–928–2316

Empire Clock Inc.
1295 Rice St.
St. Paul, MN 55117
612–487–2885

Garrett Wade Co.
161 Avenue of the Americas
New York, NY 10013
212–807–1155
General Woodworking Supply

Horton Brasses
PO Box 95, Nooks Hill Rd.
Cromwell, CT 06416
203–635–4400
Cabinet hardware for Grandfather clocks

Jeweler's Department Store
56 W.47th St.
New York, NY 10036
800–223–8960

Klockit
PO Box 636, Highway H North
Lake Geneva, WI 53147
414–248–1150

Kuempel Chime Clock Works
21195 Minnetonka Blvd
Excelsior, MN 55331
612–474–6177

Mason & Sullivan
586 Higgins Crowell Rd.
West Yarmouth, MA 02673
1–800–933–3010

Merritt's Antiques
PO Box 277
Douglassville, PA 19518–0277
215–689–9541

Midwest Importers
1101 Westport Rd.
Kansas City, MO 64111
816–753–5654

Otto Frei-Jules borel
PO Box 796, 126 2nd St.
Oakland, CA 94604
415–832–0355

Precision Movements
4251 Chestnut St, PO Box 689
Emmaus, PA 18049
215–967–3156

R & M Imports
PO Box 60
Harveysburg, OH 45032
800–762–5015

S. La Rose, Inc.
234 Commerce Pl., PO box 21208
Greensboro, NC 27420
919–275–0462

The Woodworkers Store
21801 Industrial Blvd.
Rogers, MN 55374–9514
612–428–2199
General Woodworking Supply

Timesavers

PO Box 13
Algonquin, IL 60102
708–658–2266

Viking Clock Co.
451 Pecan St.
Fairhope, AL 36533
205–928–3466

Woodcraft Supply
210 Wood County Industrial Park, PO Box 1686
Parkersburg, WV 26102–1686
1–800–225–1153
General Woodworking Supply

Woodworker's Supply
1108 N. Glenn Rd.
Caspar, WY 82601
1–800–645–9292
General Woodworking Supply

Yankee Ingenuity
PO Box 113
Altus, OK 73522
405–477–2191

Bibliography

BARKER D., *The Arthur Neagus Guide to English Clocks* Hamlyn (1980).

BROWN, W.H., *The Conversion and Seasoning of Wood* Stobart Davies (1988) (USA Linden).

BRUTON, E., *The History of Clocks and Watches* 2nd Edn (1977) Orbis 1979.

FISHER, R., *Painting Furniture* MacDonald Orbis (1988).

HAYWOOD, C.H., *Cabinetmaking for Beginners* Collins (1983).

HOADLEY, R.B., *Understanding Wood: A Craftsman's Guide to Wood Technology* Taunton Press (1980).

JACKSON, A. AND DAY, D., *Collins Complete Woodworker's Manual* Collins (1989).

JONES, B.E., *Clock Cleaning and Repairing* Cassell (1982).

JOYCE, E.: Revised by A. PETERS, *Technique of Furniture Making* Batsford (1987) (USA Sterling).

LINCOLN, W.A., *The Marquetry Manual* Stobart Davies (1989) (USA Linden).

LINCOLN, W.A., *Complete Manual of Wood Veneering* Stobart Davies (1984).

LINCOLN, W.A., *World Woods in Colour* Stobart Davies (1986) (USA Linden).

LOOMES, B., *Complete British Clocks* David & Charles (1978).

MACTAGGART, P. AND A., *Practical Gilding* Mac & Me (1984).

METCALFE, P. and the LONDON COLLEGE OF FURNITURE, *The Woodworker's Handbook*, Pelham (1984) (USA Arco).

NISH, D.L., *Creative Woodturning* Stobart Davies (1975) (USA Brigham Young).

OUGHTON, F., *The Complete Manual of Wood Finishing* Stobart Davies (1982) (USA Scarborough House).

PAIN, F., revised by J.A. JACOBSON *Practical Woodturner* Collins (1990).

PEARSON, M., *The Beauty of Clocks* Crescent (1978).

PETERS, A., *Cabinetmaking — The Professional Approach* Stobart Davies (1984) (USA MacMillan).

PHILLIPS, J., *Techniques of Routing* International Thompson (1982).

RAFFAN, R., *Turning Wood* Collins (1985) (USA Taunton Press).

ROBERTS, D., *The Bracket Clock* David & Charles (1982).

ROBINSON, T., *The Longcase Clock* Antique Collectors' Club (1984).

ROSE, R., *English Dial Clocks* Antique Collectors' Club (1988).

SMITH, E., *Clocks and Clock Repairing* Lutterworth (1988).

Taunton Press *'Fine Woodworking' on Finishing and Refinishing* (1986).

VOISEY, N.S., *Wood Machining: A Complete Guide to Effective and Safe Working Practices* Stobart Davies (1987).

Index

Books of Related Interest

World Woods in Colour *William Lincoln* — 275 commercial world timbers in full colour, describing general characteristics, properties and uses table. 300 pages.

Spindle Moulder Handbook *Eric Stephenson* — Covers all aspects of this essential woodworking machine from spindle speeds to grinding and profiling. 200 pages — 430 photos and line drawings.

The Conversion & Seasoning of Wood *Wm. H. Brown* — A guide to principles and practice covering all aspects of timber conversion from the log and dealing with proven methods of seasoning. 222 pages illustrated.

The Marquetry Manual *Wm. A. Lincoln* — This state-of-the-art publication incorporates all the traditional ideas and practices for marquetarians as well as all the current thinking, and a selection of some of the greatest marquetry pictures. 272 pages, 400 illustrations.

Relief Woodcarving and Lettering *Ian Norbury* — Caters for all levels of ability from beginners onwards, exploring the fields of low and high relief carving through a series of graded projects. 157 pages, fully illustrated.

Modern Practical Joinery *George Ellis* — This vast coverage of internal joinery includes windows, doors, stairs, handrails, mouldings, shopfitting and showcase work, all clearly detailed and illustrated with hundreds of line drawings. Nearly 500 pages and 27 chapters.

Mouldings and Turned Woodwork of the 16th, 17th & 18th Centuries *T. Small & C. Woodbridge* — This large format book presents full size details and sections of staircases, doors, panelling, skirtings, windows, together with architectural turnings and many other specific applications of mouldings.

Circular Work in Carpentry and Joinery *George Collings* — A practical guide on circular work of single and double curvature. 120 pages.

Modern Practical Stairbuilding and Handrailing *George Ellis* — Another epic work devoted especially and seriously to the demanding art of stairbuilding and handrailing. 352 pages and 108 plates.

Fine Craftsmanship in Wood *Betty Norbury* — Nearly 200 designer/makers are represented showing exacting standards of work and a creativity unsurpassed in the art of woodworking. 192 pages. Illustrated with colour and black and white photographs. Hardcover. (Published as **British Craftsmanship in Wood** in the UK).